HISTORY OF THE RHODODENDRON
SPECIES FOUNDATION

Genesis of a Botanical Garden

By

Clarence Barrett

Positive Attitudes, Publishers
Eugene, Oregon 97402

HISTORY OF THE RHODODENDRON SPECIES FOUNDATION
Genesis of a Botanical Garden

By Clarence Barrett

Published by: POSITIVE ATTITUDES, PUBLISHERS
87344 Prince Lane
Eugene, Oregon 97402

Library of Congress Catalog Card Number: 94-68481

ISBN: 0-9630292-7-4

Printed in Hong Kong by Colorcraft Ltd.

Table of contents

Dedication 5

Acknowledgements...7

Foreword...9

Founders of the Rhododendron Species Foundation 11

Presidents of the Rhododendron Species Foundation 19

Introduction 23

Part I: THE EARLY YEARS 25

    Chapter I: Pioneers 26

    Chapter II: The Search 43

    Chapter III: The Source 55

PART II: THE FORMATIVE YEARS 75

    Chapter IV: Hard Times 76

    Chapter V: The First Garden 85

PART III: THE BRYDON YEARS 101

    Chapter VI: The Brydons...102

    Chapter VII: The Second Garden 105

PART IV: THE WEYERHAEUSER ERA 115

    Chapter VIII: The Third Garden 116

    Chapter IX: Going Public 126

    Chapter X: Phase II..142

    Chapter XI: Growth 166

    Chapter XII: Security 182

Color Photo Section 193

Appendix A: Species Acquisition List 209

Appendix B: Species acquisition and inventory database 221

Appendix C: RSF - Weyerhaeuser Contract 281

Appendix D: Garden Master Plan 284

Appendix E: By-laws as amended to April 26, 1980 and
                     as revised to November 10, 1990.....................293

Appendix F: Garden Master Plan, Nov. 1, 1980 307

Appendix G: Membership list 321

Dedication

This work is dedicated to the memory of Dr. Milton V. Walker and his wife Helen G. Walker. It was they who conceived the idea of a world class rhododendron species collection in America and it was their dedication and singleness of purpose that caused the collection eventually to materialize. They envisioned a foundation to administer the collection and they contributed generously of their time, energy and money to its realization.

Acknowledgements

The author is indebted to Ian Walker for the loan of his father's voluminous files and records, without which this history would not have been possible in its present form and detail. Pamela Elms was very helpful in the early stages of the writing, for digging out information, records and photos from Foundation archives and offering other services as needed. Newsletter editor Renee Hill has been most helpful in providing information and particularly in offering encouragement from time to time.

Edith Brydon, Ruth Woods, Barbara and Rudy Mate, Nick and Evelyn Weesjes and others have kindly contributed information and the loan of treasured photos. Many key figures in current Species Foundation affairs took the time to read the manuscript and make timely and helpful suggestions and corrections. For all this help, and for the encouragement of many Foundation members who knew of these efforts, thank you so much.

Thanks are also due the American Rhododendron Society for permission to quote freely from its publications.

Unless otherwise indicated photos are from the Species Foundation archives. I regret that in many cases attribution cannot be given individual photographers since there is no record of the photographer's identity.

Clarence "Slim" Barrett
Eugene, Oregon - 1994

Foreword

In addition to its value, this is a remarkable book in two ways: It deals with an institution which is unique throughout the world, and it was produced by author Clarence Barrett without compensation at an expenditure of time and energy so great that it is hard to imagine.

The usual course for a rhododendron hobbyist is to acquire hybrids with the biggest truss and the gaudiest flowers that can be found. In time, the interest shifts to the species for the charming, harmonious unity of scale among branches, leaves and flowers, evolved through many millions of years into handsome compositions.

In harsher climates, a new trait of hardiness must be added by the breeder, but the species are still the only resource which can be used with precision, and the conscientious hybridizer must be intimately acquainted with them to reach his goal.

In 1964 the identification of rhododendron species was indescribably confused. Seeds produced in the British Isles, especially, and in the United States, were distributed with the names of the species that bore them even though they resulted from open pollination, abundantly aided by bees bearing pollen from other species nearby.

The need for authoritative, authentic specimens of the species was urgent, and so a Rhododendron Species Foundation was proposed by Dr. Milton Walker, later a generous benefactor.

As an illustration of the need, I can cite, with apologies, a personal experi-

David G. Leach

ence. In the 1950's several British publications were holy writ to scholars and students everywhere. I was in the midst of writing a book, *Rhododendrons of the World*, and the illustrator was Edmond Amateis, a world renowned sculptor and amateur rhododendron hybridizer. His beautifully composed botanical illustrations featured the identifying guideposts for each species, based on the British literature. As the text neared completion, it became obvious that there were conflicts between it and the illustrations. In the interest of accuracy, I was obliged to go to the British Isles and photograph specimens of known provenance, usually with the collectors' field numbers. Using these photographs, the patient Mr. Amateis redrew nearly all of the species illustrations. So was the utter confusion that then existed in species identification.

The History of the Rhododendron Species Foundation is abundantly illustrated with photographs and brief biographical sketches of some of the most active supporters, whose names are household words to growers of rhododendrons. Others picture the scenes as the species collection went through the three major phases of its development.

In this book will be found the difficult, sometimes agonizing labor which produced the birth of the Rhododendron Species Foundation, told mainly by the letters exchanged among those who nursed it from an unpromising infancy through the tribulations of adolescence to the sturdy, established maturity of the worldwide reputation it enjoys today.

The Foundation recently celebrated its 30th birthday, when it had in its collection at Federal Way, Washington 2,155 forms of 426 rhododendron species. Appendix A gives the sources of the collection, and Appendix B is an invaluable listing of the species in the garden.

This account of the Rhododendron Species Foundation, then, brings to life the pioneers of rhododendron culture, and underlines the value and utility to breeders and hobbyists everywhere of the unparalleled asset which the Foundation's species garden represents.

David G. Leach
Madison, Ohio
August, 1994

Founders of the Rhododendron Species Foundation

Milton V. Walker, M.D.
1903-1986

Founder

MILTON V. WALKER, M.D.

Milton Vance Walker was born August 24, 1903 in Elmvale, Ontario, Canada. When he was only three years of age his mother died of tuberculosis and thereafter he was raised by an aunt and uncle who lived in London, Ontario. He attended the University of Western Ontario, receiving first a Bachelor of Arts degree and, in 1928, his Doctor of Medicine degree. While attending this school he met the school librarian, Helen Jane Gordon Patterson, who was also the daughter of Milton's mathmatics professor, William Patterson. Helen tutored him in mathmatics and a close relationship developed between the pair and they were married in 1928. Their honeymoon consisted of a two week canoe trip through Ontario, terminating with a visit to Henry Ford Hospital in Detroit, Michigan, where Milton served his internship.

Upon completion of the internship the couple moved to Oregon, living first in the tiny community of Remote, then in Springfield, where Milton's general medical practice began. In those days house calls were frequent and one evening while attending the birth of a child to a farm couple near Pleasant Hill Milton went for a short walk and, noting the beauty of the area, congratulated the farmer, only to learn that the farmer was for financial reasons having to sell a portion of the land. Milton contacted the realtor the next day and with his last $100.00 made a down payment on what was to be the family homesite and eventual temporary location of the Species Foundation garden.

Dr. Walker's practice was busy in spite of the depression and while many of his patients lacked cash to pay for his services they were willing to work, and he made use of their labors in the construction of the family home. A patient's team of horses skidded a large chicken coop from across the road and this, when cleaned up and set on blocks, constituted the beginning of the house. Over the years the house was added to and gradually completed, with lawns and shrubbery being installed, becoming known eventually as "Glenellen". It is likely that the couple's frequent visits to Butchard Gardens near Victoria on Vancouver Island inspired their extensive flower and shrub beds and their acquisition of many different plants to satisfy their urge for creating natural beauty. At about the same time they joined the Obsidians, a hiking club, exploring the native flora and fauna. They cultivated friendships with a number of University of Oregon faculty who were engaged in the fields of botany and Helen's greatest interest, music.

In 1941 Dr. Walker's Hospital, as it was then known, was established on the banks of a mill race, surrounded by a beautiful rose garden. Dr. Walker and another doctor and a support staff of ten operated the hospital until after World War II it was converted into a clinic with a staff of doctors, each with his own specialty. The Clinic remained active for years though Dr. Walker retired from practice in the early 1960's.

It was in about 1960 that Milton's interest became absorbed in the genus rhododendron and, as so often happens, soon became focused on the species. His efforts in attempting to collect true forms of the many species were thwarted by the lack of authentic representatives in the Pacific Northwest and through a fortunate chain of events he became aware of the treasury of superior species then located in many notable British gardens. He conceived the idea of the Species Foundation, was active in its formation, supported it financially and served as its first president. With Helen's help and encouragement he devoted the remainder of his life to the acquisition of the finest species of rhododendron and their establishment in the gardens of the Species Foundation, first near Eugene, Oregon, then Salem, Oregon and finally at Federal Way, Washington. He never faltered in his insistence on the purity of the collection.

Dr. Walker died in Palm Springs, California on February 18, 1986 at the age of eighty-three. Helen survived him for five years, passing away on Oct. 21, 1991 at age ninety-six. Their substantial estate was left in a conditional trust for the benefit of the Foundation.

The Walkers had three children: Margaret, Ian and Glenn. Ian remains active in the Foundation.

Founder

EDWARD B. DUNN

"Ed" Dunn was born in Seattle, Washington in 1902, to descendants of Irish immigrants. With the exception of a stint in the U. S. Navy during World War II he lived his entire life in the Seattle area. He grew up on First Hill in Seattle, attending Summit School, and as a young man studied at the University of Washington.

Mr. Dunn traveled extensively, often in the company of friends, to gardens in Scotland, England, Ireland, Europe, China, Japan, Canada, Central and South America, Australia and New Guinea. For over forty years he carried on voluminous correspondence with rhododendron growers throughout the world.

Edward B. Dunn
1902 - 1991

Photo courtesty Dunn Estate

In the mid-1950's Ed served as president of the Seattle Rhododendron Society and subsequently he served on the board of directors of the American Rhododendron Society. He was president of that organization from 1965 to 1969 and in 1971 he received its highest honor, the Gold Medal. His involvement in horticultural organizations gained him many friends and admirers. Endre Ostbo, well known rhododendron grower and hybridizer, named his most beautiful hybrid, "Edward B. Dunn".

Edward was president of the University of Washington Arboretum in 1960. He presided over the opening of the Japanese Garden there. In 1982 he and Brian Mulligan were largely responsible for the Seattle Rhododendron Society acquiring the Meerkerk Rhododendron Gardens on Whidby Island.

Ed was active in the early group of rhododendron enthusiasts who, with Dr. Milton Walker, sought the better forms of species Rhododendrons and ultimately formed the Rhododendron Species Foundation. He served as president of that organization from 1971 to 1973 and was very instrumental in the establishment of the Species Foundation garden at Federal Way, Washington.

Ed Dunn was a gentle man. He particularly enjoyed hybridizing rhododendrons, collecting and growing woodland wildflowers, expecially erythronium, trillium and dodecatheon. His two and one-half acre garden revealed how rhododendrons can be combined with understory trees, shrubs and wildflowers. It contained a water garden, miniature orchard and seed and nut bearing trees to encourage wildlife. His garden was his pride and joy and a delight to his visitors. His gardening philosophy lives on in the Edward B. Dunn Historical Garden, a trust established in September, 1993.

Founder

CECIL SMITH

Cecil C. Smith was born in Champoeg, Oregon June 11, 1904. He attended schools in Champoeg and Newberg, and after graduating from Newberg High School, attended Oregon Agricultural College, now known as Oregon State University.

Mary L. (Molly) Smith, nee Beaty, was born and raised in Minnesota and worked there as a grade school teacher before moving to Oregon. Cecil and Molly were married in Newberg, Oregon on December 14, 1941 and two sons were born of the marriage. There are now three granddaughters. Cecil farmed grass seed with his brother, Walter, until Walter's death in 1960 and thereafter he farmed alone. The couple started their rhododendron garden in 1951 on Ray Bell Road in the St. Paul, Oregon area. Over the years they entertained visitors to the garden from England, Scotland, New Zealand, Japan and Canada, with up to 200 visitors during the spring of the year.

Cecil missed by one meeting being a charter member of the American Rhododendron Society, but for many years he was an active member of the Portland Chapter. He was on the national board of directors of the ARS for eighteen years, received the Gold Medal in 1967 and the Bronze Medal from the Portland Chapter in 1979.

Cecil Smith and wife Molly

In 1985 he was the recipient of the Pioneer Achievement Award from the American Rhododendron Society. He was a founding member of the Rhododendron Species Foundation, contributed generously of his time and substance throughout its early struggles, has served continuously on the board of directors of that organization and is presently an honorary member of the board.

Founder

WALES WOOD

Wales Wood was born January 7, 1907 in Willis, Montana. He grew up in Willis and graduated from high school there. He subsequently moved to Portland, Oregon where he attended the Northwest College of Law, receiving his Bachelor of Laws degree in 1936. He was employed in a private firm for a time, then went to work for Title and Trust Company in Portland.

Ruth was born in Wall Lake, Iowa and lived there until her early teens when she and her family moved to Montana. She graduated from high school in Montana, then attended the University of Montana, graduating with a Bachelor of Science degree in pharmacy. She was first employed in the laboratory at Providence Hospital in Portland, Oregon, then as a teacher in a dental college.

Wales and Ruth met at a dinner party while he was attending law school and the couple was married in Corvallis, Oregon on Christmas Day, 1925.

Wales Wood (1907-1978)
and wife Ruth

In 1938 Wales was designated manager of the Title and Trust office in St. Helens, Oregon and the couple lived for a short time in an apartment there. In the course of a Sunday drive they stopped at a lovely view site overlooking the Columbia River in the "Chime Crest" area north of St. Helens, where Wales examined a handful of earth and decided this was where he wanted to live. The couple bought a small tract of land where they built their home and eventually acquired an extensive rhododendron collection.

Ruth was also employed by Title and Trust Company and the couple worked together until their retirement, Ruth in December, 1965 and Wales in November, 1968.

The Woods had a remarkable rhododendron collection, were both quite knowledgeable and were in constant demand as judges and speakers at rhododendron and other horticultural events. They frequently hosted visitations by tour groups of international scope. Both Wales and Ruth served on the board of directors of the Rhododendron Species Foundation. Wales served as president for a time and Ruth, as of this writing, is an honorary member of that body.

Wales also served on the board of directors of the American Rhododendron Society, and of the St. Helens Chamber of Commerce. He was past president of the Columbia County Bar Association and the St. Helens Men's Garden Club. He passed away in Portland, Oregon, Feb. 28, 1978.

Founder

CLARENCE CHASE

Clarence Chase was born December 21, 1898, in Eugene, Oregon. He lived there all his life in an area near the present Autzen Stadium that was once called "Pruneville" because it was surrounded by many acres of orchard. Along with his two brothers he joined his father in the business of growing vegetables, most notably in greenhouses.

Clarence graduated from high school in Springfield, Oregon, and attended both the University of Oregon and Oregon State College, now called Oregon State University. He served in the U. S. Naval Reserve from 1918 to 1920. He married Marche Dahl in 1922 and three children were born of the marriage.

Under Clarence's leadership the vegetable production gradually changed to flower production and the family project became "Chase Gardens", with Clarence the general manager in 1927. At one time Chase Gardens was the largest rose producer west of the Mississippi River and the largest white orchid pro-

Clarence Chase
1898 - 1988

Photo courtesy Molly Hufford

ducer in the world. In 1948 Clarence was elected vice-president and general manager of Armacost & Royston, Inc., an orchid breeding company in Los Angeles.

Through the years Chase was an active member of the First Congregational Church, Kiwanis, Eugene Chamber of Commerce and the YMCA. He was a two term board member of the Society of American Florists and served as director of Roses, Inc., a national organization.

Somewhere along the line Clarence became interested in rhododendrons and in the natural course of events he developed a taste for the species in particular. He joined Dr. Milton Walker and the other enthusiasts in searching for the best forms and like them he became disillusioned with what he found in the Pacific Northwest. He readily supported the formation of the Rhododendron Species Foundation and served for many years as treasurer of that organization, particularly through the trying years when funds were scarce and expenses mounting.

Clarence became ill with Parkinson's disease and died October 4, 1988 at the age of eighty-nine.

Founder

J. HAROLD CLARKE

J. Harold Clarke was born in Brown County, Indiana on June 12, 1899. He grew up near Shelbyville, Indiana and attended school there, where his mother was a teacher. Upon graduating from Shelbyville High School he attended Purdue University, where he received a bachelor's degree in 1921. He next attended the University of Delaware at Newark, where he taught part time until he received his master's degree. He completed his formal education at Columbia University where he was awarded his Ph. D. in plant physiology.

Dr. J. Harold Clarke
1899 - 1990

Photo courtesy Gretchen Clarke

For twenty-three years Dr. Clarke was a professor of pomology at Rutgers University in New Jersey, where he specialized in small fruits and named five varieties of strawberries. He moved to Long Beach, Washington in 1946 to take charge of a large cranberry farm and nursery and in 1956 he established the rhododendron nursery that occupied him for the rest of his life.

Clarke married Edith Cribbs in Indiana in 1922 and two children were born of the marriage, Paul E. Clarke and Jeanne Derr. Edith was very active in the establishment and operation of the nursery until she passed away in November, 1970. Subsequently Dr. Clarke remarried, to Gretchen Sirpo, who survived him at his death in Sun City, Arizona on Nov. 7, 1990 at the age of ninty-one. He left three grandchildren and six great-grandchildren.

Dr. Clarke was a long time member of the American Rhododendron Society and served it in many capacities, as a director, secretary, president and as editor of the Bulletin. He was a dedicated rhododendron species enthusiast and served unstintingly in the formation and operation of the Foundation. He was a member of the American Society of Horticultural Science, and had served as president of the Washington State Nurseryman's Association. For six years he was chairman of the U. S. Department of Agriculture's Deciduous Fruit and Tree Nut Research and Marketing Advisory Committee. He was a governor of the American Association of Nurserymen and a member of the Evergreen Pesticide Council.

He was a prolific writer and authored two books, *Getting Started With Rhododendrons and Azaleas* and *Small Fruits For Your Home Garden*, as well as many scholarly articles in various horticultural journals. His awards included the gold medal of the American Rhododendron Society and the Centennial Medallion from the Agricultural Research Center of Washington State University.

Founder

FRED ROBBINS

Fred Robbins was born in Ritzville, Adams County, Washington, Nov. 16, 1902. He was raised in Ritzville through high school except for a year at Northwest Military Academy in Wisconsin. He was the youngest of four children.

Fred Robbins
1902 - 1989
Photo courtesy Martha Robbins

For a time he worked for the White River Lumber Company as "Bull of the Woods" but decided logging was not to be his lifelong work. He enrolled at the Universlty of Washington in forestry. But the wanderlust overcame him and in 1922-23 he shipped out on an ocean freighter, down the west coast and around to New York and eventually to the orient.

In 1928 he married Dorothy Carlson and two daughters were born to the marriage. For a couple of years he worked for a car dealer, then purchased an interest in a car dealership, where he remained occupied until World War II stopped the availability of cars. After the war, in about 1947, he sold the car dealership and purchased a shingle mill. He retired in 1957.

Before 1940 Fred grew vegetables, perennials and a few roses but about then Dorothy encouraged him to accompany her to a rhododendron show. He saw R. Brittania and Unknown Warrior in bloom and was hooked. Soon he became acquainted with Lester Brandt, nurseryman and propagator, and an interest in rhododendron species developed. He began importing plants from England but often times they did not conform to the book descriptions of species. He, like many others, became discouraged and began looking for true species.

This, of course, brought Fred into contact with Dr. Milton Walker and others interested in rhododendron species and ultimately into participating in the formation of the Rhododendron Species Foundation. He served as president of that organization during the time the Foundation garden was being established at Federal Way, Washington after moving from Jock Brydon's place in Salem, Oregon. During this time when funding was scarce and staff meager, he often worked six days a week operating the tractor, hauling sawdust, planting plants, supervising the garden plan and generally managing the total operation.

Fred passed away Sept 26, 1989.

Presidents of the Rhododendron Species Foundation

Milton V. Walker, M.D.
July,1964 to June, 1968

Wales Wood with wife Ruth
June, 1968 to June, 1970

Edward B. Dunn
June, 1970 to April, 1973

Presidents:

Fred Robbins
April, 1973 to April, 1977

Lawrence Pierce
April, 1977 to April, 1979
Photo by Olan Mills

Dr. William Hatheway
April, 1979 to February, 1980

Presidents:

Dr. David Goheen
April, 1982 to April, 1984

Jane S. Rogers
February, 1980 to April, 1982

Photo courtesy Stewart Rogers

Herbert Spady, M.D. and wife Betty

April, 1986 to April, 1988

Esther Berry
April, 1984 to April, 1986

Presidents:

David Jewell

April, 1988 to April, 1989

Burt Mendlin

April, 1989 to April, 1991

Don King

April, 1991 to April, 1994

Fred Whitney

April, 1994

INTRODUCTION

Research has revealed that the history of the Rhododendron Species Foundation may reasonably be divided into certain chronological eras:

(1) The early years, before even the thought of a "foundation" as such was formed, a time when certain active and thoughtful members of the American Rhododendron Society began comparing their species rhododendrons with each other's, and with the descriptions in the then leading books and noticing vast differences that caused them to wonder if in fact they had true species plants at all.

(2) The formative years after the Foundation was conceived and legally formalized and a general plan formulated and put into force for the selection, acquisition and propagation of materials from the finest verified species rhododendrons from many English gardens. The University of British Columbia played an important role in this era, and of course Dr. Milton Walker played a leading role.

(3) The Jock Brydon era, when the plants propagated at the University of British Columbia and established in the Milton Walker garden were transferred to the home and nursery of Jock Brydon, near Salem, Oregon. There Jock and his wife, Edith, began propagating on a sufficient scale to permit distribution of some plants, and over a comparatively short period of time the number of accessions increased dramatically.

(4) The Weyerhaeuser era when the plant collection was removed from Brydons' to the present location near Federal Way, Washington. Of course, more change and growth has occurred in the fourth era than in all the others combined, due to the remarkable effort of the many dedicated people that have made the garden what it is today with, of course, the very significant help of the Weyerhaeuser Company.

Very few of the people who participated in the activities of the first two eras are still alive and of those who are, some have a little trouble remembering and others are in poor health and have things to think about besides my prying questions. Statements have been obtained from them when possible and used where appropriate and my appreciation goes out to them for their cooperation. But most of the information pertaining to those eras came from Dr. Milton Walker's personal correspondence and articles from the Bulletins and Journals of the American Rhododendron Society, many of them written by Dr. Walker, Dr. Phetteplace, Dr. Clarke and other very literate people. (It should be noted that unless otherwise stated no attempt has been made to correct or edit material quoted herein as to grammar or punctuation, or as to language, some of which is uniquely colorful.) If the role of Dr. Milton Walker at times seems exaggerated, it should not. He was without question the driving force behind the organization and early functioning of the Species Foundation and his voluminous notes and records are virtually the only source of information concerning the early years that has been made available to this writer other than the A.R.S. publications, R.S.F. newsletters, plus minutes of board and executive committee meetings.

It seemed impertinent to attempt to paraphrase the Journal or Bulletin articles when they were so capably written, so many of them have been quoted in part, or in some cases in their entirety. While it may in some ways seem a needless duplication to repeat these articles here, they are widely scattered throughout the A.R.S. Bulletins and Journals, intermixed with innumerable other subject matters. It seemed appropriate to bring them together in the context of the Species Foundation history, where they may be easily followed in their chronological sequence so that one might comfortably watch the history unfold.

PART I

THE EARLY YEARS

CHAPTER I
PIONEERS

JAMES ELWOOD BARTO

About ten miles west of the town of Junction City, Oregon, in the eastern foothills of the Coast Range, lies a quiet wooded valley dense with third and fourth growth Douglas fir, intermixed with salal, huckleberry, sword fern, wild cherry, vine maple and alder. Forcing his way through the dense understory one finds an occasional bedraggled rhododendron, intergrown with wild blackberry brambles and crowded by competing hazel nut and vine maple. But these are not the R. *macrophyllum* that one expects to find growing throughout the Coast Range - rather they are rhododendrons of some unknown variety, obviously strange to this part of the world and their appearance in this setting seems ludicrous, to say the least.

James E. Barto
1881 - 1940
Photo courtesy Dr. Franklin West

It's difficult to imagine that this same peaceful valley once rang to the sound of an axe and the whisper of a hand saw as giant Douglas firs were felled and cut into manageable lengths so that old "Shorty" could skid them to a landing to be cut into firewood. "Shorty" was the work horse owned by the Barto family that once occupied this valley - but here is the story of James Elwood Barto, a notable pioneer in rhododendron culture, in the words of the late Carl Phetteplace, M.D. The story has been edited slightly, for the sake of brevity and clarity:

"It is with a sense of humbleness and inadequacy that the project of gathering up what information that at present seems available about the life and work of James Barto is undertaken. My own interest in rhododendrons dates back only about fifteen years, but each year as I appraise my own garden and visit those of others about the area, I am more and more impressed with the great contribution this man has made to the rhododendron world. Only now, a full twenty years after his death, are many of the fine things originating from the seeds he grew mature enough to be fully appreciated. It can now assuredly be stated that almost nothing he grew was inferior, but on the contrary, many of the species from his garden were of a quality and form that has not been equaled or surpassed by specimens that have come to us from other sources. Yet how little we seem to know about this man and how he was able, under the most adverse circumstances, to accumulate perhaps one of the most complete and choice collections of rhododendron species ever achieved by a single independent individual. At present I know of only two or three people outside of his surviving wife and two of the children who live nearby who knew Mr. Barto personally. Mr. Del James in The Bulletin of April, 1950, has given us a very valuable sketch of his work, and this has been summarized in 'Rhododendrons, 1956'. There is almost nothing additional recorded in our literature. Although the following leaves much to be desired, it is hoped it will first establish information that is to be gotten through the help of his family before even that source is lost to us and secondly, it may move others to bring forward some heretofore undisclosed information about him and his work. Although it is known that he was a prodigious letter writer and communicated thusly with rhododendron people over a large part of the world, yet at present there is only one of his letters that has ever been made available to us. This was the one that Mrs. Chauncey Craddock kindly sent to Mr. James and is included in his paper. There must have been scores of equally interesting writings to his many correspondents and it is possible that this might serve to uncover some of them.

"James Elwood Barto was born in Lewistown, Pennsylvania, June 14, 1881. As a child he was considered 'sickly' and consequently was started to school late. He made rapid progress however, and was graduated with his age group from what is the equivalent of the twelfth grade. At fourteen he moved to Kansas with his father, who was a judge. Later they moved to Joliet, Illinois, where his father died. At some time in this early period, he must have taken training as a carpenter, because he was regarded as an excellent cabinetmaker and finisher all his life.

"In 1905 he enlisted in the regular U. S. Navy where he served two enlistments ending in 1913. On November 1, 1913 he married Miss Ruth Ellen Lampson and they made their home in north Chicago. Six children were born to them, five boys and a girl. Merrill, born in 1919, Pauline, the present Mrs. Fred Sandoz, born in 1921, and Donald, born in 1928, still live in or near Eugene, Oregon.

"At the outbreak of World War I, he re-enlisted as a warrant officer in the Navy for the duration. Mrs. Barto, who still lives in the original Oregon home, states that he was always interested in flowers and shrubs, that he was an ardent reader and student, and that once he became interested in a subject, he pursued it exhaustively. Chickens, rabbits and goats of special breeds, as well as mining and minerals and honey bees were subjects explored in this pre-rhododendron time of his life.

"Soon after the armistice, he heard that certain lands in Oregon were open to homesteading for veterans. In 1920 he came west to investigate. Before returning to Chicago, he had filed on the place ten miles west of Junction City in the Coast Range Mountains which was to become the Barto home. It was entirely unimproved, rough, hilly, brush and timberland through which flowed a very small stream, called Bear Creek.

"Returning to Chicago, the children and all belongings were loaded into an old chain-drive truck and the trip westward was made, taking several weeks. They arrived in Eugene in October, 1920. A camp was made north of Skinner's Butte where the winter was spent. He was able to find employment as a carpenter building a fraternity house at the University of Oregon, Eugene. Over week ends, he was able to clear a small spot of ground on the homestead and started construction of a log cabin which they moved into in June of 1921. This was enlarged and covered with sawed lumber within the next few years.

"In the years that followed, Mr. Barto continued to work at his trade throughout the week, mostly in Eugene, but some in Corvallis and other surrounding towns, coming home week ends to work most of Saturday night, all day Sunday and then getting back to his job early Monday morning. There was the home to make more livable, accessory buildings to erect and land to clear. Mrs. Barto describes how she and the children would hold the lantern while he worked into the night. For the nineteen years of his life that remained for him, he continued this grueling existence, working at his trade to obtain the money so badly needed and pushing himself every hour available over the week ends to accomplish as much as possible about his home.

"For a time after he first became interested in rhododendrons, he also worked with many other types of ornamental plants. He imported seed and grew quite a variety of magnolias. Many tree peonies were imported from Japan, as were long lists of camellias which, by the way, proved unsatisfactory and were soon dropped. *Davidia* or dove trees, *viburnums, Gordonias, lillium giganteum, delphiniums* and holly were among the others grown to some extent. He was much interested in native Oregon plants and shrubs and collected a variety of seeds from our flora which were sent often in exchange for rhododendron seeds to correspondents, both domestically and abroad.

"Apparently the circumstances that started his special interest in rhododendrons came in 1925. He was employed by the firm of Raup and York to construct a greenhouse. Mr. Raup still operates a large greenhouse facility in Eugene, mainly growing potted azaleas for the florist trade. In his conversations with Mr. Raup, he was told that rhododendrons and azaleas were not yet fully appreciated and that they would eventually be recognized as the finest of all shrubs. Raup gave Mr. Barto some seeds which were brought home and sowed in a small box. Mrs. Barto had a small chicken incubator going at the time which was heated by a kerosene lamp. The flat of the newly acquired seed was placed on the top of the incubator and thus got bottom heat. The seedlings did well and were later moved out into a little cold frame which he built against the house.

"As he was watching over these first seedlings, he began to make inquiries as to who might know something more about these plants. As he heard of names, he began to write letters, first to those in our country and then to England, Scotland, Japan and even in China. His son, Merrill, believes that Mrs. A. C. U. Berry of Portland was the most helpful of anyone in the early period. He found that she already had a wide experience and told him of many people she knew with whom he began communicating. It is said that she recommended him for membership in the Rhododendron Association of England and this membership he maintained throughout his life. Mrs. Berry also shared seed with him which she received as a contributor to some of the major collecting expeditions into the Orient.

"Mrs. Chauncey Craddock of Eureka, California, who also had a considerable experience with rhododendrons, was much interested in his work and made a number of visits to the Barto place. She is credited with being of great help. It is believed she knew more about the material he was growing, details as to source, and the ideas and plans he had for the future than anyone at the time. The loss of such people as Mrs. Craddock before any information about him could be obtained, plus the other disastrous events near the close of his life, make it necessary to rely to a large extent on indirect information about the things he grew."

At this point Dr. Phetteplace discusses in some detail the extensive correspondence carried on by Barto, most of which adds little to the Barto story and has thus been omitted. Phetteplace then continues:

"The only additional clues we have as to sources comes from the knowledge we have of the plants he grew. There are a number of species or forms that are distinctly from certain expeditions. The lovely R. *decorum* with the small blotch in the throat, for one example, is generally recognized as the form brought out by Dr. Hu with Professor Wu. Other forms were sent by Wilson and by Kingdon-Ward, while the name of Cox is associated with the form with the greenish-yellow tint. All these variations and more have been identified among the Barto R. *decorums*.

"His collection seemed to cover the range of rhododendrons from the small *lapponicums* to a considerable variety of the so-called big leafed specimens. Among the azaleas, he had representatives of nearly all of the various subseries.

"The question has been asked, how could one man required by necessity to work full time away from home to provide necessary funds accomplish so much, starting with no knowledge at all on the subject. It is believed that while away during the week he had no more regard for sleep than he did at home week ends and did much late oil burning, studying from the numerous books he was said to possess and also carrying on his almost world-wide exchange of letters.

"The first seeds germinated over the chick incubator as mentioned were started in 1925. Within a year or so, his letters began to bear fruit in the form of quantities of seed from various sources. Any of us who have tried to grow the seeds from a few rhododendron crosses realize the pressure these growing plants can apply. They require constant care, ever expanding facilities, details of labeling and keeping records, transplanting, sorting, watering and control of weeds. Add to this circumstances of starting with no physical equipment, funds or even cleared land and the difficulties would, indeed, seem great.

"There were two favorable factors, however. First, the climate was very favorable for this type of plant, which, of course, we in the northwest all know. Second, the soil that was so difficult to wrest from the forest was ideal. It was quite virgin ground upon which leaves from the trees had fallen and decayed for many, many years. It was loose, porous and high in humus. Being on hillsides, it was well drained.

"In 1926 the first greenhouse was built. Heat was provided by a wood stove with pipes circulating warm water under the beds. Soon it was filled with flats of small seedlings carefully labeled and recorded. It was said that the flats soon presented the appearance of a green lawn. Mrs. Barto relates that she would at times hear him out in the greenhouse talking to the little seedlings as if they were people. The necessity for a lath house soon followed. The first one was built just above the house and was soon filled with plants. In the fall, not knowing how much cold the small plants could tolerate, the children sacked up and carried down large quantities of maple leaves to cover the plants for the winter.

"As the plants grew, ground must be cleared so that they could be moved out of the lath house. There was no machinery for this purpose. The trees felled were cut up into wood for the home and the greenhouse and also for building materials such as were needed. The stumps were blasted out and pulled together with the one horse they possessed ['Shorty'] so they could be burned. Eventually five patches comprising at least five acres were cleared and planted with rhododendrons so thickly that later Merrill relates that he had to cut to the ground every other plant in each alternate row because of over-crowding.

"With this, of course, was the necessity for some form of irrigation. As western Oregonians know, we have a superfluity of rainfall in the winter, but from May or June until fall, no successful gardening is done without water. Fortunately on some government land to the north there was a large spring. A water right was obtained on it for irrigation. He was able to obtain a quantity of two inch black pipe. Everyone in the family remembers the exact length of pipe first laid, 2700 feet, because this corresponded to the number of miles the family drove in the old truck coming from Chicago to Oregon. A small dam was built for storage so the spring provided an abundance of water. There was tremendous pressure on the line. Small holes were bored in the pipes that were laid down along the plantings from which the water would shoot high into the air and scatter with the air currents, giving excellent distribution. This water system was a very large project in itself for a man with only one horse for power and the children for helpers, but it was adequate as long as it worked. Simple as it appeared, however, it frequently required attention because of plugging with leaves or other problems which Mr. Barto or Merrill usually could remedy in a short time.

"As more seeds and many plants arrived a second larger greenhouse was required. There was no oil or electricity or automatic control at that time, so that the heat was maintained by a wood fire in the furnaces, often requiring getting up at night to replenish the fuel.

"Much more lath house was required, so that a second larger one was built below the dwelling near the creek. It was framed with poles and the 'laths' were not close enough to protect adequately.

"In the past women often worked out of doors much more than they do today to help wherever needed. Children likewise often worked hard as soon as they were old enough to be of help. No story of this project would be proper if it did not give some credit to Mrs. Barto and the children, especially Pauline, Merrill and even little Donald for their part in making this garden possible. Pauline (Mrs. Sandoz) states, 'The constant weeding, watering and transplanting was a never ending chore which involved the entire family'. Each week end before returning to his work, Mr. Barto would lay out instructions for tasks that should be done while he was away.

"During all of these years up until the late 1930's, there was never a thought of growing plants for any commercial purpose. It was an impelling fascination for him to collect and constantly learn more of these interesting plants and to watch them grow. As the result of his letter writing, he began to get visitors more from afar than from the local area to see what he was doing. During this time, it is Merrill's opinion he gave away thousands of plants to anyone who came and showed a kindred interest. Later in the thirties, he began to get requests for *Davidias* from such distributors as F. M Ellis urging him to propagate them freely in order to help him supply his demand."

Here Dr. Phetteplace discusses at length Barto's success in grafting plants theretofore considered not suited to this form of propagation. He then writes of Barto's experiences as foreman in a Civilian Conservation Corps (CCC) camp, where his only experiences with rhododendrons were his frequent expeditions into the mountains in searching for *macrophyllum, var. album*, usually accompanied by many of the youths from the camp. It was at this point in his life that Barto began to develop the symptoms of his final illness. Phetteplace continues:

Dr. Carl Phetteplace
Photo courtesy Lane County Medical Society

"From this point, the story is indeed a sad one. It seems that here almost every conceivable circumstance followed one after the other to work for the destruction of the fine thing he had expended himself so completely to achieve.

"About May, 1940, he was so ill that he sought admission to the Veterans Hospital in Portland for medical care. Cancer was discovered and he was never to return to his home or garden again. In June the same year, the house caught fire and burned to the ground with all his library and records excepting a few letters. The upper lath house was so close that part of it burned and some 2000 small plants were destroyed. Mrs. Barto relates that this news was kept from him for two or three months, but finally disclosed because of his frequent requests for certain books or records which he wished brought to him at the hospital.

"Later Merrill, the only boy at home really able to carry on, was called into the service in World War II. Mrs. Barto, Pauline and young Donald were all that remained to try an impossible task. Mr. Barto passed away December 22, 1940. Almost at once the irrigation system became plugged to the point where Mrs. Barto was unable to irrigate at all. Consequently the little plants that he had talked to as little seedlings suffered and many died. Mrs. Barto, seeing the hopelessness of her situation, began to sell the plants for next to nothing to the many visitors who now were coming from almost the length of our Pacific Coast. Some hauled large and small plants away in truck loads. In the lack of knowledge that prevailed at that time, it is said that some used these plants as understock for grafting with commercial hybrids. Others, upon arriving home, found that they had more plants than they could use and dumped them as garbage.

"If I may be pardoned for a personal experience, my first visit to the place was in 1944, having at the time no knowledge of rhododendrons at all. Twelve or fifteen small plants were brought home which were perhaps a foot tall. They were growing in the lower lath house thick as weeds and selections were made, attempting only to get a different appearing foliage in each plant. All of them have proved to be worthy species and some are now the pride of my garden. One, for instance, is the R. *augustinii*, variety 'Barto Blue', which many consider the equal of any of the selected forms which have come to us from elsewhere. Many others in the area can report similar examples of bringing plants home with little knowledge of what they had and finding after a few years that they had something very choice. At one time it is recalled that these plants were referred to as 'just an old Barto' when walking through someone's garden. Now, so many years later, they are sought after and referred to with pride as 'an original Barto.' The greater time necessary for species to be rewarding to the gardener as compared to our garden hybrids was not appreciated at the time. And by the same token, only with time and experience have we become aware of the superior quality of selected species over many of the hybrids which are so much more popular. And the species are often even more useful for some types of gardens."

Dr. Phetteplace discusses Barto's largely unsuccessful efforts at hybridizing rhododendrons, then summarizes:

"Actually Mr. Barto grew rhododendrons only fifteen years, during which time he was very busy collecting and it is probable that he never really got into the field of hybridizing before his untimely death. Perhaps there is much more about this man and his work that should be included in any sketch of his life, but this may serve to show something of the remarkable person that he was. Greatness, it has been said, may not be measured so much by the achievements by which one gains great public acclaim, but rather by the completeness with which he sacrifices himself without thought of personal gain for an honest cause, whatever that may be. In this respect he amply qualified. Like so many people of great achievement, he died in very modest circumstances, still reaching for higher goals when neither he nor many others realized that he had done anything of consequence.

"The question has been often asked, 'How far along would we be in knowledge and culture of rhododendrons in this area if it were not for Mr. Barto's contribution?' Someone has said that it would have taken a generation to become familiar with so much that we now know. Perhaps we might have grown hybrids rather extensively in the area because of such favorable natural conditions here, but it probably is true that our knowledge of species would have been much retarded. On the other hand, it is even more interesting to speculate on the achievements that might have been possible had he lived to grow out the hundreds of thousands of plants we know he had, and had it not been for the fire that destroyed so much, including his records. This, of course, is inestimable. Even so, there surely is cause for undying gratitude among us for the great contribution to our knowledge and enjoyment made by this humble man." (From The Quarterly Bulletin of the American Rhododendron Society, Vol. 14, No. 2 & 3, 1960.)

In the foregoing article Dr. Phetteplace expressed the hope that its publication might bring forth from readers, other letters from Barto to his many correspondents. This hope was realized when in May, 1960 Dr. Phetteplace received the following letter from Barto's East Coast counterpart, Joseph Gable:

May 9, 1960

Dear Dr. Phetteplace:

I have read with great interest your article in the Society Bulletin on Mr. James Barto and it takes me back to the beginning of things here too. I can only find three of his letters in my files but I recall many of our exchanges of seeds and plants.

I think our first correspondence started with mutual acquaintance with Mr. George Fraser of Ucluelet, B.C. and through Mr. Fraser I started a correspondence with Mr. E. J. P. Magor of Cornwall, England and received both seeds and pollen which I shared with Mr. Barto. Then I also grew many seedlings from Mr. Magor's seeds and from Dr. Rock's collection which I knew would be tender here and I recall sending him several boxes of these by express. He, as you record, wrote profusely and I was unable to keep with him in that line.

. . .There should be a list here of all the Rock numbers I sent to Mr. Barto and also of those he sent for he divided some of Rock's seeds with me that he had from Mr. Brower, but if his records were all burned these would of no value to you.

My vision has deteriorated to the point that I can only poorly decipher these letters I send and it is difficult for me to find things in my files. There may be more Barto letters taken from the files and piled into boxes or they may have been discarded in some house cleaning operation. I do not know.

From your article telling the difficulties under which he started we must have had considerable in common. I too recall referring him to F. M. Ellis as a source of *davidia* seeds. The first lot we got were both good but the second time, when I at least, invested much heavier, they all proved to be 'duds'.

Still the old hard days were the good days!

Sincerely
Joe Gable

The three Barto letters received from Gable:

Letter No. 1   Junction City, Oregon
                                                              March 20, 1930

Mr. J. B. Gable
Stewartstown, Pa.

Dear Sir:

The secretary of the Rhododendron Association [England] has sent me under my permit no. 1868 a box of rhododendron seed.

Mr. Gurney Wilson, secretary gave me your address and requested me to let you have some seed if I would. I divided the varieties that had enough seed to make fairly sure of getting plants for all. Of course, there is one more address: Mr. Ansel Brower, Hickory Hill Nursery, Newport, Long Island. I am giving the address so if your seed fails or mine we might have plants from the above.

I have seedlings of many varieties one to three years old and still am adding as fast as possible, also some hybrids. Growing the *davidia involucrata* (Dove Tree) that I received from Wilson and bulbs and rare plants that can be raised from seed and cuttings.

Respectfully yours,
J. E. Barto

Letter No. 2

Junction City, Oregon
March 27, 1930

Mr. J. B. Gable
Stewartstown, Pa.

Dear Sir:

I missed one packet of seed in same to you and Mr. Brower. I enclose it to you. If you have a packet of this species [R.*williamsianum*] please forward the seed to Mr. Brower, Hickory Hill Nursery, Newport, Long Island.

Respectfully,
J. E. Barto

Letter No. 3

Junction City, Oregon
April 10, 1930

Mr. Joseph B. Gable
Stewartstown, Pa.

Dear Sir:

I thank you for the list and will be pleased to exchange with you. I expect to have seedlings of about 300 varieties and species of rhododendrons and azaleas this fall. Perhaps we can supply each other with plants missing in our collection. Of the rhododendron you wish I have Rh. *chrysanthum* 20 plants 1 year and also germinated seed of: Rh. *haematodes, Rh. campylocarpum, Rh. lacteum, Rh. dichroanthum, Rh. williamsianum.*

Rh. *chrysanthum* is from Kew. Some from the Arnold Arboretum, Royal Botanic Garden also seeds from members of the Society. The J. F. Rock Rh. *carolinianum* interests me very much. Perhaps you might have one to spare this fall with bloom buds on. My interest is in getting the strain for hybridizing that I hope to give a great deal of attention.

Our climate is great for the erica family and I hope to take full advantage of it. Will make out a full list of species and so forth this fall that I have so we can compare lists.

Respectfully yours,
J. E. Barto

Subsequently Dr. Phetteplace received another letter from Gable,

July 20, 1960

Dear Dr. Phetteplace:

We have found some more "Bartoniania" and am sending it on to you. I had a very difficult time trying to read it over with my old eyes - or rather eye - and so I send it along to you. I wish it could be printed and wonder if the Bulletin could be persuaded to do this? It would be interesting to many members.

This has interested me in taking some backward glances too. Mr. Barto, George Fraser of Ucluelet, Vancouver Island, B.C., and Halfdan Lem, then of Ketchikan, Alaska, and Endre Ostbo were my first correspondents in the Northwest and we did a world of trading seeds and tiny seedlings. Through Mr. Fraser I became acquainted with Mr. E.J.P. Magor of Cornwall and he sent me pollen and seeds of hundreds of species and varieties. Many of these I deemed would be useless to try here and sent them west, and they sent me many things too.

... Hoping these letters will be of some use to you, I am,

With sincere regards,
Jos. B. Gable

Letter No. 4

Junction City, Oregon
February 2, 1932

Joseph B. Gable
Stewartstown, Pa.

Dear Sir:

I guess I am not much of a correspondent, conditions are somewhat to blame. The most unusual year here, plants grew fine at that. Rains stopped June 1, and 1/4 inch fell until the rains started in November. This was a long and exceedingly dry spell. Terrific rain followed one week of black cold 6 degrees F., and heavy winds most of the time. This sure cut the tender species, those surviving are worth a great deal for propagation. Most of the Rock numbers are alright so far even unprotected. Most surprising is R. 04007 *helioleplis* even only 1 year and this seedling is looking extra good.

Before I forget please set aside 2 *falconeri* series Rock 18234 for me as I am afraid my few plants are gone. After things clear up I will check your want list and see how my plants are.

At one time 4 feet of snow covered the ground, now rain, snow and repeat week on week. I do not know when it will let up. Usually the last of February is good. Rh. *dauricum, muchronulatum* for all this weather are about to open.

A Rh. *yunnanense* flowered last October for the first time with a good set of buds remaining for spring flowering.

(Paragraph about plant conditions on Mt. Hood is omitted.)

Where ignorance is bliss it is folly to be wise they say. But my ignorance saved me from the mistakes made last year and former years. My first seedlings were raised in a compost of rotten wood, sharp sand and very old decomposed litter dug out of the base of rotten centered maples. Into this was mixed more or less with a buck-shot soil that had been washed by rain into the hollow cavities on my hills. This is a very arduous job if much material is to be gathered. This mixture had its quota of weeds and required a lot of work. But all this work I attribute to the successful propagation of rhododendron here. As you know seed must be kept close, and in extreme hot weather the newspaper I used had to be kept moist by light sprinkling. This settled the paper so close to the seeds that moss would start when I used it for the beds later, and used peat moss. But my native mixture did not do this until seedlings were large enough to exclude the air. Once or twice a day weeds would gently force the paper from the compost surface airing the germinating seeds, and allowing larger mounts of water to be soaked into the porous paper. This made a balance between air moisture and the dry litter.

I have grown 'Amurisaku' and *poukhanense* 4 inches in one season from seed. On *fortunei* there were seven distinct breaks of growth in one season. All species cannot be induced to do this, yet, before a High School class R. *fortunei* made 24 inches of growth at the end of a second season. The plants were less than 1/2 inch in height when they were planted. The use of tweezers to pull weeds is best. Take hold at ground level, this prevents breaking of the weeds and removing their roots and at the same time not moving the compost.

Due to losses in bank failures and lack of business it is hard to keep up with expenses. I may not be able to supply all of your want list as the outcome of last winter cannot be assessed. The surviving plants should be hardy elsewhere, or with just a little protection, as they are growing here unprotected. You may be sure if you follow Wilson cultural ideas for producing hardiness, means terrible losses, sometimes 1 oz. of seed only produces a very few plants from a tender species. However in the long run, I will not be disappointed after years of labor if a species proves unsatisfactory.

I would like financially to aid in the forming of a U. S. Rhododendron Association, but cannot do so now. Yes, the slopes of five pass caravan route in Kashmere look good to me. The highest range 18,500 feet may yield something hardier for the U. S. I would very much like to aid in the exploring of this region, *betula* and evergreens cover the slopes as nearly as I can find out.

I wonder if the trade of plants I furnish you enough to repay plants from you. As it is now I could do no other way. I have never visited your section of Pennsylvania, not having gotten so far south, but can judge conditions fairly well. My boyhood was spent near Williamsport, then Philadelphia, Pittsburgh and Annapolis. I visited many cities when I was with the navy.

Enclosed is a leaf of a very hardy Rh. *racemosum* with a white edge of underside showing. In not so severe winters a lovely foliage form. I wonder if you have this. Hope to have rooted cuttings of this this coming fall. A few Rh. 'Loderi' are hardy, some lost a seasons growth. Others with hardy branch buds seem OK. This and some Rh. *falconeri*, Rh *lacteum* and others a *lapponicum* with lavender flowers in late July were lost. They were from Rock 1929.

I would like 2 plants each in trade for plants I have Rh. *aechmophyllum, adenogynum, agastum, carolinianum album, dentosum, falconeri* series Rock 18234, *floccigerum, intricatum, racemosum* 19404 Forrest and *traillianum*.

I am enclosing a packet of seed of Rh. *californicum* [*macrophyllum*] which I gathered on Mt. Hood near Government Camp about 4000 ft. It should be hardy if wood is ripened before freezing. … Are you in on the Rock 1932 expedition. I could not make it, not enough business.

Rh. *oldhamii* 1 year cuttings did not lose their leaves so far. The older plants did but appear to be alive. This species is sometimes deciduous and should not be as tender as rated but is well worth all the care since it is such a lovely thing.

A large rose double flowered Indica x *oldhamii* looks as it will be as good a doer as *oldhamii* which will be good. Rh. *occidentale* x 'Loderi' and other crosses are interesting and a large magnifying glass discloses a great difference of leaves. Rh. *californicum* x *thomsonii* has glands above and below a red undersurface. The Rh. *californicum* was a good pink 3 1/2 inch flower, with crepe like petals of good pink flowers. They were 21 - 27 to a truss.

Respectfully yours,
J. E. Barto

Letter No. 5

Junction City, Oregon
July 8, 1932

Mr. Joseph B. Gable
Stewartstown, Pa.

Dear Sir:

I thank you for your list, however, I am afraid it was destroyed in some manner as it is nowhere to be found. The list enclosed is of species and hybrids I have in numbers of one to a thousand or more. Rh. *racemosum oleofolium* in flower only two years from seed. *oldhamii* in four years, *japonicum* only four years to flower and lovely now. Also some American azaleas and imported hybrids in flower at this date along with Rh. *maximum*.

Rh. *maximum* does not do well as a rule on the Pacific coast is the information I can get, yet it is a good grower with me. No species or series compares to Rh. *fortunei* and its s.s. One species Wilson sent me seed of is a good variety, supposed to be a deep red and it is a wonder. Now 18" to 30" in only two years. Plant leaves 8" long and throwing side shoots. Several of these I disbudded to induce branching, but think that will be no advantage. Rh. 'Beauty of Tremaugh' is another extra good one 16" to 24" in 2 years. Rh. *fortunei x thomsonii* will make 12" to 18" 2 year Rh. *davidsonianum* makes 12" in a year. Rh. *arboreum* seem 18" to 36" in 4 years also seems a good one and apparently hardy here. The *triflorums* are inclined to grow too late and are therefore sometimes with blackened tips. I believe this is my fault by forcing growth too late.

It is developing my trade as a carpenter took me to the outposts of settlement. The coast and high mountain areas. While at Waldport on the coast moving a house I heard of a pure white rhododendron, and next season discovered this plant. Only one man knew of it and he was dead for several years. According to Wilson it is the missing species reported by Menzies over 150 years ago. Also in Alsea Bay the salt spray carried overhead and falling as rain tasted brackish. Rhododendrons live in it all around. Every house here had its boat tied to the porch in preparedness for the ever expected tidal wave which inundated this town periodically. All this site is a wonderful rhododendron area. Therefore salt is a good thing for rhododendron *californicum* and also I believe for every rhododendron in existence. A close study here shows rhododendrons in nature grow only on westerly slopes, facing the Pacific even if only a few yards from the edge of a bluff, along the ocean front or even two hundred miles inland. Our winds and rain from the ocean carry salt high in the air in a liquid state from the storm centers at sea. The leaf mould here has not broken down, but is forming a peat colored mulch of many years harvest, and sometimes 12" deep on the west slopes and on east slopes only one third that. This is a wonderful study to me and proving itself by the responses of rhododendrons that I am growing. The foliage color is all it could be and more. It is good to see growers almost gasp when entering my lath houses. I do not think the application of salt is good in the plant growing season, but in winter when nature in her moods and gales does it it cannot be wrong. I was born upstate from you and as you know a good Dutchman would not put in an asparagus bed without 2" of salt 18" below the surface of the ground. My theory is that salt adds to an acid soil and should aid as lime does to an acid soil. The doctors of science here at the Dept. of Agriculture wonder if other methods of culture should not be tried, since my plants show so well.

The hardiness of plants in the English yearbook does not hold good here. Some hardy so called showed the freeze. Rh. *maximum* in Portland for one was badly hurt. This brings us down to position, exposure and hardening, where individuality of the plant in the series may be taken into consideration. Ripe, hardened wood must be there regardless. The *lapponicums* are rather exacting in this respect. The *grande, falconeri, lacteum,* supposed to be tender are hardy if ripened. I had a lot of unnamed varieties of seed sent to me by Wilson and by using his ideas they were left out all winter. The first year showed a loss of 75%, however I will have no fear of the remaining plants since the tender ones have been weeded out by nature. When I received the names a year later you may imagine my surprise. This was a lesson not to be lightly taken or easily forgotten. I will profit by it in the future.

I do not know if it is customary for species to break or make more than one growth. Some have broken seven times in a single season. Rh. 'Pink Pearl' made 24" in 2 years from cuttings, breaking time after time with over 18 branches. It may be the salt and aluminum sulphate in conjunction with ripening of the wood by withholding water that is doing it. Of course, I spray them on the foliage as orchids are done, and there almost seems to be a link with orchids in this spraying the foliage.

If you have another copy of the list I would appreciate another one. I am much interested in hybrids, our own crosses. Rh. *occidentale* is a swamp azalea in some places here, and is growing in running water 7 or 8 months of the year. I do not think the roots would stand deep freezing.

J. E. Barto

Some interesting observations can be drawn from Mr. Barto's letters, perhaps many more than this writer can venture, but here are a few. There seems to have been no awareness of, or concern for, the fact that the seed obtained by Barto and Gable from English gardens and arboretums here and abroad were undoubtedly the result of open pollenization, hence of at least questionable authenticity. This, of course, was the very sort of activity that led eventually to the formation of the Rhododendron Species Foundation. However, a great deal of the seed was received from Rock and Forrest expeditions and having been gathered in the wild, was of unquestioned authenticity but largely unidentified. A long list of rhododendrons raised by Barto was attached to his Letter No. 5 but was not included here as it adds little to the story. It contains many Rock and Forrest collection numbers, unidentified as to name. An interested reader will find the list on pages 230 to 232 of Vol. 14, No. 4 of the ARS Quarterly Bulletin.

It is apparent that rhododendron enthusiasts' proclivity for experimentation and speculation has changed little in the last sixty years. Barto's speculation that R. *californicum* (*macrophyllum*) grows only on the western slopes, even 200 miles inland seems not to be borne out by my observations. His use of salt as an aid to rhododendron culture is interesting and seems to make some sense considering the apparent health of plants growing in seaside mists, although this writer is not aware of any grower who follows the practice today.

It seems that many of the subjects introduced rather abruptly by Barto were probably answers to questions posed in a past letter by Gable. It is a sign of changing times that even after over two years of friendly correspondence and an exchange of countless seeds and plants the correspondents still restricted themselves to the use of formal last names and the salutation "Dear Sir."

- - - - - - - - - - -

JOSEPH B. GABLE

Earlier in this chapter Joseph B. Gable was referred to as Barto's East Coast counterpart. While Gable's history is not as familiar to westerners as to those who live in the Eastern U. S., Gable certainly was as much a pioneer in rhododendron culture in the East as was Barto in the West. In Vol. 36, No. 3 of the Journal of the A. R. S. (Summer, 1982) Gable was announced as the first recipient of the Pioneer Achievement Award. While Gable was perhaps known more for his hybridization than his work with rhododendron species, still his earlier efforts dealt abundantly with the raising of species and portions of the condensed version of his lifelong efforts and accomplishments in both areas are worth setting forth here:

With all our respect and love we honor Joseph Benson Gable, a great and gentle man, a true pioneer in the Genus Rhododendron by awarding him the Pioneer Achievement Award for:

His vision and unswerving conviction of the prodigious potential in the Genus for diverse and untapped beauty and uniqueness.

For the creation of beautiful, novel plants adapted to growing conditions in gardens in the Eastern United States, and throughout the world.

For his innocent and humble perseverence despite intolerant climate and generally unavailable knowledge.

For his keen observation and constantly open mind.

For his infinite patience and dedication to the improvement of the Genus.

For his accumulation of knowledge heretofore unknown to his part of the world at that time.

For his meticulously kept records.

For his selfless sharing of knowledge and plants with others.

For his understanding and evaluation of the many species, which became his building blocks.

For his hybrids which in turn became building blocks for scores of plants in an ever wider and more diverse climate.

For the beauty he created.

For the many friends he made.

JOE GABLE - THE MAN: (Excerpts from selected writings)

"... gentle perceptive seeker after all that is beautiful on God's green earth." - From Gable's Memorial Service.

"... remember the dinner when Joe was given the Rhododendron Society Gold Medal and when he smiled (or giggled) that he didn't know why he should be given a medal for doing just what he wanted to do." - John and Gertrude Wister, Swarthmore, Pa.

"To those who knew him, Joseph B. Gable of Stewartstown, Pa., was a slight, shy, gentle man with thinning grey hair, weatherbeaten and unpretentious in his gardening clothes; not much of a business man, but totally consumed by the desire to create new, better colored strains of azaleas and rhododendrons hardy in the colder parts of the country." - Edward W. Weingartner, Gable Azaleas in the Olive W. Lee Memorial Garden, ARS Quarterly Bulletin.

"I must say that Joe had a good, long, wonderful life filled with enthusiasm for people, music, flowers and family. What more did he have to look forward to other than sharing God's kingdom?" - Ernest Yelton, Rutherfordton, N. C.

"It has been a privilege to walk with Mr. Gable in his gardens, and catch a bit of his quiet enthusiasm for the new plants." - Elizabeth and Lorenzo Kinney, Kingston, R. I.

"... he so distinguished himself because he was so dedicated and devoted to his ideal, and that always involves a personal sacrifice and often greater for the family." - David G. Leach, N. Madison, Ohio.

"... he served as an inspiration to others who have continued this work". Robert L. Tichnor, Aurora, Oregon, President of the ARS.

"... for decades I had depended on him more than anyone else for information about Rhododendrons, and I am proud that our names have become so universally linked." - Guy Nearing, Ramsey, N.J.

"In town he is known as a man who helps his neighbors, pays debts, and keeps his word." Margaret Kantress, granddaughter, at 14 years.

"I am thinking that dad was rich in good friends." - Caroline Gable.

JOE GABLE - THE PLANTSMAN: (Excerpts from Gable's letters and catalogs.)

May 15, 1930 - "Over 200 kinds of rhododendron seed have been received from plant expeditions, friends and other sources."

June 2, 1930 - "Received pollen from England." (R. *haematodes* and others.)

Jan. 30, 1931 - "… raising 10,000 *racemosum* seedlings …"

Feb. 9, 1931 - "Some *lapponicums* survive in shaded beds … *impeditum* dies in two summers … first knowledge of Magor's listing …"

May 12, 1931 - "… Rock 59717 small flowers, deepest color, hardiest form …"

May 6, 1932 - "Some seedlings of cross between Forrest *racemosum* 19404 and Rock 59717 are tall while others are low and dense."

Oct. 15, 1932 - On subscribing to Forrest expedition, "Please don't mention the price of the seeds before my wife as that will surely get me into trouble."

Nov. 20, 1932 - "… *neriiflorum* series will be the source of color and dwarfness in hybrids of the future. No other species with so many brilliant colors."

May 23, 1933 - "Received 350-400 packets of seed from Rock collection."

Jan 12, 1936 - "… *chrysanthum, fauriei* and *brachycarpum* are but three points in a gradually changing form of a Japanese species."

July 26, 1937 - "… started using indolebutyric acid for rooting hormone."

Dec. 16, 1942 - "… it doesn't matter what color a hybrid is as long as it's red.…"

JOE GABLE - HIS ACCOMPLISHMENTS:

Fall, 1933 and Spring 1934 catalogs list 105 species and 41 hybrids.

Grew seed from 346 species and subspecies.

Introduced 111 named rhododendron hybrids, 45 named azalea hybrids; grew 33 azalea hybrids named and introduced by others.

JOE GABLE - HIS HONORS:

1938 - Jackson Dawson Medal from Massachusetts Horticultural Society, for original contributions to Horticulture.

1953 - Gold Medal, American Rhododendron Society. The citation read in part, "The Gold Medal is also made in consideration of your pioneer investigations of a multitude of Asian Rhododendron species and their hybrids to determine their adaptability to the climate of the Eastern United States. The hardy forms isolated in a score of species grown from seeds provided by collectors in Asia have enriched the horticultural resources of the East.…"

1954 - Citation, Certificate of Merit, from Pennsylvania Horticultural Society for "… distinguished contribution to Horticulture in growing and hybridizing Azaleas."

1954 - March 24 edition of Saturday Evening Post featured "The Flowering Forest of Joe Gable."

1968 - Elected Pennsylvania Nurseryman of the Year by the Pennsylvania Nurseryman's Association.

Joe Gable died July 20, 1972.

Joe Gable, left, with Ted VanVeen (Sr.)

Joe Gable with George Grace, left

Photos courtesy Ted VanVeen

CHAPTER II
THE SEARCH

In 1961 Dr. Milton Walker and Dr. Carl Phetteplace of the Eugene area, together with their contemporaries in the then young American Rhododendron Society, having become dissatisfied and discouraged in their efforts to accumulate respectable collections of true species of rhododendrons, took the matter to the national organization. Dr. J. Harold Clarke, the then President of the A.R.S., responded by appointing a committee to study the matter, the committee to be chaired by Dr. Walker. In the spring of 1962 Dr. Walker filed the following report:

"A prominent species grower remarked recently that he was sure that over the years, he had discarded more plants than he now had in his garden. Why? Probably, because like many others, he found that he had bought not a true species, but a poor hybrid. Species enthusiasts are not interested in just garden plants but collect species for the beauty of the plant and the exquisite quality of the better forms.

"All collectors of species have experienced the difficulty of finding good forms, and of even knowing that what they buy is typical of the species. The reason for this we believe is twofold. First, there is no authoritative list published as to where one may locate typical, or very good forms of a particular species; and second, there is no unanimity of opinion as to what constitutes the typical, or what are exceptionally good forms.

"In an attempt to do something about this problem, The American Rhododendron Society has set up a Species Project Committee. This committee has initiated a pilot study, which is now under way with the cooperation of chapters in Seattle, Tacoma, Portland and Eugene. At the suggestion of Mr. Clarke, the study is being limited for the time being, to the above four centers, and will be expanded as soon as some of the problems inherent in a new undertaking are solved.

Arthur Childers
1914 - 1992
Photo courtesy Maxine Childers

"The committee decided that the first step would be to locate where species are being grown, and by whom. The ten species they selected for the pilot study are R. *souliei*, R. *wardii*, R. *calophytum*, R. *fargesii*, R. *haematodes*, R. *didymum*, R. *barbatum*, R. *strigillosum*, R. *augustinii*, R. *hippophaeoides*. At the present time local chairmen are collecting data on the above listed species. Arthur Childers, chairman of the Eugene Committee, got his questionaires out at the February meeting, followed closely by Merle Cisney at the Portland Chapter meeting. Ben Nelson of Seattle and Charles Edmund of Tacoma are heading up the project in Washington, and report a good deal of enthusiasm for the attempt the A.R.S. is making to bring a little order out of the present confusion.

"The ground work for this project, which is being done by the local committees, is of inestimable value. It is they who will search out each owner of a mature plant of the species under study, and they who will have the task of filling out a very complete report on the plant (See Figure 1). This may involve more than one visit in order to get detailed measurements of leaves, anatomical description of flowers, and if possible photos of the flowers, leaves and plant. This report is not in any way an evaluation of the plant, but simply a recording of factual information. Too much credit cannot be given to those who are serving, and will serve on the local Project Committee.

"When the detailed reports on these species come in to the A.R.S. Committee, we will have the help of some of the older more experienced growers, who are being mobilized into Evaluation Teams. It will be the function of these teams to study and compare the reports on the plants in the various species, go out and examine as many as possible, and come up with recommendations as to which plants in their opinion, are truly representative of the species; which are varieties of the typical, and which are very good forms of the species. The Evaluation Teams have the final responsibility in this far reaching project.

"When Dr. Clarke appointed the undersigned Species Project Committee, he stressed the organizational function of the committee. We were first asked to study the project and provide the President and Board of Directors with a suggested organizational plan, if the project seemed of value. After three months study, the committee recommended that the project be undertaken, and a plan of organization was submitted. The Board of Directors approved the plan at the December meeting of the A.R.S. And so a pilot study, as outlined above, has been set up, and is now in progress.

"The Species Project Committee would be glad to receive constructive suggestions from any interested members."

Frank D. Mossman, M.D.,
Secretary
304 E. 10th St., Vancouver, Wash.

Arthur K. Harris, M.D.
Box 708, Camas, Wash.

The foregoing was from The Quarterly Bulletin of the American Rhododendron Society, Vol. 16, No. 2, p. 93, April, 1962. In the succeeding issue of the Bulletin, Vol. 16, No. 3, July 1962, at page 178, Dr. Walker offered the following report on the progress of the Species Committee. It is interesting to note that the committee, now facing actual plants in the gardens of the Northwest, is beginning to have frustrating problems in defining the boundaries of their search, that is, in finding plants that purport to belong to a certain species, then deciding if they are within the allowable parameters of variation for that species, if in fact the parameters themselves can be established.

Dr. Walker: "In the late afternoon of a wet day, a grower of many years' experience was heard to remark - - 'I didn't expect to get anything out of today's trip except pneumonia, but I've learned something and it was fun too.'

"Such remarks are not unusual among Species Committee members who often have gone out on inspection trips with one foot dragging, only to find that visiting gardens in search of unusual or better forms of the Species Rhododendrons is both instructive and fun indeed. There seem to be still a great many unanswered questions [regarding] species, at least for some of us. Here are a couple.

"Rh. *haematodes* is usually considered to have a rather obovate or oblong leaf with the apex quite rounded. However, we have found in many gardens, a form called by the owners, 'Exbury' *haematodes* that differs in leaf shape. It is actually more elliptic than obovate with an acute apex, some leaves being almost lanceolate in their narrow tapering.

"We find on checking *The Species of Rhododendron*, 2nd ed., that the leaf is described as oblong and obovate, with the apex obtuse to rounded. No statement is found of variations in the leaf shape that might be construed to fit the elliptic shape and acute apex of the so-called 'Exbury' form.

"The question therefore arises - - should we who are growing this 'Exbury' form consider it a hybrid, or is it possible that it is a form of Rh. *haematodes* with a leaf shape differing from that described as typical? It seems almost sacrilegious to question such an authoritative book as *The Species of Rhododendron*, yet when it was published some thirty-two years ago, the editor himself said in his introduction to this monumental work - - 'It is therefore with no idea of finality that the present book appears.'

"The efforts of the Species Committees, in the four selected areas, have been limited these first few months, to just locating the ten species under study. No attempt has been made as yet to evaluate the plants recorded. While it is hoped to uncover 'better' forms of the species and eventually make them available to everybody, at the present time we are concerned with just being able to recognize plants that are representative of the species. This in itself presents problems.

"In the garden of Halfdan Lem of Seattle is a plant that in most respects fits the description of the species *cardiobasis* and yet we had thought the Rh. *cardiobasis* was no longer in cultivation. This beautiful mature plant, standing eight feet tall, and as much across, looks like a huge Rh. *orbiculare*. In fact it was so labeled in the garden of James Barto of Junction City, from whom Mr. Lem secured the plant. Mr. Barto must have prized this plant because '... it was in his private garden close to the steps leading into his home,' according to Mr. Lem. So many unusual species have come from Mr. Barto's collection, that it is quite within the realm of possibility that we have stumbled onto a species that was thought not to have been in cultivation.

"As we search for descriptions of this plant, we find that it is not described in *The Species of Rhododendron*, 2nd. ed. but that the *Rhododendron Handbook* 1956 describes it as follows, 'A shrub up to ten feet, resembling Rh. *orbiculare*, with round stiff leathery leaves, heart-shaped at the base. The flowers with 7 lobed corollas are large, white or rose colored, 6-7 in a loose truss.' Mr. Lem's plant fits the above description perfectly, except that every truss has 15-18 flowers, not 6-7.

"This question of a species having more flowers in a truss than the described plant was discussed with Ben Nelson in Seattle, and a trip was made by the writer to the Nelson garden in Suquamish. Here Mr. Nelson pointed out a plant labeled Rh. *argyrophyllum*. We counted 23 flowers in every truss on this plant, which certainly had all the other outward appearance of Rh. *argyrophyllum*, but which the Species book says should have only 6-12 flowers in a truss.

"These are examples of some of the interesting problems that have presented themselves to the members of the Species Committee. Even the recognition of plants truly representative of their species is not always a simple matter. It may be that there are certain variations from the described characteristics of a species that we will have to recognize by describing different forms of the typical species. But just how much variation from the published botanical description will be permissible? These and other questions that have arisen are making the species study stimulating and exciting."

Interestingly, in the same issue of the Journal, in the section entitled Rhododendron Notes, an item by the then Editor, Rudolph Henny, observes that, "Many of the forms of the *triflorum* series in this country were originally grown from seed obtained from collectors. We have often thought some of these selected forms are superior for this country, to those imported from England. This is particularly true of Rh. *augustinii*." Immediately following is an article by Bob Bovee stating, "There are many good species in this country which have been checked and found true to type." Contrast these statements with the previous and following articles by Dr. Walker. Both Bovee and Henny were prominent nurserymen and respected for their knowledge of rhododendrons. One wonders if they were in contact with the Species Committee, which was at the time having such difficulty finding true species or even defining "true." It is interesting to note that the committee is now studying twenty species rather than the original ten.

"In the search for the truly diagnostic marks that establish unmistakably the true type species, all the available published literature on the twenty species presently under consideration has been studied, charted and condensed. An effort has been made to put in writing the essential characteristics of each species as a guide for members who are engaging in the Species Project. After much effort and study, the data assembled was found wanting in many aspects by the committee.

"Much of the literature studied follows the original publication, and little effort was ever made later to narrow or broaden the latitude that is so evident with the often variable species. Where is the line drawn on what constitutes the so called type species? It is true that in some species as in the Rh. *fortunei* group are remarkably uniform in foliage, bloom and habit, with the absence or presence of scales as described, and no difficulties are encountered. In the *neriiflorum* series, sub-series *haematodes* or the sub-series *sanguineum*, to name but two, much the opposite prevails. Foliage shape and size in some instances do not follow any known description, nor does the absence or presence of light or heavy indumentum, or the wide range of corolla coloration shed any light as to a positive identification. This leads to the real reason for the huge undertaking of the Species Project - - the cataloging of known plants of the true species wherever possible, finding the best forms, and making both available. We know the job will take many, many years, but feel that it will be worth every effort expended.

"Thousands of seedlings of species have been grown from seed, here and abroad, very rarely hand pollinated, and as a result much hybridity is in evidence. It is now very difficult to tell a species from a hybrid. What will be the answer say in another twenty-five or fifty years? Will the true species have disappeared? Much discussion and feeling is already leaning in that direction. True, the bees will sometimes produce an outstanding cross that will be a delight to a gardener, but while one good hybrid is being accidentally grown, thousands and thousands of other plants are being mistakenly grown under a species label that is entirely false, and are of such poor quality that they are fit only for the fire.

"Now, the local Species Project Committees are busily at work trying to sift the wheat from the chaff, all the way from Victoria and Vancouver, B.C., under the guidance of Mary (Mrs. Ted) Grieg, to San Francisco, where Ed Long and Jock Brydon are really fired with zeal to identify and properly label their fine collections of species. The committee in Seattle is doing an outstanding and very thorough job with the whole area divided geographically, and worked by teams. The committee met weekly for some time, with members travelling long distances to attend, and help set up the machinery for the 'bugging' as they call it, or detail reporting of the various species. Another enthusiastic member is J. A. Witt, the Assistant Director of the University of Washington Arboretum. He has contributed hugely of his time and knowledge particularly in regard to the outstanding collection of species at the arboretum.

"Many members of the society have urged the release of information we have gathered so far, but the Species Project Committee has been very reluctant to assume the authoritative position of labeling plants as 'typical' or 'superior forms', until more study has been done, and more plants inspected. However, we do plan to start publication of a tentative descriptive list of good forms, and where they may be seen, with the next issue of the Bulletin, and continue in subsequent issues." (From The Quarterly Bulletin of the American Rhododendron Society, Vol. 17, No. 2, April 1963.)

In keeping with the foregoing promise, in the ensuing issue of the Bulletin, Vol. 17, No. 3, July, 1963 Dr. Walker presented the following: "The Species Project of the A.R.S. would like to make available some of the information gathered by local committees and checked by members of the A.R.S. Committee with the full knowledge of its incompleteness. In the short time the Committee has been functioning it has been physically impossible to locate all the best forms of a given species even in the Pacific Northwest, or to definitely state which ones are 'typical' or representative of the species. However, many fine forms have been found and we have been asked to publish a short description of these plants and state where they may be seen and studied.

"The plants described below, by their growers in most cases, are fairly mature plants according to our standards in the U.S.A. In the Committee's judgment these plants are outstanding representatives of the species and conform to the published botanical descriptions. Undoubtedly there are many others just as outstanding and one reason for starting publication of our findings is to uncover other fine forms.

RHODODENDRON CALOPHYTUM - This plant was grown from seed by the late James Barto with no existing record as to the explorer or its number to identify its source. It is probably 30 years old and began flowering 15 to 18 years ago. It has missed a year occasionally but generally is covered with trusses. In February, 1962 it was very heavily budded and almost ready to flower when the temperature suddenly dropped to 15 degrees Fahrenheit. Although the plant has never shown any injury, this unusual cold destroyed all the flowers and there was only one truss that year.

Calophytum means "beautiful plant" and it is that indeed. The fine plant now growing in my garden near Eugene, Oregon is presently about 10 feet tall and 14 feet across. Although one of the fortunei series it is considered one of the "big leafed" species, with leaves 14 to 16 inches long and 3 to 3 1/2 inches wide. A characteristic is the collar-like arrangement of the leaves on the branches.

The truss is rather flat topped and has 25 or more florets. This specimen has especially deep pink flowers which are accented by the almost red pedicels, which are 1 to 1 1/2 inches long. There is a rather prominent deep maroon blotch in the corolla. Another distinctive characteristic is the stout style capped by a discoid stigma 1/3 of an inch across. The leaf scales are red and the new growth is striking with the bright green upper surface and white floccose undercoating which is quickly lost.

R. *calophytum* is such an outstanding rhododendron that it probably should be used more in hybridizing. Two of its progeny are "Avalanche" and "Calstocker", both fine varieties for the larger garden area. Carl Phetteplace, M.D., Eugene, Oregon.

"With the exception of a very large and very fine plant in the garden of Mr. and Mrs. Ted Greig at Royston, Vancouver Island, B.C. the plant described above is, in our opinion, one of the finest now growing in the Pacific Northwest. Other very good forms may be seen at the U. of W. Arboretum, the Test Garden in Portland, Oregon and at Hendrick's Park, Eugene, Oregon. Variations in color from the usual pink shade, which may be very light to a dark pink, may be found in plants growing in the gardens of Halfdan Lem of Seattle, Wash., and H. J. Larson of Tacoma, Wash. (M.V.W.)

RHODODENDRON THOMSONII - A rhododendron *thomsonii* was given to us by some friends about 1947. The plant was then about 2 1/2 feet tall and possibly around 10 years old. We have grown it in full sun until the last 3 years when we moved it to a position where it gets afternoon shade. It has now reached 6 ft. tall, 11 ft. wide and 25 ft. in circumference 1 ft. above the ground. Our plant has been blooming for about 8 years only sparingly, however it bloomed profusely one year. The flowers are a good red and a little larger in size than the typical, as described in the "Species of Rhododendron." The leaves of our plant correspond to the usual description of a somewhat orbicular lamina with rounded apex and blunt mucro.

Kingdon-Ward in his book *Rhododendrons* says that Rhododendron *thomsonii* forms a handsome shrub 10 to 20 feet high and almost as much through. He could be describing the plant now growing in our garden in Seattle. The local species committee tagged this plant as a superior form on its habit alone. Ralph C. Jacobson, Seattle, Wash.

"Most plants of R. *thomsonii* checked by the A.R.S. Committee were found to be tall, rangy and not particularly attractive as garden plants. Occasionally we found a compact and well shaped plant, usually growing in more sun than the average, but in one garden two plants growing side by side showed definitely different growth habits leading us to wonder if there are actually two forms of R. *thomsonii*. Let readers be advised that 'full sun' as described by Ralph Jacobson above, is for the Seattle-Tacoma area and is equivalent to probably half sun in the Portland-Eugene area.

"We have selected the plant described by Ralph Jacobson to bring out the difference in growth habit and to emphasize the fact that a well grown and cared for plant of R. *thomsonii* can be an exceedingly handsome shrub as well as breathtakingly beautiful when in the full bloom of maturity.

"Many of the fine specimens of R. *thomsonii* to be found in the Seattle area originally came from an exceptional batch of seedlings grown by Herb Ihrig, Bainbridge Island, near Seattle. Mr.Ihrig received his seed from Darjeeling, India in the early 1930's. He has kept a few plants, and now has some extraordinarily beautiful ones 10 to 12 feet tall and as much in diameter. The writer had the great privilege of seeing these plants in full bloom this spring. The beauty of the large ruby red waxy flowers will long be remembered.

"In Tacoma, Wash. good forms may be found in the gardens of Herbert Bowen, H. J. Larson and others. The late Rudolph Henny had a good R. *thomsonii* in his garden and other good ones may be seen in the Test Garden in Portland and in the garden of Dr. Carl Phetteplace of Eugene, Oregon. (M.V.W.)

R. YAKUSIMANUM (sic) - Our plant of R. *yakusimanum* F.C.C. was obtained from E. R. Peterson about 1954. He received the cuttings from George Grace, to whom they had been sent by Francis Hanger from Wisley in 1950. The Wisley plant came from Exbury as a layer from the original plant imported by Rothschild from Wada in Japan.

Our plant is now about thirteen years from a cutting and is about thirty inches high and fifty-six inches wide. It is dome shaped and very compact. It buds well every year, and many buds are removed in the fall to keep them from being too crowded.

It is exposed to the summer sun from about nine in the morning until three in the afternoon. The temperature may go above 90 degrees as many as fifteen times during the summer with daytime humidity in the twenties and some-times lower. These low humidities are pleasant for people but a test for rhododendrons. R. *yakusimanum* appears to stand more sun than the great majority of the genus. The foliage is a little larger and darker on the north side of the plant than on the south side. Perhaps the ideal exposure would be in the open except for light shade for four or five hours in the middle of the day.

R. *smirnowii, R. metternichii, R. makinoi and R. degronianum* require more shade than R.*yakusimanum.*

This plant has good drainage next to a four foot dry rock wall. It is in silty clay loam with some fir sawdust incorporated and has a constant mulch of fir needles. Nitrogen and sulfur are added once a year in March. It has had no die-back and the leaves stay on for six years, the longest time that I have observed in either species or hybrids.

The horticultural virtues of R. *yakusimanum* have been so thoroughly aired in the literature the last few years that I shall make only a brief summary. (There follows a lengthy description of the plant that is only too familiar to all rhododendron enthusiasts so it will not be repeated here.) Cecil C. Smith, Aurora, Oregon.

"Mr. Jock Brydon imported from Exbury a plant now in the garden of Bob Comerford of Marion, Oregon, and from which many plants now growing in this vicinity owe their origin. All are alike, but none we think are as beautifully grown as the one described above. The only plant of any size we have found north of Portland is a very nice one growing in the garden of Fred Robbins of Puyallup, Wash. (M.V.W.)

R. METTERNICHII var. TSUKUSHIANA - This plant was purchased in 1946 from a row of seedlings grown by H. L. Larson of Tacoma, Wash. It was about 8' tall, compact and supposedly a dwarf type of rhododendron well suited for a sunny location. It was about 8 to 10 years old at the time of purchase. Two or three years later when it bloomed for the first time we identified it from the Species Rhododendron book as R. *metternichii*. Mr. Larson later confirmed this identification and then gave us the Japanese varietal name of '*Tsukushiana*'.

Our plant has been grown where it receives only early morning sun. It puts out from 4 to 6 inches of growth a year and now stands a full 6' tall and 8' in width. The mature leaves are 6" long with a dark-green, glossy surface. The underneath is a beautiful, tawny color, the indumentum being so fine it gives the effect of a hard, shiny surface. The prominent mid-rib is a light green color.

The flowers are campanulate, light pink in color with a few reddish freckles. They are 7 lobed, 9 to 12 in a truss, each floret supported on a 1 1/2" pedicel. This is an excellent foliage plant as well as one having beautiful flowers.

At the time we purchased this plant there were six others purchased by members of my family; however our plant seems to be superior to the other six, though they are all beautiful specimens. Four of these plants are now to be found growing in the National Test Garden in Portland, Ore. Two are at the top of the rockery and two are located in the species plantings along the west side of the island. Ruth M. Hansen, Portland, Ore.

"Mr. H. L. Larson of Tacoma has three distinct forms of R. *metternichii* growing in his garden, all of them very beautiful either in full bloom or as an interesting foliage plant. In the Eugene area Dr.Phetteplace has a good plant about 5 ft. tall and in Portland there are the plants in the Test Garden but none as fine as the one described above growing in the garden of Ruth and Ted Hansen. (M.V.W.)"

The following article, written by Dr. Walker some two years following the activation of the Species Committee, marks the beginning of a change of orientation from seeking out true species in the gardens of the Pacific Northwest, to a recognition that the ultimate source of the finest species was to be found in the British Isles:

"The chairman of the Species Project had the great privilege this past summer of seeing the Species Collection at Windsor Great Park in England. The size and maturity of these plants was most impressive. We, here in the United States, are so used to our small and very young plants, we are not prepared for the majestic beauty that maturity brings to rhododendrons. The plants at Windsor are well spaced and arranged in Series, with not one or two forms of a given species, but often a dozen different forms, all carefully and legibly labeled with name and collector's number. To see thousands of these species plants growing superbly in a natural woodland setting was a sight never to be forgotten. Sir Eric Savill and Mr. T. H. Findlay have made a tremendously important contribution to the Rhododendron world in bringing together these several thousand Rhododendron Species plants for study and preservation.

"In a previous issue of the Bulletin a start was made by the Species Committee to report on the location of good forms found, and the growers were asked to write short descriptions of their plants. Many complimentary comments have been received, obviously from members who either had bought what they were told was a good form and it turned out to be worthless, or were honest enough to admit they didn't know a good form from a poor one. These people are serious in their desire to know where they can go to see what we consider a truly representative plant of a given species.

RHODODENDRON BARBATUM - This plant was grown by the late James Barto from seed sent him from one of the expeditions to China. Records of the explorer or number were lost at the time of the fire that destroyed the Barto home. (See 'The Life and Work of James Barto', A.R.S. Bulletin, April p. 67 and July p. 147, 1960). It has been in my possession about 15 years, and probably flowered for the first time about then. It is now 9 1/2 feet tall and would have been 7 feet across without misfortune. In March it is such a spectacular sight with its glowing red trusses and deep green foliage that on three separate occasions passers-by have rushed from their cars and cut good sized branches to take with them. This is almost the only vandalism that has ever been committed in my garden, and it is my belief that this has been motivated, not by evil intent, but rather by the attraction of such a striking appearance of a large shrub in full flower at a time of year when such things are uncommon.

The bark is smooth and dark mahogany brown in color, quite handsome in itself. Like all rhododendrons with such bark it does not break out with new growth below the point where branches have been cut away, hence the damage from vandalism causes permanent disfigurement.

The leaves are 3 to 5 inches in length and 3/4 to 1 1/2 inches in width, slightly cordate at the base with moderately acute apex, deeply veined above and with prominent mid-rib and lateral veins below. The juvenile leaves have bristles on the petiole and mid-rib, but at maturity there are only sparse hairs in this specimen.

The truss is compact and rounded, approximately 5· inches across, with a dozen or so deep crimson or blood red florets. Though the weather is often inclement at blooming time, the plant is attractive at a distance for as long as 6 weeks, the trusses even enduring light frosts.

It will not strike root by layering, and I have had no success with the few cuttings I have tried. It does graft in early spring quite successfully, however. There seems also to be some difficulty in getting seeds. Although several attempts have been made to hand pollinate, no seeds have germinated, for me at least. The plant has never shown injury with temperatures we have had here, occasionally to about 0 degrees Fahrenheit. A picture of the plant in flower was shown on the cover of the Bulletin for April, 1962. More serious effort than I have made to propagate it should be carried out, as it would be a credit to any garden. Carl H. Phetteplace, M.D., Eugene, Ore. [Editor's note: This particular plant was subsequently killed to the ground by a severe freeze. Fortunately a number of plants propagated from it survive.]

"The 1956 freeze must have been especially hard on the R. *barbatums* because they have nearly all disappeared. The plant above described is the only one of any size we have found in the northwest, outside of a pretty fair sized plant in the Arboretum at Seattle. Dr. Phetteplace has moved his plant to a situation more remote from vandals and it is becoming adjusted to its new surroundings very well. Unfortunately, as he says, it seems particularly hard to propagate. (M.V.W.)

R. CAERULEUM ALBUM - The plant of R. *caeruleum album* now growing in the Portland Test Garden was recently acquired from Mrs. Rae James of Eugene, Ore. It stands about 7' high with a spread of 4' to 5'. Its flowers are pure white, with small red spots in the throat. The leaves are 1 1/2" long, 1" wide and glabrous on both sides. The upper surface is almost a bluish green, the under surface more of a whitish color. It is without doubt one of the most attractive forms of this species in cultivation.

This R. *caeruleum album* came from Barto's many years ago. It was selected out of a whole group, while in bloom, as a superior plant by Mr. and Mrs. Del James when they were real beginners. Ruth M. Hansen, Portland, Ore.

"Del and Rae James had two forms of R. *caeruleum album* both obtained from the Barto collection. Some say that the form that was lost due to overzealous weed spraying by city employees was better than the one described. If so, it must have been a superb form because the one donated to the Test Garden by Mrs., Rae James is the most beautiful specimen of R. *caeruleum album* we have seen. (M.V.W.)

RHODODENDRON STRIGILLOSUM - The clone of R. *strigillosum* to be described was obtained from Royston nursery on Vancouver Island, in 1955, as a seedling about 4 years old. It bloomed in 1962 and 1963, starting twelve years from seed. Several people who have seen a number of clones of this species say that this one is typical, and one of the more desirable expressions of R. *strigillosum*. The plant is now about four feet wide and five feet high with one main trunk and branching from the ground. The leaves are dark green and about six inches long. They scorch badly in full sun here in the

Willamette Valley, even when the plant is well established in one location.

Some people do not care for it as a foliage plant. I think it is very distinctive with its oblanceolate leaves, with a cluster of long coarse hairs on the leaf stalks, or petioles. The young growths have many long bright red bracts on the stems, over the long, frosty white bristles covering the stems and leaf stalks. The bristles on other good clones have a reddish tinge. On still others the bracts are a pale green, giving a much less desirable effect.

Our plant has from ten to thirteen flowers in a truss. They are cup shaped, and a clear bright red, about two inches wide. The pedicels are not as long as are those on many plants of this species, and as a result, a dome-shaped truss is formed and the corollas look right out at you. To get a top quality plant of R. *strigillosum*, the buyer should see it both in bloom and in new growth. It is especially desirable that the better clones of this species be located and propagated. Cecil Smith, Aurora, Ore.

"There are many good *strigillosums* to be found in gardens of the Northwest besides the one described above. Most have excellent color, and a few, like the ones grown by Cecil Smith, Ben Nelson, H. L. Larson, and Wales Wood have extremely attractive foliage with a thick nest of hairs formed by the radiating leaf stalks. As Cecil Smith points out, this species does much better in almost complete shade, in the Willamette Valley, and even in the Puget Sound area Ben Nelson's beautiful plant is grown in almost complete shade. (M.V.W.)

RHODODENDRON INSIGNE - Our Rhododendron *insigne* was purchased from the Layritz Nurseries in Victoria in 1957. We were informed at the nursery that the plant had been imported from England in 1937. Under good garden conditions it has doubled in width and is now 4 feet by 4 feet. It is indeed a slow growing plant. The flowers are pink and the truss is firm and rounded, with about fifteen flowers making it an attractive display. The plant is worth growing for its form and plastered coppery indumentum alone. Ralph Jacobson, Seattle, Wash.

"David Leach describes this plant as a 'handsome, neat, slow-growing shrub' and says that in cultivation it usually reaches only 6 to 9 feet in height. Despite the fact of its being typically slow in growth, the plant described by Ralph Jacobson is unusually small for its age. There are very few plants of R. *insigne* in good form to be found in this region but we think this one is a good representative of the species. There are no others that we know of outside of the Seattle - Tacoma area that are typical. (M.V.W.)

R. AUGUSTINII FORMS - There are a number of excellent forms of R. *augustinii*, some of which are now being grown commercially, others not yet on the market. These forms vary from light blue with a greenish blotch to a deep purple with reddish-brown blotches. One of the most confusing classifications is the distinction between R. *augustinii* and R. *chasmanthum*. The difference, according to the Species book is so minute that I fail to see any actual variation between the two forms; therefore in the following list no distinction will be made between the two so-called species.

There are now three Barto raised plants of R. *augustinii* which have been recognized as superior forms and which have been given varietal names. They are as follows: 'Barto Blue' selected and named by Dr. Carl

Phetteplace of Eugene, Ore.; 'Marine', selected and named by Bob Bovee (deep purple); 'Summer Skies', selected and named by Ben Lancaster, Camas, Wash. Other selected forms are: 'Lackamas Blue', selected and named by Ben Lancaster, Camas, Wash.; 'Blue Cloud', listed as R. *chasmanthum,* selected and named by Ruth M. Hansen: The original plant was purchased by Mrs. Sophie Cason in 1928 and is still growing in her garden in Portland, Ore. Flowers are unusually large, about 2 1/2 inches across with greenish markings, and light blue in color; 'Caprice', selected and named by Ruth M. Hansen, same source as above. Original plant was killed in the 1955 November freeze. Flowers large with dark markings.

From this same collection is a plant with the RHS-HCC color Imperial Purple 33/1. This has never been named or propagated for commercial use but it is an outstanding deep color and of good garden value. Another R. *augustinii* plant of excellent light blue quality was obtained many years ago from the Esch Nursery. This has large flowers, greenish markings and deserves recognition. Robert Whalley grows a beautiful light blue form which has almost a white striping down the center of the petals. It is quite outstanding. Ruth M. Hansen, Portland, Ore.

"The Species Committee has included R. *augustinii* in this report to draw attention to this species as being one of the best of garden rhododendrons for ease of growing and beautiful massed effect. There are many very inferior seedlings being grown although there are a dozen or more very excellent forms available, propagated by cuttings, and therefore just as good as the best grown anywhere. (M.V.W.)"

H. L. Larson, Ben Nelson, Mr. Whitney and Dr. Walker
evaluating plants in April, 1963, for Species Committee

Milton and Helen Walker
on a collecting trip
Photo courtesy Ian Walker

CHAPTER III
THE SOURCE

Dr. Walker's visit to Windsor Great Park described in the beginning of the foregoing article triggered some thoughts that led him to plan a more protracted visit to the British Isles the following summer. In anticipation of this trip he contacted Mary Grieg of Vancouver Island, Canada to inquire as to whom in Canada might be able and willing to take on the project of handling propagation of any materials he might arrange to have shipped over from Great Britain. Mary Grieg wrote the following letter as a result of the inquiry:

Feb. 29, 1964

Mr. Herman Vaartnou
Supervisor of Grounds,
University of British Columbia
Vancouver 8, B.C.

Dear Mr. Vaartnou,

We had a letter from Dr. Milton Walker of Eugene, who is the chairman of the American Rhododendron Society's species project. This, as you may know is an effort to find, list and if possible acquire the best forms of a selected list of species each year.

On the 18th of March Dr. Walker is going to England to see "every private garden in Britain that has outstanding forms of the species". Sir Eric Saville, Mr. Findlay, Patrick Synge and Dr. Fletcher are arranging their itinerary and they plan to remain over there until May 27th. Dr. Walker asks if we can suggest anyone who would grow on scions and cuttings which they hope to acquire, as he says the U.S. would fumigate them, and Canada does not. They would have to be kept here for at least one year, and possibly longer. Do you think it would be worth your while to cope with the considerable amount of work in exchange for a proportion of the resulting plants? If it can be handled, we think from the University's point of view it is a chance not to be missed. And if Nick [Weesjes] and Evelyn [Jack] can't get results, no one else is likely to!

Of course we know you could not answer Dr. Walker without conference with powers that be, but at least it seemed worth writing to you ... perhaps you would write to Dr. Walker, R.R. #2, Box 455, Creswell, Creswell is just outside Eugene, Ore.

We are sending a copy of this letter to Miss Jack for her information.

Yours sincerely,
/s/ Mary Grieg

Endorsed on the bottom of Evelyn Jack's copy, "Dear Evelyn, This might be exciting indeed - do hope you can swing it! M G"

Walker toured a number of gardens as planned and conceived the idea of a large permanent collection of species rhododendrons in America, under the auspices of some sort of "foundation". During the course of this tour, and as a direct result of it, he compiled what he called a "Species Location List" or "Species Acquisition List" in which he recorded the location of what he and his advisors had determined to be the very best forms of the species in the British Isles and elsewhere. The original list is set out in full in **APPENDIX A** at page 209 of this book, although it was amended from time to time.

Unfortunately there seems to be no direct record of the trip, all the gardens visited or the people encountered, although the following letter from Dr. Walker to Sir Eric Savill and Mr. Findlay upon his return to the U. S. gives us some idea of the nature of his visit and the rapport established with his English friends:

June 23, 1964

Dear Sir Eric and Mr. Findlay:

I hope you will not mind a combined letter because after just completing eight double paged letters to Directors of the new Rhododendron Foundation, I am not about to abide by formalities. You two are so closely associated and my thanks are for both of you that made our stay in Great Britain so enjoyable.

I cannot in any way express our gratitude for your help and generosity. Helen and I enjoyed so very much having lunch with you again in your home, Sir Eric, and it was always a pleasure to run into you as we walked in the gardens. Not until afterward did we realize who Sir Frederick Stern was, when you introduced him to us. Now as we read about him we can recall meeting him and Lady Stern. We have so many memories of pleasant times spent with Mr. Findlay, not only at Windsor but in Cornwall, Wakehurst, Leonardslee and the various shows that we feel that he is a good friend. I hope you didn't mind my pulling your leg once in a while - I only feel I can tease friends I know pretty well. I especially enjoyed our visit together at Caerhays and if I had any doubts before as to your ability to recognize plants, that day made me admire your knowledge tremendously. I do hope that you will be given an opportunity of helping them at Wakehurst sort out the wheat from the chaff.

There is a real potential there for a fine garden.

We have the Articles of Incorporation ready to file for the Species Foundation and I plan to go to Salem this afternoon for this purpose. Seven men, some at least quite outstanding, have consented to be directors of the Foundation. Besides the President and Executive Secretary of the American Rhododendron Society, we have an attorney and former A.R.S. Director, one of the oldest growers of Species and a present Director of the A.R.S., a retired lumberman of considerable business experience and wealth, and a friend of mine who has extensive business interests as well as being a Director of several national horticultural societies. We will hold an organizational meeting on July 11 and have a tentative set of by-laws drawn up ready for the meeting. We plan to enlarge the board of directors to probably 25 eventually. So far I have to do most of the work but hope that after we get going someone else will help out. At least this job keeps the days full to overflowing.

I do want you to know how very much Helen and I appreciated your help on our recent trip, and also that we are convinced that there are no finer gardens in the world than at Windsor.

Cordially yours,
Milton V. Walker, M.D.

Within a few days of the writing of the above letter Dr. Walker and Fred Robbins met at the University of British Columbia, with Leon Koerner, Dr. Hawthorne and Dr. Prink of the botany department, and arrangements were finalized for the propagation of all the cuttings to be received from the English gardens, as well as the care and growing on of the plants for up to two years. The propagation was to be done under the supervision of Mr. Herman Vaartnou, supervisor of Grounds at the University of British Columbia.

In July, 1964 Mr. Vaartnou obtained from the Canada Department of Agriculture a waiver of phyto-sanitary certificate requirements and agreement from customs officials to forego lengthy quarantine and inspection procedures, thus allowing rhododendron cuttings nearly free entry into Canada from the British Isles. British donors were requested to mail cuttings on a Monday so they would reach the University of B. C. before the following week end. Cuttings thus handled were sometimes a little wilted but usually were capable of being revived sufficiently to propagate. Miss Jack was slated to do the hands-on propagation work, which began that August. Meanwhile, Dr. Walker had been grafting particularly fine varieties on his own and had about 100 grafted plants for the new collection in British Columbia.

Dr. Walker realized that by using standard propagation procedures it was going to take a lot of time to accumulate enough plants to stock the Foundation garden or gardens, to say nothing of plants for distribution to the membership and even to the public through the nursery industry, so he began to make inquiries regarding a new procedure of which he had heard, propagation by means of meristem tissue culture. A Mr. Barry Jasper of Long Beach, California, having done much research on the subject and having succeeded in propagating orchids by this means, offered to attempt to develop the process with rhododendrons, with no guarantee of success, but required a fee of $3,000, which of course the Foundation didn't have. But Dr. Walker entered into an agreement with Mr. Jasper, stating, "… if I have to foot the bill myself." It is not clear from Walker's records exactly why the arrangement didn't work out but in July 1965 the agreement was terminated with Jasper being paid the sum of $250.00. So meristem tissue culture propagation had to wait for a second abortive attempt.

In early September, 1964 Dr. Walker wrote letters to the following, requesting rhododendron cuttings :

Mr. Julian Williams, Caerhays Castle, Cornwall, England.
Mr. John Basford, Brodick Castle, Isle of Arran, Scotland.
Mr. Frank Knight, Director, R.H.S. Garden, Wisley, Woking, England.
Wing Commander F. L. Ingall, Corsock House, Castle Douglas, Scotland.
Mr. John Hanvey Sen., Leggygowan, County Down, North Ireland.
Mr. Archie Gibson, Glenarn, Rhu, Dunbartonshire, Scotland.
Mr. M. Colledge, The Gardens, Logan House, Wigtownshire, Scotland.
Mr. R. Shaw, Younger Botanical Garden, Benmore, Argyll, Scotland.
Mr. Archie Kenneth, Stronachullin, Nr. Ardrishaig, Argyll, Scotland.
Sir George Campbell and Ilay Campbell, Crarae Lodge, Argyll, Scotland.
Mr. R. J. Wallis, Wakehurst, Ardingly, Sussex, England.
Dr. Harold Fletcher, Royal Botanic Garden, Edinburgh, Scotland.

These selections were made from the SPECIES LOCATION LIST that had been prepared as a result of Dr. Walker's visits to Britain and which is set forth as **APPENDIX A** at page 209 of this book.

At this time the new Foundation had a total of $700 in its treasury, mostly the result of a fine gift from Ernest Yelton, M.D. of North Carolina, and the board members began thinking seriously of a permanent home for the anticipated collection of species rhododendrons. Perhaps it would be more accurate to say they were considering at least three locations - one approximately in the Eugene area, one somewhere between Vancouver, B.C. and Portland, Oregon and one on the Pacific Coast in southern Oregon or California for the anticipated tender varieties. There was no unanimity on this point, however, Dr. Walker and others favoring the idea of multiple gardens while Dr. J. Harold Clarke and others felt this would dilute the efforts of the Foundation and that one central garden should be constructed, with all efforts directed to its financing, completion and maintenance.

Correspondence became preoccupied with a search for wealthy prospective donors to build the million dollar endowment it was anticipated would be required to finance the acquisition of land and construction and maintenance of the gardens and their supporting structures and facilities. Negotiations were actually undertaken with wealthy landowners, with the goal of transferring ownership of their property to the Foundation while they retained a life estate and the right of possession and management of their gardens and plant collections during their lifetime. None of these negotiations bore fruit, however, and the search for financing went on. Dr. Walker made a trip to the East Coast in November of 1964 for the express purpose of interesting some very wealthy easterners in serving on the board of directors and, particularly, in making substantial donations to the Foundation. These efforts were in vain, from a financial standpoint, and on December 5th Treasurer Clarence Chase notified Dr. Walker that he could not reimburse Walker's trip expenses since there was only $29.67 left in the Foundation's bank account. But the trip had been successful in one sense; three very influential men agreed to serve on the board of directors - Mr. Henry du Pont, Dr. John Wister and Dr. Henry Skinner, with a tentative agreement from Mr. W. R. Coe, Jr.

One of the prominent board members wrote a lengthy letter to Dr. Walker, suggesting that Dr. and Mrs. Walker actually donate or devise their home near Eugene to the Foundation for purposes of the initial garden, a proposition often repeated and to which the Walkers tentatively agreed, subject to certain limitations and conditions. This idea went through a number of stages, including temporary codicils to the Walkers' wills and an eventual contract of purchase from the Walkers, but nothing came of the transactions and Walkers eventually sold the property to private parties after the species plants were moved to the Jock Brydon property near Salem, Oregon.

Meanwhile the officers of the newly organized Species Foundation decided it was time to let the A.R.S. membership know what had been developing. This was not an easy decision and resulted from months of debate over the question of timing - some believing it should be delayed until prospective large donors had been approached, others arguing equally adamantly that the announcement would encourage large donations. Finally, in the January, 1965 issue of The Quarterly Bulletin of the American Rhododendron Society, Vol. 19, No. 1 the editor, Dr. J. Harold Clarke, published the following article, entitled THE RHODODENDRON SPECIES FOUNDATION, Development of the Idea:

"About three years ago the American Rhododendron Society, because of the rapidly increasing interest in species rhododendrons, and because of the scarcity of good true-to-name species plants, started the 'Species Project'. The purpose was to first locate and label individual plants which appeared to be typical of the species as far as could be determined, and later to mark plants considered by the committee to be superior forms of the species. This project, under the chairmanship of Milton V. Walker, M.D., was active in some of the western chapters of the Society, many species clones were studied and some were discussed in the A.R.S. Bulletin.

"**Breeding Material Needed** - Interest in rhododendrons is at an all time high, not only in this country but in Germany, the British Isles, New Zealand, Australia, Japan, and possibly other countries. Most of this popular interest so far has centered around the hybrid varieties, many of which are quite old; some which have been around 50 to 100 years are still being planted. They were quite valuable in their time but have their limitations. Many people are now becoming interested in the breeding of rhododendrons in order to produce varieties which are of better color and more beautiful but particularly, varieties which are hardier, more resistant to heat, to alkaline soil conditions, and to attacks by insects and disease pests. There is also an awaking interest in rhododendron varieties which will force readily for the florist trade. The background of hybrid rhododendrons, of course, is the list of species which have been used in breeding and hope of the future lies in the genetic makeup of these and other so far unused species.

"**Species Highly Regarded** - It has been true in the British Isles and is becoming quite evident in this country that many rhododendron fanciers who may first have been interested in the available hybrid varieties soon desire to grow the species plants from which the varieties were originally developed. Some become collectors of species in general or in one particular series. In any group of advanced rhododendron enthusiasts the conversation will usually turn to the species which are valued so highly for their intrinsic charm, their natural but restrained beauty and the ease with which they can be worked into the landscape in very satisfying ways.

"**Superior Forms Important** - The fact that plants of a given species may show a considerable amount of variation has been both a curse and a blessing. It provides the excitement and the promise of superior individuals to be earnestly sought and treasured. On the other hand the number of really superior forms in a species is likely to be very limited, and the average quite below the quality of such superior forms. The problem is to find available plants or propagating material of the superior forms. Of course the problem of finding any true-to-name plants of a given species is not always easy. It has been stated that probably not more than 30%, if we include the azaleas, of the listed species are available for purchase in the United States or Canada. Many rhododendron enthusiasts have purchased plants of species only to find that they are inferior forms and fit only for the discard. Many others have found that the plants they purchased were incorrectly named, most frequently because the plants from open pollinated seed, were actually hybrids, and unselected hybrids at that.

"It is generally known in the Rhododendron world that a very large number of species have come from Asia, and particularly from western China, southeast Asia and Japan. Most of the species now available were sent to British financial backers of the plant expeditions which located them. There was no particular urge to propagate and make available to the general public the superior forms which a few of these original sponsors were keen enough to collect. Usually a certain amount of the seed of these importations went to the Botanic gardens at Edinburgh, Kew, or other such institutions. The species plants of the Asiatic types being grown in North America have mostly come from open pollinated seed, collected in these Botanic gardens from the plants originally grown there from seed furnished by the collectors.

"**What Happens To Superior Forms** - It is not necessarily the responsibility of a Botanic garden to do a great deal of selecting in order to obtain a very good form of a particular species. Such an institution may be interested in maintaining a plant or two of a species although possibly concerned less about the superiority of the form than its conformity to the type specimen. Furthermore, Botanic gardens are under many pressures. As administrations change interest in certain groups of plants may wax or wane. A Botanic garden becomes famous for its rhododendrons because someone in charge was particularly interested in that genus. The next administrator may be interested in an entirely different group of plants, the emphasis changes, and over a period of years the collection gradually dwindles both in number and in excellence.

"There have been many good forms, and some quite superior, selected by individual fanciers on the larger estates in the British Isles. As time goes on, however, the identity of many of the outstanding plants will be lost. In many cases the clone itself will disappear as large estates are broken up, for housing developments, or to permit payment of inheritance taxes.

"The tendency in the nursery trade has been to propagate species rhododendrons by seed and of course there are economic reasons for that. As this goes on, however, the true identity of the original species will be lost in a swarm of open pollinated and hence possibly cross pollinated seedlings. The breeder, wishing to introduce certain characters into his progeny then cannot rely on a particular parent plant transmitting characters which he desires. The parent may be a complex hybrid rather than the true species which the breeder wants.

"**The Collection At Windsor Great Park** - The very fine collection of species at Windsor Great Park in Great Britain not only constitutes the largest and most comprehensive collection of species Rhododendrons in the world but as a part of the Crown Estate may also have the greatest prospect of permanence. The gardens were laid out under the sponsorship of King George V and Queen Mary and were brought to their present state by King George VI and Queen Elizabeth. The real contribution to the gardens, from the Rhododendron standpoint, came with the acquisition of the famous Stevenson Collection in 1950, including over 2000 plants of about 460 species. The Species garden, and the Savill garden, named after Sir Eric Savill who laid it out, will probably be able to maintain this collection more or less indefinitely. Many of the famous private collections, like the Stevenson Collection, will eventually be dispersed or lost as economic pressures develop.

"In the summer of 1963 Dr. Walker visited Windsor Great Park in England and was impressed by the fact that a very large number of fine forms of species Rhododendrons were growing there, mostly from the Stevenson Collection, were well arranged and displayed, and the idea immediately occurred that a similar collection in this country would be very desirable.

"Contact was made with Sir Eric Savill, who was largely responsible for the development of the gardens, and Sir Eric most generously promised that any desired propagating material would be made available. He stated, however, that there were many other desirable species clones in private gardens in the British Isles, and Dr. Walker was urged to return the next spring and examine them.

"In 1964, therefore, Dr. and Mrs. Walker spent several weeks in England, Scotland, and Ireland, visited many gardens both public and private where fine species Rhododendrons were being grown, and received very friendly cooperation with respect to arrangements to secure propagating material.

"Where Might A Similar Collection Be Established? - Much thought is being given to the location and maintenance in this country of a somewhat similar collection where one to several superior forms of each available species might be seen, and studied by those who are interested, and from which propagating material might be furnished to various institutions, and to the nursery trade so that these superior forms would be available for purchase by individuals. A number of different alternatives were considered.

"At first it seemed that some public place, such as a city, or state park, or a university grounds, might be desirable, because of the possibility the site might be made available at no cost and because public funds might be used to provide maintenance. However, there are definite objections to such a location. Arrangements made with one set of administrators may not be looked upon favorably by their successors. The administration of such a collection in a public place would have to be shared with those responsible for the public interest in the institution or park. It would be difficult to prevent the collection area from being used by people who come solely for relaxation, and are likely to give their children free rein to play among the plants. Somewhat the same may be said of universities and botanic gardens. There would be pressure against expanding to additional areas and in time it probably would be difficult to hold areas already planted if some new and very worthy project were to develop.

"Site Should Be Owned By Rhododendron Minded Group - After considerable study it seemed that the acquiring of suitable acreage under the complete supervision of a Rhododendron minded group of directors was the only solution. Development on this basis would be very expensive as money would be needed not only for acquisition of the property but for maintenance over an indefinite period. It would be possible, however, for those who are deeply interested in rhododendrons to control the establishment and development of such a collection, and to propagate and distribute to various institutions, and to the public through the nursery trade, without the limitations often imposed by already established procedures in public or semi-public institutions.

"Why The Foundation Was Needed - Although the American Rhododendron Society had set up the Species Project it was not in a financial position to support the project beyond its original concept of volunteer work within certain chapter areas.

"It is obvious that to bring a large number of rhododendron species clones (mostly as cuttings) to this continent, propagate them, secure a suitable site and establish them in a permanent planting, provide continuous maintenance, and eventually make propagating wood available, would be quite expensive. It seemed, however, a very desirable objective and, as the only possible means of achieving it, on a stable and permanent basis, a non-profit 'Rhododendron Species Foundation' has been incorporated in the state of Oregon. The Foundation has been set up as a separate and distinct entity from the American Rhododendron Society, and the Society has not been obligated in any way. The Foundation, in turn, is in no way responsible to the Society.

"Purposes Of The Foundation - The purposes of the Foundation, as set forth in the Articles of Incorporation, are to conduct scientific research and educational activities in the field of horticulture, primarily with species rhododendrons, to include the study, analysis, and classification of species rhododendrons, and the location, selection and propagation of the very best forms, and to make such knowledge available to all persons interested in the culture of species rhododendrons. The activities of the corporation shall be broad in scope, and may include the establishment, maintenance, and operation of a garden, or gardens, and other facilities for the testing, growing and propagation of species rhododendrons and other allied or companion shrubs, trees, or other plants.

"Foundation Goals - To acquire land and to establish plantings, and then to maintain them in satisfactory condition would involve an endowment in the neighborhood of $1,000,000. The rhododendron gardens at Windsor Great Park cover over 35 acres. To accomplish its purposes it would be necessary for the Rhododendron Foundation to have at least that much and preferably a larger area. There should be space for the plants to be grown without crowding so that plant characters as well as flower characters could be easily studied. There would need to be not only labor for maintenance but technical supervision so that the plants could be under continuous observation by trained personnel. It is hoped that acquisition of superior forms would be more or less continuous after the more readily available forms in Great Britain are brought to this country. New species are still being found and described, and if western China emerges from the communist cloud additional explorations there will undoubtedly provide additional new species.

"Plant Material Is Available - The ground work has already been laid with permission for the obtaining of propagating material from Windsor Great Park, and with similar whole hearted cooperation from many other institutions and private gardens in the British Isles. Such an opportunity may not come again. The plant material is available if we can provide a place to establish the main collection and provide maintenance so that it will be a continuing inspiration to rhododendron enthusiasts and a source from which breeders and fanciers can actually obtain the material they need and desire.

"Generous Gifts Needed - It is realized that a project such as this cannot be achieved by small contributions. A membership arrangement would involve an annual membership campaign which would be costly in terms of money and of the time of personnel who would be diverted from the broader objectives of the Foundation. An annual campaign for a nationwide Foundation by volunteer help would probably fluctuate greatly in overall effort and effectiveness.

"It was decided, therefore, that the Foundation would have no members. Instead there will be a board of directors, of approximately 25 carefully selected individuals, representatives of the various parts of the country where rhododendrons can be grown. The directors will guide the development of the Foundation and the raising of an endowment fund which, it is hoped, will enable the Foundation to accomplish those objectives for which it was established.

"Generous gifts will be necessary if the Foundation is to meet the challenge of the situation and become a vital factor in the finding, preservation, study and dissemination of rhododendron species. The Foundation is set up in such a way that money, securities or real estate may be received by donation, by bequest, or other arrangement. Arrangements are being made with the trust department of one of the larger banks to serve as trustee of endowment funds.

"Directors And Officers - Obviously the success of a project such as this, and the attitude and confidence of possible donors, will depend upon the men and women who serve as officers and directors. A small preliminary task force has been working on the general organization of the Foundation. Various influential people are being approached to serve as members of the Founding Board, charter members of the Foundation's Board. A complete list of the officers and board members will be published in the very near future, as soon as the makeup of the organizing board has been completed."

The initial officers and board of directors were announced in April, 1965 and were as follows:

> President - Milton V. Walker, M.D., Creswell, Ore.
> Vice president - Mr. Wales Wood, St. Helens, Ore.
> Secretary - Mr. Fred Robbins, Puyallup, Wash.
> Treasurer - Mr. Clarence Chase, Eugene, Ore.
> Honorary Vice-president and Director - Sir Eric Savill, The Great Park,
>   Windsor, England.

> Directors:
> Dr. J. Harold Clarke, Long Beach, Wash.
> Mr. Edward B. Dunn, Seattle, Wash.
> Mr. Henry DuPont, Winterthur, Del.
> Mr. David Leach, Brookville, Pa.
> Dr. Henry Skinner, Washington, D.C.
> Mr. Cecil Smith, Aurora, Ore.
> Dr. John C. Wister, Swarthmore, Pa.

Although the Rhododendron Species Foundation had now been formed and arrangements had been made to import the finest forms of the species from English gardens, the Species Location Committee continued to function as a part of the American Rhododendron Society with the following members: Ben Nelson, Chairman, Cecil Smith, Mrs. E. J. Greig, Milton V. Walker, M.D., Carl Fawcett, Ed Long, Paul J. Bowman, M.D. and Gordon Jones. However, there seems to be no information recorded regarding the subsequent activities of this entity.

Dr. Walker was invited to deliver an address concerning the beginnings of the Species Foundation to the 1965 annual meeting of the American Rhododendron Society in New York. Fortunately the presentation was recorded and later published in the Bulletin, Vol. 19, No. 3, July, 1965. Though a bit redundant it is believed worthy of inclusion here, inasmuch as it explains the source of expected plant material, and effectively summarizes the accomplishments of the past, the present status of the Foundation and the future plans of the organizers. Besides, it is a nice first-person account of his experiences in Britain.

Genesis of the Rhododendron Species Foundation and Rhododendrons in Great Britain

"I consider it an honor to be asked to address you on the Species Foundation and Rhododendrons in Great Britain. I cannot pretend to be an authority or an expert, despite having recently had the rare opportunity of seeing thousands of species plants in British gardens. At a time like this, I like to remind myself of the definition of an expert - 'An expert is quite an ordinary fellow, away from home.' Many of you know me too well, for me to pose as an expert.

"Let me first direct your thinking to a group of men to whom we owe a debt of gratitude - the plant explorers, who brought from Asia those species we now enjoy and without which we would not have our splendid hybrids. Hybridization of rhododendrons only started 139 years ago with the blooming of that spectacular blood red R. *arboreum* which had been introduced from India 15 years previously. Plant exploration commenced in earnest with Sir Joseph Hooker, who in 1847 pioneered a hundred years of explorations that gave us most of the rhododendrons we are growing today. Among Hooker's introductions are to be found some of the finest we have like R. *thomsonii* and R. *falconeri*. Fine old patriarchs from Hooker seed growing at Stonefield in the west of Scotland, and at Rhu near Glasgow, are sights long to be remembered.

"E. H. Wilson pioneered a new period in plant exploration which resulted in the astounding discovery by him and his contemporaries, Forrest, Farrer, Rock and Kingdon-Ward, of more than 600 new species in the first 40 years of the 20th century. Unfortunately, both Farrer and Forrest died in the field. Our debt to these men has been very graphically pointed out by David Leach in his book *Rhododendrons of the World* where he says, 'The journeys of the plant explorers into the mountain wildernesses of India, Burma, Tibet and China, were high adventures of courage and endurance, of disappointment and discovery, of exalted experience and overwhelming disaster.' I am glad the fine tradition established by the early plant explorers is being carried on today, by Peter and Patricia Cox and their friend P. C. Hutchison, who are now collecting in Bhutan and by Francis DeVos in Nepal.

"Financial Backers of Expeditions - Travel in the mountainous regions of Asia was arduous and dangerous 50 to 60 years ago and it took financial backing to undertake an expedition then as it does today. Let us think for a moment of these fine people who financed the intrepid explorers with their own money. At first there were individuals like Veitch and Sons, and Arthur K. Bulley, founder of Ness Gardens. Later there were syndicates composed of larger numbers of contributors as the costs increased. Mr. Bulley alone financed George Forrest's first two expeditions and was also a member of each syndicate financing the last five expeditions of Forrest. We must not forget these financial backers who made the explorations possible.

"Growers of Seed - Who grew out all the seed sent back by these explorers?

Probably thousands of packets of seed were sent back in the course of just a few years. We know that in a ten year span no fewer than 312 new species were discovered. J. B. Stevenson, of Towercourt, and his wife were among those who not only backed the plant explorers financially, but grew out seed from probably every one of the expeditions. Euan Cox writes me that this enormous influx of seed between 1922 and 1938 was 'handled like an efficient business concern. Jac Stevenson as it were ran the office, keeping a very careful record in what came to be a dozen or so notebooks - Mrs. Stevenson undertook the practical work, sowing every seed, and did most of the pricking out and ultimate planting in the nursery bed.'

Helen Walker, left, with the Harrisons

Photo by Milton Walker

"Last spring I sat on a bench in the garden of General and Mrs. Harrison, (the former Mrs. Stevenson) while she told me it was her daily job, after Mr. Stevenson went to the office, to transplant 250 seedlings from each batch of numbered seed. Later I wrote Mrs. Harrison for more information about Towercourt and was amazed to find that, from the records, she had evidently sowed and cared for a total of 2,942 packets of rhododendron seed. The amount of work is staggering to the imagination. The bookwork to keep the records straight was in itself no small job. As the seedlings grew, there was the problem of selecting, discarding and finally describing the new species as they came into bloom. The plants in the Stevenson collection at Towercourt made possible, in large measure, the description of the species in the first Handbook. We do indeed owe a great debt of gratitude to the plant explorers and to the financial backers of the expeditions, but I feel we are equally indebted to people like the Stevensons who did the less exciting but very essential labor of growing out these hundreds of thousands of seedlings.

"**Species Project** - A few years ago while Dr. Phetteplace was visiting Mrs. Stevenson, she expressed to him her real concern over the loss of carefully selected forms of the species, due to the breaking up of fine collections growing in the gardens of private individuals. She pointed out the confusion that was becoming worse each year with the growing of multitudes of open-pollinated seedlings under species labels, (when in the main they were hybrids and not true forms of the species.) Mrs. Stevenson predicted utter chaos in 25 years, unless something was done soon to preserve and propagate the true forms. This comment, made by such a respected and knowledgable woman as Mrs. Stevenson, led first to the A.R.S. Species Project, then this past year to the Rhododendron Species Foundation under whose guidance there is now taking shape in America, a collection of authenticated true forms of the species.

"For more than three years, groups of people working on the Species Project, have visited gardens in the West Coast, seeking to locate good forms of the species. In doing so, we have formed a much better idea as to what were forms truly representative of the species. The conclusion was reached that many of the species we were growing were poor forms and possibly not true forms at all. The most unfortunate aspect of our findings was, I think, the realization of the many years of wasted effort in bringing into bloom inferior plants from open pollinated parents, when at the same time in Great Britain there were being grown hundreds of true species of remarkable beauty with the owners quite willing to share their treasures with us.

"**Stevenson Collection** - Two years ago, while on a European trip, I made a point of going to see the part of the Stevenson Collection of Species that had been moved to Windsor Great Park. While I had read about it in Lanning Roper's excellent book, I was not prepared for the magnitude of the collection, the size of the plants nor the number of different forms of each species. Here were gathered together, so it seemed to me, all of the best forms in the world. Later I was to learn that this was not strictly true, although I may be forgiven when you realize I was looking at the results of nearly 50 years of work in germinating seed sent back from expeditions, of growing out these seedlings, of sorting, discarding and saving only the truest and best forms in a lifetime of work for Mr. and Mrs. Stevenson. The thought naturally occurred to me - 'How wonderful it would be if we in America could have a collection like this.' I wondered if we could get cuttings and scions and discreet inquiries revealed that it might indeed be possible. After considerable correspondence, a meeting was arranged with Sir Eric Savill of Windsor Great Park, for September on the way home from this trip.

"Mrs. Walker and I were invited to have lunch with Sir Eric at his home in Windsor Great Park and we found him to be a most friendly and genial host. High point of the meal was a delicious brown trout that he himself had caught the day previous. After lunch we had about an hour's discussion of the Species Project in which Sir Eric displayed a very real interest, and about which he seemed already to be informed. Suddenly he turned to me and said, 'Dr. Walker, you may have anything we have - anything.' After a moment of thought he added, 'You would of course be foolish to take anything and everything, because we have a lot of poor things here. The private gardens of Britain have many fine forms that you should also have, and you ought to

have only the best for your collection.' Later after we had discussed some of the problems of importation and had agreed that the sending of cuttings and scions would be most feasible, Sir Eric again turned to this matter of private collections. 'I would suggest that you come back next spring during the blooming season,' he said, 'and plan to spend 2 to 3 months visiting private gardens and selecting the best forms for your collection.'

"To be able to visit private gardens would be a privilege indeed, but to select the best forms was, I knew, beyond my knowledge and capability. Do you see how easy it is for 'quite an ordinary fellow, away from home' to be treated as an expert? I thanked Sir Eric and said that even if these private owners would be so kind as to offer cuttings to a stranger, which I doubted, I wouldn't be capable of selecting the best forms. On the first point, I remember he said something like, 'Tut and nonsense, we'll see that you get into every private

Mr. T. H. Findlay

Photo courtesy Royal Horticultural Society, Lindley Library garden that you want, and Mr. Findlay and I will see that you get whatever cuttings that you want too.'

"**Planning** - The winter after this conversation with Sir Eric was spent doing a great deal of reading about British gardens and trying to figure out just how we could accept the wonderful opportunity presented. Somehow a list of the good forms in the gardens to be visited both public and private, would have to be compiled so as to know what to look for when we visited them, and eventually to use if we were to request cuttings and scions later. By spring, I had notes on over 60 rhododendron gardens in Great Britain, at least twice as many as it would be possible to visit. How was I to know that the species described in the literature were true forms? I would certainly have to have the assistance of authorities like Mr. Davidian and Mr. Findlay. Suppose these people were good enough to offer to send us cuttings, how were we to get them into the States without preshipment inspection of the parent plants? Sir Eric had told me that such inspection was quite impossible because of the distances involved in getting inspectors to come from London. Could anything be done to prevent the losses some of us had experienced with entry fumigation? And just supposing we were able to get a sizeable number of cuttings in, who could be trusted to propagate them? Who would grow them on? Wales Wood and Dr. Clarke agreed with me that somehow a way just had to be found to get these fine species for the rhododendron buffs in America.

"We realized that eventually a permanent garden would have to be established so that these outstanding forms would never be lost. To do this would take a great deal of money, and someone suggested a non-profit corporation in the form of a foundation that would be able to receive tax exempt gifts. Wales Wood, who is fortunately an attorney, went to work on this angle while we traveled to Great Britain last spring. We were most hospitably received and saw some wonderful species in bloom. Maybe you would enjoy seeing some slides now of the gardens visited and a small fraction of the species seen. After you have seen the slides, I will continue with my talk by telling how we have attempted to solve some of the problems I have sketched for you. (75 slides of outstanding forms of species and general scenes of a few of the very beautiful gardens visited were shown at this point.)

"At the beginning of this talk your attention was drawn to some of the pioneers to whom we are greatly indebted - the plant explorers, the backers of the plant expeditions and particularly to those dedicated people like the Stevensons who grew the seed sent back, sorting and discarding those plants that were not, in their opinion, true species. Mention has been made of the beginnings of the A.R.S. Species Project, sparked by Mrs. Stevenson's concern over the loss of true species and the chaos that was resulting from open-pollinated seed being grown under species labels. The unplanned but very fortunate visit we had at Windsor Great Park and later the very generous offer of Sir Eric Savill has been related. And just now you have seen a sampling of the very fine forms of the species that are being offered to the Foundation so that we too may enjoy their superb beauty. How we have met some of the problems inherent in this amazingly generous offer remains to be told.

Dr. H. R. Fletcher
Photo courtesy Royal
Horticultural Society, Lindley Library

Sir Eric Savill
*Photo courtesy Royal
Horticultural Society, Lindley Library*

"You will remember Sir Eric's recommendation of a visit to private gardens so that I could see for myself the fine forms in bloom and select the most valuable for our collection. No one realized more than myself how inadequately prepared I was to undertake such an assignment. Very fortunately I had available the constant assistance and encouragement from men of knowledge and authority. With the help of Sir Eric Savill and Mr. Hope Findlay from Windsor, Dr. Harold Fletcher and Mr. Davidian from Edinburgh, and Mr. Patrick Synge, Editor of the Royal Horticultural Society, Mrs. Walker and I were able, last spring, to visit 30 private gardens and several large nurseries. We also spent many days studying the plants at Windsor, Wisley and the Royal Botanic Garden in Edinburgh. We traveled over 3000 miles by car, and what seemed like 30,000 miles by foot, as well as going by train and boat as we crisscrossed all of the United Kingdom of Great Britain and Ireland during a visit that extended for two and a half months. With the help of the men just mentioned, a list of what were considered the best forms in each garden was compiled. Then this list was checked by Mr. Findlay and Mr. Davidian for purity and it is from this list that during the past year we have requested 322 different species or forms for our Foundation Collection. The University of British Columbia through Mr. Leon Koerner, a very generous benefactor, offered to receive and propagate any of the species we wished to have sent to them. They even agreed to grow on for a period of two years the propagated plants and to forward them at any time to any destination we desire. All they asked in return, was the privilege of keeping one plant of each species to establish a Canadian Species Garden. They have agreed to assume the complete financial responsibility for that garden.

"This heaven-sent offer relieved us of the pressing problem of immediately locating somewhere to put the plant material that was already being mailed to us. After all, you cannot say to someone offering you plants that you want very badly, 'Sorry, I'd like to have them but I don't have a place right now to put them. Would you send them to me in a year or two?' We felt it was up to us to find a place right then for this very generous gift or the opportunity might be lost forever. Fortunately the importation arrangement between Canada and the United States is such that we anticipate no difficulty in bringing these plants into this country as soon as we have a place to put them.

"**Foundation** - While we were in Great Britain last spring Mr. Wales Wood drew up the Articles of Incorporation and in June of last year a non-profit corporation to be known as the Rhododendron Species Foundation, was registered with the Corporation Commissioner of the State of Oregon. An organizational meeting was held in July when officers and directors were elected and by-laws adopted. I might mention just a few items of policy and organization that may interest you. It was agreed at this first meeting that the Species Foundation should complement and extend the functions of the American Rhododendron Society, and in no way be in conflict. It should not be responsible to the A.R.S. and likewise the A.R.S. should not be responsible financially or otherwise for the Foundation.

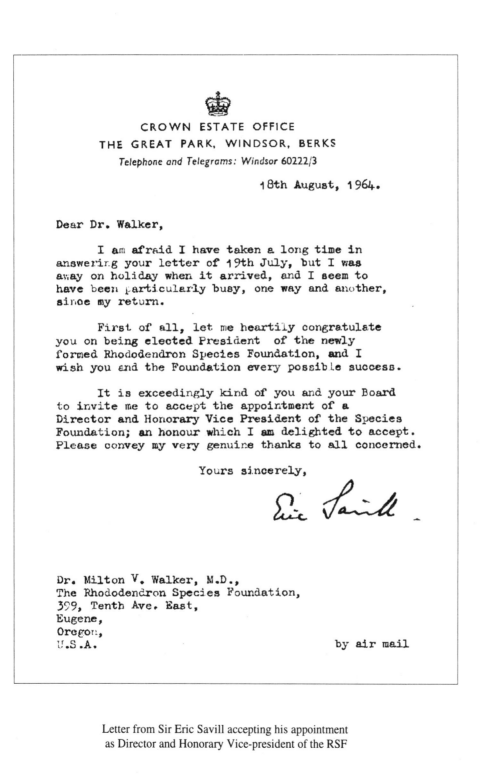

CROWN ESTATE OFFICE
THE GREAT PARK, WINDSOR, BERKS
Telephone and Telegrams: Windsor 60222/3

18th August, 1964.

Dear Dr. Walker,

I am afraid I have taken a long time in answering your letter of 19th July, but I was away on holiday when it arrived, and I seem to have been particularly busy, one way and another, since my return.

First of all, let me heartily congratulate you on being elected President of the newly formed Rhododendron Species Foundation, and I wish you and the Foundation every possible success.

It is exceedingly kind of you and your Board to invite me to accept the appointment of a Director and Honorary Vice President of the Species Foundation; an honour which I am delighted to accept. Please convey my very genuine thanks to all concerned.

Yours sincerely,

Eric Savill

Dr. Milton V. Walker, M.D.,
The Rhododendron Species Foundation,
399, Tenth Ave. East,
Eugene,
Oregon,
U.S.A.

by air mail

Letter from Sir Eric Savill accepting his appointment
as Director and Honorary Vice-president of the RSF

"The by-laws do not provide for a general membership. It was felt that a large membership with dues and yearly fund raising activities was not indicated and that the objectives could be well served by a board of directors if very carefully chosen. It was thought advisable to have a board of considerable size, maybe 25 eventually, with all but the original directors to serve for a period of 5 years in order to assure as much permanency as possible. We realized that we had to have a core of directors living in the Northwest, but wanted all sections of the United States and possibly Canada represented. We wanted the A.R.S. to be fully represented on the board but not to overweigh it. We recognized our primary need for business men with experience in public relations, insurance, stocks and bonds and real estate. We would need a great deal of legal counsel and so the legal profession should be well represented on the board. We most certainly needed men who could, by personal contribution or influence, help in raising the endowment of a million dollars that was considered absolutely necessary to the successful achievement of our objectives. We fully realized that the success of the Foundation depended on the board of directors who should be men of national stature in horticulture and business, men of recognized integrity and leaders in their field and men willing to give liberally of their time and substance.

"Founding Board of Directors of the Rhododendron Species Foundation - [Editor's note: Only those preceded by (*) were actual directors, the remainder having been honorary appointments.]

> *Milton V. Walker, M.D., President, Creswell, Oregon.
> Sir Eric Savill, Honorary Vice-president and director, Windsor, England.
> *Mr. Wales Wood, Vice-president, St. Helens, Oregon.
> *Mr. Fred M. Robbins, Secretary, Puyallup, Washington.
> *Mr. Clarence A. Chase, Treasurer, Eugene, Oregon.

Directors:
> Mrs. Prentice Bloedel, Bainbridge Island, Washington.
> *Dr. J. Harold Clarke, Long Beach, Washington.
> *Mr. Edward B. Dunn, Seattle, Washington.
> Mr. Henry F. duPont, Winterthur, Delaware.
> Dr. H. B. Hawthorn, University of B.C., Canada.
> Mrs. Henry Issacson, Seattle, Washington.
> Mr. Gordon E. Jones, Oyster Bay, N.Y.
> Mr. David G. Leach, Brookville, Pennsylvania.
> Mrs. Pendleton Miller, Seattle, Washington.
> Dr. Henry Skinner, Washington, D. C.
> *Mr. Cecil C. Smith, Aurora, Oregon.
> Dr. John C. Wister, Swarthmore, Pennsylvania.

"Board meetings have been held in July, October, March and the annual meeting was held last evening. Besides electing the Founding Board of Directors just enumerated, one or two important items of business deserve mention. Last evening at the first annual meeting of the Foundation, it was decided to establish an advisory council for the Foundation. The suggestion had been made that there are many good men and women who are interested in the Species Foundation whose advice and guidance would be most helpful, but for various reasons are not able to consider a position on the board of directors. We feel that the addition of an Advisory Council will greatly strengthen the organization of the Foundation.

"As you no doubt realize, a foundation cannot function without tax-exempt status. At the October meeting of the Board, the Bank of California was selected to act as trustee for the Foundation. When we met with the trust officers of the bank, one of the first questions asked us was, 'Have you filed your application for tax exempt status with the Internal Revenue Service?' Actually we hadn't at that time. We asked to be advised on this matter, and the trust officers strongly urged us to engage the services of a competent tax attorney, because of the complexities of the laws and the recent changes in these laws. We did engage the services of a highly recommended tax attorney, and after 5 months of careful preparation of the application, and the assembling of supportive data the application was filed on March 26th of this year. Action on these applications normally can be expected in about a year and some have taken over 3 years. I am happy to report to you that the Foundation has already received notification from the Internal Revenue Service of tax exempt status. The communication says in part, 'you are exempt from Federal Income Tax as an organization' and also 'Contributions made to you are deductible by donors.' I am sure you will agree with me that a major obstacle has been overcome and the road ahead should be clear going to the achievement of our goal of a million dollar endowment.

"**Objectives** - I would like to outline for you the broad objectives of the Foundation. Leaving aside all the legal and technical language in the Articles of Incorporation, I would say that the objectives could be summarized as threefold. 1) Making available true forms of the species - both type and outstanding forms. 2) Preservation of these forms so that they will not be lost, and 3) Research and educational activities in the species of rhododendron.

"I have told you how we are solving the immediate problem of importation and propagation. By present methods I am afraid it will be years before these good forms are propagated in sufficient numbers to be generally available. We have given a good deal of thought as to the best and quickest way to make these species available to everyone as soon as possible. In fact we are already financing a research program in the meristematic culture method of propagation which, in orchids, makes it possible to reproduce 10,000 plantlets within 12 to 18 months from a single cutting. The purpose of the research is to devise a process for the rapid propagation of rhododendrons by cell culturing procedures. The overall plan is to set up gardens in strategic locations, so that while these true forms of species might not be available for everyone for some little time, they will be found in Foundation Gardens and be available as a source of pollen and for study.

"A large central or main garden located either in Oregon or Washington seems climatically best suited for the greatest number of species and has priority in our planning. Subsidiary gardens are planned to eventually exhibit species suitable for those particular climates and to maintain stock plants for the propagation which will probably be carried on at the main garden. Subsidiary gardens have been suggested for Vancouver, B.C.; San Francisco Bay area and the California or southern Oregon Coast for the more tender varieties and the large leafed species; Hamilton, Ontario, Long Island, N. Y., Pennsylvania and perhaps North Carolina for species suitable for those particular climates. These subsidiary gardens would not be owned by the Foundation but would be located at, and maintained by, botanic gardens or other institutions, by special arrangement. It is anticipated that only the main garden would be owned by the Foundation.

"The main purpose of the gardens would be to carry out the objectives previously outlined. We feel that each garden located as conveniently as possible to a population

71

center, should exhibit true forms of the species suitable for that particular climate. And that these should be accurately named and provide comparative standards for study. The gardens would be primarily for study and research and definitely not display gardens. We think that such gardens will be of inestimable help to hybridizers as a source of pollen. Many men have found it difficult to be sure of the parentage of the plants they are using in their planned programs of hybridization. Large scale propagation facilities and possibly a meristematic culture laboratory will have to be set up at the main Foundation garden. We hope the scientific activities of the Foundation will not only encompass research in the identification and reclassification of the species in their series, as is now carried out at the Royal Botanical Garden in Edinburgh. Permissible limits of variation in the different species and the many questions concerning natural hybridity are intriguing lines of research. In order to aid the Foundation in its scientific activities, it would be advisable to provide specialized training specifically in the genus rhododendron, to otherwise qualified botanists. And to provide a start in this training we must find an adequately trained taxonomist.

"Our immediate problem is to find and finance the purchase of property suitable for the Foundation main garden. In two years time at the very most, we must have a home prepared for our rapidly enlarging collection of species.

"I would like to point out that the project undertaken by the Foundation is not a West Coast one, not even a national one but is international in its scope. Dr. Harold Fletcher, Regius Keeper of the R. B .G. sent me a copy of a paper he had written for the International Association of Botanic Gardens and Arboreta, and read during the tenth International Botanical Congress held in Edinburgh in August of last year. In the opening paragraph of this paper Dr. Fletcher said, 'If accurately named living plants are to be found anywhere they ought to be found in botanic gardens. Yet it is clear that the percentage of wrongly named plants growing in botanic gardens is high. Even so, seeds from these plants are distributed to botanic gardens and horticultural establishments - seeds, moreover, from incorrectly named plants which have been openly pollinated.' To quote further, 'Thus for ages, botanic gardens have been distributing incorrectly named material throughout the world. Obviously it is high time this practice stopped and the only way to stop it is to make available for distribution, viable seeds resulting from controlled pollination of authentically named vegetative propagations of such material.'

"By way of illustration he cites how 'an authentically named reservoir of living material of the genus rhododendron could be built up and the material distributed to interested parties.' He suggests one collection in Great Britain and one in America. In his letter to me Dr. Fletcher says, 'As you see, the whole matter ties up with what you are intending to do in America.' All of us I know have the greatest respect for Dr. Fletcher because of his horticultural knowledge and achievements. It is therefore a source of great satisfaction to have his wholehearted support and outspoken approval of what the Foundation is attempting to do.

"The support and interest in the Foundation both here and abroad is very gratifying. I have had letters from people all over the United States and Canada who have heard about the Foundation. I have been asked to speak about the Foundation in a number of places. I greatly appreciate the opportunity tonight of being able to tell you something about the genesis and the objectives of the Foundation. There are many men right here before me who have made great contributions to horticulture. We do hope their names will not be forgotten nor the results of their work lost. Neither should the sacrifices and discoveries of the early plant explorers be lost nor the work of people like the Stevensons be wasted. We want to avoid that chaos referred to by

Mrs. Stevenson with the loss of the true forms of the species and the confusion that was resulting from open pollination.

"From a more personal standpoint, an opportunity has been presented to us, of not only being able to preserve these good forms by establishing them in a collection here in America, but someday to have them in our own gardens. Will you help us in our efforts to make the best possible use of the opportunity presented?"

Dr. Walker, center, with Ewen Cox, left, and his son Peter Cox of Scotland

Frank Knight of Windsor Park

PART II

THE FORMATIVE YEARS

CHAPTER IV

HARD TIMES

In 1964 and early 1965 negotiations had been progressing with a wealthy Seattle area benefactress who was interested in the Species Foundation and apparently willing to donate a substantial parcel of land located on Bainbridge Island and of great value. In his correspondence Dr. Walker once stated that this donation "would largely dispose of our problems with an endowment fund." So it is not surprising that the board was greatly disappointed and discouraged to learn, in the summer of 1965, that title to the land would be withheld until the Foundation could show itself to be financially sound and capable of clearing the land and constructing necessary improvements, which, of course, the Foundation was unable to do.

In a letter to J. Harold Clarke, Executive Secretary and Editor of the A.R.S. Bulletin and member of the board of the Foundation, Dr. Walker wrote, "Frankly I'm quite discouraged with the help I have been getting. I have had some business problems that have required my almost constant attention the last number of weeks. I have not been able to arrange even a meeting in Seattle with interested parties. ... There has been no money come in whatever. I have stopped paying for the meristem research which helps some, but I need at least $100.00 to send out requests for September cuttings. I have unpaid bills amounting to about $1,400.00 I presume. Don't you think I have reason for discouragement? The only encouraging thing I can report is that as a result of the printing of my talk in the Bulletin I have found a lawyer in Eugene who is interested and willing to work despite lack of knowledge."

The lawyer mentioned in Dr.Walker's letter was Clarence Barrett (this author), who offered his services as an attorney or layman. Walker, having just dispensed with the services of a California botanist in the effort to adapt meristematic tissue culture techniques to rhododendron propagation, immediately inquired as to Barrett's background in botany and was assured he had none. This didn't deter either party, however, and Barrett willingly (and naively) took on the job, establishing a crude laboratory in a spare bedroom in his home. At the time Walker assured Barrett, "Slim, if you succeed in this venture I can assure you you will achieve much more notoriety than you could ever achieve as an attorney."

Since the Foundation was without funds and in debt at the time, Dr. Walker, because of his conviction that this process was crucial to the timely advancement of rhododendron propagation procedures, personally provided the funds for the acquisition of laboratory glassware and other basic equipment, chemical ingredients and building materials to construct the necessary sterile chamber and laboratory tables.

Knowing nothing of the technicalities of plant tissue or meristem cultures, Barrett consulted with Dr. Wimber of the botany department at the University of Oregon, who guided him in the selection of equipment and chemicals, in appropriate study avenues and in the basic techniques of isolating meristem tissue particles and establishing cultures. A month or so of concentrated research enabled Barrett to proceed on a limited basis, but within a few months, and after some preliminary success, he was served with divorce papers and a petition to sell the family home. The experiment came to a sudden halt, never to be resumed. This was extremely unfortunate for as Dr. Walker wrote to Corydon Wagner, "During the past summer the project has been taken over by an attorney in Eugene who is accomplishing much more than Mr. Jasper did and at a fraction of the cost."

In the fall of 1965 requests were sent to the following gardens, nurseries and individuals, for cuttings or scions of many additional varieties:

Sir Eric Savill, Windsor Great Park, England.
Archie Gibson, Glenarn, Glasgow, Scotland.
Charles Puddle, Bodnant Gardens, England.
John Basford, Brodick Castle, Scotland.
Sir George Campbell, Crarae Lodge, Argyll, Scotland.
G. Needham, South Lodge, Horsham, England.
Royal Botanic Gardens, Surrey, England.
Borde Hill, Sussex, England.
Sunningdale Nurseries, Surrey, England.
Kew Gardens, Kew, England.
Major E.W.M. Magor, Cornwall, England.
Sir Giles Loder, Leonardslee, Sussex, England.
Mr. John Hanvey, Sr., Co. Down, Ireland.
Corsock House, Castle Douglas, Scotland.
Caerhays Castle, Cornwall, England.
Major G. A. Hardy, Kent, England.
Mr. Archie Kenneth, Stronachullin, Argyll, Scotland.
Younger Botanical Garden, Argyll, Scotland.
Royal Botanic Garden, Edinburgh, Scotland.
R.H.S. Gardens, Wisley, England.
Peter Cox, Glendoic, Scotland
Rowallane
Wakehurst

With each request was enclosed a one, or sometimes two-page letter of instruction as to Dr. Walker's preference concerning hardness of the wood, wrapping and shipping details, and a discussion of the Foundation's progress to date, all laboriously typed, individually. And each request contained a $5.00 bill to cover postage and handling, which was always gratefully acknowledged.

The first shipment of cuttings from Brodick arrived in Vancouver in September, 1964. By October of 1965 Miss Evelyn Jack of the University of British Columbia had developed a full scale propagation effort in behalf of the Species Foundation, receiving the cuttings and scions from England, Scotland and Ireland, noting their condition and deciding how to proceed with each. From her notes and correspondence it is interesting to consider her observations and procedures, some of which are excerpted:

Oct. 4, 1965: "So far we have received cuttings from five sources with more arriving today.... The majority are good cuttings but there is the odd species which is rather too poor to expect it to root. The cuttings are placed half in mist and half in a closed frame, except the alpines which are on a cooler, open bench. I graft only when the cuttings look too anaemic. I am using the system Leach advocates - soaking in an indolebutyric acid solution for 18 hours. I also use a fungicide dip before sticking the cuttings, and supplemental lighting.

Nick and Evelyn Weesjes
Photo courtesy Evelyn Weesjes

"I notice that whenever the cuttings are issued phyto-sanitary certificates in Britain, there seems to be quite a delay between the time of taking the cuttings and mailing them. ... Our plant inspection authorities agreed to waive phyto-sanitary inspection requirements for cuttings, so I think this is an unnecessary delay.

"Letters of acknowledgment are sent out either the same day or the day following the arrival of the parcel.... It lets the sender know within a week that we have received the cuttings. All the plants from the fall and spring shipments are planted out in frames with the exception of the tender species. They have not made enough growth to take cuttings from them."

Oct. 6, 1965: "Parcels received Oct. 4, 1965:
     Lochinch Castle: 16 cuttings. Arrived in good condition, except R. *charitopes* which had black leaves. Parcel first sent to ... Edinburgh for phyto-sanitary certificate.
     Borde Hill: 26 cuttings. Arrived in very good condition.
     Wakehurst: 54 cuttings. Cuttings arrived a bit crushed and manila envelope badly torn in transit. R *hypoglaucum* arrived with black leaves."

Oct. 13, 1965: "The cuttings from Edinburgh were very well packed in a box and arrived in perfect condition, however, the 2 packages from Leonardslee arrived by surface mail although the postage was for airmail. Since they were three weeks on the way, they looked a sorry mess. I may be able to save R. *cinnabarinum roylei*, *R. linearifolium, R. serpyllifolium* and one of R. *trichocladum's*. There was no differentiation between the 2 groups of R. *trichocladum* but one was completely dead. Mr.Puddle sent 2 cuttings of R.*lanatum* as he had noted we had lost it…"

Oct. 26, 1965: "So far we have received thirteen shipments of cuttings. The latest to arrive were from Wisley - mostly replacements of last year's shipment and this time arrived in good condition; a 3rd package from Leonardslee, mailed the same time as the previous two packages, but taking four weeks to arrive, also in a deplorable condition. Here again, they had enough postage for air mail but perhaps because it wasn't labeled as such, it came surface mail. The latest to arrive, and this time sent by surface mail, was from Sandling Park (Major A. E. Hardy) and it took three weeks to arrive. The cuttings were packed in wet grass in a plastic bag and by the time they arrived, the cuttings were mostly defoliated and the grass wet silage. I have tried to save some but I think they can be written off."

Looking back at her experiences in behalf of the Species Foundation, Miss Jack (now Evelyn Weesjes) shares some recollections:

> We had splendid co-operation from the Customs Branch of the Vancouver post office. Mr. Ron Hurley would phone us directly a package arrived and we would have it picked up within an hour or two of his phone call. The result of such co-operation was that the cuttings could be grafted or in the rooting bed just three days after they had been taken in Gt. Britain....

> At first I tried grafting many of the species and because of the short time to prepare for the imports arriving, we used many kinds of understock, even *ponticum*. If I had had more experience with species at that time, I probably would have treated more as cuttings. The cuttings were sent in fall, September to November, and then again in February for grafting.

> By 1968 there were several hundred RSF species planted in the lath house at the nursery. That winter was most severe and we lost a lot of plants. It

Nursery at University of British Columbia - *Photo courtesy Evelyn Weesjes*

happened at Christmas with a sudden drop in temperature. With everything closed for the holiday, Nick (Weesjes) finally got some bales of alfalfa from the UBC farm and we did our best to cover up the rhododendrons. It helped somewhat but was not sufficient to give a complete cover. There wasn't too much else we could do at the time.

> ...In 1967 I took over the requests and paid the money for the cuttings. There were no imports in 1968 or 1969. In 1970 Dr. Walker resumed requesting cuttings, this time in conjunction with Dr. Roy Taylor of the UBC Botanical

Garden. Shortly after that my connection with propagating for the RSF ceased.... There were times when Dr. Walker gave the impression that he personally owned the RSF collection and in retrospect he probably had the right to think so after having put so much of his own money and time into the project.

Dr. Walker kept urging me to progapagate from the established RSF plants as quickly as possible. He wanted a large number of plants built up, probably to help finance the RSF. This posed a dilemma for me because by 1966 there had been great changes in the office personnel and no one was left who knew of our arrangement with the RSF. Herman Vaartnou left in 1966. It was taking considerable of my time to propagate and look after the collection and I was afraid the new superintendent would not approve. On more than one occasion I had to ask for help from Dr. H. Hawthorn, an RSF director and professor at UBC. Thank goodness, he was also a good friend and greatly interested in rhododendrons. In 1968 Dr. Roy Taylor became the head of the renewed Botanical Garden and in 1970 took over the RSF from me.

There was always a lot of pressure from rhododendron people on both sides of the border to get RSF cuttings from me. I suppose many thought I was unreasonable in refusing their request - but that was part of my agreement with RSF. I got so I didn't go to rhododendron meetings and didn't encourage rhododendron visitors. …

Peter Cox with Helen Walker
Photo by Milton Walker

One little anecdote occurred, possibly around 1971, during a visit by Peter Cox and his wife. They came to the nursery accompanied by Dr. Roy Taylor. Peter Cox was very interested in the rhododendrons in the lath house, probably recognizing some of those he had sent. Because Dr. Taylor was also present I didn't dare let it be known that we still had species so I tried my best to lure them out of the lath house. Anyway, I hope I made it up to Peter when we spotted an eagle quite low in a tree and he eagerly photographed it. I was most impressed by his powers of observation. I had mentioned sometime earlier that we had a R. *campanulatum* Cooper form and I wondered which form it was. On the tour, I forgot about my request but in the middle of a conversation while walking about, Peter pointed to the plant in question and said, "that form is called Roland Cooper."

Now that brings me to another little story. You will see mention of it in a letter from Dr. Walker. It seems Dr. Walker had no use for Leonard Frisbie of the Pacific Rhododendron Society and probably the feeling was mutual. Anyway, Dr. Walker understood from Frisbie that the latter was going to get a set of the RSF plants from us. Post haste Dr. Walker was up in Vancouver and very agitated. Of course, there was no substance to the story but whether it was a misunderstanding or Frisbie wishing to cause mayhem, I have no way of knowing. Dr. Walker did blame Frisbie for not being able to get much cutting material from Bodnant. It seems Frisbie got there first.

I have reservations that I was the best one for the job of propagator for the RSF but with my limited knowledge I did the best I could. Together Nick and I at least laid the groundwork for the RSF.

[Note: Evelyn Jack eventually married Nick Weesjes and the couple now lives near North Saanich on Vancouver Island. They have a large garden known as Towner Crest, a natural garden containing over 3000 plants, in which 250 species and 300 hybrid rhododendrons are represented. The author is greatly indebted to Mrs. Weesjes for the above information, most of which is in her own words, and other documentary material furnished.]

On October 18th, 1965 Dr. Walker wrote to Ed Dunn complaining of the lack of funds and $1,500 in indebtedness and suggesting that a professional fund raiser be hired, to be paid a percentage of the funds raised. On the same day he wrote a more positive letter to Fred Robbins, stating, "At last report we now have 417 different forms in the Foundation Species collection. Pretty good don't you think for about 18 months work? The problem now is that I have run out of species to ask for except in about three of the larger gardens. I hate to quit enlarging the collection when I know that there must be at least 300 to 400 more forms that we could get just for the asking...."

At the end of November several board members met in Seattle with three wealthy prospective donors in hopes they could be induced to make substantial contributions to the Foundation. Alas, it was the consensus that "... no one is going to contribute a large amount of money right off the bat for this Foundation. It is their feeling that this may come in time but that right now sights should be lowered to a more modest fund and a more gradual beginning of a garden ... it is only when something tangible is started that donors can really come into the picture." (Letter to Dr. Walker from Ed Dunn, Dec. 2, 1965.) One of the prospective donors was the husband of the benefactress who had offered land to the Foundation earlier. The land was still available on the same conditions, but with a possible lease at one dollar a year during development. The board members examined the land on this occasion and found it suitable but requiring extensive development. And there was still no money for that purpose.

Due to the lack of development funds and the urgency of obtaining a home for the newly propagated species plants, Dr. J. Harold Clarke renewed his often repeated suggestion that the Walkers donate their home near Eugene, Oregon for that purpose, inasmuch as it was already partially developed and the Walkers had previously stated their willingness that it ultimately be used for Foundation purposes, one way or another. On December 11, 1965 Dr. Walker responded,

I appreciate your comments about our own garden in Eugene. Naturally I am very fond of it and agree with you that it has everything that is necessary for the Foundation Garden with the possible exception of size. I think the 25 acres that I sold could be repurchased for about $30,000, making a total of 50 acres which would be adequate. The point you bring up about supervision is very important and would be a real problem on Bainbridge Island. The cost of buildings and equipment and water would be no small item. However, I can't do anything about my place. You might if you cared to. There are many ways that Helen and I could be assured of staying off relief but it is not my place to urge such things.

Just to give you an example of my thinking - I have a half interest in the Medical Arts Building in Eugene as well as the old Clinic property. We have been offering it for sale at $1,200,000 with my equity of $225,000 to go for $212,000. If Mr. Wagner or Mr. Bloedel [wealthy prospective benefactors] or someone else would purchase my equity and pay it out over a period of say 15 years, it would give me $14,000 per year sure to live on. I could then afford to turn over my home and garden which is valued at $75 to $85,000 to the Foundation right away. As it stands now I have property but no money and no prospects of making any return on the Medical property for several years. It however is a sound investment and 10 years from now will make the owner a lot of money.

There are many other ways of financing the Eugene home property but the above illustration is sufficient. I probably shouldn't have written the above but I know that you are aware of my *intention to leave whatever I have left to the Foundation on Helen and my death.* All we need to do is protect ourselves for our few remaining years. (Emphasis added).

Dr. Clarke answered, "I realize that you might be somewhat hesitant about discussing your own property and I think I see the picture pretty well. This is something I might be able to discuss in a discreet way with some of the other Board members if the opportunity arises. I can appreciate your feeling that you should have some security for yourself and Mrs. Walker in the future."

Dr. Clarke

While this type of dialogue was common (but somewhat private and often subtle) among various board members in their frustratingly slow progress toward securing financing and a garden site, negotiations continued for the possible acquisition of the Bainbridge Island property and Dr.Walker frequently mentioned in his voluminous correspondence with acquaintances throughout the U. S. and abroad, the likelihood of establishing the garden there. He always pointed out, however, the great expense that would be involved in improving the land and constructing appropriate facilities, and usually included a subtle (and sometimes not so subtle) suggestion that a substantial contribution from the recipient would be appropriate and appreciated, as well as tax deductible.

On December 15, 1965 Dr. David Leach of Brookville, Pa. wrote to Dr. Walker to report the ineffectiveness of his efforts at fund raising. "These men seem to be deluged with appeals for every conceivable cause, all tax-deductible, of course. I suspect that at present our project appears somewhat nebulous to a non-specialist, since we have no site as yet, no staff and no financial commitments. These fellows may be wary of contributing to a program that they think might not get off the ground. Perhaps when it becomes perfectly apparent to all, as it is to us, that real progress has been made and that the Foundation is a practical reality with a promising future, we can expect a more encouraging response." Dr. Leach also suggested the possibility of offering a reciprocal "gift" of new species rhododendrons to those who made a substantial contribution to the Foundation but Walker seemed to find this unacceptable.

On the same day, as though to punctuate Dr. Leach's musings, Walker received a letter from Prentice Bloedel of Bainbridge Island, stating in part, "… my wife and I will make a planting site available to the Rhododendron Species Foundation on … the [following] terms and conditions:

1. That the Foundation *be well enough financed to begin with* to have some promise of permanence. (Emphasis added)

2. We would propose to limit the acreage contributed at this time to your actual requirements for the next few years with provision for additional acreage as demand arises with an agreed maximum.

3. We would further propose that the Foundation's tenure be by way of lease at nominal rental for a term of, say, 30 years; after which if the Foundation were still in existence and active and required the site, it would be deeded to the Foundation. There would be a further provision that the site would revert to us if during the life of the lease the Foundation became inactive, were liquidated, or did not use and require the site.

Another matter to which I hope you can give some consideration is the suggestion that the tract be in some way linked with the name of my wife, Virginia Merrill Bloedel."

Corydon Wagner of the Seattle area had been approached with a plea for financial assistance and while he appeared tremendously supportive of the idea of a Foundation garden, he thought perhaps to begin with it would be possible, and advisable, to establish the garden in conjunction with the University of Washington Arboretum, with the understanding that it could be moved from there when separate facilities became available. This information was conveyed to Dr. Walker by Fred Robbins and Walker's discouragement was evident in his reply:

The interest shown by the group up there is very encouraging and I think we all appreciate their help. However they have not worked with this project as long as we have and consequently do not have the long range thinking that we have. From a practical standpoint, it may be necessary to call on the Arboretum for help when the time comes that the U. B. C. wants relief from the load of plants that they are caring for, and if we do not have a garden ready to receive them. If that happens I have a premonition of the ending of our grand plans. True we will have introduced rare forms into both Canada and the U.S.A. but have failed in making them generally available to growers. From the experience in Great Britain it would seem that eventually with the change in Directors of those two gardens, the species would be eventually lost, and all our work be for naught. I know that this proposal is considered just a temporary one, but my experience is that these temporary arrangements often become permanent and the original plan is shelved. Sorry to be such a wet blanket but I would not be honest in not stating my present feelings.

I admit I would feel much more optimistic if we had our present debts paid. I now have the unpleasant task of writing to Brunne and Meysing [attorneys] and telling them their May bill for $1,059.90 still cannot be paid. At the meeting was there no discussion or suggestion how we could raise the $1,500.00 we need to get out of debt and maybe another $1,000 to run on? If we cannot raise such a small sum without trouble, I think we will have to go slow in incurring more indebtedness.

To exacerbate the frustration of the situation there was a letter from Sir Eric Savill of Windsor Great Park, stating that while he admired the concept of the Species Foundation Garden, he felt it would be foolhardy to consider a garden of less than 150 acres. On a happier note, Brunne and Meysing agreed to a several month deferral of payment of their account.

In the spring of 1966 Dr. Walker underwent surgery, which slowed his activities for a time. In June various board members made generous contributions to the Foundation and Walker was able to pay off all outstanding indebtedness. However, he complained in his letters to many people that the board at its last meeting apparently was not interested in addressing the problem of large scale fund raising for purposes of purchasing or developing a garden. He feared they favored moving the plants to the University of Washington Arboretum.

Young Dr. Walker in his office in the Walker Clinic in Eugene, Oregon - 1950's
Photo courtesy Ian Walker

CHAPTER V

THE FIRST GARDEN

By late 1966 word had spread that the Foundation had succeeded in bringing a great many of the finest forms of species rhododendrons to Canada from the British Isles. A list of species and forms then accumulated at the University of British Columbia may be seen in **APPENDIX B, COLUMN "V"** at page 221 of this book. Consequently Walker and other members of the board were inundated with requests for donations of plants to "worthwhile" public gardens and for sale of plants to private gardens and individuals, all of which had to be deferred until a sufficient stock was accumulated. During that same year Dr. Walker, being somewhat preoccupied with personal matters and having become a bit discouraged with the board's lackadaisical attitude toward large scale fund raising, halted his own efforts to raise money via correspondence. Also, being at such a distance from the University of B.C. and the plants themselves, he largely abdicated his responsibility for requesting additional plant materials from British gardens to Evelyn Jack and the U. of B.C. staff. He felt, reasonably, that they were more in touch with the needs.

Board meetings became infrequent during 1966 and 1967 and the meetings that were held were not well attended. Enough voluntary donations somehow arrived to cover current administrative expenses and the Foundation limped along, continuing to exist but without any really enthusiastic participation by anyone other than Evelyn Jack and her staff. Meanwhile, the existing plants continued to grow and more cuttings and scions were accumulated and added to the collection in Vancouver, B.C.

In August of 1967 the Internal Revenue Service notified the Foundation that it had failed to file the necessary tax returns for the years 1965 and 1966 and that it was in danger of losing its tax-exempt status as a result. Walker responded with an apology and an explanation that the failure to file returns was a result of the resignation of the Foundation's Treasurer, Clarence Chase. This omission was somehow cured and the Foundation retained its tax-exempt status, although the files do not indicate who eventually took responsibility.

In October, 1967 Ed Dunn, then President of the American Rhododendron Society and Foundation board member, wrote to Dr. Walker:

Dear Milton:

Is there anything new with the Species Foundation? I haven't had a chance to get to Vancouver to see the plants or to talk with anyone there but I heard from Mr. Bloedel the other day that the cuttings seem to be doing pretty well but that they (U.B.C.) *rather figured they owned them.* (Emphasis added) .

I wonder if there isn't some way that we can get these plants down here before they disappear into the Canadian wilderness? I know there is still interest on the part of the Bloedels and the Wagners and there must be some way that we can utilized this interest and start our garden if even in a small way.

I hope things are going much better for you at this point and I would like very much to hear from you as to what we can do with these cuttings.

Dr. Walker replied from Palm Springs, California:

Dear Ed:

It was real nice to hear from you a few days ago. Helen and I miss having you drop in on us and hope that business or pleasure will bring you down this way.

To answer your first question - there is nothing new with the Species Foundation. For all intents and purposes the Foundation is inactive, or so I keep insisting to the Internal Revenue Service and to the State Registrar [of corporations]. Of course this is not 100% factual as one of our purposes was to bring in and make available new and better forms of the species and this is being done after a fashion. We can hardly justify our tax free status as a scientific and research organization so I presume it will be just a matter of time before we will be put out of business if we don't voluntarily disorganize.

When Miss Jack visited us here in Palm Springs last winter she told me there were a few of the *maddeniis* that were large enough to distribute but outside of yourself, no one has shown any interest in getting them and propagating for distribution. The other species that have been propagated, maybe two or three of a kind, probably are not large enough yet from which to take grafts or cuttings. I have had no intimation at all that as you say - "they rather figured they owned them." To the contrary, the last time I was up there, they gave me the impression that soon the plants would have to be distributed because of lack of space. They have never been told and never have said that they expected more than one from each form propagated.

Maybe the Bloedels got a cool reception because there have been a great many people who have been nosing around wanting to see the collection and wondering aloud if they couldn't get a cutting or two. Miss Jack has evidently been trying to avoid too much publicity.

I do think that this coming spring something definite will have to be done about dissolving the Foundation or rejuvenating it with a complete new set of officers. I am more than willing to step aside if it would do any good.

Even more dire did the straits of the Foundation seem when in February, 1968 Dr. Walker dispatched the following letter to Evelyn Jack:

Dear Miss Jack:

I have finally got some of my own personal problems solved so from now on will, I hope, be able to give some attention to other things.

Two of the Directors, Cecil Smith and Fred Robbins, have recently visited with us here in Palm Springs and we seem to be in agreement that now is the time to wind up the affairs of the Foundation. It is apparent that we will not be able to raise sufficient endowment to maintain a Foundation garden, even if the property were to be donated free and clear. I am deeply disappointed because I had great plans for a real research institution.

Our arrangements with you as I remember, is that the U.B.C. was to have a start of every plant that we brought in from Great Britain. At our annual meeting next May, we will have to come to some decision as to what to do with the Foundation plants, and get them moved. As you are aware, many people covet these new forms but the objective of the Foundation has been and still is, to make them available to as many people as possible. We feel that the best way to do this is to put all of them in the hands of a commercial propagator, who will then wholesale them to the trade. We do not want any one person to get them, and keep them for selfish reasons.

I was particularly disturbed when Fred Robbins told me that Mr. Frisbee of Tacoma had personally told him that he was purchasing a complete set of the Foundation Species. This man has been a thorn in the flesh of the American Rhododendron Society ever since he broke away and formed his own Pacific Coast Rhododendron Society. His activities made my work in Great Britain very difficult. Please reassure me that my information is incorrect. [She later reassured him on this point].

If you have any good ideas as to how we can distribute these forms, so as to do the greatest good to the greatest number, I would appreciate your suggestions.

In April Walker again wrote to Miss Jack, this time informing her that because of age and health he and Helen were selling their home and garden. "The Foundation has been toying with the idea of purchasing it but I am afraid they will delay too long despite a very generous offer on our part."

And generous it was, for the Walkers, through their realtor Oscar Spliid of Eugene, had received an offer to purchase their property for the sum of $100,000.00, with $25,000 payable upon acceptance by Walkers and the balance payable at $17,820 per year. Earnest money had been received on this offer and it awaited only the Walkers' signatures. At this late moment, Walkers were withholding their signatures on the Earnest Money agreement, pending a decision of the Foundation Board of Directors on Walkers' offer to sell to the Foundation for $50,000.00, just half the amount they would receive on the Spliid transaction. Furthermore, since the Foundation had no funds for a down payment, Walkers agreed to borrow $25,000 from a local bank, which loan the Foundation could assume as the down payment, and the remaining $25,000 would be payable on monthly terms. Thus the Foundation would be getting the property for half its market value, without any cash investment. In addition the Walkers agreed to sell a tractor and considerable other personal property required for the maintenance of the property for the further sum of $8000, also payable in installments.

Generous as the offer may have been, it was not sufficient to convince all the board members of the wisdom of the purchase, as evidenced by this letter from Carl Phetteplace:

> I am afraid that I may not have made myself entirely clear in some of the conversations we have had about the Foundation and the possibility of purchasing Dr. Walker's place, and especially about my regard for Dr. Walker. My only concern was that from several sources, including one conversation with Dr. Walker a few years ago, I have the impression that the water situation in the Pleasant Hill area is very variable and there are places where they had serious difficulty getting more than enough water for ordinary household use.
>
> I have also wondered if members of the Board had really gone over the property sufficiently carefully personally, so as to be sure that this would be well suited for the Foundation's needs over a long period of time. I do think that the price that Dr. Walker has placed on the property is exceedingly reasonable. I know of other property that could be considered quite comparable which has sold for substantially more than he is asking for this, so that is no problem.. But whatever the price on the property might be, the most important thing is whether or not it best suits the needs regardless of how reasonable the price might be.
>
> Secondly, I want to have no misunderstanding about my high regard for what Dr. Walker has done. For years various people have tried to jar some of these plants loose from British gardens and have met with the coolest kind of reception. His accomplishments have been tremendous. He has spent a great deal of money as well as time, and I know that it has been very close to his heart and that he is willing to make even still further substantial contributions, probably in his will or some other way financially. I am sure we would have no species project had it not been for him and I think this is extremely important, because I have had some information that these gardens were falling to pieces in Britain and this may be the best chance of preserving them for anyone.
>
> Believe me, I would be very happy to see the Walker place the "home" of the species project plants if it has what is really needed to carry on. I suppose I have been just a little over-zealous in probing to see if we had enough information to go ahead with it. I am sorry if I have rubbed anyone's hair the wrong way or by my actions seemed to imply a lack of confidence. It just seemed to me that if I had anything to say about it that now was the time to do it, rather than later on.

In May Dr. Walker sent notices to all directors that a special meeting was to be held June 3, 1968 for the purpose of considering the purchase of the Walker property by the Species Foundation. In the same notice he pointed out that his term as president of the Foundation was expiring and he urged that someone else be elected to fill the position. The board obliged him by electing Wales Wood, attorney from St. Helens, Oregon, as the new President. Others elected were Clarence Chase, vice president; Fred Robbins, Secretary; Ed Siegmund, Treasurer; Directors: Cecil Smith, Ed.

Dunn, Dr. Milton Walker, J. Harold Clarke, Alfred Martin, James Blackford, and Dr. Carl Phetteplace. Following is President Wood's inaugural message:

Greetings:

After a lull for the past two years there has been a great deal of activity in the last few weeks.

Wales Wood

Photo courtesy Ruth Wood

At the annual Board Meeting last month, the members learned that the President's [Walker's] home and beautiful gardens were to be sold. For a number of years many of the Board members have felt that this would make an ideal garden for the Foundation Species Collection. The imminent sale made it imperative that the directors at this time consider any possible available locations including this property.

Another factor that entered into the urgency of a decision was the imperative need it seemed of bringing the Species Collection from the University of British Columbia to the United States this summer if at all possible.

After weighing all the suggested locations for a Foundation garden, it was the unanimous decision of the Board of Directors, that the Walker property be purchased at the offered price and terms. During all the discussions, Dr. Walker absented himself from the meetings.

Having made the decision to purchase the property, pledges were given by a number of the Board members to handle most of the expenses during the first two years. This is an encouraging start, but only a start, and we will need the interest and financial help of each director and his friends.

Dr. Walker resigned as President prior to the discussions about a possible purchase of a garden site. He has consented to remain for the balance of the summer to direct the care of the garden and the moving of plants from Vancouver. It is hoped he will be available for the continued direction of the garden.

I have accepted the responsibility of guiding the Foundation as your new President. I ask that each of you give me your whole hearted support in establishing a Foundation Species Garden that will serve the whole of the United States and Canada.

One of the first acts of newly installed President Wales Wood was a response to the above letter from Dr. Phetteplace:

If the selection of Doctor Walker's place is wrong, then I think most of the members of the Board are to be blamed because most of us have applied pressure on Doctor Walker to establish the garden there. Doctor Walker has over the past three or four years devoted hours and days of his time to the

Foundation as well as a sizeable amount of financing. He has carried most of the burden in the formation of the Foundation and its development into a very workable institution with an excellent Board of Directors.

Some $8,000 had been pledged and letters went out to the board members, reminding them of their pledges and the urgency of their response. It was anticipated it would require about $18,000 a year to operate the garden and retire the indebtedness. In July the final papers were signed for the purchase of the Walker property and arrangements were commenced for the removal of the Foundation's plants from Vancouver. Happily, the University of British Columbia indicated its willingness to continue the fine relationship with the Foundation and the Foundation, in turn, decided to make the U. of B.C. the first Foundation Subsidiary Garden site, an "honor" the University declined for the moment for political reasons.

When in October, 1968 the time came to move the plants from Vancouver to the new garden near Eugene, timely advance arrangements were made so as to simplify the passage through Customs at the border between the U. S. and Canada. But these well made plans, like many others, went awry as Dr. Walker's account of the trip indicates:

Bob [Mazaney] and his friend from the Parks Department [in Eugene] drove the 18 foot van up from Eugene and we met them Thursday evening and had dinner together - and really celebrated I can tell you. Friday morning with the help of four men from the U.B.C. and the four of us we had the truck loaded by 8:40 and were on our way. About 15 miles out of Vancouver the truck had a broken water pump and we had to get it hauled back into the city for repairs. We started out again at 12:30.

Despite our careful preparation in July for the Customs, I had a bad time and was referred from one official to another and from one border crossing to another until we had wasted 2 hours and had to hire a broker to go bond for us. I think it will all come out right but it sure was touch and go for a while. I had to promise to send to the chief deputy officer copies of the Constitution and Bylaws, Incorporation papers, dates of the I.R.S. tax exempt status and date of registration as a Charitable Foundation in the State of Oregon etc.

We picked up 20 good sized plants at Fred Robbins and got home at midnight. Saturday morning Bob Mazaney brought the truck out to the garden and we unloaded and Bob took the truck into town.... Bob and his friend Greenwood had taken three full days off their vacation to do this job for us and warrant a very warm word of thanks. Without

Plants being moved into Walker garden
Photo by Milton Walker

Bob's experience in packing plants we would never have got the 800 plants in the 18 foot van let alone the 20 big balled plants from Fred Robbins.

Saturday we had some help but spent all day sorting the plants and placing them according to series in the lath house and according to tenderness as well as utilizing all the space - or better, not wasting any. Sunday it rained but we had 9 helpers and worked all day planting. Most of the plants came through fine and looked in good condition. The only ones that I saw that didn't look good were a few very small *russatums*. Many were four to five feet tall and too many were of the tender varieties. Miss Jack evidently disregarded my suggested list where I had eliminated all the tender ones this time.

Special thanks might be made to Ed Siegmund for taking time off to go up to Vancouver and do all the driving as well as working Saturday and Sunday planting - Bob Mazaney and Greenfield who drove the van up to Canada - Jim Gossler and two kids and Kurt Huey who helped with the planting, also Cecil Smith who came over on Sunday to help.

A list of the plants received by the Walker garden from the University of British Columbia may be seen in **APPENDIX B, COLUMN "W"** at page 221 of this book.

Retrospectively, an idea expressed in a letter from Dr. Walker to Ed Dunn in December, 1968 is worth noting for its ironic implications. The letter involved primarily the Foundation's unsuccessful efforts to find, and afford, a full time person to look after the garden. Walker states:

Dr. Walker and Kurt Huey
sorting plants

> I understand that Jock Brydon is coming back to Oregon and will run his fruit orchard near Salem. It seems to me that this will be too big a change from the responsible job he has at the Arboretum [Strybing Arboretum at Golden Gate Park in San Francisco, California] and I doubt if he will be happy leading that kind of life now. I wonder if he would like to move into our house at the Foundation Garden and be a Director, in charge of the garden. There are many things to recommend such a move, such as from his standpoint the contact with so many of the horticulturists he knows all over the world, a challenging project in building the only Species Garden in the U.S.A. and directing the propagation and research.

Ed Siegmund

> If you think this idea is worth pursuing would you like to write Jock or recommend someone who is closer to him. If we had someone like Jock living on the place and enjoying a certain amount of physical work, a full time caretaker would not be necessary. Otherwise we will have to find someone full time and depend on the local

committee for supervision, not as good a solution in my humble opinion.

The irony is in the fact that Jock Brydon did not move into the Walker house but instead, eventually moved the entire Foundation collection to his fruit orchard near Salem, Oregon. That is the subject of part III of the History of the Rhododendron Species Foundation - The Brydon Years.

The winter of 1968-69 was a winter of much snow. Dr. Walker and his wife left the garden soon after the plants were brought in from Vancouver and spent the winter at Palm Springs. In the absence of a full time caretaker, board members Ed Siegmund and Kurt Huey looked after the garden, taking cuttings for propagation and rendering first aid to the plants when they suffered snow damage. Only 18 plants were lost but in the absence of proper supervision of the facility one of the outbuildings was entered during the winter and vandalism and theft committed. So, in June, 1969 Dr. Walker hired a Mr. Boyd to be a full time employee of the Foundation at an annual salary of $7,500, payable at $625 per month, with the provision that if the Foundation was unable or unwilling to pay the salary, Dr. Walker would do so personally. Such was the will and dedication of Milton Walker.

As a first signal of the financial crisis faced by the Foundation with regard to the purchase of the Walker place, on December 18, 1969 Dr. Walker received a letter from the bank from which he had secured the loan assumed by the Foundation as a down payment. It noted that the Foundation was two months in arrears and nearing the third month of delinquency, which, if that occurred, would result in their calling the loan. They pointed out that the loan had been made to him personally and they would look to him for payment in full. Fortunately the next day's mail brought a check in the sum of $5,000, representing donations received by the Finance Committee, and the default was cured at once - for the time being.

It seems important at this point to summarize the financial plight of the Foundation, and Treasurer Edward E. Siegmund's financial report issued to the board on April 1, 1970 accomplishes that:

Cash on hand 4/1/69 $ 75.98

    Receipts:

Donations	$11,419.79	
Rent received	2,213.57	
Insurance claim proceeds	118.30	
Equipment sold	475.00	
Dividends	15.81	
Loans	3,250.00	

                                             17,492.47

                                             17,568.45

Disbursements:

Labor	5,248.84
Equipment repair	314.07
Repairs	268.29
Utilities	347.95
Gas & oil	72.62
Supplies	554.69
Office supplies	189.99
Interest	4,131.13
Mortgage	1,715.15
Insurance	408.88
Freight	100.30
Repay loan	250.00
Taxes	1,475.92
Bank charges	15.72
Bank loan payments	2.008.10

17,111.65

Cash on hand 4/1/70   456.80

In spite of about $14,000 income from donations, rental and sale of equipment, it was still necessary to borrow $3,250 in order to pay expenses. A nagging thought intrudes here: In the contract of employment of Mr. Boyd, the gardener, which was negotiated and entered into by Dr. Walker without the board's authority, Walker agreed to pay Boyd's salary if the Foundation was unwilling or unable to do so. The written contract was part of the Foundation's records, yet apparently no one saw fit to pursue this avenue in spite of the Foundation's dire financial condition which threatened its very existence. Perhaps due to the Walkers' already extensive involvement in the Foundation's finances and operation, the board's collective conscience would not permit the exercise of this literal interpretation of the contract.

In May Dr. Walker reported to the board that the general condition of the garden was good despite extensive storm damage, mostly snow which broke off limbs but killed few plants. In March there had been 1948 plants at the U. of B. C., representing 387 different species or forms, and after bringing 803 plants to the Walker garden there remained in Vancouver 1145 plants, leaving 758 plants yet due the Foundation, strictly speaking. In order to make more room in the garden and decrease the work load the following had been accomplished:

Over 500 large hybrids had been removed by Walker
Ground cover propagation had been eliminated
Day lillies and perennials removed and beds made available
Rose beds emptied for alpine rhododendrons
Lath house beds were emptied, reworked and fumigated before U.B.C. plants installed
Many azaleas given away as gesture of good will

Dr. Walker had donated 564 plants to the Foundation in 1968-69, representing 168 different forms. There were now 530 different forms in the Foundation Collection.

The annual meeting of the Foundation was held in Tacoma, Washington on June 6, 1970 with the following officers, directors and guests present: Mr. and Mrs. Wales Wood, Clarence Chase, Mr. and Mrs. Ed Siegmund, Dr. and Mrs. Milton Walker, Mr. and Mrs. Jock Brydon, Dr. Harold Clarke, Ed Dunn, Mr. and Mrs. Pendleton Miller Fred Robbins, Corydon Wagner, Dr. Roy Taylor of U.B.C. The Treasurer, Ed Siegmund, reported that the financial condition of the Foundation had worsened since the end of the fiscal year with taxes of $1000 delinquent since last November, outstanding loans of $1000 overdue and unpaid, mortgage and note payments delinquent for 3 months, all amounting to over $3,200.00 with only $800.00 on hand to pay them and current payroll and operating expenses. The Finance Committee's report, on the other hand, delivered by Pendleton Miller, indicated $9,500 had been donated during 1969, with pledges of $8,000 for 1970 - far less than would be required to retire existing indebtedness and pay operating expenses. The Committee felt that the purposes and objectives of the Foundation did not have a wide enough appeal to make an endowment campaign successful, and that long range financing would have to come from an organization like the American Rhododendron Society or the Garden Clubs of America.

The following officers were elected: Ed Dunn, President; Dr. J. Harold Clarke, Vice President; Ed Siegmund, Treasurer, Dr. Milton Walker, Secretary. The following Directors were elected: Mrs. Prentice Bloedel, Gordon Jones, David G. Leach, Mrs. Pendleton Miller, Dr. Henry Skinner, Mrs. Corydon Wagner, Dr. John Wister; and the following nominated: George Clarke, Mrs. Emil Hager, Jr., Kurt Huey, Hadley Osborn, and Theodore VanVeen.

Dr. Walker, Chairman of the Garden Committee, reported that while the Foundation now had about 1500 different varieties, they had only 274 of the 545 species listed in the latest Handbook, and that they were then about halfway to the goal of gathering a representative collection of all species. He also stated that, "For the first time it has been possible to do our own propagating and we are glad to report that the greenhouse is nearly full of beautifully rooted little species plants. Out of the 2758 cuttings put in from our own and four other gardens, we have just about 1800 ready to put out or distribute."

He also reported that during the past year he and Mrs. Walker had donated 1500 rhododendrons and camellias to the Foundation, comprised of 100 selected specimen hybrid rhododendrons, 154 camellias and 1246 species rhododendrons.

By the end of 1970 the financial condition of the Foundation had deteriorated even further and it owed Dr. Walker $2,500 for funds he had advanced, plus 10 payments on the land sale contract for the purchase of the garden, several payments on the purchase of the equipment, all totaling $6,200. Also the Foundation was 6 months delinquent in the payment of the bank loan assumed as the down payment, and two years taxes, with penalty and interest, had accumulated, for a grand total of $9,345.20 of indebtedness. There were no prospects for raising enough money to pay the indebtedness, let alone continue the operation of the garden. It was an inescapable decision that the garden must be given up.

On January 5, 1971 J. Harold Clarke wrote to Dr. Walker as follows:

Ed Dunn stopped in about three days ago and we discussed some of the problems of the Species Foundation. As you know, I was unable to attend the last meeting of the Board of Directors and had read with some dismay the report of that meeting. I felt badly about it for two reasons. One, of course, was the danger that the species collection could not be maintained permanently in one place. The second thing was that you and Mrs. Walker had spent so much time, effort and money and the rhododendron world in general did not seem to be giving the support it should be giving. I do not know what can be done but I felt that I should make some comments.

I had hoped that an appeal to the general membership of the A.R.S. would bring some results and I still feel that it would. Just why the brochure authorized at the last A.R.S. Board meeting was not sent out, I am sure I do not know. I still think it might have some effect and might possibly turn up a few large contributors which is what we need. Of course it is more difficult to get contributions in our present situation where we are in default on the payments. People like to give to something they feel is already a success. Under the circumstances I see no real alternative to turning the property back to you. However, frankly I am hopeful that this will not be the end of the Species Foundation.

From the very beginning I had felt that the logical place for this collection was your garden. I had hoped that arrangements could be made whereby you would simply retain your residence at the garden, oversee the collection with enough money being contributed by others to take care of the extra care and the propagating. Judging from conversations with you I had gathered that you had considered leaving the property eventually to the Species Foundation but, as I said before, I had hoped that you would continue to live in the home there, own the property and simply be caretaker or overseer of the collection with labor and materials being contributed by the Foundation.

At this stage of the game it is asking a great deal, of course, to suggest that possibly the same arrangement could be made. Would it be at all possible for you and Mrs. Walker to consider taking back full title to the property but still permit the species collection to be quartered there with money being raised by the Species Foundation for expenses of maintenance? It seems that the Foundation could raise perhaps eight or ten thousand dollars a year which should take care of any extra expenses involved in maintaining the collection.

Hopefully you might agree to bequeath the property to the Foundation and so the Foundation could solicit funds to provide the necessary annual maintenance. I realize that this is more than we have a right to ask but you have already contributed so much that I am encouraged to at least make the suggestion. I know that others have placed the Foundation in their wills so that eventually there will be a considerable amount of additional money available, but that does not solve the problem at the moment.

As you probably know there has been some discussion of the idea of finding another place for the collection if you take the property back and the plants have to be moved. Apparently Jock Brydon is willing to take over the collection but it would probably cost somewhere between eight and ten thousand dollars a year and there would still be no permanent home. That would simply be on an annual maintenance basis and then presumably at some time in the future another move would have to be made to a permanent home.

I think it is quite essential that we have a permanent garden where these plants can be grown on to mature size, and from which propagating material may be available for the indefinite future. The whole collection could be disbursed now to people who are very much interested in species but, if that were done, within twenty years probably 90 percent of the plants would be either dead or the identity lost, or at least not available to the general rhododendron public. In other words it seems to me that it is more important to get the collection permanently established some place than it is to get the plants propagated and distributed.

I realize that if you should consent to some such arrangement it would be over and beyond the call of duty and I feel somewhat embarrassed at making the suggestion, but after you have put so much time and effort into this project I do hope you can figure out some way that it can be maintained in the best interest of the rhododendron public even though that public may seem relatively uninterested.

Dr. Walker's disappointment and disillusionment, even bitterness, are evident in his reply on January 14, 1971:

Your worry that the Species Collection cannot be maintained permanently in one place now that the garden is being given up is also uppermost in my mind. I agree that this very important objective of the Foundation seems to have failed and we can only hope that the U. of B. C. will preserve these rare forms. When we started, Windsor was the only public garden with prospects of being able to preserve their fine collection of species indefinitely. Now I am glad to say that Wakehurst and Nymans are both making a start in making a very complete collection of true forms of the species. However, I am a bit chagrinned to think that such a wealthy country as the U. S. A. has not seen fit to support such a modest but very worthwhile project. I am sure we in the A.R.S. are to blame for not being able to convince people of the value of our undertaking.

I am really not too surprised that the excellent brochure that you prepared and spent many hours of work on the preparation, was not sent out. My understanding was that it was to have gone out by separate mailing the early part of December. It would have and still could do a great deal of good. The suggestion was made last year for a "Foundation Notes" page in each Bulletin of the A.R.S. and I said to Carl Phetteplace that Jock Brydon didn't seem very enthusiastic and I wondered if it would actually appear. [Jock Brydon was then the Editor of the A.R.S. Bulletin]. Carl's reply was to the effect that he would personally see that it was done. It hasn't. You also mention that you still think it would increase interest in the collection of species if a list and descriptions were published in the Bulletin. Didn't you know that at Jock's request I prepared 20 some pages listing alphabetically with sources, etc., all of the plants received from abroad? It was a long and time consuming job but was done by the allotted date as I remembered it. Jock had not made the date needed clear or had forgotten what he told me so he said it would have to wait and it has never been published much to my disgust.

I know that you have always wanted Helen and I to continue to live in the

Pleasant Hill home and exercise supervision over the garden and we appreciate your understanding about a person's giving up their home of many years. We haven't done so, to avoid even the suggestion of some benefit to us and to assure that others would assume responsibilities so easily left to us.

To illustrate how little local people realize the hours of work Helen and I still put into the garden during the summer, they have suggested that they could take over the care of the garden with its 5000 plus plants with a part time man and volunteer help. We have practically no volunteer help and have had to dip into our own pocket for necessary expenses. Do you realize that we have not been reimbursed for even postage and a little petty cash expenditure now amounting to well over $150.00? I will be sending in my resignation soon as secretary of the Foundation so that someone else may have the opportunity of paying the postage, etc.

In order to keep a man on the place we have advanced the Foundation in the form of loans that now cannot be repaid according to Ed Dunn - $2,500. Delinquent payments to us on the contracts bring up the amount owing to us at this time to the sum of $6,213.00. Taxes and delinquent payments to the bank on the mortgage bring the total indebtedness of the Foundation to at least $9,345.20 according to my figures.

You are right in your assumption that Helen and I expected to and actually did have a codicil added to our wills leaving not only the property at Pleasant Hill to the Foundation but the whole residue of our estate, amounting at that time to over a half million dollars. However, there were stipulations attached, such as the Foundation must be a going and viable organization and there must be matching funds pledged. I think you realize that we have tried by example and urging to get others to participate and we are more than glad to help but others must do their share. I am not offended in any way by your suggestion that we deed the property without restrictions to the Foundation and hope that money will be forthcoming to maintain it. Experience has shown that it hasn't been done in the past, with no payments on our contracts for 10 and 11 months, none to the bank for 6 months and taxes delinquent for 24 months or more. Even without these payments it took loans of $2,500.00 to keep a caretaker gardener on the place. It just does not seem reasonable to expect the picture to change no matter how you and I would like it to change.

There is a solution to the difficulties of the Foundation and it is the same solution I suggested at the meeting in New York nearly six years ago. I refer to the raising of an endowment without which such an organization as ours will expire. Even to raise $500,000 would be sufficient and it needn't be in cash but in pledges or wills or property. Surely there are five people in the whole of the United States who could be persuaded to leave $100,000 to the Foundation or 10 people to leave $50,000. With what Helen and I are prepared to do, the Foundation would be on a firm and permanent basis indefinitely. What we need is the type of leadership that can find just a few wealthy and interested persons.

Interestingly, Dr. Walker makes no mention of his agreement to pay the salary of the gardener if the Foundation was unable to do so; nor does he seem to recognize that the conditions he attached to his devise of his estate to the Foundation are the same conditions to be expected from prospective donors, namely that the Foundation be a "going and viable organization and there must be matching funds pledged."

On February 12, 1971 President Dunn sent the following message:

TO: DIRECTORS OF RHODODENDRON SPECIES FOUNDATION

As directed at the last Board meeting, the Foundation garden and equipment at Eugene are being quit-claimed back to Milton V. and Helen Walker. Your president appointed a committee chaired by Corydon Wagner, to seek out a means of preserving the Collection upon removal from the Walker property. This committee has recommended a proposal made by P. H. Brydon. As most of you undoubtedly know Jock now has a beautifully situated cherry orchard and farm just outside Salem. He has room for the Collection and the Committee found the conditions just about ideal for rhododendrons. The proposal is:

'The Species Foundation would pay me $600.00 per month and in return I would provide my services, the lease of the property (the exact dimensions to be determined and eventual boundaries marked), plus additional day labor to be contracted and paid for me, the use of small tools, power lawn mower, small power cultivator, taxes and utilities.

'The Species Foundation would agree to pay for supplies, such as peat moss, ground fir bark, fertilizers, insecticides and fungicides; also the construction of a lath house, and greenhouse. In the event tractor work would be necessary for clearing stumps, brush, etc., this would be paid for by the Foundation. I do not think that the Foundation should invest in any major power equipment at this time and any construction that is done should be limited to what is necessary, but built so that it can be added to at a later date.

'It was indicated by some of the Eugene members that they would be willing to assist in the transfer of the collection to Salem. If any expense is incurred, i.e., rental of a truck, etc., the Foundation would pay for this cost. If you agree in principle to this very rough proposal and we prepare a detailed agreement, I would suggest that we proceed on a one year basis, after which we could evaluate the whole situation and adjust financial matters to correct inequalities which may have developed.'

As much as we all hate to give up the Eugene garden, this proposal appears to be a fine solution for the present and should enable us to carry on with propagation and distribution of the plants, as well as continue in our endeavors to establish an endowment fund and a permanent garden.

Jock Brydon

As time is short and it does not seem possible to have a Board meeting in the near future, I ask that you indicate your approval or disapproval of this proposal, using the enclosed envelope by return mail. If you have suggestions or modifications of the plan, please send them on and they will be considered in the final agreement made with Jock. More plants are due to come down from Vancouver on the first of March and these should be delivered directly to him so, definite arrangements should be completed before that date.

It is estimated that an annual budget of $10,000.00 would cover the expenses

It is estimated that an annual budget of $10,000.00 would cover the expenses and many of us feel that this is reasonable. It is less than one half of the former budget and seems within reach. We hope that support from the ARS, various Botanic gardens and individuals will enable us to better this figure.

Brydon's proposal was accepted by the board of directors and on April 23, 1971 the Foundation and Walkers entered into a Memorandum of Agreement whereby the Foundation conveyed back to Walkers the garden and all equipment and personal property, including the plants theretofore donated to the Foundation by Walkers, but retained the right to remove the Species Collection plants. Walkers assumed and agreed to pay all current and delinquent taxes and payments of all kinds, thereby relieving the Foundation of any financial obligations, present or past. The effort had failed; this era had ended, but the Foundation was again solvent.

Dr. John Wister, left, and John Knippenburg

Percy Hadden "Jock" Brydon
1906 - 1990
Photo courtesy Edith Brydon

PART III

THE BRYDON YEARS

CHAPTER VI
THE BRYDONS

Percy Hadden Brydon was born November 15, 1906 in Edinburgh, Scotland. Times were hard after World War I and as a boy of nine he helped the family expenses by being a "message laddie", delivering groceries in a basket for a neighboring grocer after school and on Saturdays.

His father was a commercial traveler for a wholesale grocery company. Dressed in a stiff collared shirt, bowler hat and an umbrella over his arm, he went by train around Scotland. At each stop he would hire someone to carry his samples in a cart as he visited his customers. On one such trip he complained to a fellow traveler that it was almost impossible to find an opening as an apprentice for his son. This man happened to be Mr. Cuthbertson who was senior partner of Dobbie & Co. of Edinburgh - the largest seed and nursery company in Scotland.

Without considering aptitudes, personal wishes or other considerations, young Percy started and completed seven years of apprenticeship at six shillings a week. For part of each day he was taught to grow, harvest and clean vegetable and flower seeds; for the rest of the day he was taught to grow, propagate and sell nursery stock. During this apprenticeship he also studied botany and horticulture from 8 to 10 o'clock each evening three nights a week at the East of Scotland College of Agriculture. During these years he was often sent to London to help put up displays of flowers at the Chelsea Flower Show.

After completing his apprenticeship in 1927, Percy joined a fellow apprentice and moved to the United States of America. He worked at Stump & Walter Seed Co. in New York City for seven months before going to California where he worked for a seed company in Gilroy for a time. He then became propagator at McLellan Co., wholesale florist, and installed tropical plants in greenhouses at the Schilling estate in Woodside. In 1932 he was hired as propagator at the University of California Botanical Gardens in Berkeley. He remained there for ten years, becoming manager the last few years.

During these years Percy propagated ornamental plant seeds from Dr. Rock's expeditions to China in 1932-33-34, and seed from Dr. T. H. Goodspeed's expeditions to the Andes in South America. He also helped to install exhibits at the Treasure Island World Fair and many flower shows and started the Rhododendron Dell at the Botanic Garden in Berkeley. During these years he was active in the beginning of the

California Horticultural Society in San Francisco and was editor of the early California Horticultural Quarterly. By this time his nickname, "Jock", was firmly established, it having been used to separate him from the English players on the Sons of St. George Soccer Team in San Francisco.

In 1934 Jock married Edith Findley from Salem, Oregon - a marriage that lasted 56 years until his death in 1990.

Jock's apprenticeship and other training in Scotland had not prepared him for advancement to Director of the University of California Botanical Garden, so in 1943 the couple moved to Lompoc, California where he worked for a time for a seed company. Then the couple moved to Granger, Washington, near Yakima, where they had 30 acres of cherry, apricot and peach orchards.

Jock's horticultural background caught up with him when he was asked to serve as Vice President of the new American Rhododendron Society which was starting in Portland, Oregon. In 1946 the orchards were sold and the couple moved to Salem, Oregon, where Jock joined in partnership with John Henny in the growing and sale of rhododendrons. This partnership ended when Jock recognized the need for a good retail plant nursery and started Brydon's Nursery and Seed Store in Salem. In 1950 he started a mail order business in rhododendrons and azaleas. For seven years he had an exclusive right to plants from Rothschild's Exbury Estate. Many Exbury plants were introduced into the trade and Jock's catalogs sold plants clear to the East Coast.

During all these years Jock presented many lectures and slide shows, judged many flower shows and made many friends. His humor was marvelous and he had a rare gift of words as he wrote many articles. He gave many plants to Bush Park in Salem and for the State Capitol. He was President of the Rotary Club and enjoyed playing golf.

In 1960 old friends from San Francisco suggested Jock's name for the position of Director of Strybing Arboretum in Golden Gate Park. This was something he could not resist so - back to San Francisco. By this time the eldest of their two sons was grown but the move was difficult for the younger, 13 year old.

Jock had many plans for projects he wanted to accomplish at Strybing Arboretum and in the ten years he was there, with the splendid help of the Arboretum Society he completed the following programs: The Conifer Trail; the John Muir Trail; the Redwood Trail; the Sunset Demonstration Gardens; the Native Garden; Garden of Fragrance for the Blind, etc. Started was the Docent program, the cacti and succulent garden, and a program devoted to teaching teachers - who then transmitted their botanical information to their students with dramatic results. During these years the couple visited many British gardens which resulted in making many new friends and taking thousands of pictures to be later shown to many garden clubs.

While the Arboretum experiences were never to be forgotten, the couple decided in 1970 to return to Oregon so they bought 35 acres of country property containing 20 acres of cherries near Salem. (The author is indebted to Edith Brydon for the foregoing account of the Brydons' background, the same having been taken almost verbatim from Mrs. Brydon's writing. The conclusion of her account is set forth in her own words):

It is hard to believe that anyone could be thrust without choice into a profession at an early age and find such lasting enjoyment. Sometimes I think that we all enjoy endeavors at which we excel. It is a great privilege for a wife to be a helper to such a person. Our work thrust us into such a multitude of marvelous experiences - so many lovely friends, such beautiful gardens, such grand memories - too many to mention.

And now I must get to the dictionary to correct the spelling for Jock couldn't abide misspelled words and he is no longer here to make necessary corrections but — he is with me, never-the-less. Edith Brydon.

"Jock" and Edith Brydon on their 40th wedding anniversary
1974
Photo Courtesy Edith Brydon

CHAPTER VII

THE SECOND GARDEN

Months before the Memorandum of Agreement was signed by the Foundation and Walkers, it was apparent to everyone concerned that the Walker garden was being abandoned in favor of Jock Brydon's cherry orchard and that early spring was the best time to move the plant collection. As early as February 14th, 1971 Dr. Walker wrote to Jock Brydon regarding this matter:

Dear Jock: I am glad to hear thru Ed Dunn that you are going to take care of the Foundation Species Collection. It is too bad that only part of the collection will be moved but it will be the most important plants - those originating from plant material sent from Great Britain and those given directly to the Foundation by Robbins, Wood, Smith and Phetteplace I understand.

The majority of these plants are under 2 feet I would say and in the lath houses. Ed said that you were planning to wait until I return to move the plants but I told him I saw no necessity for that. The sooner they are moved to be under your care and before the hot weather, the better. The date of our return is very uncertain and may be as late as May or even June. The remainder of the plants out in the garden may be a bit difficult to identify so could wait until we get back as there are not so many of them.

On the same day Walker dispatched a letter to Harold Greer of Greer Gardens in Eugene:

You probably know more than I do what is going on in regard to the Foundation Species Collection, but in case you don't I thought I would drop you a line.

Jock Brydon has agreed to take care of the plants that have come from plant material sent from Great Britain and those plants given directly to the Foundation by certain Americans - Robbins, Wood, Smith & Phetteplace. This leaves hundreds of good forms that I had given to the Foundation by collecting both here and abroad. These remain my property to somewhat compensate me for the approximately $30,000.00 loss I have suffered.

I will be selling the majority of all my plants and specimen trees and I want to give you first chance to take whatever you want at a reasonable price....

Similar letters went out to a number of prospective purchasers over the next few weeks, from Hadley Osborne in California to the University of British Columbia in Vancouver. The following letter of February 28 to Ed Dunn, fellow board member and long-time personal friend, indicates the extent of Dr. Walker's impatience:

Dear Ed: On January 17th I wrote pointing out that the month of January was then over half gone and I would like very much to get this matter cleared up. A copy was sent to Pendleton Miller. Six weeks have now gone by and still I have had no action. What must I do? It surely strains a friendship of many years.

I have written to Jock and have had no answer nor even acknowledgment of my letter. I have prepared a list of approximately 500 plants that he can pick up right away. I have had two inquiries concerning the purchase of part or all of the remaining plants. I want to sell these at once but my hands are pretty well tied until the plants the Foundation wants are removed. Please let us have some action.

A partial explanation for the delay in moving the plants came in a letter from Jock Brydon dated March 3, 1971.

Dear Milt: Little did I know when I retired from the Directorship of Strybing that I would be deep in plants again within two and a half years!! There are still some loose ends blowing in the wind, but it looks as though the Species Collection will be under my care as soon as the weather moderates.

We have had some snow and there is still about 9 inches in the orchard. Jim Gossler has gone up to Vancouver and is bringing back plants this week. They will be left at my place and as soon as the ground dries out somewhat I hope to go to Eugene and commence hauling the balance.

Snow covered Brydon orchard
Courtesy Edith Brydon

On March 5th Ed Dunn answered Dr. Walker's rather curt letter demanding action:

Dear Milt:... If you are resigning as Secretary - after the necessary papers are signed conveying the property back - I hope you will turn over to me, or the new Secretary, the vital documents covering the Foundation. We have a rather informal organization but, perhaps, it needs a bit of tightening up.

Sorry about the delay and your frustration over the transfer of the deeds, etc., but these things must be done in a legal manner, apparently. I told Pen [Pendleton Miller] that you wanted action and that you did not want to incur further legal expense from Donald Husband [Walker's attorney in Eugene] and suggested that I call Jim Blackford and ask him to get the necessary forms. Pen said no, that he wanted to handle it as per his letter to Husband and if there is a fee he will pay it rather than start over again. If Wales [Wood] is down there, maybe he can furnish Pen with what he needs and speed things up a bit. After all, we are dealing with Oregon law.

The Board has approved the arrangement with Jock and I believe that he can take the plants pretty soon - if the snow is off the ground....

On March 13th Jock Brydon informed Walker, "The delay now is weather. It is pouring now and has been gusting and raining for quite some time. Even the natives can't recall such a sustained stormy spell. In some spots on the north side of hills and barns, there is still snow in evidence."

Again, from Palm Springs, California, Walker wrote to his attorney, Donald Husband, in part:

Maybe you do not realize that in June of last year, the decision was made to return the property. It was put off until a supposed September meeting of the Board and when it finally was held I agreed to wait until January 1, 1971 for the return of the property to give them every chance to raise money. All these documents etc., should have been prepared three months ago. It is a very unbusinesslike and inexcusable delay.

Consider then, the following letter to attorney Donald Husband, indicating a copy having been sent to Dr. Walker. It is dated Sept. 28, 1970 and is from the Walkers' tax accountant, C.P.A. Robert H. Lemon:

I have a copy of the letter which you wrote to Mr. Edward B. Dunn, President of the Rhododendron Species Foundation concerning the reacquisition of property sold by Dr. and Mrs. Walker.

I suggest that the property not be reacquired by the Walkers before 1971. The reacquisition may well result in taxable income to the Walkers and they would be much better off to have this occur in 1971.

I also suggest that if the Foundation is unable to pay the property taxes on the property that Dr. and Mrs. Walker make contributions to the Foundation to enable them to pay the taxes in 1971. Dr. Walker cannot obtain an ordinary tax deduction by paying the taxes on property he has sold, but he may be able to obtain a deduction for a cash contribution in 1971. His contributions in 1970 have probably reached the limit of that allowable.

It is regrettable that it is necessary to take back this property but apparently it is the only answer. **My primary suggestion is that the reacquisition and all other points of settlement occur in 1971 and not in 1970.** (Emphasis added).

In the middle of April the Walkers' gardener, Wayne, wrote to say that Brydon had started hauling plants from the lath houses, but he complained that the weather was still very wet and unsettled and that there was still snow on the ground in places.

Greer Gardens, a Eugene nursery, had been employed a year or so earlier to propagate plants for the Foundation on a contract basis. Hundreds of plants and rooted cuttings were at the nursery awaiting the move to Brydon's when weather permitted. These plants were mainly destined for eventual distribution rather than inclusion in the Species Collection. At the August, 1971 board meeting it was resolved that plant distribution might commence, with distribution to be through nurseries. Nurseries which contributed $50.00 or more to the Foundation would be permitted to participate by purchasing surplus plants at cost of propagation. The following year the board concluded that participation by nurseries had been negligible, so discontinued the policy, deciding, instead, to make plants available to anyone who contributed over $100.00. Ultimately another policy change dictated that those contributing over $250.00 might buy plants, with a minimum order of 25 plants and a requirement that all rooted cuttings bear Foundation furnished tags, available for fifty cents each.

At this board meeting Treasurer Ed Siegmund showed cash in the bank in the sum of $1,725.31. At the time of the following board meeting in April, 1972, the balance of cash on hand was $5,584.13 and a savings account had been opened. Of course, by now all plants had been removed to Brydon's and in addition he reported 2300 cuttings were in the benches, plus over 300 grafts.

Concerning the move, Jock Brydon reported in the October, 1971 issue of the A.R.S. Quarterly Bulletin, Vol. 25, No. 4: "Almost constant rains delayed transplanting until late April and, were it not for the yeoman labors of the Eugene Chapter members, this task could not have been completed before the hot weather which began in June. Some two thousand plants were dug and lined out temporarily in nursery beds over which sprinkler systems had been installed. Since then a 60' x 60' lath house has been built and partially filled. At present, a 30' x 17' propagating house is under construction. The collection comprises some 515 accessions with 380 in Salem and an additional 135 yet to come from the University of British Columbia in Vancouver, Canada, making a total of 384 species, subspecies, and selected clones.

Brydon home near Salem, Oregon
Photo Jock Brydon

"The new site is on a wooded slope facing east and situated some 5 miles west of Salem. Shade and protection is afforded by native stands of Garry Oak (Que*rcus* *garryana*), Madrone (*Arbutus menziesii*), Douglas Fir *(Pseudotsuga menziesii*), with occasional specimens of Oregon Maple (*Acer macrophyllum*) and some Vine Maple (*Acer circinatum*) interspersed with Lawson Cypress (*Chamaecyparis lawsoniana*). About four acres of wooded garden are available for eventual display. The topography of the land and variance in amounts of shade offer many different exposures for the species, some of which demand full sun, and others dense shade. The native soil type is Aiken or, as the locals call it, 'red hill dirt'. It is friable, deep, well drained and on the acid side. Air drainage is excellent and the 30 acre cherry orchard, which is part of the property, has never been known to be affected by late spring frosts. Springs provide irrigation water for the garden and the overflow is impounded in a reservoir with a capacity of 500,000 gallons."

A list of species plants moved from the Walker garden to Brydons' may be seen in **APPENDIX B, COLUMN "X"** at page 221 of this book. As propagation facilities were completed and expanded, Jock Brydon proceeded to dramatically increase the number of cuttings rooted and grafted, as well as to continue receiving new material from Britain. As the cuttings became established as plants capable of surviving on their own, they were made available for distribution and board meetings seemed preoccupied with devising new distribution methods, but nothing innovative occurred and it took time for an effective plan to evolve.

Cutting beds in Brydon greenhouse
Photo Jock Brydon

Meanwhile, beginning on Dec. 7, 1972 a devastating freeze struck the entire Oregon Willamette Valley, including the Brydon garden and the Foundation's collection. Jock reported the effects in Vol. 27, No. 2 of the Quarterly Bulletin, at page 85:

"RHODODENDRON SPECIES FOUNDATION - A PRELIMINARY REPORT ON FREEZE DAMAGE. Beginning December 7th, 1972 and continuing for four successive nights, the official low temperatures at the Salem, Ore., Airport were -4 degrees, -12 degrees, -5 degrees, -2 degrees and -3 degrees F. Our last severe cold spell was in 1950 when -10 degrees F. was recorded and this recent -12 degrees F is a record for the Salem area. Fortunately for the Rhododendron Species Foundation

Planting beds at Brydon's

Yard and planting beds during freeze
Photos Jock Brydon

collection, my garden is some 200 feet above the airport in altitude and slopes sharply to the East and North with excellent air drainage. This, combined with an 11 inch snowfall, somewhat moderated the intensity of the cold. Our lowest temperature in the garden was -5 degrees F. and due to variations in topography, tree cover, etc., our temperature range during the cold period varied from -5 degrees to +10 degrees F. It is still too soon to give an accurate account of the damage, since many of the species which appear to be dead have green wood below the snowline. Occasionally latent buds will break into growth after the plant has been cut back and, in some instances, adventitious buds will appear on older wood.

"This report is primarily concerned with the larger plants out of doors. The smaller plants under lath were completely covered with snow and many otherwise tender species survived where their older counterparts succumbed in the open. Speaking of the larger leaved species the probability for loss is greatest in the Maddenii, Grande, Falconeri, Arboreum, and Irroratum Series, in that order. The highest survival percentage seems to be in the Taliense, Fortunei, Ponticum and Thomsonii Series. The smaller leaved and dwarfer species in the Lapponicum, Saluenense, Uniflorum and Campylogynum series ware practically untouched due to the snow cover. How they would have fared without a snowfall is another question.

Brydon lathhouse during freeze
Photo Jock Brydon

"All of us have a tendency to try border-line plants and push the limits of their cold endurance beyond their capacity to survive. At times we succeed for a few years and enjoy some of the more exotic species and then the "unusual" happens. Such species in the Maddenii series as *carneum, parryae, veitchianum,* etc., are in the H-1 and H-2 category for hardiness and the inevitable happened; but, even if they get frozen once in a while, many of the Maddenii group have the propensity to grow again from the base and regain their former size in a short time. This spring will tell the tale. In this Series, *ciliatium, fletcherianum,* and *valentinianum* appear to have weathered the storm but will need some light pruning to remove frozen wood.

"In the Falconeri Series, *fictolacteum, galactinum* and *hodgsonii* are untouched but *falconeri, basilicum, arizelum* and *eximium* look quite dead. (The small plants which were under the snow in the lath house are all right.) Although I know that the chance of these large-leaved species pushing from the base is slight, I have not given up hope, not while there are latent buds on the lower 12 inches of growth. In the Grande Series all of the species out of doors have lost their leaves and the upper branches are completely dead. However, as in the Falconeri Series, I shall hold on until spring before discarding them.

"Species in the Arboreum Subseries are apparently more tender than those in the Argyrophyllum Subseries. In the former, *arboreum, lanigerum, niveum* and *zeylanicum* will have to be cut back quite severely, whereas, *argyrophyllum, floribundum,*

111

hunnewellianum, hypoglaucum, insigne, ririei and *thayerianum* are relatively unblemished.

"Members of the Irroratum Subseries as *hardingii, laxiflorum, irroratum, pankimense, ramsdenianum* and *shepherdii* show extensive leaf injury but, *aberconwayii* and *anthosphaerum* are not harmed too badly. R. *venator* is the only member of the Subseries Parishii which seems to have come through, although *elliottii* may break from the base.

"R. *camelliiflorum*, an H-1-2 is dead which is expected, but I was agreeably surprised to note that *wilsonae*, also an H-1-2, is completely untouched. This member of the Staminium Series was sent to us from Wakehurst and flowered last year. It is a low spreading plant, ultimately reaching six feet, with bright shining green leaves and 2-inch lavender-pink flowers which are delightfully fragrant.

"We expected R. *campanulatum* and its var. *aeruginosum* to survive and they did. Another of this series, *fulgens*, also came through without a blemish but *tsariense* was burned above the snowline. The Carolinianum, Dauricum and Ferrugineum Series were not affected, but all the species in the Cinnabarinum Series were damaged although the wood looks green and fresh and there is a strong possibility that they will break again in the spring. In the Subseries Barbatum, both *barbatum* and *smithii* are completely defoliated, perhaps dead. Other species in the Barbatum Series such as *bainbridgeanum, crinigerum, glishrum, habrotrichum, spilotum, vesiculiferum, pachytrichum* and *strigillosum* were badly leaf scorched. The "toughies" in this group are *anwheinse, maculiferum, pseudochrysanthum*, and *morii*. They lost neither leaves nor buds.

"The Fortunei Series came through in fine shape - *diaprepes* and *griffithianum* were defoliated and possibly bark-split. All the others seem to be in good shape, particularly *orbiculare, fargesii, calophytum* and *praevernum*.

"Those species in the Neriiflorum Series such as *chamae-thomsonii* and other low growing types were quite safe from injury under the snow but the larger leaved and taller growing species as *mallotum, beanianum*, and *catacosmum* were partly defoliated. The only species showing damage in the Ponticum Series is our native *macrophyllum* and I am certain it will recover. None of the Taliense Series were affected. However, in this Series, the Foundation has but 15 species out of a possible total of some 50. While many of them are not in cultivation and some merely botanical curiosities, there are a number of excellent foliage plants and we are continuing our efforts to introduce them from various gardens both here and abroad.

"There were few casualties in the Thomsonii Series. All forms of *wardii* did not seem to mind the cold. By contrast *campylocarpum* was damaged in flower buds and foliage. The upper leaves of *stewartianum* were quite black whereas *stewartianum* var. *aiolosalpinx* was unhurt. All other species in the Thomsonii Series seem to be in good shape with the exception of *cyanocarpum* and *viscidifolium*, both of which have lost their upper leaves.

"Surprisingly enough, the larger plants of *augustinii* and its many forms survived remarkably well. The only weak sister was *augustinii* 'Electra' which lost its leaves to the snow line but should recover rapidly. The various forms of *davidsonianum* did not fare so well and are completely leafless now but should come back from the base. With the exception of *concinnum, keiskei, hanceanum nanum* and *lutescens* which were unharmed, most of the species in the Triflorum Series lost their leaves to the snow line.

"A more specific account of the December freeze damage is being prepared in tabulated form for the next issue of the Bulletin and by that time we should be more fully informed on such details as flower bud survival, bark split and regeneration from the older wood." [Note: a reasonable search has turned up no subsequent report.]

By the fall of 1973, under the care and direction of Jock and Edith Brydon, the number of accessions had increased so dramatically and the number of propagated species plants raised by Brydons had accumulated so prolifically that it became obvious that very soon more space and labor would be required than was available in the Brydon garden. Accordingly, Corydon Wagner arranged a meeting between a Foundation committee and Mr. George Weyerhaeuser. The committee consisted of Wagner, who was a relative of Weyerhaeuser, Fred Robbins and Jock Brydon. It was hoped that Weyerhaeuser might consider providing facilities for the garden in part of the large Weyerhaeuser campus connected to the corporate headquarters at Federal Way, Washington, near Tacoma.

To the committee's delight Mr. Weyerhaeuser and his staff received the committee's presentation with great interest. At a special meeting of the board of directors of the Foundation on Nov. 11, 1973 the board unanimously approved the plan and instructed the committee to proceed with negotiations with Weyerhaeuser. Before adjourning the board optimistically set the next meeting for May 8th at Weyerhaeuser headquarters at Federal Way. There was now $8,050.80 in the treasury.

Weyerhaeuser corporate headquarters near Federal Way, Wash.

Negotiations proceeded much faster than anyone had believed possible and another special meeting of the board was called February 19, 1974 in order that the board might consider and discuss the details of the proposed agreement with the Weyerhaeuser Company which had already been formulated and awaited only their approval. Subject to minor changes the board instructed the appropriate officers to execute the agreement, but due to President Robbins being in Europe at the time the agreement was not signed until his return soon after the May 8th annual director's meeting. This most fortunate agreement may be read in its entirety in **APPENDIX C** at page 281 of this book.

Basically, the agreement gave the Foundation the use of approximately 24 acres of prime land ideally suited to rhododendron culture with a few alterations, most of which the Weyerhaeuser Company agreed to accomplish. The company was to provide the funding and equipment to clear, grade and contour the area, to add the necessary soil amendments in the form of partially decomposed sawdust and nitrogen, to build foot paths and service roads and to fence the entire area with chain link fencing for protection and security. They agreed also to fund the construction of a greenhouse, lath house, office and equipment storage building, all to the Foundation's specifications, and to install water and electrical services and provide those utilities at the company's expense. In return the company required only that the Foundation assume responsibility for its own insurance and liability problems, that it proceed to enlarge its plant collection, that it operate according to its tax exempt status and that the company have the right to buy the plant collection in the event the Foundation should ever elect to terminate the agreement, a right which it might exercise upon the giving of 24 months notice in writing.

Beginning to develop the new garden

PART IV

THE WEYERHAEUSER ERA

CHAPTER VIII

THE THIRD GARDEN

The site was typically beautiful native woodland, inhabited by second growth Douglas Fir, with occasional understory trees of vine maple, dogwood and madrona. Some selective cutting was required to provide the necessary variety of growing conditions with regard to sun and shade and air flow. In addition, initial preparation would involve the removal of blackberry vines and other underbrush while retaining salal, ferns, Oregon grape, trilliums, huckleberry and natural ground cover whenever possible. Boulders, windfalls and rotten logs were to be carefully retained to add to the natural woodland setting.

Design and construction characteristics of required structures were certainly not left to chance but were meticulously detailed by knowledgeable people within the Foundation:

Lath House: Shall be 78' x 60', in 3 sections, each 78' by 20' with 8' clearance at eaves and 12' at peaks. The laths to be l" x 4" and running North and South so that the sun will cross laths to provide moving light and shade. The base of the lath house should have 9" of coarse gravel over which beds are laid. This to provide maximum drainage and allow water to drain rapidly in a vertical direction and reduce the occurrence of various root rots to which the young plants are most susceptible. Each bed should be 6' wide and retained by 2" x 10" cedar boards. The soil mixture has been specified. Two Skinner System Sprinkler lines should be suspended beneath lath house roof, each line 78' long and activated by two oscillators. (Approximate cost $500.00 for Skinner System)

Propagating House: Shall be located adjacent to the lath house and approximately 60' x 32'. Construction should be steel framework with fibre glass cover. Interior benches should be of 2" cedar. Propagating benches to be heated by resistance lead cables. Entire house vented by exhaust fans and louvres. (Approximate cost $15,000.00)

Office, Potting Shed & Tool Room Combination: Approximately 60' x 24' constructed of wood with cement floor. (Approximate cost to include heat, water and light $14,000.00)

Tools and Machinery: A small tractor (e.g. Mitsubishi R 1500) equipped with hydraulic hoist, fork lift, and trailer is essential for moving and transplanting larger plants and for the preparation of rough land. (Approximate cost $4800.00)

Staging Area: A 1 1/2 to 2 acre site within easy access to lath house and greenhouse, etc., for assembling plants prior to being placed in their permanent locations. Covered by sprinkler system consisting of 30 Rainbird Sprinklers on 3/4" pipe stands. (Approximate cost $450.00)

Small hand tools, hand rototiller for use in nursery area to be supplied by Foundation.

The first order of business was to prepare a place for the collection which was soon to be moved to the new site from the Brydon garden near Salem, Oregon. A tract of approximately two acres was cleared, graded and sawdust added to a depth of about five inches before it was treated with fertilizer and tilled into the soil, thus creating a friable planting bed. Construction commenced almost immediately on the lath house and greenhouse with the tool house and office building not far behind. Overseeing the entire operation on a daily, almost constant basis was President Fred Robbins, with Jock Brydon being at hand a great deal of the time.

New greenhouse from above

At a board meeting on May 8, 1974 one of the first serious discussions was had of the need for an endowment fund to be established to hold funds, the principal of which would hopefully be untouched for operational expenses, with only the income being available if needed. This was an objective that had been repeatedly stated by the Walkers from the inception of the Foundation, and one they had frequently brought to the attention of the board, usually without effect. A decision was made to study the prospect

View of new lath house

and a committee was named by the President. At the following meeting on August 18th a formal resolution was adopted authorizing the establishment of an endowment but legal advice was to be sought as to the wording and form of the document itself. Some board members felt the endowment corpus should be untouchable under any circumstances, while others felt only the income should be used as a general rule, but that in an emergency the corpus could also be used. Eventually it was decided to authorize both forms, with each corpus to be held separately. Although the Foundation now had cash on hand of about $32,500.00, it was many months before the legal details were implemented and funds actually deposited.

At the August 18th meeting Jock Brydon, who had for the last few years been overseeing the collection, suggested that everyone be on the lookout for a person to take over the management of the garden. During the fall of 1974 a gardener was hired. His name was Kendall Gambrill, he was 29 years old, had an avid interest in rhododendron species, had been employed by VanVeen Nursery for two years and seemed eminently qualified. In November, 1974 President Robbins announced to the board that the greenhouse, lath house, office and tool house were almost completed and that eleven volunteers from the Tacoma Study Group had hauled two huge truck loads of plants from Salem and planted them in the newly completed beds, where they would spend the next couple of years while their permanent planting sites were prepared and organized. He also particularly recognized Briggs Nursery of Olympia for the use of the truck and Ray Swanson of the Olympia Chapter of ARS for loading and driving the truck. Jock Brydon also commented on the faithful volunteers from Eugene and Salem who dug, balled and burlapped some 2000 plants in preparation for the move.

Rear view of new facilities. Roof beyond lath house covers new tool house and office.

Dr. Walker, living in far away Palm Springs, California but wanting to be involved still, went about securing a list of appropriate trees and companion plants to be eventually worked in with the rhododendron collection. He was assisted in this project by Brian Mulligan. By the end of November all plants had been moved from Brydons' with the exception of rooted cuttings in the greenhouse and year old plants in the lath house, about 2000 plants all together. They would wait until the following spring for removal. Alders and other weed trees were being removed by Weyerhaeuser employees who were expected to complete this phase by the first of January, 1975.

Meanwhile, due to the publicity attending the establishment of the new garden so near the largest population center in the State of Washington, the persistent appeals of the financial chairman Corydon Wagner for funding, and active recruitment activities by many of the leading board members and officers, there was a surge of new interest in the Foundation and new board members were continually being added to the roster. In addition, director Betty Miller had suggested another potential body to be known as an "Advisory Council" and to consist of people who were vitally interested in the Foundation but for some reason were not able to serve on the board of directors. While President Robbins saw these developments as healthy advancements, leading to eventual leadership in the hands of younger, capable people, his views were not universally accepted, as appears from this letter from Dr. Walker, purporting to speak for his wife, Helen, and his friends Wales and Ruth Wood, who had now moved to California and were living near the Walkers:

Palm Springs, CA.
November 28, 1974

Dear Fred: (PERSONAL)

I would like to make a few comments to you personally so that you are aware of some of the things Helen and I are discussing with Wales and Ruth Wood. I think I can say that they are in agreement with us in general. In some instances they feel more strongly than we do and in others less.

We are in agreement that with the enlargement of the Board of the Foundation, the general direction of the Foundation is in danger of veering from our original purposes. We are at a loss to know why some of the new members wanted to be elected, let alone being elected to a species organization. We would suggest caution and thorough investigation of proposed members to the Board or we will find ourselves outvoted, our purposes and objectives changed and finally be taken over by the Rhododendron Society.

Betty Miller's suggestion of an Advisory Council for those not able to be active directors, sounds good on the surface. However, there are many of us who are physically unable to attend many Board meetings but are a great deal more sincere in our concern for the Foundation than some of the recently elected and attending Board members. Wales Wood and Ruth feel that they are no longer any use to the Foundation and should resign from the Board. I have argued with them that their steadying influence and singleness of purpose over the years are just what the Foundation needs at this time. My experience with an Advisory Council has been purely from a prestige standpoint and they have never been seriously asked to ADVISE. [Editor's note: Compare this attitude with that expressed in his speech on page 39, i.e., "We feel that the addition of an Advisory Council will greatly strengthen the organization of the Foundation."]

I note in the minutes that the Executive Committee is to act as a nominating committee "to present names at the Annual Meeting". We are strictly opposed to open election of members to the Board because the tendency is to elect by popularity and not by ability. We think election of members should be only at the Annual Meeting and by ballot sent out beforehand. This would also apply to the endowment fund committee.

In talking to Wales just now he thinks that visitors invited to Board Meetings be restricted strictly - say to picnic meetings but not to any meetings where business is discussed. Helen and I agree. I hope that you will give serious thought to some of these points that we down here in Palm Springs feel are

Clearing the land

important to the welfare of the Foundation.

Cordially yours,
Milt and Helen Walker

President Robbins's reply a month later was restrained but in his usual tactful way, made his point quite well:

December 24, 1974

Dear Milton, Helen, Wales and Ruth:

The questions you brought up in your recent letter are problems that up to now we have not been able to solve. Mr. Wagner is covering a lot of territory in our attempt to get enough money to do our share at the Weyerhaeuser garden. So far he has sent 500 letters to various lists of garden clubs, and he plans to send another 1,000 or so before we are through. Out of these lists we hope to come back and check out people who can well afford to contribute to the Foundation. In opening up the list to so many people we are in turn going to require a much larger staff of volunteers to take each of these various segments of the organization and help separate the load of operating the Species Foundation.

The recent spring meeting brought up very clearly that our entire Board is getting along in years because, of all the volunteers able to work, only Warren Berg, Martha and myself represented the Species Foundation. The big problem right now is how to organize and get younger people on the Board who can take over this work. Both Cordy [Wagner] and I are having a good time developing the garden, but it is only a short time before someone else is going to have to pick up the load.

Jock Brydon was in the hospital for several days with diverticulosis and has been unable to do very much since our executive meeting, which brings the question to where the possibility of our having to have an immediate solution, should any of us get into any serious trouble, is needed. The Board is scattered and mostly inactive. We are trying to resolve how we can use the various local study groups because they have by far the most people with the most knowledge and are anxious to get involved and help. Presently we have set up a breakdown of contributors of Supporting at $25 per year, Sustaining at $50, Contributing at $100, and Developing at $500 and up per year.

The ideal solution is to find another Jock and Edith Brydon, and that won't be easy to do. With that type of setup the President could be located most any place because most everything was taken care of by Jock and Edith.... Kurt Huey has resigned, which leaves a vacancy not easy to fill, as he was a natural to take over the Presidency. However, the garden can't be operated from Eugene so we feel that most of the officers should be local so they will be available.

... Our present Executive Committee, which I appointed at the meeting, is not large enough, as we are becoming involved in too many things; for example, investigating trust funds, various methods to raise money, getting our publicity together so that we don't find a half dozen people making various statements, and trying to consolidate and get younger members in to really run this whole thing.

Our lath house is working out beautifully. The greenhouse is 95% finished, and our work shed and office area will be ready in a week or so. We have had problems in drainage in the nursery, but have solved it temporarily. More work must be done on our drainage.We will again start taking out stumps and clearing of the entire area now, though we will slow down some of our developments because of the slow economy and the request that we postpone some of our spending for a year.

I hope this answers some of your questions and would appreciate everyone getting together and giving some workable suggestions as to how to handle the Board. We must keep the voting board small enough to be effective, but we must make some sort of arrangements for some of the other people who are good contributors, are very interested, and like yourselves, have much experience and basic sound thoughts as to how to hold this thing in a compact management arrangement and still have a large membership....

> Sincerely yours,
> The Rhododendron Species Foundation
> /s/ Fred Robbins
> President

It seems significant that while Dr. Walker's letter was pointedly marked "personal" and enclosed with another, more business oriented letter, the reply is equally pointedly a formal Foundation communication. The two letters serve to point out the concerns of two long standing and active but aging members of the board, the reluctance of one to accept change in his beloved project, and the acknowledgement of the other of his vulnerability to the aging process itself.

Britt Smith recalls an incident having an interesting bearing on this difference of opinion:

> In 1974 the first group to visit Sikkim for the purpose of trekking in rhododendron areas was returning to Seattle via non-stop flight from London. All but two of the twenty-six who made up that group were on board and, by chance, Fred Robbins and his daughter Martha were also on board. During the course of the flight Fred invited every member of the group, I believe, to come to sit beside him and talk. Martha had vacated her seat for that purpose. He wanted to talk about the then relatively new Rhododendron Species Foundation, and it is assumed that all of those conversations were similar. As I recall, Fred asked me what I thought of the Foundation and what I thought about joining it, and then he listened patiently as I recited my thoughts to him.

> I told Fred that the idea of the Foundation was interesting, but that I felt excluded by the then common understanding abroad that membership was sought from those who could contribute $1,000 per year or more.... Fred said that he had an idea that the concept of requirement for ability and desire to contribute substantial sums of money had developed, but was not really true. Then he indicated that the reason for his talking to members of the Sikkim group was to allay that impression and to replace it with a new understanding that the Foundation was interested in developing a broad membership of those of modest financial means who were interested in rhododendrons. It seemed that only a short time after that a new impression of the Foundation did develop and that the growth of membership accelerated.

In separate letters the Walkers and the Woods continued to prod the board toward more firmly establishing the endowment fund by depositing money therein, but President Robbins continued to report that while the endowment had been created, there was a feeling that present funds must be reserved to cover operating expenses until a current fund drive by treasurer Wagner was completed. Dr. Walker made his annual donation to the Foundation in the form of two checks, one for $500.00 to be used for operating expenses and the other for $500.00 marked solely for a permanent endowment fund, not to be used for operating expenses. This money was held by the Foundation in a separate savings account pending the opening of an endowment account.

At the annual directors meeting on May 15, 1975 it was reported that the balance of the plants from the Brydon garden had now been moved to the new garden, again thanks to Ray Swanson and Briggs Nursery. In addition Ken Gambrill reported over 2000 cuttings and 500 grafts in the benches. 230 new trees had been donated to the Foundation by Milton Walker and Fred Robbins. A surprising statistic: Weyerhaeuser estimated that completion of their work and improvements would amount to a capital investment of $385,000.00!!

A special board meeting was called for July 15, at which time it was announced that the compound around the buildings had now been blacktopped and plans were underway to complete the main roads before winter, with secondary roads to be completed and gravelled the following year. Gambrill was complimented for his excellent work in propagating grafts and cuttings. But the substance of the main announcement was contained in the following letter:

WEYERHAEUSER COMPANY
Tacoma, Washington 98401
July 11, 1975

Mr. Fred Robbins, President
The Rhododendron Species Foundation
P O Box 99927
Tacoma, Washington 98499

Dear Mr. Robbins:

Weyerhaeuser Company will make cash contributions to the Rhododendron Species Foundation in order to assist the Foundation in defraying expenses to be borne by the Foundation.

The company agrees to match, dollar-for-dollar, any funds raised by the Foundation other than funds contributed to the Foundation for endowment purposes. This commitment ends December 31, 1977. The maximum contribution to be made during each calendar year 1975, 1976 and 1977, is $15,000 or a maximum contribution of $45,000 during the three-year period based on equivalent contributions for operating purposes being raised by the Foundation.

By way of illustration, if the Foundation raises $13,000 in 1975 for operating purposes, Weyerhaeuser Company will match the $13,000. If in 1977 the Foundation raises $20,000 for operating purposes, the Weyerhaeuser grant will be $15,000. These grants are in addition to Weyerhaeuser Company obligations under the Agreement between Weyerhaeuser Company and the Foundation dated June 13, 1974. It is the expectation of the company that the Foundation will be in sound enough financial condition by 1978 so that no further grants similar to those described in paragraph two will be expected.

Yours truly,

/s/ Rowland Vincent

With this encouraging information at hand the board proceeded immediately to establish a two-part endowment: A. In the absence of restraints imposed by a donor, this fund should pay the income annually to the Foundation and, in the event of the board's determining an emergency to exist, pay all or any part of the corpus to the Foundation; and B. In the event of the imposition of restraints by the donor, this fund would be responsive and compatible with such restraints. $15,000 was authorized to be deposited immediately in Fund A. Dr. Walker's $500 donation was placed in Fund B.

By November, 1975 all the main roads were in, about 1200 small plants were available for distribution, about one third of the entire area had been covered with sawdust to a depth of 9 or 10 inches and 500 to 600 pounds of ammonium sulfate per acre had been spread. It was hoped that the water system would be established in the entire garden by the following fall so that permanent planting could start. New by-laws were proposed that for the first time would permit general memberships to be established. They were accepted in principle, with details to be worked out before the annual meeting the following spring. Thus the concept of the Foundation representing a rather exclusive, elitist club composed only of very wealthy and/or influential members theretofore envisioned by Walkers and Woods, was effectively concluded. And justly so, for it had fostered a very limited support base, nearly leading to the demise of the Foundation itself. In addition, it was apparent that the organization needed input from people with expertise in the fields of law, accounting, finance and management, as well as an interest in rhododendrons.

The financial report submitted at this time by Treasurer Corydon Wagner for the first nine months of 1975 is interesting in that it reflects the vast change in the Foundation's financial agenda since the garden had been moved to Federal Way. Note particularly the expense entries for consultants fees, secretarial services, wages and payroll taxes, and the whopping bank balance of almost $45,000. The Foundation had become a going concern.

FINANCIAL REPORT
January 1, 1975 Through October 31, 1975

Cash in Bank 1/1/75		
Checking account, Eugene	$ 184.46	
Checking account, Tacoma	4,216.28	
Cash savings, Eugene	2,389.73	
Cash savings, Eugene	3,088.20	
Savings Cert., Eugene	1,699.20	
Time deposits, Eugene	20,000.00	$ 31,577.87

Receipts
    Donations   28,960.43
    Interest   1,035.33
    Dividends   63.00   30,058.76
                                        $ 61,636.63

Disbursements
    Garden supplies   1,287.16
    Consultants fees   2,400.00
    Lease-rent   1,600.00
    Legal & accounting   66.50
    Miscellaneous   141.28
    Office supplies   442.07
    Plants   609.50
    Payroll taxes and insurance 730.92
    Secretarial services   1,617.50
    Travel & transportation   53.00
    Telephone   124.80
    Wages   7.717.90 $ 16,790.63

Cash in bank 10/31/75
    Checking account, Tacoma   29,560.96
    Savings account, Tacoma   13,500.00
    Savings Cert., Eugene   1,785.04 $ 44,846.00

Stock held
    60 shares Potlatch $1,455.00
    100 shares Talley   1,175.00

                      Corydon Wagner, Treasurer

Gathering in new lath house
Recognizable are Jock Brydon, Esther Berry, Ed Dunn, Lawrence and Mrs. Pierce

CHAPTER IX

GOING PUBLIC

The change in by-laws was approved by the Board in the spring of 1976 and provided for seven membership classifications: Individual, $25.00; Supporting, $100.00 to $500.00; Sustaining, $500.00 to $1,000.00; Patron, $1,000.00 to $5,000.00; Life, $5,000.00 to $10,000.00; Benefactor, $10,000.00 to $15,000.00; Endowment, $15,000.00 or more. For reasons of health, Corydon Wagner had retired as treasurer of the Foundation and Joe Nolan, who had been elected to succeed him, reported that at a cost of $840.00, some 4600 solicitations had been mailed. 115 responses had been received to date totalling $5,350.00. In view of the expanding membership the board decided it would be wise to increase the number of authorized directors to 60 and the by-laws were again amended to so provide.

At an earlier date Jock Brydon, being ever mindful of the ultimate goals of the Foundation, had suggested three possible planting options for the collection, once the grounds were prepared for planting, and had asked the board to poll its membership to determine which option should be adopted. The options were: (1) According to Series and Subseries, showing their relationship, (2) According to the geographic origin of the species, or (3) According to their cultural needs, i.e. sun, shade, etc. He personally favored option 3 as being most practical and presenting a more pleasing aesthetic effect. At the annual board meeting in April the results of the poll were announced; the board had elected to adopt option #2, arrangement by geographic origin, the major such geographic areas being: 1. China, 2. Tibet, 3. Nepal, Sikkim, Assam, Himalaya & Bhutan, 4. Japan, Korea & Formosa, 5. Burma, 6. North America, 7. Europe, Caucasus, 8. Student's garden. At this same meeting Karen Gunderson was named as assistant secretary with responsibility for keeping the Treasurer's books and taking care of most of the correspondence and details of the new membership campaign.

In response to the board's choice of a planting option, Jock Brydon prepared a comprehensive Master Planting Plan:

> At the new site of the Rhododendron Species Foundation it is estimated that approximately 450 species can be grown out of doors. This number does not include sub-species, varieties and cultivars but in estimating the areas assigned to each geographical group, space for the various botanical forms has been included. A very small percentage of the species may need winter

protection and, in some instances, additional wind protection may be necessary. Furthermore, various micro-climates may become evident as plantings proceed and from time to time, adjustments will be inevitable. However, these changes should be minor and will not significantly affect the overall planting scheme.

Important considerations in the planting plan are as follows:
The total available space at the site is 23 acres
The greenhouse, nursery, lath house, plus the adjacent area (not in condition for planting at this time) occupies approximately 4 acres
The estimated space in windbreaks, roads, paths, and natural cover is 4 acres
The remaining area left for planting rhododendron species, companion plants, etc., is approximately 15 acres

Within this area the species should be arranged in an orderly manner where they may be easily found for study by visitors. Each geographical group should be assigned sufficient space at the outset so that future acquisitions can be accommodated. To reduce maintenance to a minimum, the plantings should commence at the North end and proceed South as more plants are acquired.

There are eight groups in the planting arrangement, seven are geographical and one is for demonstration purposes (the Student's Garden). The number of species in each section is based on a personal judgment of which will survive in the Tacoma area. Some of the species (i.e. R. *grande*, R. *macabeanum*, etc.) may be on the tender side, but the percentage of tender species on the list is quite minimal, and because of their importance, it was thought that a little extra effort to provide protection would be worthwhile.

Since we are including various geographical forms and cultivars of the species, I have estimated an average of 5 forms per species and 3 plants of each form, thereby multiplying the number of each species by 15 to arrive at a total number of plants to be accommodated in one geographical area. Inasmuch as rhododendron species vary in size from dwarf shrubs to forest trees, the ultimate space requirement per plant has been based on an average of the square feet required by a mature plant. For example, R. *impeditum* may need 10 square feet in 20 years whereas R. *calophytum* may occupy 100 square feet in the same period. I have therefore allowed an average of 60 square feet per plant in the formula for space requirements. For example, there are 250 species in the China section, hence the formula is 250 species x 15 forms x 60 square feet which equals 225,000 square feet or 5.6 acres net. Based on the above formula, the species may be apportioned as follows:

GEOGRAPHICAL AREA	# OF SPECIES	ASSIGNED SPACE
CHINA	250	5.60 acres
TIBET	63	1.25 "
NEPAL, Sikkim, Assam, Himalaya, Bhutan	46	1.00 "
BURMA	22	.50 "
JAPAN, Korea, Formosa	42	1.00 "
N. AMERICA	24	.50 "
EUROPE, Caucasus, etc.	10	.25 "
STUDENT'S GARDEN		1.00 "
TOTAL NET ACRES		11.60 Acres

The above leaves a balance of 3.40 acres out of the total net of 15 acres for planting. This would be used to accommodate various trees, shrubs and ground covers, preferably those species which are natural companion plants for the rhododendron species or, at least native to the same geographical areas. For example, R. *campylogynum* occurs in the Southwestern Chinese Province of Yunnan but also is found in S. E. Tibet and W. Burma. Where this occurs and we have the collector's number to identify the particular forms, it will be necessary to place them in their proper sequence.

Brydon then proceeds to suggest how various garden or ethnic groups might choose to underwrite the care of certain of the areas in which they may have a primary interest. He also informs that of the 250 Chinese species 171 are presently on hand; of 46 Nepal, Sikkim, etc., species, 35 are on hand; of 43 Japan, Korea, etc., species 34 are on hand; of the 24 North American species 12 are on hand; the one Alaska species is on hand; of 4 European species 3 are on hand; and of 5 Caucasus species 4 are on hand.

Well thought out though Brydon's proposed planting plan was, it was not adopted outright by the board and even Jock himself strongly recommended the employment of professional assistance in arriving at a final plan. So a committee was appointed to study the matter. Esther Avery was to be in charge of the study garden and she proceeded with plans to develop this area. Meanwhile the President pointed out the need for a full time garden manager, to be in charge of all business and horticultural operations. It was rumored that President Robbins was tiring and considering curtailing his activities at the garden somewhat. After all, he had been running the garden almost single handedly since its establishment at Federal Way.

Another matter mentioned by the President at the board meeting was an article that was soon to appear in the University of Washington Arboretum Bulletin, Vol. 39, No. 2, Spring 1976, written by Foundation member Doris Butler. Much of the information contained in this beautifully written article has already been set out above but with the kind permission of Doris Butler and the Editor of the University of Washington Arboretum Bulletin, a portion is reproduced here inasmuch as it reveals many of the Foundation's plans at that time, and the attitude of the community toward the garden.

... With the removal of much undergrowth allowing circulation of air and penetration of light, the remaining trees began to respond and now form the background of protection and aesthetic appeal for the garden.

A perimeter road and the necessary service roads were installed. A 10-foot chain-link fence surrounds the entire garden. Plans are to make the fence unobtrusive by planting material adjacent to it to fit the woodland setting. Cedar and redwood split rail gates provide entry to the property. Footpaths will allow visitors to enjoy the garden at leisure.

... Of the three buildings, each of significance to the program, perhaps most impressive is the greenhouse. Much planning went into its construction, resulting in a superb facility for propagating species. Six long benches provide room for cuttings. One bench is equipped with 100% humidity to facilitate grafting. Some material is difficult to root, though the goal is to obtain all plants from cuttings. Three mist systems are controlled by timers, as are light, heat and humidity controls. The elaborate switchboard has controls for each bench, for heaters, blowers, and for the pad pump and damper at the opposite end of the greenhouse.

This facility will enable the Foundation to raise between twelve and fifteen thousand cuttings a year of the finest forms extant today. Surplus plants are presently being offered at cost of production to Foundation members who have donated $100.00 or more. As stock enlarges, plants will be made available also at cost to the entire membership of the Foundation, to members of the Rhododendron Society chapters and to the trade.

One other structure, a gazebo, has been erected at the highest point of the garden. A special gift from interested Board members and friends, the gazebo will provide a view point for the entire garden, a gathering place for tours and will house educational exhibits and information for visitors. [This paragraph was added in a later update of the article.]

As impressive and important as the preliminary work funded by the Weyerhaeuser Corporation is, the most important part of the garden development is presently beginning. The collection of plants formerly grown in Eugene and Salem have been maintained in the nursery area. Others have been added. There are now over 350 species, combining 300 clonal forms and 40 varieties for a total of some 10,000 plants. Over 6,000 plants, some 2 - 4 feet, others 4 - 5 feet, are ready to be planted. Additional material is being propagated and will become a part of the garden as size and conditions permit.

The nitrogen enriched sawdust spread on the entire acreage has sufficiently decomposed to permit planting to begin. Much planning and coordination has preceded this activity, with members of the Board responding to questionaires regarding the proposed arrangement of plants. The curators of such gardens as Windsor Great Park and Kew in England and the Royal Botanic Garden in Edinburgh and other knowledgeable horticulturists and botanists have been consulted. Study groups have submitted their ideas. All are agreed that the Species Foundation has an unprecedented opportunity to create an outstanding garden, perhaps the finest of its kind anywhere in the world. The arrangement of plants however, has not had the unanimity of opinion. [The substance of Brydon's proposed plan is here discussed and will not be repeated.]

The Student's Garden will be primarily a demonstration garden with representatives of the 75 series and sub-series preferably arranged to show their phylogenetic relationship. It will be useful for study group purposes, but will also benefit the individual visitor to the garden who wishes to identify, compare or learn more about the genus.

The proposed plan utilizes the remaining 3.40 acres for natural companion plants - trees, shrubs and ground covers - which preferably are indigenous to the same geographic area as the rhododendrons with which they will be planted. Being planted now are young trees of *Acer ginnala, A. griseum, A. grosseri, A. nikoense, A. palmatum dissectum, A. p.d.* 'Omatum,' *A.Amelanchier* 'Saskatoon Berry,' *Cercidiphyllum japonicum, Cornus* x 'Eddie's Wonder', *C. kousa, C. mas, Enkianthus companulatus, Fothergilla monticola, Hamamellis mollis, H. intermedia* 'Jelena', *Magnolia kobus,*

Stewartia monodelpha, S. pseudocamellia, and *Styrax obassia.* Other material is included in future plans.

Future plans also include construction of a glasshouse and a coldhouse, enabling the Foundation to grow the exciting Malesian species and other tender species such as some of the Maddenii series which would not survive in our climate without special consideration. These plans, however, will await the completion of the present garden.

What is important about the garden is that here will be room for only the top forms. Every form planted will be an A. M. (Award of Merit) form earned against competition, or a top form from private and public gardens of the British Isles, Japan, America or elsewhere, or that obtained from today's plant hunters, for some feel that many species remain to be discovered. Each plant will typify the finest form available. All will be forms recognized as authentic species; all will have been keyed or identified by authorities.

Important also is the fact that this is a Species Foundation garden. It will, therefore, have unanimity of direction and a singleness of purpose as well as an international outlook. The garden will be developed and maintained by the Species Foundation with total control being provided by the officers and board of that organization. To date costs have been borne by a small group. The collection now has a permanent home and the garden is rapidly becoming an observable entity. Currently the Foundation assumes responsibility for all costs of future development and maintenance. It must be self sufficient and self supporting. A broad base of memberships in the Foundation would help to insure the necessary funds for the garden. All memberships, gifts and endowments are welcomed and are tax deductible.

...What an exciting concept this garden is and how fortunate we in the Northwest are to have it at our doorstep! Nothing like it exists anywhere in the world. With the gradual demise of famous gardens elsewhere for tax reasons, this garden can assume even greater future importance, for it will be a repository of the best forms available anywhere - a living museum.

As the garden matures and receives worldwide recognition, the proximity to an international airport adds another dimension to its value as a garden and to the opportunities for service. Plants from any area of the globe can be dug, transported by air, and replanted in the garden within a twenty-four hour period. As trade with China, Indo-China and the Far East is re-established, new species discovered can be brought to the garden for study, propagation and dissemination. Scientists, botanists and experts, whomever they may be and wherever they may be, can be flown to the garden to view and check new and existing material. The garden can become the Mecca - the place in the future where rhododendron species can be seen, studied and authenticated.

People of the Pacific Northwest can feel pride in this innovative undertaking. They can be participants by lending their support as members of the Foundation. The garden's potential is great. It will be an outstanding contribution to the horticultural life of the Northwest, and obviously, as it matures, it will become an item high on the list of tourist attractions in our area.

In August, 1976 the first mention was made of a Foundation Newsletter and the President suggested perhaps one of the directors would be appropriate to the job of editing the same. In fact, it was felt that board members should be involved in many more activities than they had been and there was a prolonged discussion of prospective committees to handle various aspects of the Foundation. There was also a prolonged discussion of possible planting arrangements, particularly since Warren Berg had just submitted a new proposal with a flexible series arrangement emphasizing landscape design. The matter was shelved for further study in hopes the Brydon and Berg concepts could be combined or compromised. At the same time the President made it very clear that the study garden was the sole province of Esther Avery and that she was to have the last word in that matter.

While Esther Avery was in charge of the study sarden, Warren Berg worked very closely with her and the two of them supervised about 30 volunteers. As a result, by the time of the October board meeting, the work had progressed to the point that they were able to invite the directors to view the result. In addition Esther advised the board that the people who had participated in the study garden had now formed a Study Garden Committee. Concerning the overall plan of the garden, the latest garden design map prepared by an architectural firm, Sasaki-Walker, was shown to the board.

The President introduced to the board the newly hired garden manager, Jack Hirsch. He appeared to be well qualified, having acquired an Associate Degree in applied ornamental horticulture from S. U. in New York at Farmingdale, and attended Iowa State University, majoring in horticulture with a botany minor. He had worked at Queens Botanic Garden and later managed a tree service, as well as having been assistant grower at Country Gardens Nursery.

Jack Hirsch

By the spring of 1977 thirty-two tour groups had signed up to visit the garden, including one group of 500 or more people, Garden Clubs Of America. It was important under those circumstances to arrange training sessions for tour guides, as it was felt that very large groups should be divided into more manageable subgroups of twenty or so. Jane Rogers was placed in charge of this program and by April she was desperately seeking more volunteers. 23 tours had been arranged for a short period of 15 separate days. The garden's fame was rapidly spreading, although there were those within the Foundation who would have waited at least a couple more years to allow the plants to reach a more impressive size before welcoming visitors in such numbers.

With the aid of a grant from the Stanley Smith Horticultural Trust in Scotland in the amount of $10,000, work had been progressing rapidly in the garden. The winter had been mild and volunteers had pitched in from twelve plant-oriented organizations: Arboretum Study Group, Niphargum Society, Northwest Ornamental Horticultural Society, Pacific Rhododendron Society, Portland Garden Club, Seattle Rhododendron Society, SRS Study Group, The Tacoma Species Associates, Tacoma Garden Club, Tacoma Chapter, A. R. S., Olympia Chapter A. R. S., and the Tacoma Rhododendron Study Club. In addition to the existing collection, plants had been received from Mrs. A. C. U. Berry's garden in Portland and over 750 plants had been received from Western Washington Research and Extension Center in Puyallup, representing some 50 species and consisting mainly of 12 year old plants. Two temporary gardeners were hired to work with the volunteers, all under the direction of Jack Hirsch.

Robbins wrote a progress report to Dr. and Mrs. Walker, who had been absent from the garden for quite a time:

Dear Milton and Helen,

Our meeting was very good with about 120 people attending. The early minutes, 1961 and on, gave information to most of the people that was new. Cecil Smith, Harold Clark and Ed Dunn were the only charter members who attended. Ed Siegmund had a slight stroke and was in the hospital for a few days but is home now. I don't know, but I sense a bad feeling from the people in Oregon. I don't know whether they resent our not joining the A.R.S. or what. I have ignored them along with every one else, while I was building the garden. It does seem odd.

The physical part of the garden is complete. Weyerhaeuser has to grade and clean up the roads, put the fence back around the nursery and blacktop from the entry down to the shop.

The gazebo is complete - very handsome and cost $10,038.00 to be subscribed from Weyerhaeuser people, 23 of them. Most of them have not been contributors and hopefully we can get a foot in the door. It will take 5 - 10 years to complete the planting. We had to clean the nursery out so the sprinkler system could be installed which meant getting everything out. All the geographical areas received the plants which they were native to but all the dips and hollows can be fitted into individual spots for landscaping and that will take a lot of time. Hopefully they don't decide they are capable and not hire a competent professional.

You and Helen should come North and see the garden while the blooming season is on. The garden is outstanding and very exciting.

Best regards.
Fred

The completed gazebo

In April 1977 Fred Robbins retired as President and Lawrence Pierce was elected to replace him. Pierce immediately announced that the themes of his term in office would be the financial stability of the Foundation and the implementation of an educational program. Renee Hill had now been acting as Editor of the Foundation's quarterly Newsletter and had just completed the second issue. Pierce suggested that Renee, Doris Butler and Rick Billings, head of the Weyerhaeuser graphics department, serve as a publicity staff for the Foundation. Many local newspapers and other publications were now eager to print articles concerning the garden and it seemed only appropriate that staff be empowered to deal with them.

During the tour season that spring Milton Gaschk of Tacoma, one of Milton Walker's correspondents, wrote to Walker, his letter expressing perceptions perhaps typical of tour participants:

> First of all, the Species garden looks great. Went on a tour about 10 days ago in company with the Northwest Ornamental Horticultural Society (Seattle). Everything is in the ground that is big enough to show. Much is just in the ground to get it there, and will have to be moved later into permanent positions. There was some color but nothing like it will be later. Some very attractive landscaping vignettes, using stone and dwarf material, accented with a Japanese maple or two. Karen Gunderson tells me that there will be much emphasis on landscaping. I'll keep you posted. Not much in line of trees or shrubs planted as yet, presumably this will come after the basic material is planted. Many tours visiting the garden - if this continues, and I'm sure it will, it will be a busy place.

Dr. and Mrs. Walker now came up with yet another innovative proposal - That a Foundation library be established. They offered their complete rhododendron slide collection, together with a projector and screen, as well as books, records, correspondence and so on. Dr. Walker took many library items to the Foundation office in August and was able to see the garden for the first time in two years. He was somewhat overwhelmed by the changes that had taken place.

Consideration was being given to the construction of a separate facility to house a library as well as other facilities, but for the time being President Pierce agreed to store donated items in his home. Meanwhile, a sale of surplus plants by the Species Associates of Tacoma netted $700 for the library fund.

Early in August a special meeting was called of the Executive Committee, consisting of President Pierce, Warren Berg, Jane Rogers, Mrs. Hugh Baird, Mrs. Charles Hyde, Fred Robbins and Corydon Wagner. The meeting was also attended by Joe Nolan and by Jock and Edith Brydon as guests, and Karen Gunderson as secretary. The purpose of the meeting was to formulate a Master Plan for the Foundation for the ensuing fifteen years. The meeting lasted for two full days and was in effect a brainstorming session, out of which emerged lists of Foundation priorities:

Immediate - 5 years 1977 to 1981
1977
Revision of By-laws
Annual operations budget
5 year budget projection
Temporary structure for tender plants
Monthly or quarterly newsletter
Signs, fountains, benches, etc., for garden

Semiannual meetings with Weyerhaeuser
Parking facilities - 6 to 10 spaces
Mounted map for garden
Library
Landscape designer
Permanent committees

1978
Information kiosk
Garden brochure
Lecture program
Units or study groups
Calendar of events and tour dates
Tour guides orientation program
Plant of the week or month sheets
Restroom facilities
Enlargement of office space
Plant distribution expanded
Plant sales during tours
Improved labeling for plants sold
Education program - seminars
Additional equipment
  Engraving machine
  Copy machine

1979
Garden director
Additional office staff

Intermediate - 10 years 1987

Publications on species
Pollen bank
Seed exchange
Herbarium
Staff size increase
Computerized record keeping

Long Range - 15 years 1992

Visitor's center with atrium
Glass house or conservatory

Permanent committees envisioned were education, finance, publications, publicity and membership. Brydon felt a high priority item was the employment of a Garden Director to authenticate the species, for public relations, to acquire companion plants, to begin and oversee an education program, for the distribution of plant material and pollen and to advise on and supervise additional physical structures. It was anticipated that improvements envisioned over the period of the plan would be from $250,000 to $350,000 with the exception of the conservatory, which was estimated at $750,000. The President was authorized to spend $4,000 to employ the firm of Peterson & Associates to implement the plan.

The proposed Master Plan formulated by the Executive Committee was presented to the full board of directors at the October meeting and the board adopted the plan by unanimous vote, authorizing the President to spend $5,000, if needed, to implement the Master Plan by the use of professional assistance. The Master Plan is set out in full in **APPENDIX D** at page 284 of this book.

Several old friends of the Foundation had found it increasingly difficult to attend meetings for some time now, and for good reason. Wales Wood had a respiratory problem and needed to be near his oxygen tanks most of the time. Dr. Milton Walker had undergone surgery and lived in Palm Springs, California, a great distance from the Foundation. His wife, Helen, had a heart condition that did not permit him to be away from her for long. Dr. Carl Phetteplace had now retired from his medical practice and, while recuperating from a heart problem, was spending his time tending rhododendrons on his five acre garden at Leaburg, Oregon, also a great distance from the garden. All were aging and none were comfortable with the long drive to Federal Way. A letter to Dr. and Mrs. Walker from their close friend, Dr. Phetteplace indicates the nature of his situation:

The young Dr. Phetteplace
Photo courtesy Sacred Heart Hospital

Nov. 15, 1977

Dear Milt and Helen,

It was good to receive your note and good wishes. I have a problem in that I do not feel tired when working about the place until a day, or even two days after the fact. So on two occasions now I have gone into fibrillation - evidence of decompensation or failure. Quinidine apparently has no effect on me except some unpleasant ones. Consequently they have sent me off to the hospital for electroconversion. The first time it was difficult for me to think of having 110 volts of electricity shot through my myocardium but it was so simple, not especially unpleasant and instantly effective that I did not resist this time.

Everything is fine now and I'm back at digging around as usual. Probably I'll get into this fix again 'ere long because I somehow can't realize that each year my tolerance for work is less than the year before. There is about 5 acres here, half of which is rather intensively planted to something or other and there seems always to be something or other that ought to be done. Getting help is very difficult. The young boys that are available are unreliable to say the least and 16 year olds and older are all looking to the woods where they can make 6 or 7 dollars an hour. Older men are generally content to live on their Social Security and take it easy.

I'm becoming very much aware that I have a "bear by the tail" here as soon I will be unable to take care of it or no longer here and my children even if interested are not financially able to do much with it. And I do not have the liquid reserves to give them the funds that would enable them to hire someone to take charge of it. My principal assets are the place and it in fact becomes a liability after I'm gone. So it will in the not too distant future become another of the Barto, Gick, James, Rudolph Henny and similar places that "have been". And why should I be concerned about that? The original idea was to provide enjoyment and happiness for myself (and Edith) and the public who enjoyed it. That has been accomplished amply so let the future take care of itself.

I think you have realized this years ago and so we now have a Species Foundation. That is the only way of continuing anything of this kind for future generations. It was a wonderful vision that you had. No one else had ever even hinted at such a project so far as I know. It is certainly firmly established now and can do nothing but grow and expand. Who knows of all the fine things that can develop out of this Foundation over the generations to come? I am sure it should expand in scope in many directions from this basic original idea of collecting and preserving the now known rhododendron species. It should last as long as man himself and should be considered a monument to you two.

Happy Holiday season to you both.

Edith and Carl

This writer is confident there are many among the readers who can relate to Dr. Phetteplace's feelings of frustration in having laboriously built a large garden and accumulated a large plant collection only to realize during their senior years, the impermanence of their lives and the likelihood of their efforts being lost to posterity.

An exchange of correspondence in early 1978 serves to underscore the continuing importance of purity in the minds of most of the people involved with the garden. In February Dr. Walker wrote to Esther Avery,

Wales and Ruth Wood have written to me saying how pleased they were to have been able to donate some plants to the Foundation.... Carl and Edith Phetteplace have spent a month in Palm Springs and I have had an opportunity of discussing donations with Carl. He has not been at all well and since his return to Eugene is back in the hospital. I am sure Carl would consider donating a number of his plants, most of which are from excellent sources.

This brings me to the main point of this letter and is I think of some importance. I will grant that the Woods' and the Phetteplace plants probably are true forms of the species as far as they know. But are they? There will be other donations from lesser gardens and who will say whether they are true forms or not? That is why I am very much interested in your proposal of a Fellowship Group. If it functions properly it will be the most important factor in the success or failure of the Foundation itself. I shudder at the responsibility of the chairman who I assume will be held responsible for saying in writing that to the best of his knowledge every plant distributed by the Foundation IS A TRUE SPECIES. If plants are propagated that later turn out to be hybrids in the judgment of the Fellowship Group, there will be some red faces and a massive recall of plants that will compare to the automotive industry. The damage done to horticulture and to the Foundation could be catastrophic.

Esther Avery replied,

Your interest in the Fellowship Group proposal was a real boost to me...

Regarding the Species you mentioned, I do believe that the beautiful old plants from your Foundation members should be put into landscape areas called "The Founders Garden" on the Foundation grounds, and not have to be put to overly CLINICAL SCRUTINY at this time.

It will take the work of ANOTHER WHOLE GENERATION OF MEN to provide an updating and the <u>PROPER PRINTING</u> for a "<u>STANDARD OF SPECIES AT THE FOUNDATION</u>". Besides that, the collection that has been brought together over the last 25 years SHOULD REMAIN INTACT AND INVIOLATE. I believe that most of us who have worked to make collections, go this way in our thinking.

For all these past years - people have driven hundreds of miles - annually - to see the plants and gardens of Dr. Phetteplace, Cecil Smith, your own collection, Mr. Robbins collection, and Wales Wood's garden, etc., and they will do the same now, should the Foundation be lucky enough to acquire those plants. People will always be thankful for the work that has gone into the Foundation collection, and the contributions of the men who have made it all possible.

I DO NOT THINK ANY PERSON SHOULD WORRY THAT A PLANT MIGHT NOT BE TRUE ENOUGH, BUT LET TIME AND CAREFUL WORK SELECT OUT THE BEST FOR DISTRIBUTION, AND LET THE REST REMAIN TO ENHANCE THE FOUNDATION GARDEN. [Emphasis is Esther Avery's]

Dr. Walker expressed his concern over this matter to Fred Robbins who replied,

In regards to true forms of the species in the garden, we are so far advanced from the days before it was moved to our present location there is little comparison. Remember when your "Butterfly" took a blue ribbon for *wardii*? [Pardon the author for inserting a reminiscence here. Many years ago he saw the most magnificent specimen of a R. m*acrophyllum* truss which had just won a blue ribbon in a Eugene show, and immediately purchased the plant from the nurseryman-exhibitor for $8.00. Upon cleaning up the root ball in preparation for planting he found the tag imbedded in the stem below soil level, "Antoon van Welie".] All these study groups have been working six or eight years taking each individual in every series and really working them out. In addition we have had the benefit of the best experts in the business check the garden: Davidian, Cox, Wada, Philipson, Suzuki, Brydon, Bryan Mulligan, as well as Jack Hirsch and Ken Gambrill. Several species cannot be finally proven until they have bloomed and been studied under a microscope. We do not have a meeting of the minds with the botanists and horticulturists....They have changed 3 times in the last 20-30 years. I feel we are as clean on pure species as any garden in England - Scotland and better than most. I have bought plants in the last 4 years from England which are wrong. Remember they are the ones who have been distributing open pollenated seed all over the world for the last 20 -30 years and our little darlings, the A.R.S. is continuing the good work even though the R.H.S. have stopped. [R.H.S. = Royal Horticultural Society]

Could anyone overlook the sarcasm directed at the then fledgling A.R.S. seed distribution program? Sadly, the same letter informed Dr. Walker of the death of Wales Wood a couple of days earlier.

Informal study groups having been successful and popular during the past fall months, President Pierce named an Education Committee in the Spring of 1978 and a course was planned for the fall months to be known as "INTRODUCTION TO THE SPECIES RHODODENDRONS", and to consist of information on the place of rhododendrons in the plant kingdom, activities of plant collectors, terms used to describe the plants and rhododendron culture. The course was designed to meet in four two-hour sessions in October and November and to be self supporting financially. In addition a TAXONOMY DISCUSSION GROUP was organized with over fifty members enrolled.

A Research Committee was formed, chaired by Dr. R. Lee Campbell of the Western Washington Research and Experimental Station of Puyallup, with Dr. George Staebler of the Weyerhaeuser Company also on the committee.

The office building was rearranged to accommodate the library and the President appointed a library committee to sort, catalog and record the accumulation of books, slides, papers and reference materials that had already arrived due to the generosity of a number of members. Founding members of the committee were Karen Gunderson, chairman; Esther Avery; Dr. and Mrs. Robert Glock; Margaret Johnson; Barbara and Rudy Mate; Mrs. James Level; Janet Binford and Margaret Young. The committee immediately adopted a statement of purpose: "To acquire, catalog and make available books, publications and other resource material on the subject of the genus rhododendron and to make such information available to those interested." Arrangements were made to place rare books and items of particular value in the vault in the Weyerhaeuser administration building.

Concerns had been expressed within the board as to the somewhat "temporary" nature of the Foundation's tenancy within the Weyerhaeuser campus, and the possibility of expanding the garden to adjoining vacant acreage. In response to President Pierce's inquiry the following response was received from Weyerhaeuser:

Weyerhaeuser Company
Tacoma, Washington
April 13, 1978

Mr. Lawrence J. Pierce, President
Rhododendron Species Foundation
9343 Fauntleroy Way, S.W.
Seattle, WA 98136

Dear Mr. Pierce,

It is the purpose of this letter to set forth my current thinking with respect to future improvements and expansion of the Foundation's program here at Corporate Headquarters. We understand that in order to generate significant contributions, it is important for you to be able to show a higher degree of permanence and stability at the current site than is possible under our existing agreement. For that reason, and in order otherwise to update the agreement, we have agreed to redraft the agreement in the form of a lease and to provide for a rolling ten-year termination period.

I again want to emphasize that we continue to desire to support the Foundation, the nature of our support being in the area of the provision of the real property and the bearing of certain limited costs associated with operating at that site. On the other hand, we believe that it is the responsibility of the Foundation and its members to raise the funds necessary for operations and future improvements. Although Weyerhaeuser Company may, from time to time upon submission of appropriate requests, make contributions of cash, property or services in excess of that to which we are committed under the new lease, we want to emphasize that it is a matter of periodic review and discussion and not a commitment.

Finally, with reference to the future expansion of the site and the new proposed visitors' center, we will remain willing to provide additional real property to you located in the general area of the present premises for the purpose of adding to the plant collection, such property to be added by amendments to the lease at such time as appropriate proposals are submitted to us for the expansion. Although we are currently bearing the costs of power, water and property taxes associated with the existing site and will continue to do so under the present lease, I do point out that this is inconsistent with our basic view that the operating costs of the Foundation ought to be borne by the Foundation. In the event of any expansion we would intend to re-examine the question of whether Weyerhaeuser Company should continue to bear these particular costs.

As to the visitors' center, this raises another series of questions which we think it appropriate to deal with at the time you present to us more formal proposals with respect to the construction of the visitors' center. At that time it would become appropriate to consider the question of access to the premises, responsibilities upon termination of the lease, the duration of the lease and the relative cost to be borne by each of the parties. We do not feel it is appropriate or necessary to decide between us those questions until such time as your visitors' center plans become more developed.

Mr. George Weyerhaeuser
on a visit to the garden

Sincerely,
/s/ George H. Weyerhaeuser

In June the very knowledgeable and capable garden manager, Jack Hirsch, resigned, stating that,

"I found I was getting involved in so many different programs that were eating up too much time, and the mental stress worrying about these problems was getting to me. The main problem I believe was the executive committee, when trying to define my job, didn't realize how it would develop. Two positions are needed: One as garden manager to run the physical side, the planting, the weeds, equipment, irrigation, volunteer help in the garden; the other a garden director, one to handle lectures, tours, publications, etc. I was trying to do both and with all the different phases going you were jumping from job to job not getting or spending enough time on each. I tried to correct the problem with Mr. Pierce but did not have any success in resolving the problem.... I will continue to help the Foundation in any possible way I can on a volunteer basis."

Hirsch was replaced by Steve Whitcher, who was hired as "groundskeeper". A new organizational chart was prepared, indicating the groundskeeper to be responsible for the garden and shop area, gardeners, nursery, greenhouse and lathhouse, coolhouse, plant collection & herbarium, plant distribution and records system.

During the summer Mr. Albert Nerken of New York, believing special protection should be afforded the more tender varieties at the garden, offered the sum of $7,500 toward the construction of a cool house if the Foundation could secure donations and pledges to cover the rest of the projected approximate $10,500 cost. His generous offer was accepted, although completion of the cool house and its automatic heating system was not accomplished until January, 1979, and not before a number of days of very cold weather during which many tender plants were badly damaged. The eventual cost was $18,000 including the heating system. Fred Robbins was steadfastly opposed to this expenditure, feeling the money should be used for other drastically needed facilities.

Of interest to those of us involved in the affairs of the Foundation as of the time of this writing, is the following letter from President Pierce to Dr. Walker in August of 1978:

You will be pleased to know that your son, Ian, has consented to have his name submitted to the Board of Directors in October as a future director of the Rhododendron Species Foundation. We hope that he can spend time away from his busy profession to attend at least the board meetings and our annual membership meeting. Perhaps, as he gets older, he will become even more interested in rhododendrons.

Fred Robbins had something to add regarding this matter,

Your thinking on Ian being on the board is correct. He knows your feelings about the garden and I feel it quite a sacrifice on his part to take the time to learn about the operation. It is not necessary for him to be an accomplished gardener. Our need is to get a younger age group with good business sense who can judge the operation from the outside and give a better balance.

An early photo of the Walker family, courtesy of Ian Walker. Helen is in the center, Milton at far right. Ian is at far left.

Of course the board of directors approved Ian Walker's position on the board and he serves to this date with great distinction.

In the fall of 1978 a number of significant announcements were made. The cool house would be completed by Christmas and sufficient funds had been donated to cover the entire cost. During the spring season the staff and volunteers had hosted over 4000 visitors to the garden. Over 3000 plants had been sold at a nice profit. Memberships in the Foundation had increased from 285 to 455. The Education Committee's fall course had been attended by 30 members and thirty-five members had been studying the new taxonomic system proposed at last summer's conference in New York. In addition, Professor Lu-cheng Chong of the University of Washington and Judy Young, one of the members of the Foundation, had agreed to translate into English the rhododendron key included in the Chinese publication, "Iconographia Corophytorum Sinicorum" and the Publications Committee had raised over $3,300 for this project.

Molly Smith, Ruth Olsen, Ruth Wood and
Mildred Berthelsdorf, in the lath house

Ben Nelson, left, with Dr. Walker

K. Wada, Molly Smith, Helen Walker and Jim Russell

CHAPTER X

"PHASE II"

In the spring of 1979 the Foundation was entered upon what President Pierce had liked to call "PHASE II" of its development. A great many changes had taken place during his administration and more were occurring daily. The Foundation now had a 20 year leasehold interest in the real property rather than a simple tenancy at sufferance, thus could assure potential donors of the permanence of the operation. Outright ownership of all the physical facilities on the premises, including the greenhouse, cold house, lath houses, office and storage facilities, garden equipment, irrigation systems, fences and all improvements to the garden, had now been transferred to the Foundation from the Weyerhaeuser Company, items whose value was estimated at over $340,000. Plant sales for the previous year had exceeded $21,000 and were expected to reach $25,000 in the current year.

Ken Gambrill was sent on a tour of German and British gardens to meet their curators, maintain relations and seek new accessions for the garden. He succeeded most admirably, bringing home some 380 cuttings and a number of small plants from such gardens as Borde Hill, Glendoick and Royal Botanic Gardens at Edinborough.

The library was growing, now under the able chairmanship of Barbara Mate, with new donations of books, papers and other appropriate materials. Substantial cash contributions from various persons and horticultural groups were making it possible to acquire filing cabinets and other paraphernalia necessary to the proper arranging and storage of materials. The education committee had been active and all classes presented were well attended.

Unfortunately the news that spring was not all good. During the winter there had been almost a month of very cold weather, dropping to eight degrees for over two weeks, followed by winds that took down a number of trees and damaged but did not destroy a number of valuable plants.

A number of people who had heretofore played significant background roles in Foundation activities were suddenly thrust into the fore by being nominated and elected to positions of leadership. Dan Morris was now Treasurer and in April, 1979 announced that the Foundation had a net worth of over $152,000. Mrs. John (Renee) Hill who had been Editor of the Newsletter (and continued in that capacity) was elected Secretary. Mrs. N. Stewart (Jane) Rogers was elected vice-president and the

Great beauty often results from winter weather,

. . . but so can damage or destruction.

new President elect was Dr. William H. Hatheway. Dr. Hatheway was professor of forestry at the University of Washington and also associated with the University of Washington Arboretum. He appointed as his Executive Committee, in addition to the aforementioned new officers, Mrs. Pendleton Miller, Fred Robbins and Mrs. Hugh Baird.

A formal and equitable division of responsibility had now been established and Ken Gambrill, as curator, was responsible for the collection, propagation and distribution of the plants. Maintenance, weed control, water systems, fertilization and other garden and building maintenance was the job of Steve Whitcher, grounds keeper. Policy and long range planning of the garden was the responsibility of the Garden Committee, with garden development, replanting and redesigning of the garden being the combined effort of the Garden Committee and the Foundation staff. Kelly Dodson was added to the staff as a horticultural assistant, to help the curator in all phases of that work.

During the spring E. White Smith was in the Study Garden to work with anyone interested in the field study of rhododendrons. This experiment was expected to continue in future years, under the auspices of the Education Committee. The activities of that committee were now expanding rapidly. A novice level course was offered by Esther Avery and an intermediate one by Bob Badger. In addition Bob Badger was offering a course designed for members who have just decided to collect and grow species rhododendrons. Dr. Herbert Spady was offering a two-hour class on photography in the garden, covering techniques to be used to capture blooms at their best.

Ken Gambrill reported there were a great many plants as yet not placed in the garden due to the lack of a master garden plan. On October 9, 1979 the Executive Committee met and adopted a "Statement of Proposed Garden Objectives:
    1. The garden must provide a way of introducing the interested novice to the genus rhododendron. This person's interest must be captured and maintained. This means that the garden must be informative and have strong aesthetic appeal.
    2. The garden must be of value to persons who want to study the genus rhododendron at a beginning to intermediate level. The existing Study Garden is designed to meet the needs of this class of users. Representative species in each of the important series which can be grown out of doors in our area are arranged in a taxonomic grouping which is designed to meet the requirements of our educational program.
    3. The garden must be of value to experts in the genus. This objective is consistent with our by-laws, which state, in part, that our Foundation 'should create one of the outstanding centers in the world for the acquisition of rhododendron species and the study, cultivation, display and distribution thereof, and to disseminate knowledge relating thereto.... To provide space and facilities for scientific research in the field of horticulture, primarily species rhododendron, and for the study of the habitat, selection and propagation of superior forms.' Good scientific research on rhododendron species should, of course, include work on the classification and relationships of the species. To accomplish this effectively, closely related species should be planted near one another, so that visual comparison of living plants becomes possible.

    "Proposed Garden Master Plan: An acceptable master plan must take all these objectives into consideration. It is not our wish to create a garden for experts which intimidates or in any other way tends to repel the novice - or, in fact, any other person with a genuine interest in our goals, nor is it our intention to create a garden of outstanding beauty that is of little or no scientific or educational value. We refuse, at this stage, to admit that the three goals we have put forward are incompatible with one another or, in fact, with much (but not all) of the planting work which has already been accomplished. What we will require of a planner is technical competence in landscape and garden planning, understanding of our goals, knowledge of plant materials (including species rhododendrons and acceptable companion plants, as well as their cultural requirements), a sense of taste compatible with that of our members, and considerable imagination. Clearly, this is a great deal to expect of any planner. Accordingly guidance and expertise will be provided by an *Ad Hoc* Committee for Garden Planning appointed by the President and approved by the Executive Committee."

The *Ad Hoc* committee was composed of Dr. Hatheway, Jane Rogers, Jock Brydon, Ken Gambrill and Betty Miller.

In early December, 1979 a disagreement over some "technical question" and as to lines of authority arose between President Hatheway and the curator, Ken Gambrill, as a result of which the President asked for Gambrill's resignation on December 5th. Gambrill resigned, as requested, but a furor resulted, with telephone calls and letters from directors and others indicating their disapproval of the President's action. The President referred the matter to the Executive Committee, which, though without unanimity, agreed with Gambrill's point of view. Hatheway referred the "technical matter" to special consultants, who found also in Gambrill's favor. Hatheway then recommended that Gambrill be reinstated as curator. He also proposed a modification of the By-laws defining the authority and responsibility of the President but his proposal was rejected by a majority of the Executive Committee, though again not with unanimity.

Ian Walker, having been directly involved in the controversy, recalls the incident:

The issue between Ken Gambrill and Bill Hatheway was over fertilizer. For several years there had been a simmering dispute over the shavings into which the rhodies had been planted. The issue was that the shavings were not breaking down to make humus and therefore the rhodies were nothing more than healed in, and no root system was developing. When Bill was president, the issue came to a head and Bill contacted the Forestry Research Group to recommend a nitrogen fertilizer dosage which would speed the decomposition of the shavings into humus. A dosage was recommended and Bill gave directions to Ken to have that amount applied. Ken said that he did not agree, that it was too heavy a dosage and refused to apply the fertilizer. Bill took this as a direct assault to his authority and wanted to sack Ken immediately. There was a meeting held at the home of Joe Nolan with Bill and myself in attendance to discuss the issue. I recommended that the issue be brought up before the executive committee for discussion before a final decision was rendered; however, I was outvoted. It was rather a peculiar state of affairs as I had been identified to be a cohort of Bill and Joe, yet I needed to be accepted on an ongoing situation with the members of the other side of the issue. It was a little difficult at times to convince Jane [Rogers] and the others that I was a friend to both sides.

President Hatheway, feeling he could not serve as President under the Executive Committee's interpretation of his authority, resigned as President and as a member of the Executive Committee, effective January 16, 1980, whereupon Vice-president Jane S. Rogers became President. Fred Robbins also resigned as a member of the Executive Committee, thus leaving two vacancies on that body. Both Robbins and

Hatheway, however, retained their seats on the board of directors.

This controversy brought sharply into focus a potential problem that had existed for some time due to the Foundation's financial inability to employ an Executive Director. Historically, Presidents had pretty well taken charge of hiring, firing and general supervision of the entire operation, a great many functions that would normally have been assumed by an Executive Director, had there been one. But then no one had ever questioned the procedure before. Now it was in question.

Hatheway's position was that the Foundation should be operated much as a small non-profit business, or a university botanical garden or arboretum. The President should be the chief executive officer and should have general authority and control over Foundation affairs and over its agents and employees, subject to the board of directors. The board of directors should be responsible for the management of the business and affairs of the Foundation and the protection of its property. The principal surrogate for the board is the Executive Committee. Since neither the board nor the Executive Committee is capable of carrying out these responsibilities, they delegate these responsibilities to others who act as their agents. When broad powers are delegated to the President, he is in fact the chief executive officer of the Foundation, responsible for the day-to-day conduct of its business and has the authority to hire and fire agents and employees in order to achieve its goals. Powers not so delegated should be reserved to the Executive Committee and the board.

The position of the majority of the Executive Committee was that the President did not have such broad powers; that the agents and employees of the Foundation were responsible to them rather than to the President, and the President therefore had no right to hire and fire. They felt the Foundation should be operated on the model of certain museums, in which the Executive Committee takes a very important part in the ordinary management and operation of the business, including supervision of paid staff. Both sides agreed that many of the functions under dispute would ordinarily be handled by an Executive Director, if there had been one. But since he would also be paid staff, to whom would he report - the President or the Executive Committee? A question that needed to be addressed and resolved by the board of directors.

Not only the Executive Committee was concerned with the seeming lack of direction in the Foundation, as witness the following letter from one of the founding members:

Jan. 26, 1980

The Rhododendron Species Foundation
Executive Committee
Post Office Box 3798
Federal Way, WA 98003

Dear People:

Today I received a letter from Jane Rogers on behalf of the RSF executive committee. At last we are informed officially of some of the actions of the executive board.

I attended the painful board meeting last fall and learned, to my astonishment, that there were still no general plans for the garden, let alone detail plans. Up to that revelation everything was supposed to be going fine in spite of the barren landscape and evidence that there had been some shifting of what comparatively few plants had been planted.

After the board meeting I visited the foundation headquarters and talked to several people who wanted to volunteer to help in the garden but wondered when the board was ever going to give them directions. Unbelievable! I hope that not too many of these people have been discouraged.

I understand that there is great variation in the depth of sawdust applied to the planting area. With greater depth there is apt to be a smaller percentage of breakdown, available nitrogen being uniform, thus requiring a great variation in the amount in different areas. It would be impractical to find and analyze each variation in depth of sawdust. The amount of N to apply evenly over the whole area would have to be estimated. Perhaps one closely associated with the conditions might make a better guess as to the amount of N to apply than would the professors.

Later I began receiving reports of dissension within the executive committee and to my amazement the firing of Ken Gambrill who, as I see it, has done a phenomenal job of propagating. The distribution of fine species had been the chief object of the founders. The establishment of a showplace was secondary. I suggest that the promotion of tours be dampened down a bit until there is something more to show. A number of people have wondered what they came up there for.

There have been rumors of personality clashes with the personnel. I cannot imagine a curator being happy managing a garden that has not been provided with a plan by the people in charge at this late date.

I have had phone calls and letters from the East Coast as well as locally inquiring about the rumored deep trouble of the RSF. Until now I have not been able to confirm these rumors.

It seems to me from here that the executive committee could not have contrived a more ingenious method of disrupting the RSF if it had planned it that way!

I thought several years ago that there had been a compromise plan worked out showing the relations of the species to each other and showing the country of origin.

If the board is split down the middle in this wrangling I fervently hope that each side will not draw a new member and remain split. Has it occurred to you that, if you proceed at the planting speed that you have so far, Weyerhaeuser might boot us out?

Yours truly,

One of the six founders,
Cecil Smith

At a special meeting of the board of directors called by President Jane Rogers on February 23, 1980 Mrs. Rogers made her report to the board. It is well worth setting out here in its entirety, for its wisdom and clarity in stating the problems and the means of solution:

I became President on January 16 when Dr. Hatheway resigned. His resignation letter and that of Fred Robbins, as a member of the Executive Committee, are in the Secretary's hands if you wish to read them. The Executive Committee met on January 18 and because of the large number of letters from directors and members, all of which are here if you wish to read them, acted to reinstate Ken as Curator. Since that time there have been a number of things that have happened this past month, many of which had been pending or awaiting signature. The Garden Enterprise proposal was approved by the Executive Committee on December 6 and the agreement was signed January 18. You will hear more about this from Pat Gutter. The Weyerhaeuser transfer of assets has been completed. We continue to lease the land, however we have now been given the buildings and improvements inside and including the fence. The other side of this is, as the buildings and other assets are now the property of the Foundation, we are now responsible for the maintenance, repair and insurance, all of which was previously taken care of by Weyerhaeuser. The Trust Fund Agreement setting up the Endowment Funds with Pacific National Bank of Washington has been restated to comply with IRS. This agreement was also signed the end of January. As Ian Walker pointed out we are now at work on job descriptions, areas of responsibility, lines of authority, job performance evaluation. In a volunteer oriented organization it is difficult to have continuity in the management when the President and Executive Committee changes. We are now trying to establish descriptions and lines of authority to clarify the problem.

There has been a great deal of discussion about what the Rhododendron Species Foundation is and how it should be run. What it is not, it is not a profit making corporation. The original founding members felt they could handle and finance the organization with endowment funds only. This was not the case. Since 1976 we have had a membership organization. We now have about 500 members. We are a plant society, but in addition to being organized for the love of one type of plant we have a plant collection and a garden. To a degree we are like a museum, a living museum. We are not an arboretum or botanic garden dependent on state or city fathers and bureaucracy. Obviously, we have some elements of all of these. We are privately funded instead of going to the legislature for tax payer's money. We are heavily dependent on volunteers both for their money and, if you have been listening to all of the committees, for their time and effort. If we had to pay for all of this time our budget would be enormously more than it is.

The question on how to operate the Foundation and Garden has come up in some depth in recent months. And the Directors must decide how you want it operated. The real question is how much authority should be given to the President by you, the Directors, as opposed to how much is reserved by the Directors and by their representative group, the Executive Committee. The means of doing this will be by clarifying and revising the By-laws at the annual meeting of the Board of Directors in April. Dr. Hatheway's position as I understand it is that he feels the President should have broad powers and should be able to run the organization and the garden as the President sees fit. The majority of the Executive Committee in this question feels that major actions, significant expenditures should have the approval of the Committee before they happen. In the three years that I have been on the Executive Committee this has been the precedent. In the minutes of the prior Executive Committee meeting it states that any expenditure over $100, should have the Committee's approval. The way to solve this is to carefully look at the By-laws, consider how you would like to change them, or not change them. We will soon be sending to you a copy of the By-laws with a request that you return your input. The by-laws changes will then be presented to the Board at the April meeting. Any suggested changes will be sent out to you before the April meeting. There are a few changes in awkward wording and procedural changes, such as terms of committee chairmen.

As far as the Master Plan for the garden, again the Directors will need to make some key decisions before we get much further. The Directors will need to decide the priorities, the purposes, the goals of this garden. I expect to write to you asking for your input on these matters. This is your garden, how it should be done is up to you.

Warren Berg and Ian Walker were elected to fill the vacant positions on the Executive Committee.

As mentioned above, the Executive Committee had in January approved a proposal by the landscape architectural firm of Garden Enterprises, Inc., of Seattle, to develop a master Plan for the garden. The architects, John Ullman and Pat Gutter, had begun work on the project which was expected to take about 4 months. It was hoped the detailed plans would be ready in time for the fall 1980 planting season.

At the April board of directors meeting Jane Rogers was retained for a new term as President, with Renee Hill also remaining as Secretary, while Dr. David Goheen was elected Vice-president and Ian Walker, Treasurer. The new Executive Committee consisted of the elected officers, together with Esther Berry, Edward Dunn and Ernest Dzurick. As was promised and expected a revison of the by-laws was on the agenda and Dr. Hatheway's position and proposed form of revision was prepared by Joe Nolan and submitted for the board's consideration. It was no surprise that his proposal was rejected and the office of the Presidency was weakened rather than strengthened by the revision finally adopted. The complete set of by-laws, as thus amended, is set forth in **APPENDIX E** at page 293 of this book.

The reader is admonished that it is to be expected that additional revisions will take place over the years and the by-laws set forth in the appendix will not necessarily be those in effect at the time of reading the book. To relate the revision to the resolution of the controversy described in the foregoing pages, the new language added to paragraph VII.2 President is set forth in bold type.

Early in the Spring of 1980 a questionaire had been distributed to the members of the board of directors regarding their preferences in the way of garden design. The responses, when tabulated, indicated the directors preferred some arrangement other than by the geographic concept. The study garden was strongly approved in its then existing design and the use of hybrids in any capacity was overwhelmingly rejected. Indicated were the need to stress efficient management, cultural conditions, aesthetic appeal and ease of comparative study while minimizing educational features, conformance to botanical standards and accommodation of visitors. The garden should be designed to accommodate the scientist, the rhododendron expert and the fancier.

In June, 1980 the landscape firm of John Ullman and Associates presented the board with their Garden Master Plan, which had taken the above questionaires into consideration, along with many site considerations and considerable input from staff and individual board members. Their recommendation was that the garden be rearranged to botanically emphasize microclimate potentials; to provide a path through the collection with provision for points of emphasis and enrichment and to provide an improved area for plant sales and visitor seating inside the entry gate. Their recommendations were accepted by the board of directors on motion of Dr. Herbert Spady.

In the spring of 1980 Secretary Renee Hill wisely saw the need to collect and preserve the historical record of the Foundation, and with that in mind she dispatched inquiries to certain persons who had played key roles. The replies are pertinent and interesting, recalling in the very words of the parties concerned the early struggles and triumphs of the Foundation, each from his own personal perspective. Three of the respondants, Dr. Walker, Wales Wood and Jock Brydon, have since passed away.

Dear Renee: We were happy to hear from you. I only wish that I had saved notes on the activities of the beginning years of the Species Foundation. As is known, Milt Walker conceived the idea of the S.F. and rounded up several of us who had problems in getting good species. We called him "the needle", because he kept punching us until we agreed to help in forming some kind of organization. I hope that one of the others has saved Milt's long letters discussing the advantages of organizing.

The concept was:
    1. To acquire species which had the greatest horticultural value, as they are found in the wild.
    2. To propagate and distribute them.
    3. To acquire a site where they could be grown uncrowded, to show their natural growth habits.
    4. To preserve those plants for identification purposes.
This has been a dream through the years.

Within two or three years after the Walker property was acquired, both Dr. and Mrs. Walker, due to health problems, began spending their winters in a milder climate. Propagation came to a standstill. We were not getting anywhere. A number of crisis meetings were held, and the thought of folding up passed through our minds, but someone always brought up something new to try. The late Wales Wood was particularly adept at hanging tough.

The chance to move the plants to the Brydon garden saved the RSF from terminating its activities. It was a great day to help move some of the plants to their new home. Jock B. started to propagate rapidly, and gave the organization a life-saving boost. It was on its way at last. Jock was born and raised in Scotland, and attended the University of Edinburgh. Because of his connections, he was able to acquire cuttings from a great number of fine species. He opened the door to many more Scottish and British gardens.

At the time of the organization of the RSF, imported plants and cuttings were heavily fumigated, and the casualties were high. That is why arrangements were made with UBC to grow plants there. At that time there was no problem getting them into this country. The arrangement was not entirely satisfactory.

Wales Wood was the first president of the RSF [Editor's note: Actually Dr. Walker was the first President], and as a lawyer helped in legal matters.... The late Jim Blackford of Eugene made the RSF tax exempt. I heard him say that he had no idea when he started on the work involved in making contributions tax free.

I wish that I could give you some documented information, but this is the best I can do.

                        Sincerely,
                        Cecil C. Smith

St. Helens, Oregon
June 11, 1980

Dear Renee:

Thank you for noticing that I have not been able to make it to the meetings recently. I was on my way to the February meeting with Molly and Cecil Smith but we had a car accident in Longview and mangled their beautiful Mercedes. Only recently is it back in order. I do not drive in heavy traffic and that is most inconvenient.

There are stacks of RSF material, mostly copies of minutes, here in this house. One of the first things I found was an article in Wales' handwriting that reports on the early days of the RSF. I am enclosing a copy. It is possible that this has been published some place but, if so, I do not know where. [The article referred to follows immediately after this letter. - Editor].

In the early days there were not all that many really good species to be seen so we were eager to meet in the homes of places that were near the gardens. This was especially true when the garden was at Walkers and at Brydons. After while, so that it would not be too much of a problem for Edith Brydon she had a caterer come in. During inclement weather meetings were sometimes held at part way points to equalize driving time and distance.

Meetings were always very informal - sort of a family affair. In most instances both husband and wife were so active that no one paid any attention to which one was listed as director. You could discuss RSF business with Helen or Milton, Molly or Cecil, Fred or Dorothy, Jock or Edith. I believe you could still do this with the Pierces, the Averys, the Wagners (Sr.) or the Pendleton Millers. Several years ago one wife used to try to get some other wives to eat with her away from the mob so that she would not have to listen to rhododendron talk all the time. She had trouble finding cohorts.

For a while at the beginning the Clarence Chases, the orchid people, were active but apparently the orchids won out. Grace and Jim Blackford of Eugene both contributed a lot of hard work in the early days and we must continue to be thankful for the Ed Siegmunds, Curt Huey and Dr. Carl Phetteplace.

I have many years of happy memories and it is astounding how large a proportion is in some way connected with rhododendron.

Sincerely,
Ruth M. Wood [Mrs. Wales Wood]

Wales Wood's handwritten notes:
During the spring of 1960, Mrs. Wood and I had the opportunity of spending considerable time in the rhododendron gardens of Scotland and England and with the great people associated with these gardens. We were impressed with the quality of the rhododendron species in these gardens and we thought it was so unfortunate that so many rather ordinary hybrids had been imported into the USA and so few of the fine species. It was on this same visit to England in the garden at Towercourt and in our presence that Mrs. Stevenson made the comment about growing species from seed to Dr. Carl Phetteplace which observation Dr. Milton Walker gives credit for the formation of the Rhododendron Species Foundation. Really, I have always felt that the purchase of a very

inferior plant of R. *strigillosum* at a rather large price had as much to do with the formation of the Foundation. The plant was a very bad form both in foliage and color of bloom, bereft of bristles and a dirty pink in color of bloom. Dr. Walker is a person who likes to get value received for his money.

1961 was the year of the International Rhododendron Conference in Portland and again we were made aware of the great species in Scotland and England as projected on the program, particularly the part given by Dr. Fletcher. It was during this time that we had the opportunity to get acquainted with Dr. Walker and his wife, Helen. During 1962 and 1963 we had various visits to the Walkers' garden and they to our garden. There was much discussion on species. The American Rhododendron Society's Species Project never 'took off' as hoped. I guess there were not enough true purists as we have been called. As species enthusiasts, we could see no other way to go. Compromise was impossible.

Rudolph Henny's death in June 1963 was another factor in moving the species project out of the ARS. Rudolph was the balance wheel for the ARS and without his guidance there was much dissention among various groups and members across the United States. Also, the ARS took action to support a seed exchange program* which was in the exactly opposite direction to the purpose of the Species Project.

During February, 1964, while I was recuperating from surgery, Mrs. Wood and I were often with Dr. and Mrs. Walker in their home in Palm Springs. Much more discussion on rhododendron species took place. We had an opportunity to see how thoroughly Dr. Walker did his homework in preparation for a trip to the British Isles to secure scions of outstanding plants. In early March, 1964, Dr. and Mrs. Walker and Dr. J. Harold Clarke visited our home and garden. The Walkers were soon leaving for London and the gardens in the Brisish Isles to secure the cuttings as indexed in the records compiled by Dr. Walker.

It was Dr. Walker's desire that I prepare the articles of incorporation and by-laws for the Rhododendron Species Foundation, the same to be presented at an organization meeting to be held after they returned from London. During the Walkers' absence we had the priviledge of meeting Fred and Dorothy Robbins and Warren and Pat Berg.

The first meeting of the Rhododendron Species Foundation was held July 12, 1964 at the Multnomah Hotel in Portland. At this time, officers were elected and the articles of incorporation and by-laws were adopted. Dr. Walker had made arrangements with the people associated with and in charge of the University of British Columbia Botanical Gardens for the propagation of the scions from Great Britian. This arrangement was to cover selections made in the spring of 1964 and on subsequent trips to the British Isles.

The following years, 1965 through 1967, were busy years securing scions from selected plants in the British Isles and from gardens of the United States. The time was also filled with developing the mechanics of the Foundation such as choosing new directors, making business contacts that would possibly lead to financial security for the organization. I remember a trip that the directors made to Bainbridge Island, Washington, to view a beautiful parcel of land generously offered to the Foundation for a garden by Mr. and Mrs. Prentice

Bloedel. We had to refuse the offer because we did not have the finances to develop the land into a garden and to purchase the equipment and buildings to make it operational. Lack of finances was a continuous problem and the project's appeal was limited to a very small group of far-sighted men and women. David G. Leach, author of *Rhododendrons of the World* and a director of the Foundation, in his New York Times article on the Foundation's garden put it very well when he wrote, "It was a novel farsighted effort which few thought could succeed."

Now that the Foundation's future and its garden seem assured, we hear comments from the former doubters saying, "At last the Foundation is making progress." They cannot seem to realize that it took ten years of work and financial sacrifice by the directors and a very few loyal friends to build up the collection to put into the Weyerhaeuser Garden. Without the collection there would have been nothing to offer the Weyerhaeuser Company.

The move of the collection from the University of British Columbia Botanical Gardens to Dr. and Mrs. Walker's garden near Eugene was begun in 1968 and later moved to the garden of Mr. and Mrs. P. H. Brydon near Salem. These moves and the later move to the Weyerhaeuser Garden near Tacoma have been well covered in various articles about the Foundation.

It was a great privilege for me to work with the other Foundation directors during the organization's formative years. All made their contributions in money and time without any thought of personal return other than the establishement of a collection of superior species in a garden in the United States. And here I want to give special credit to three men in particular for the success of the project: Dr. Milton Walker for his vision, his initiative and hard work in starting the organization and securing the plant material; Fred Robbins for his excellent business judgment, his organizational ability and his hard work and management in establishing the Weyerhaeuser Garden; Mr. Corydon Wagner for his financial advice and assistance. These same three men have made large financial contributions over the years.

Wales Wood

* [Editor's note: The author, on his only meeting with Mr. Wood, naively commended the ARS for its foresight and good judgment in finally adopting a seed exchange program, whereupon Mr. Wood, with scorching disdain, informed the author that such a remark was totally out of place in his presence.]

From Dr. Milton V. Walker: June 30, 1980

I'm glad to help in your history project of the RSF and will send (sometime) my files of the early years which are voluminous!* If you really need them soon, I might be able to get them off on one of my infrequent trips to Palm Springs but I don't loiter with temperatures 110 to 120 degrees. Let me know.

Factual history is usually dull reading and I would suggest a few human interest items like the luncheon meeting at a private club in Seattle to which a few prominent men were invited. As President I started to speak of the need for an endowment fund - when a chair scraped back and a visitor got up and left saying in a voice loud enough for all to hear, something like, "Might have known there was a catch in a free lunch invitation." Such experiences in my opinion paint a true and interesting history.

Let me hear from you.

> Cordially yours,
> Milton V. Walker, M.D.

*[Editors Note: Dr. Walker's files for some reason never reached Renee Hill, but they were indeed voluminous and in fact formed the basis for a great part of this history. The author is indebted to Dr. Walker's son, Ian Walker, for the loan of these invaluable records.]

Letter to President Jane Rogers from Jock Brydon: September 11, 1980

When I retired from the Strybing Arboretum, nothing was further from my mind than to become re-involved with ornamental horticulture. But, somehow, a curious set of circumstances came together in the spring of 1969 when I joined the Rhododendron Species Foundation as a director. Shortly thereafter, Dr. Walker was unable to continue his stewardship of the collection and, since I had extra garden room in the cherry orchard, Fred Robbins and Cordy Wagner prevailed upon me to assume the responsibility for the species collection and presto, I was back into rhododendrons once again!!

In retrospect, I break out in a cold sweat thinking of the problems that had to be overcome. Of primary importance was an adequate supply of water since the fifty foot well with four inch casing was only enough for the house and garden. Fortunately, we had a year around creek on the place which, when dammed, provided an acre pond and enough volume for the incipient collection of Rhododendron species. Booster pumps were installed to lift the water some 50 ft. in elevation and 500 ft. in distance to the proposed nursery area. A larger transformer had to be installed by the P. G. & E. and the power lines moved underground.

The collection at this time was mostly in the 9 to 12 inch grades with a few plants in the larger sizes. Therefore, after establishing an adequate supply of water, the next consideration was to construct a lath house, glasshouse, and a nursery area. At this point, we were fortunate to obtain the services of Andy Evans, a retired farmer, who appeared faithfully each Monday, Wednesday and Friday mornings from 8 A.M. until noon. Andy, Edith and I constituted the entire staff and turned our hands to any task, electrical, agricultural, and structural with Edith pinch-hitting in the secretarial department!!!

We built a 60 ft. by 60 ft. lath house and a 30 ft. by 17 ft. glasshouse, each equipped with the necessary power and water systems. We felled large oaks and fir trees to provide more light for the young plants. Soil amendments such as peat moss, leaf mold, and sawdust were hauled in to provide a more friable medium for the small plants. Secondary pipe lines were installed so that all plants could be reached by sprinklers.

When the collection was moved from Dr. Walker's place at Pleasant Hill to my home in Salem, members of the Eugene Chapter were most helpful, particularly Curt Huey, Ed Siegmund and Winston Hanke. Until 1975, when the plants were transferred to Tacoma, we had the plants all to ourselves. This was a blessing in a way since it allowed us to "gang oor ain gait" as my grandmother used to say, and we were far enough from the beaten track so that visitors were a rarity, although I could always provide shovels, axes, etc., in the event that a volunteer was so inclined!!

Few members of the RSF realized that I owned and operated a 35 acre cherry orchard in conjunction with my home and garden. When I agreed to assume responsibility for the Rhododendron collection, it was necessary for me to hire the work that I had been doing in the orchard so that I could assume this new responsibility. Fortunately, the RSF, chiefly through the efforts of Fred Robbins and Cordy Wagner, was able to provide me with a monthly check for $600.00 to help pay for the expense of utilities, Andy's salary, repair and use of equipment, additional tools, and a portion of the orchard upkeep so that Edith and I could devote our time to the collection.

Funds were scarce, but necessity was the mother of invention and I recalled that the Saratoga Horticultural Foundation partly solved their financial problems by selling propagations of clonal selections to interested nurserymen. With some modification, we finally evolved the scheme of distribution for our surplus propagations to interested species buffs and the resulting revenue was certainly welcome.

In April and May of 1971, approximately 1000 plants were transplanted to my place from Pleasant Hill. 200 of these were subsequently returned to Dr. Walker's garden since they were dug by mistake in his absence. In addition, 106 plants were hauled from the University of British Columbia Botanical Garden, courtesy of Jim Gossler. Unfortunately, many of these were found to be infested with root rot when inspected by Oregon State plant pathologists and subsequently destroyed. Fortunately, the plants had been temporarily heeled in and after their removal, the soil was fumigated with Methyl Bromide to prevent further infection. I do not have an accurate record of the surplus small plants which Dr. Walker gave to Harold Greer prior to 1971. These were mostly rooted cuttings which I moved to my place from Greer's Nursery in Eugene and included with the surplus propagations which were subsequently distributed to donors. Incidentally, duplicate copies of the plants shipped to donors were sent to Tacoma shortly after the collection was moved from Salem. By summer of 1975, the entire collection had been moved to its present location. In this connection, I note that included in my records is a list of Rhododendron species, Japanese Maples, and miscellaneous trees and shrubs. These I donated to the garden and were acknowledged by Fred Robbins but have not been recorded. They were grown from cuttings and scions which I received from friends prior to becoming involved with the RSF and, when we decided to sell our orchard, I had no further use for them.

I cannot speak too stongly of the tremendous contribution which British gardeners have made to the RSF. Totally unselfish, they sent in scions year after year, particularly when the material went astray in the mails or was needlessly delayed by the U.S.D.A. and arrived dead. Members of the Eugene Chapter were especially appreciated, particularly during the interim period when the transition from Salem to Tacoma was in progress.

When it became apparent that the collection had outgrown our limited facilities in Salem and the future of the RSF was in doubt, we were indeed fortunate to have Fred Robbins and Cordy Wagner to provide a solution and arrange for a permanent home for the collection. All of us owe a great debt to Fred for his efforts and dedication to the preservation of the RSF for without his determination we would not be where we are today.

Finally, I must say that it was indeed a great privilege for Edith and me to have the plants in our garden during those early years. Few gardeners have the opportunity to enjoy a collection of this magnitude in its formative years and we do want to express our appreciation for this experience. We received about 800 plants from Dr. Walker and, during our stewardship we managed to increase the collection to about 4000 plants plus whatever plants were distributed to donors as surplus. It is with regret that we cannot be more active in the affairs of the Foundation but the distance between Salem and Tacoma seems to grow greater each year!

P. H. ("Jock") Brydon

In April 1981 it was announced that the Foundation sponsored publication *Rhododendrons of China* had been completed and that of the 2,000 copies printed over 1,300 had already been sold, for an income of $15,600. A new RSViP program for volunteers was instituted and the first orientation meeting was attended by over 40 volunteers. Office space was running short and it was hoped that space theretofore occupied by Weyerhaeuser could be vacated and remodelled to fill this need.

The education program had now been expanded to provide some correspondence courses as well as the usual personal attendance courses taught at the Foundation gardens. For a number of years the personal attendance classes were well attended but eventually the local market became saturated and the Education Committee, under the chairmanship of Dr. Spady and with the support of his able wife, Betty, and other committee members, put together a course specifically designed for those persons outside commuting distance or for various reasons unable to attend classes at the Foundation. The course included printed materials prepared by committee members, slide presentations also prepared by committee members, and references to standard works on rhododendron nomenclature, taxonomy, history and culture. The course was designed to be the equivalent of a three hour college level course, although participants could study at their leisure. Over the years it is estimated that over 200 persons completed this course, many individually but some in groups.

Most of the plants had been moved out of the meadow area in preparation for the removal of trees, existing service roads and the existing irrigation system, all to accommodate the new garden plan. It was hoped replanting could be done in the fall. The Garden Planning Committee consisted of Esther Berry, David Goheen, Ken Gambrill, Betty Miller and Dan Morris. At the annual election the existing slate of officers and Executive Committee members were retained for another year. Trust funds had now accumulated in the total sum of over $122,000 and the Foundation now had a net worth of over $553,000.

Garden tours hosted by the Foundation attracted over 6,000 visitors that spring and summer, with 85 volunteers assisting the staff in this regard. Surplus plants were sold to visitors with $11,900 being realized. Plant distribution sales brought in just under $30,000.

Two new proposals were submitted to the board at the October meeting, one to authorize the collection of pollen from verified species plants in the collection, for sale to members for a price in excess of the cost of collecting and processing same. This proposal was easily adopted by the board. The other proposal, however, was for the self pollenization of selected, verified species plants and the collection and the sale of the seed. This proposal had received some advance support in the form of a letter from Ken Gambrill to the board in which he advocated acceptance of the proposal and argued its merits. This was not acceptable to many of the older members who remembered the results of the seed program once offered by the Royal Horticultural Society in England, with countless hybrids being grown by unsuspecting recipients over the years. Dr.Walker expressed his objection to the President,

> This [Royal Horticultural Society] has been and still is one of the most honorable and highly respected Horticultural Societies. Probably the seed distribution started out with hand pollination under just as strict controls as Ken Gambrill has in mind, but this is an example of what CAN happen over the years. Some of us that raised R.H.S. plants for 25 years and then found that we had been caring for just another hybrid, will never forget this lesson.

> … Incidentally I think it was very poor judgment on Ken Gambrill's part to send out a propaganda letter pertaining to a project that would enlarge his responsibilities. He is an employee of the Foundation and the officers and directors are responsible for decisions in regard to Foundation policies and projects.

Ruth (Mrs. Wales) Wood complained,

> The seed distribution project makes me almost ill but there seems to be little I can do about it. With open membership and even many of the older supposedly loyal members eagerly supplying pollen and seed to the ARS promotions the outlook seems hopeless. I dare not mention the topic to Cecil [Smith]; I have not seen Carl or the Siegmunds for a long time. Have you heard anything from Fred [Robbins] regarding the matter? There has been tension between Fred and Ken [Gambrill] for some time. I am afraid that Fred may feel almost as helpless as I do and he is right there in constant contact.

> We did the best we could for the good of the order and we were paid in precious friendships and memories. We do not agree with the way things are being run now but we are being forced to give priority to other matters - especially health.

The seed program was rejected by the board, and Ed Dunn wrote, "As you undoubtedly know, the proposal for a seed distribution program was soundly killed. Only a few members besides Marshall Majors and Esther Berry seemed disappointed at the outcome."

Fred Robbins's attitude is stated in a letter to Milton Walker,

> I have given up on the Foundation. It has been taken over by what I call the professional garden clubbers. I do not feel that there is adequate management for any large sum of money, so I have advised against putting money into any trust fund. The board is now composed of American Rhodo Society people and it is just a question of a short time when there will be talk of merging. The A.R.S. has little going for it.

In the spring of 1982 Weyerhaeuser finally vacated the north portion of the office building, thus releasing it for use by the Foundation. It offered a 24' x 24' area that was soon remodelled into a multipurpose room, storage and additional office space, mostly utilizing volunteer labor, thus enabling the construction to be done for less than one-third the contractor's estimated cost. Garden development was on schedule with the meadow area planted and only signs and benches to be added. Drawings for a new entrance building had been completed and were awaiting only the approval of the county building department before construction could commence. Cost was estimated at $120,000 and a fund raising effort was under way to provide financing for the building. The pond area was designed with the help of a $2,000 grant from the Tacoma Garden Club and the Wagner family had signified their desire to fund the pond area in the sum of $32,000 as a memorial to G. Corydon Wagner, who had recently passed away. Construction was planned to begin immediately and be completed before fall.

Over 100 new members had enrolled since the first of the year and it was decided to computerize membership records to facilitate paperwork. Mrs. Gunderson was given the task of sifting through all the old Foundation records and coming up with a Policy Manual as a result of the Hatheway - Gambrill flap. The task proved unworkable manually, so the computer was again brought into play and was used to sort information and provide summaries to facilitate the job. But there were found to be gaps, inaccuracies and outdated policies and it was necessary to refer the matter to the Executive Committee for revision and clarification.

The pollen program had been used on a very limited basis - only seven requests had been received, for a total of 45 items, of which about 30 were fulfilled. The profit was only $300.00 but many good reports were received from members, welcoming this program as a boon to hybridization, particularly in the Northeastern states where hardiness was crucial.

A great deal of seed was received from the Sino-British plant expedition to China and for the first time the Foundation was engaged in raising seedlings on a large scale, from 50 packets of seed representing 26 different species.

In April 1982 a new slate of officers was elected, namely Dr. David Goheen, President; Esther Berry, Vice President; Britt M. Smith, Secretary; and Ian Walker, Treasurer. John Eichelser, Herbert Spady, M. D., and Jane Rogers were elected to the Executive Committee and Dr. J. Harold Clarke, P. H. Brydon and James Caperci were elected as honorary directors. Unfortunately the press of personal business soon required Ian Walker to resign as Treasurer.

A Foundation sponsored tour of British gardens was so enjoyed by 24 members that an additional tour, this time to Japan, was planned for the Spring of 1984. The Photography Committee, under the chairmanship of Art Dome had been producing color slides to document the unique features of the plant collection. Over 100 species was photographed and the slides catalogued. The committee was working on slides needed by the Education Committee. Over ten members were participating in the Photography Committee. The Library Committee reported that a total of 745 books had now been received and processed. The books were appraised at $10,756.61, periodicals at $6,148.75 and equipment at $5,689.62, for a total value of $22,594.98.

A proposal was made that the board consider establishing a group within the Foundation to be known as Educational Fellows of the Rhododendron Species Foundation and that an original group of about twenty individuals be picked on the basis of:

     a. An intense interest in the study of species rhododendrons,

     b. A significant period of study of species rhododendrons shared with others as demonstrated by:

1. Published articles in papers
2. Lectures and slide shows
3. Direct personal discussion with others
4. Other appropriate means.

It was suggested that the group be self-perpetuating, that it elect members on the basis of qualifications and procedures to be adopted with the approval of the board, and that new memberships be referred to and approved by the board. It was also suggested that the chairperson of the Education Committee be a member as a matter of policy and that the chairperson might appoint committee members of his choice from the membership of the Foundation. This was not a new concept. It had been mentioned in correspondence between Esther Avery and Dr. Walker in February, 1978, although no details of the idea were expressed at that time. The proposal was tabled for further consideration but due to a lack of support within the Executive Committee it was never implemented. It was the feeling of the majority of the committee members that such a group would tend to be elitist and therefore in conflict with the general membership concept prevailing in the Foundation.

The January, 1983 issue of the RSF Newsletter announced the death of long time member Dr. Carl Phetteplace of Leaburg, Oregon. Dr. Phetteplace had donated many fine old specimen species plants to the Foundation garden and had served for many years on the board of directors. Dr. Carl Heller's death was announced in the same issue. Sadly, news also arrived of the death at age 95 of Dr. John Wister of Swarthmore, Pa., an honorary director of the Foundation for many years and considered by many to be the 'dean of American horticulture'.

The Foundation acquired its own computer, an Apple III Professional compatible with the programming already completed by the Foundation, dealing with the plant collection inventory, plant distribution lists and membership records. The purchase was made possible by a grant from Mr. Albert Nerken and the Nerken Foundation of New York in the sum of $12,585, together with a 'seed' grant from Warren Berg. The Nerken Foundation and Albert Nerken were the same benefactors who had so generously funded a large part of the cost of the cool house, some years earlier.

A decision was made to begin charging visitors an admission fee in order to help offset the additional cost of staff to supervise visitation. During that first spring there were 2,882 paid visitors, generating $4,360 in addition to plants and publications sold. And to reopen a previously rejected concept, E. White Smith, chairman of the Collected in the Wild Committee, submitted to the board a proposal for the distribution of rhododendron seed collected in the wild. Bill Tietjen, chairman of the ARS Seed Distribution Committee suggested a joint ARS - RSF seed distribution program. Both were tabled for further study by President Goheen due to the board's decision in April, 1982 not to participate in a seed program.

At the April, 1983 meeting Dr. Goheen was retained as President for another year; Britt Smith was elected Vice President, Marshall D. Majors, Secretary and Ralph H. Shumm, Treasurer. Administrative staff now consisted of Karen S. Gunderson, Administrator; Carrie M. Wolfe, Secretary, Margaret Johnson, visitor and volunteer coordinator; and Honore' Hacanson, bookkeeper. Garden staff now consisted of Ken Gambrill, curator; Kelly Dodson, horticulturist; and Tim Dunford, groundskeeper, replacing Steve Whitcher who had left for other employment.

The board also adopted a Development Plan for the Foundation. After reviewing at some length the history of the organization and its accomplishments to date the plan summarizes the present status of the plant collection as, "... the most comprehensive and diverse in North America and compares with the best in Britain. The more than 25,000 plants represent 600 species including nearly all in cultivation which can be grown out of doors in the Pacific Northwest..." The Foundation held associate memberships in the following organizations with whom it exchanged information on a regular basis:

> Alpine Garden Club of Vancouver, B.C.
> American Horticultural Society
> American Iris Society
> American Primrose Society
> American Rock Garden Society
> Australian Rhododendron Society
> Denver Botanic Garden
> New Zealand Rhododendron Society
> Northwest Ornamental Horticultural Society
> Pacific Horticulture Foundation
> Pacific Rhododendron Society
> Rhododendron Society of Canada
> Royal Horticultural Society
> University of Washington Arboretum Foundation

Membership now totalled over 600 internationally, with members in fourteen foreign countries. The reference library contained over 900 hard bound volumes, as well as periodicals, all professionally arranged and catalogued. The Foundation had sponsored the publication of two major books, *Rhododendrons of China*, translated from Chinese by Judy Young and Chong, and *The Rhododendron Species, Volume Il, Lepidotes*, by H. H. Davidian. Plant materials for research purposes were regularly furnished to, among others, Western Washington Research & Extension Center, for root weevil research; University of Minnesota, for cold hardiness studies; University of Washington, for cold hardiness studies; U. S. National Arboretum; North Carolina State University; Boskoop; Goteborg Botanic Garden; Moscow Botanic Garden and Las Cruces Tropical Botanic Garden. While the usual goals of financial sufficiency, continued acquisition of desirable species and expanded membership and facilities were announced, the primary goal was the hiring of an Executive Director as the Chief Operating Officer of the Foundation.

Pond area
gazebo in distance

The Pond area was completed in time for the April meeting and President Goheen dedicated it to the memory of G. Corydon Wagner as planned. Planting was completed on the Hillslope area, while in the Forest Glen Area oaks were planted and the area was ready for rhododendrons. A plan for the Alpine Area had been developed and accepted and rock work was planned for the summer, with planting to take place in the fall. It was hoped that all re-working of the garden would be completed by the following spring. But funding for the proposed new entry building had still not been arranged. Two major grant proposals had been submitted with great hope, but both resulted in disappointment.

As the garden developed and grew and the number of visitors received and services offered continued to grow, the role of volunteers became more apparent. Administrator Karen Gunderson, in July of 1983 acknowledged that so far that year over 100 volunteers had contributed their time and effort to committee work, activities in the garden, office, library and a number of special projects. The volunteer organization 'RSViP' inaugurated its own monthly NEWS NOTES as a means of keeping volunteers informed of jobs in progress, expected or planned.

In October the question of distributing rhododendron seed again arose, along with the possibility of distributing plants raised from seed collected in the wild and germinated at the Foundation facilities. It was decided that seed would not be distributed to individuals and that the Foundation would grow on as much seed as it could accommodate, disbursing the seedlings and any surplus seed to botanical gardens.

Mr. and Mrs. Thomas Atchison offered a $50,000 endowment for the Foundation's library. It was requested that the library be named in honor of Mrs. Atchison's father, Lawrence Pierce, past president of the Foundation. As a result President Goheen requested the Library Committee to prepare short and long term development plans for the library. They complied and the board accepted the proposals and also accepted the endowment offer made by the Atchisons. The library would henceforth be known as the Lawrence J. Pierce Rhododendron Library.

A new publication that had long been in the planning and preparation stage under the editorship of Judy Young, finally became available to members in January of 1984. *RHODODENDRON NOTES & RECORDS: Journal of the Rhododendron Species Foundation*, Volume I, 1984 was published as a technical botanical offering with an impressive array of advisors, such as David F. Chamberlain, Royal Botanic Garden, Edinburgh; Peter A. Cox, Glendoick, Scotland; August E. Kehr, North Carolina; Peter F. Stevens, Arnold Arboretum, Zhang Aolou, Kinming Institute of Botany, Academia Sinica, and RSF's own Kendall W. Gambrill. While this book was well organized and presented, it, along with the two previous publications sponsored by the Foundation, was never to prove successful from a financial standpoint.

Speaking of Ken Gambrill, perhaps not many of us think like a curator, as will be made apparent by a reading of his report to the membership in the April, 1984 issue of the RSF Newsletter. The reader may wish for orientation purposes to consult the Garden Master Plan in **APPENDIX F** at page 307 of this book.

GARDEN REDEVELOPMENT
12 MONTHS AND COUNTING

This spring the Alpine Area, centerpiece of the Garden, is the focal point of planting. The relocation of the mostly dwarf and mostly high-altitude rhododendrons to this area and the hoped-for completion of the Forest Area by late April will accomplish the major aspects of the organization and display of the collection according to the 1980 Garden Master Plan. The big job remaining to be done before the April 27, 1985 Garden Dedication will be the construction of the Visitors Center in the Entry Area.

Alpine Area work commenced last summer with site clearing, including tree removal, in July and August. Prentice Landscape constructed the rock outcrops and recontoured the area to create a setting of high mountain character. At the time of last October's Fall Foliage Festival, visitors viewed the unadorned rocky skeleton, a landscape of boulders up to five feet tall, rubble stairways of stepping-stone sized pieces, and dry water courses of gravel. A few weeks later came the good news from the Stanley Smith Horticultural Trust of a $10,000 grant for work in the Alpine Area. Thanks to the strong support of Betty Miller and the diligent participation of members of the Garden Planning Committee, we started the new year with the required funding and plans.

We began planting at the top of the site near the Gazebo with the several specimens of Mugho pine, originally placed in the 'Europe' part of the garden, and R. *cuneatum*, the atypical tall member of the Lapponicums, to form a buffer between the rocks and the wooden structure. In early February the plants of the Saluenense group were brought from the nursery and holding areas. Most of these species are represented by numerous individuals of several clones, especially R. *calostrotum*, *keleticum* and *radicans*. They form low mounding masses among the larger boulders at the top of the rock work. The Anthopogons occupy the adjacent lower 'cliffs', with R. *anthopogon* and *trichostomum* at the upper levels and R. *sargentianum*, *cephalanthum* and *kongboense* in rocky terraces. The next group to complete the west side of the 'valley' is Ferrugineum, in a location with the character of less rock and lower elevation in the area where most visitors will enter Alpine Section. The largest and most difficult to place group is the Lapponicum series, which will cover much of the east side of the area and extend along the lower border also. The large group of R. *russatum* and *scintillans* serve as the upper and lower anchors respectively. Planting the remainder of the Lapponicums, plus the Uniflorum, Lepidotum, Camtschaticum, and Campylogynum series, is the task for the remainder of March. Locating and adding companion trees must be done at the same time, in order to achieve a preliminary stage of completion by mid-April. The selection of smaller companion plants will be postponed until summer, when the needs of the rhododendrons and the plantings can be assessed better.

The other area of extensive planting is the Forest. We resumed the Thomsoniis in January, moving in R. *williamsianum*, *souliei*, *puralbum*, *campylocarpum*, *caloxanthum* and *callimorphum*. As soon as the burn pile does actually burn, we will finish with the Selense group species. That will leave the large blank space between the Irroratums and the Hillslope Area for the frantic mid-April planting of the Neriiflorums, so that the rhododendrons will be in place in time for this year's Annual Meeting on the 21st.

In sharp contrast with this apparently optimistic outlook was the written curator's report submitted by Gambrill at the April 21, 1984 board meeting:

I can not say that this has been a satisfying year. In the nursery operation we continue to succeed in establishing new acquisitions and thus expand the collection. But we are increasingly plagued by greenhouse equipment failure and the field is still over-crowded. In the garden there is the skill and desire to maintain high standards, but the manpower is lacking.

Garden development has been frustrated by lack of funds to proceed with

Preliminary work in the alpine garden, and . . .

. . .the result.

plantings according to schedule. All work was stopped in May, 1983. There was limited resumption in June to prepare for the Alpine Area, but Alpine rock construction was postponed from July to September. Forest Area planting has lagged, with partial planting of the Irroratums and Thomsoniis in early summer. There have been no funds for pathway gravel, or bark, or soil to complete the Thomsoniis and Neriiflorums, and none for additional companion plants. There are no funds for labor - either extra springtime help or to fund the third quarter of the permanent horticultural assistant planned for this year - to carry out capital projects.

There is an increasing emphasis on administrative and organizational activities rather than the horticultural side of the Foundation - in staff and budget. The staff reorganization adopted last November is intolerable. There is still a failure to support and give credit to the horticultural operation, and disruptions and irritating meddling have increased.

I was struck by the closing words of a letter which I recently received from the Curator of a major botanical garden in Europe. "My confidence is completely drained - and by comparison with ... knowledgeable, capable, and active people who are encouraged to get on with the profession they were trained for... I feel like a shrivelled cabbage. I find myself these days speaking and thinking with all the bitterness of such a vegetable...."

I fear that under the present staff organization of the RSF, I would find myself expressing similar sentiments before very long. Therefore, I have decided to resign from my position effective at the end of June.

It must be noted that for a considerable period of time a controversy had existed between Gambrill and Executive Manager Karen Gunderson that had been destructive of staff morale and burdensome to President Goheen, who as a result found it necessary to make almost weekly trips from his home in Camas, Washington to the Foundation to arbitrate disputes between the two parties and keep the operation functional. In effect there had been two bosses, an administrative supervisor and a garden supervisor, with equal power, conflicting interests and a failure to communicate. The board could not elevate one above the other for fear the other would quit. So the result of Gambrill's resignation, regrettable as was the loss of his admitted expertise, was to release funds and give the board the opportunity to employ an executive director - a single boss.

At the same board meeting President Goheen announced that the Executive Committee had approved the holding of an International Rhododendron Conference (International Rhododendron Species Symposium) to be held the following April and May in association with the American Rhododendron Society's meeting. Membership in the Foundation had now reached 750. Funding had still not been arranged for construction of the new entry building.

Esther Berry was elected President for the ensuing year, with Britt Smith remaining as Vice President, June Sinclair elected as Secretary and Ralph Shumm returning as Treasurer. Reacting to Gambrill's announcement of his resignation, President Berry commented, "As your new President I come into office at a time of some travail. No doubt you have heard that Ken Gambrill has tendered his resignation and will be leaving us at the end of June. Due to some apparently unresolvable differences, he feels unable to continue. We, at the Foundation, are sorry to lose him. During the past ten years, he has become a valuable staff member and we say goodby with regret."

Kelly Dodson, Tim Dunford and David Gwinner issued the following statement:

> In view of Ken Gambrill's recent resignation, the horticultural staff would like to express our appreciation for all he has done. The opportunity to be closely associated with an individual with Ken's unique talents and clear perceptions has enriched us all. His wonderful understanding of plants and planting relationships, his unpretentious supervision, and, certainly, his lofty ideals for the garden will be his legacy and our inspiration.

All three employees soon left their positions with the Foundation.

Ken Gambrill among the R. catawbiense
at Mt. Mitchell, above and left

Tim Dunford

CHAPTER XI

GROWTH

In the fall of 1984 Richard V. Piacentini was employed as the long awaited Executive Director of the Foundation. Richard was well qualified for the position, having earned a Bachelor of Science in pharmacy and Master of Business Administration from the University of Rhode Island and a Master of Science degree in botany from the University of Connecticut.

Richard Piacentini

Douglas Burdick, with a degree in horticulture from Oregon State University, was hired as horticulturist while Brian M. Hansen, who had previously worked at the Rare Plant Nursery in Chehalis was a new gardener now working with Steve Whitcher, garden keeper. The administrative staff consisted of Karen Gunderson, Executive Manager; Pamela A. Hanson, Administrative Secretary; Barbara Mate, Volunteer Coordinator; and Honore' Hacanson, Bookkeeper.

The new director found as his most urgent projects the completion of the Garden Master Plan, grooming of the garden in preparation for the forthcoming spring season and most important, planning for the International Rhododendron Species Symposium being sponsored by the Foundation at nearby Tacoma, Washington April 29 and 30, 1985. And prior to the symposium, on April 27 the newly arranged garden was to be dedicated in connection with the annual meeting, featuring Keshab Pradhan from Sikkim as the honored guest speaker. The following day, April 28, would celebrate the official public opening of the redesigned and rebuilt garden, to which the public and all garden groups were invited, including the entire American Rhododendron Society which was holding its annual meeting immediately following the symposium.

By the time of the spring meeting the garden was again in fine condition to receive its many expected visitors. Piacentini had been busy throughout the winter learning the intricacies of the Foundation and getting acquainted with staff, directors and procedures. The Foundation was twenty one years of age and had been at its present location for eleven years, an appropriate occasion for celebration. A number of notable developments had appeared: The Vireya Vine was being published on a regular basis and a mini study course was being offered on Vireyas, consisting of slides and reference materials. The Photography Committee under Barbara Mate's guidance had now catalogued and filed all the 35 mm. slides and stored them in easily accessible storage cabinets where they would be kept locked to prevent loss. An independent study course was being offered by the Education Committee, under Betty Spady's direction, offering fourteen units of study for those living outside the Foundation's commuting area or unable to attend regular classes.

For the 1985-86 term Esther Berry was again elected President, Dr. Herbert Spady, Vice President; Gwenn Bell, Secretary and Ralph Shumm was retained for another term as Treasurer. In addition to these officers, the Executive Committee consisted of David Jewell, Britt M. Smith and June Sinclair, with Jane Rogers and Dr. David Goheen ex-officio members.

The Rhododendron Symposium was certainly a cultural success, if not a financial one. It cost over $20,000 and the Foundation suffered some loss on the venture. But it was attended by 337 people, the lectures and demonstrations were interesting and many notable people visited the garden during the festivities. Tony Schilling of Wakehurst, England spent an afternoon discussing the Pond Area and the garden in general. David Chamberlain of Edinburgh went through the collection, verifying some of the questionable species. Members of the delegation from the People's Republic of China spent several days photographing and studying plants. Graham Smith of Pukeiti, New Zealand offered some new ideas on the cultivation and display of the Vireya collection.

Hideo Suzuki of Japan offered suggestions on the cultivation of species native to that country. He also presented to the garden plants of the white form of *pentaphylum*. Dr. Van Elk of the Netherlands spent a good deal of time with Doug Burdick concerning the propagation of rhododendrons. Mr. Pradhan of India brought seedling alpines from the Himalayas as well as rhododendrons from Sikkim, and spent a good deal of time touring the garden and offering helpful suggestions. John Womersley of Australia offered some excellent ideas on the Vireya collection, while Bjorn Alden of Sweden brought cuttings from Goteburg Botanic Gardens and offered many useful and informative suggestions on the garden in general. The garden itself had never looked better, with small wonder. Barbara Mate revealed that over 200 volunteers had contributed to the effort.

From a social standpoint the symposium was a resounding success. A welcoming reception at the Tacoma Sheraton Hotel was hosted by the Weyerhaeuser Company, with hors d'oeuvres and cocktails while the Tacoma Youth Symphony String Ensemble entertained.

With the festivities over it was back to the real world of financial problems and unending labor. In spite of substantial donations of money and splendid returns from plant and pollen sales, payroll expense and the symposium shortfall had created a deficit which Director Piacentini addressed as his major concern in the oncoming months. Karen Gunderson, long time executive manager, had been considering retiring for some time but had generously agreed to remain until Piacentini was comfortably situated in his new position as director. She now submitted a letter of resignation, ending nearly ten years of service to the Foundation. Her farewell message to the membership was touching:

Karen Gunderson with Don King

As this newsletter reaches your hands I will have completed my final days as Executive Manager of the Rhododendron Species Foundation. It was with a great deal of thought and careful consideration that I submitted my resignation to RSF Director Richard Piacentini, effective October 12, 1985. Out of concern that a smooth transition be made from a past, to the now present staff configuration, I agreed to remain through the end of the year.

Having worked in several capacities at RSF during nearly ten years, I have witnessed, perhaps from a unique perspective, phenomenal progress in the Horticultural and Administrative programs of the Foundation. The major development to the garden which occurred during this same time period has been the most gratifying aspect of my career with RSF. From my first position as Executive Secretary, In May, 1976, to Office Manager, Administrator and Executive Manager each phase of my work has been a challenge. Being caught up in the dynamic force of the Foundation, as it has grown and prospered in developing the species collection, garden and administrative programs, has given me a sense of participation, not only in something of importance and lasting value, but in helping to shape the Foundation's history. This will be, and has always been, the cause for my dedication to the goals of RSF.

Though time has quickly passed, having been on the site often and over a long period of time, I have come to have a unique perspective of progress. I know how much progress has been made, because I have seen it accomplished. I know how hard others, like our professional staff and volunteers have worked, because I have worked beside them. I am most proud of what has been accomplished and I give full credit to you, the RSF members. I am excited about what lies ahead for the Foundation. I believe new thoughts and perspectives will bloom profusely in the next few years. Goals set, some long ago, are about to be set in place. These are things about which all RSF members can be proud.

In September, 1984, the RSF Executive Committee agreed, on my recommendation, to hire a director to oversee the day to day operation of the Foundation. During this past year it has been my pleasure to have worked with Mr. Richard Piacentini, RSF Director, acquainting him with RSF policies, procedures and most importantly the people who are the Foundation's most valuable resource. For, if it is plants that have made this Foundation and its garden great, and this is surely so, it is also true that it is the people who have seen to the task.

Working under the direction of six RSF Presidents, before the arrival of our new Director, and in close coordination with the Board of Directors and Executive Committee, I have come to know the meaning of personal commitment and generosity. My association with these individuals will be an inspiration in all that I choose to do in the future.

RSF. Three letters that have become inscribed in the hearts and minds of the Gunderson family. From the inception, much like an intra-marital affair, my work has been enhanced by my husband, Stephen and daughter, Annmarie. They have been at my side volunteering to photograph, plant, host, build, repair or what ever the task at hand. In 1976, Mr. Fred M. Robbins, then President of the Rhododendron Species Foundation, and Mrs. William Avery, an RSF Director, urged me (perhaps coerced a little) or at least helped pursuade me to come up and help "organize" a newly acquired Rhododendron office in Federal Way. I agreed to give it a start, and stayed on to gain far more insightful knowledge than could ever have been afforded me elsewhere.

Also in this same year, Mr. Robbins instructed me to organize a membership program for RSF. A cosmos of individuals came together to form what is now the strong and vital body of the Foundation. To each of you I give my thanks and send best wishes with all cordiality for your help, inspiration, energy, generosity and devotion. For each of you and RSF I am hoping for a very Happy New Year. Karen S. Gunderson.

Compounding this loss was the announcement from Margaret Young that new family priorities had forced her to submit her resignation as manager of the library. She had almost solely taken on the responsibility for cataloguing the collection now located in the Lawrence J. Pierce Library. Margaret, a perfectionist, with great patience and skill had sought out the best classifications to make the sparse resources fill the potential growth of the library and the immediate needs of the patrons. This had involved many trips to the University of Washington and other libraries and a constant vigilance as to the quality of books sought for the collection. She commuted from Port Gamble on a regular basis - a round trip of some 60 miles. Due largely to her efforts and those of the Library Committee the collection now contained 1,280 volumes.

Financial desperation had caused the Foundation to use restricted funds to cover day to day operational expenses and this practice had undermined confidence in the organization. In an effort to restore confidence and get the Foundation back on a safe financial footing, cost-consciousness became the new byword as Piacentini sought to economize in all phases of the Foundation operations. The propagation greenhouse was caulked and insulated to conserve energy, with funds provided by the Weyerhaeuser Company. A 14 x 96 foot plastic house was donated by Briggs nursery and installed by all volunteer labor. Donations of companion plant materials were actively sought in order to avoid having to purchase the same. New fund raising activities were planned, including two concerts in the garden for the coming season and an intensified membership drive. A gift store was planned, to be operated by volunteers.

Despite the heroic efforts at economy and fund raising, by the spring of 1986 the financial plight of the Foundation was critical and the director reported to the board of directors that it had been necessary to reduce the garden staff to a single person, who now had responsibility for the entire garden maintenance operation - an impossible task. Office staff had been reduced and printing and mailing expenses had been curtailed. But the Foundation had shown an operating loss of over $46,000 in 1984 and an additional operating loss of almost $28,000 in 1985 and there were no longer cash reserves to cover the losses and provide operating funds. The organization simply could not survive another deficit year. In an effort to alleviate this situation a new Development Committee was named, with Larry McManus as chairman, and Stu Rogers, Ed Dunn, Curt Huey, Bob Franz, Fran Rutherford, Esther Berry, Herb Spady, and Piacentini as members, to assist and advise staff in ways of raising funds.

More sad news came in the announcement of the death of Dr. Milton V. Walker on February 17, 1986. But with that announcement came also the news of the creation of a substantial Walker trust for the benefit of the Foundation, to vest after the passing of both Dr. and Mrs. Walker. Characteristic of Dr. Walker's dedication to the goals and principles of the Foundation was his insistence that this trust not be announced until after his death, although it had been created many years earlier. Similarly, when in 1970 the board had unanimously adopted a resolution naming the garden in honor of Dr. and Mrs. Walker he had declined the honor, stating, "So many others have made the species collection possible that we would be embarrassed to have it named for us. We do not desire any publicity for something that has given us untold hours of pleasure."

At the April meeting of the board of directors, Dr. Herbert Spady was elected President, David Jewell, Vice President; June Sinclair, Secretary and Fran Rutherford, Treasurer. The winter had been a severe one, with the temperature dropping to 5 degrees F., and this had taken a toll of the more tender varieties. In July, when the damage could be accurately assessed, it was determined that 62 varieties had suffered at least some extensive damage, some killed outright. Eventual assessment revealed that a substantial number of species were lost completely, except for cuttings or scions that had been placed in the protection of the greenhouse, so that none was totally lost to cultivation. Yet the spring bloom had been exemplary, but enjoyed by a disappointingly reduced number of visitors. For various reasons the garden concerts planned for June and July had to be cancelled, but another was planned for August featuring the Emerald City Brass Quintet.

The Foundation sponsored a tour of China from April 30 to May 30. It was a grand success with sixteen cities being visited as well as seven botanical gardens. Arrangements were made for the exchange of wild collected seed and the eventual exchange of wild collected live plant material.

Rick Peterson, gardener

Budgetary restraints had reduced the number of surplus plants for sale and this deficiency was addressed by the hiring of a new propagator, Clarice Clarke. Richard Peterson became the gardener and thanks to a student intern program funded by the Bloedel Foundation the staff was able to accomplish more than had been expected. All efforts of the Executive Committee and the board were now focused on financial problems. Warren Berg was in charge of the Membership Committee and through some innovative concepts new membership categories were devised and wider appeals made to attract new members. Membership had made up about one third of the operating budget, so was crucial to the operation. A new policy was recommended by President Spady and adopted by the board, providing special benefits to persons who contributed substantial amounts to the Foundation.

For the third time a seed distribution program was introduced to the board and this time there were many voices in favor and none in opposition and the proposal was unanimously adopted. It was stressed by all that it would be essential to use heroic efforts to avoid mistakes and contamination and that only verified true species, and the best forms at that, would be used. Only qualified people would be permitted to do the self-pollination and they must adhere strictly to certain rules and methods. It was felt this program would increase public interest in the Foundation and encourage new memberships, thus providing financial rewards. In addition it would provide a major gene pool for plants lost in their natural hibitat and provide Eastern hybridizers with new, hardier material.

Dick Booth was placed in charge of the Seed Committee. Seeds were to be distributed to volunteer growers who would grow the seeds and, for some selected seed lots, return half the seedlings in two years. Some of the returned seedling would be grown on at the Foundation for verification and evaluation for potential incorporation into the collection. The balance would be sold to the general membership as seedlings. Complete instructions were to be provided to each grower, who was to be charged $5.00 per year to cover mailing and handling costs. The first season got the program off to a good start with wild collected seed from over 50 species being distributed to RSF members. But it proved difficult to get volunteers to pollenize species located in the garden.

The spring of 1987 saw a marked improvement in the Foundation's financial picture. The director reported an increase of almost $10,000 in operating income and a decrease of over $46,000 in operating expenses due to the austerity measures adopted during 1986. In addition the endowment funds had grown from $23,265 to over $67,000, an increase of $46,000. So the Foundation had begun the year 1986 $12,000 in debt and with only $702 in the bank and finished the year with $33,857 in the bank and no outstanding indebtedness other than payroll taxes. This had resulted, however, in the garden having been merely maintained, with no new construction or additions to speak of. Some improvements and additions were badly needed. But the garden had remained presentable and over four times as many visitors as usual visited the garden.

The Pond Area underwent a major renovation by Lynn Sonneman of Sonneman Design in Seattle, to correct some design flaws and to provide a more pleasing and natural effect. Leaks were fixed, the rock work was redesigned to better integrate the pond with the surrounding area and numerous habitats were created for aquatic plants and shoreside marginal aquatics, such as bog plants. Two new plastic houses were completed to house newly propagated plants for eventual distribution. And in the realm of public relations, the board of directors sponsored an evening social at the annual meeting of the American Rhododendron Society in Eugene, Oregon, attended by over 800 conference participants.

In March, 1987 Barbara Mate submitted her resignation as Volunteer Coordinator, effective the following June. Barbara and Rudy Mate had served the Foundation for many years and in a number of capacities, paid and as volunteers. Barbara, in keeping with her friendly proclivity for dispensing kudos, made the following statement:

> As I sort piles of accumulated paper and try to set up some aids for the future, I
> am humbled by the support and generosity you have all displayed for the Garden.
> A list of "Thank you's" only pin point the unnoticed, selfless acts we have taken

Barbara Mate visits with garden crew

for granted over the years as the program has grown. A few bits of history are an indication - Art Dome's, Fran Rutherford's and Steve Gunderson's marvelous additions to the slide collection; now Hal Reese's multiple trays will be added. Pearl Nelson and Connie Koeniger have seen to the cataloging; Diane Cornish and Linda Draper started the collection process.

The "Association" - that early group of volunteers who saw the need to fund projects, have a resource of volunteers, held auctions, plant sales and helped start the library. The logo "RSViP" designed by Nancy Hill and funds for the first 2,000 pins and labels raised by Karen Gunderson. The aprons we love, with pouches for all our props - a gift from Marlene, Pat and Nadine. The benches built by "Buff" Buffington. The cart made by Roy Hacanson, only one of the million little projects that have Roy's stamp on it, some major repairs, the desks we sit at.

E. White Smith's, Fran Rutherford's and Bob Badger's tender collecting and care of the R. vireya species and the "Vireya Vine" missle. Esther Avery's remarkable collection of Xerox color sheets - "next best thing to an herbarium." The blinds, the meeting room, the stand for the projector, the books, the vertical files, the book cases and the atlas stand, the years of cataloging, typing and computer work done by Margaret Young, Elizabeth Yuell, Janet Binford and Peg Johnson.

June Sinclair's grasp of the staff's needs; the way she slips into whatever is needed - always approachable and supportive. Joan Martin's photo collection for the sales area, fading now with years of use, but invaluable for enticing the novice to try a plant not in bloom. The plants themselves, each a gift, each a special way to say, "It was all worth doing."

George Ryan's fine collection of selected periodical articles. The extra hours, thought and performance of Jane Rogers and Esther Berry; Marge Baird's marvelous drawings; Judy Young's creative editing. How many miles and overnights for Presidents Goheen, Berry and Spady? Warren Berg, volunteering since the first days of maneuvering the original tractor. Thank you for all of us.

But in a year or so Barbara was back at her post at the Foundation, saying, "I just couldn't stay away." In a recent reminiscence she recalled a senior citizen who toured the entire garden with awed interest and many questions but was disappointed that the foundation did not have tomato and impatiens plants for sale. And the busy Sunday when Dottie Amundson lifted a pot from the stack and uncovered a swarm of baby mice that scattered in all directions. Then there was the parrot that toured the garden accompanied by three humans.

In July of 1987 a tour to Australia and New Zealand was announced for the months of September and October, 1988, to be hosted by Richard Piacentini. The tour included attendance at the Fourth International Rhododendron Conference in Wollongong, Australia.

The computer that had been used to store and process garden, administrative and financial records was reaching its capacity and needed to be replaced by a larger unit, estimated to cost about $10,000. Fortunately the Seattle Foundation offered a grant of $6,500 toward the purchase of the new computer, and none too soon for during the installation of the new system the old broke down - for good. The breakdown and new installation resulted in a two week delay in publishing a new plant catalog but no data was lost. At about the same time the Weyerhaeuser Company came up with a $13,500 grant to improve marketing of the visitor program. The grant funded improvements in parking, road signage, the gift shop and publication of a new brochure. Piacentini's penchant for raising funds for special projects had scored again.

As a result of the tour of China in 1986 and subsequent correspondence the Foundation was invited by the Chinese Academy of Science, Institute of Botany and the Chinese Botanical Society to visit their new rhododendron garden in Western China, to provide technical assistance and establish a long-term, friendly relationship. It was anticipated there would be exchanges of personnel, seeds, seedlings and specimens. The Chinese offered to pay all accommodations and travel expenses within China for the RSF delegation, so the Foundation's only cost would be air fare to China. It was believed the RSF was the first botanical garden in the West to be offered such an exchange.

This generous offer was accepted and a delegation consisting of Piacentini, horticulturist Clarice Clark, President Herb Spady and Mrs. Judy Young made plans to visit the West China Center for the Conservation of Rare Plants from April 24 to May 10, 1988. Since the Chinese were paying all expenses within China, air fare for RSF staff people was donated by various ARS chapters and individual members, thus not taxing the RSF budget with the unexpected expense. Dr. Spady and Judy Young paid their own air fare. The trip was a great success and upon return, Dr. Spady and Piacentini gave an informative report of their visit.

At the April, 1988 board meeting David Jewell was elected President; Burt Mendlin, Vice President; June Sinclair, Secretary; and Fran Rutherford, Treasurer. 1987 had been a good year financially. The endowment fund grew to over $200,000. Operating revenues also increased and the Foundation was able to expand many of the programs and introduce some new ones. A new Program Coordinator, gatekeeper and gift shop sales person were added to the staff. Needed repairs and improvements in the garden were undertaken and yet they were able to finish the year with a modest surplus. But expenditures were being undertaken slowly and cautiously, the staff ever mindful of the near disaster of a couple of years earlier.

In October, 1988 Director Piacentini was able to announce to the membership that a $25,000 conservation award had been received from the prestigious Institute of Museum Services. These grants were awarded to provide matching funds for collection surveys and long-range plans. The Foundation's award would allow for a survey, computer mapping and re-inventory of the entire collection of over 8,500 rhododendrons. The project would also allow for staff time, updating computer equipment and additional interns to work on the project.

January, 1989 began the Foundation's 25th year! Membership now was at the 1000 mark, with members representing fifteen countries around the world. The garden contained 2,200 forms of 503 species. Volunteers had given a surprising 2,870 hours of time to the Foundation in 1988 and the Volunteer Fund gave the garden a new riding lawnmower and the lumber for a shed to house the mower. Wes Tarpley, a volunteer, designed the shed and built it with the aid of three other volunteers. Another construction project taken on by a volunteer was a custom-made observation platform where visitors might stand to survey the collection. The deck was designed and donated by Mark Lembersky, President of Innovis Interactive Technologies, a Weyerhaeuser company based in Tacoma. Later that year Lembersky designed and built two additional structures for the Foundation, a garage and a shed.

Wes Tarpley in action

An additional construction project that had been in the planning stage for years but only partially funded, so put on hold time and again, was the entry building. It was estimated that the building would cost about $85,000 but only $25,000 was available. It was predicted that such a structure would hold a gift shop in addition to an entry to the garden and as such would be an excellent source of income for the Foundation, so Director Piacentini pleaded for the board members to push for funds to complete this project and the board responded by adopting a resolution to go ahead. Pledge cards were handed out to board members and over $20,000 was raised. It was also announced that the Pacific Rim Bonsai Collection was to be situated near the entrance to the garden and the notoriety of this collection was expected to draw a great many new visitors, thus emphasizing the importance of the new entrance building and gift shop facility.

The winter of 1988-89 was a severe one for the garden. On February 6th the temperature dropped below ten degrees for five days in a row. Water pipes in the office and shop building froze and burst, causing over $35,000 in damages, all but $250 being covered by insurance, fortunately. The office was in turmoil for over a month while records, library books and periodicals and office and library equipment were removed and stored in order to allow for cleanup and repairs. Plant damage was held to a minimum, largely due to the fact that most of the susceptible plants were housed in the plastic "hoop-houses", where temperatures never dropped below 17 degrees. This experience underlined the need for additional plastic houses to expand propagation for distribution, which, together with irrigation facilities was expected to cost $6,500.

It was hoped that the student intern program could be expanded, thus adding to the educational aspect of the Foundation while providing additional help for the garden, which was sorely needed. The program was open to students in botany and horticulture and was geared to students with a definite interest in rhododendrons. Cost of the program was $43.00 per day per student. North Kitsap Chapter of ARS presented $1,500 toward this program and it was hoped others would follow suit. Additional support for this program was received from the Bloedel Foundation and the Chiles Foundation.

At the April board meeting it was announced that the endowment fund now had reached over $270,000 and that it, together with certain restricted funds on hand, was generating interest of about $22,000 a year. Officers elected for the ensuing year were Burt Mendlin, President; Don King, Vice President; June Sinclair, Secretary; and Fran Rutherford, Treasurer.

The Weyerhaeuser Company decided to construct facilities for the Pacific Rim Bonsai Collection immediately adjacent to the entrance to the Foundation garden. It provided a paved entry courtyard, public restrooms, a meeting room, passenger drop-off point, handicapped parking and improved access to visitor parking. The new RSF entry building and gift shop were to be part of this general complex. The bonsai collection was to consist of 50 to 60 plants and to be open to the public year around at no charge, beginning in October, 1989. At the annual meeting of the Foundation membership the RSF presented an "Award of Appreciation" to Mr. and Mrs. George Weyerhaeuser in recognition of their outstanding support for the Foundation.

Suzanne Hattery at the computer

In May an additional grant from the Institute of Museum Services in the amount of $17,442 was received. As a result of this grant and anticipated revenue from the bonsai collection a number of staff changes were announced. Suzanne Hattery was named Assistant Director, in which position she would assist in directing the bonsai garden, garden development, maintenance, curating and mapping of the collection. Clarice Clark, current horticulturist was named Educational Specialist, in which position she would rely on her past teaching experience to develop new interpretive materials for the garden and exhibits, be involved in developing classes and educational programs at the garden as well as for members who live out of state. Dennis Bottemiller was appointed *may 1989* horticulturist and Barbara Mate was promised more hours to develop a larger volunteer program. Gift shop salesperson Bobbie Gojenola would now also assist with office work. A little later on a contract was signed with Weyerhaeuser to reimburse RSF for direct and indirect costs in managing the bonsai collection, so David DeGroot from New Orleans was hired as curator of the Bonsai collection.

The Pacific Rim Bonsai Collection was dedicated on a cool, misty day in early October. The largest private bonsai collection in the West Coast open to the public, it was also among the most extensive in the world. The beautiful bonsai, each individually displayed to its advantage, captivated visitors with their form and beauty. Demonstrations by members of the local bonsai groups were presented throughout the day. Weyerhaeuser hosted the dedication in beautiful tents in the lower garden. A chamber music concert added to the festivities, as did a champagne brunch that was served.

Fred Robbins and Jane Rogers, both of whom were past presidents of the Foundation, passed away in the fall of 1989. Since the new entrance building had now been completed it was decided by the board to name the building for Jane Rogers, who had been one of the strongest supporters of the project and a valued and most effective member of the garden. Of Fred Robbins, Warren Berg wrote:

Fred Robbins truly loved species rhododendrons. He spent many years persistently collecting and growing one of the finest collections in this country. Because of his determination to grow only true, authentic species he joined Dr. Walker as a founder of the RSF and was directly responsible for the importation of many of the finest forms growing in our garden today. He also donated large quantities of plant material from his own garden.

As the collection grew, Corydon Wagner and Fred, who had become President of the RSF, met with George Weyerhaeuser and came up with the present 24 acre site. Developing the garden became a full time job of negotiations, clearing land, planting, training employees and - you name it. He was certainly not afraid of hard work and long hours, working six days a week. Fred was not only a real "hands-on" President for three years (1973-76), but was most generous and instrumental in obtaining financial help as needed, particularly during the bad times of the early '80s.

We have a lot of fine people to thank for the wonderful garden we enjoy today. Fred Robbins was certainly one of those at the very top of the list. He will be sorely missed.

At the November meeting Director Piacentini announced that the Foundation was now in the best financial position it had ever experienced. Operating income had exceeded expenses by over $10,000, the endowment fund totalled over $310,000 and the new entrance building, gift shop and bonsai display were attracting many more visitors and increasing revenues dramatically. He stated that the Foundation had operated at a profit every year since 1985 with the result being expansion of programs and dramatic improvement of the garden. In another declaration of some significance, Dr. Ned Brockenbrough pointed out the importance of recording the history of the Rhododendron Species Foundation, not realizing that a proposal for the preparation of such a history was in the offing.

Now that the new entrance was completed, the bonsai collection in place and finances in good shape, the director announced many new garden projects for the ensuing months. With an increasing emphasis on greater public involvement the entrance took on a new importance. Plans were developed to integrate the new building and courtyard into the garden plan, this to include new paths, courtyard, plant sales area, benches and tour staging areas. The last spring several portions of the upper and lower Study Gardens had been closed to visitors for safety reasons, exposed roots and slippery paths having made these areas dangerous. The lower Study Garden had been renovated to eliminate these problems and the same treatment was planned for the upper Study Garden.

In the Alpine Garden there were still a few beds that needed to be redone with a new soil mix and rhododendrons and companion plants were necessary in some areas. New perennial areas were to be added in certain places that were subject to excessive sun. They add color and interest during the summer months. Heathers were donated by the American Heather Society and Heather Acres Nursery and a reference collection of hardy ferns was being added to the Study Garden by the Hardy Fern Foundation.

Propagation activities had escalated until in January, 1990 it was reported by Dennis Bottemiller that over 7,000 rooted cuttings had been already transplanted from the rooting beds and were growing nicely, with 3,000 cuttings remaining in the beds. Most of these would be available for distribution in 1992. For the third year an annual photography contest was sponsored by the Foundation with first prize a $100 gift certificate. The old gift shop area adjacent to the office had now been converted into a permanent home for the Lawrence J. Pierce Library, with newly constructed display shelves, and locked cases for rare books. A group of long time volunteers surprised Esther Avery with a party and presented her with a bench they had purchased as a memorial to the late Dr. William Avery, to be installed in the Study Garden Esther

Marlene Buffington, Nadine Henry and Pat Nelson

and Bill had worked so hard to realize. Pat Nelson, Marlene Buffington and Nadine Henry composed the following tribute to Esther Avery:

"When in doubt as to the proper pronunciation of a botanical word or phrase, say it comfortably to your ear and tongue and with authority. People will know you are correct." These words of encouragement were said by Mrs. Esther Avery: Rhododendron ebullient.

You can find this lady of rhododendrons on her tractor surveying her collection of species and hybrid rhodies at Olalla if she isn't at home in Tacoma, Washington.

Mrs. Avery and her husband, Dr. William (Bill) Avery traveled the world over in search of one more rare plant. Her photographic memory has served as a library, history, an archive to all bewitched and entranced by the rhododendron, Washington's state flower.

Dr. Bill, affectionately called by all that knew him, passed away in 1981. Esther has carried on their dreams, inviting all to share her enthusiasm. Her warmth has encircled a bevy of sleeping bags of snoring women on the floor of her cabin at Olalla, a tea of delightful goodies for a chosen few, (brought to us on the front scoop of her tractor), an International Plant Collectors seminar. She sees no walls and is a friend to all.

Esther entangled all that were privileged to study the rhododendron with her. Her tutorial widened the universe of all that know her. She still carries in her the strength of the young, small town school teacher in the long-ago town of Morton. Esther will always share her ability to learn with others.

Developing a technique of color zerox using the plant foliage was a milestone in Esther's desire to perpetuate a new and true color style herbarium, of actual plant foliage.

Sharing plants for all to enjoy was one of her many theories of nature's flora. Her songs are those of the birds that surrounded her gardens. Her music is the winds in her trees from far away places. Her poetry is in the shadows of the

Himalaya Mountains, the Salween, the Yangtze, the Mekong, the mystic Yakushimanum. All Esther's trove.

How old is Esther Avery? Somewhere between the beauty of the first rhody that graced our earth and the last floret to bloom before the sun goes down forever. We three co-authors are rich in memories of our teacher, Esther Avery.

Barbara Mate and her husband, Rudy, both for many years highly active in RSF affairs, Rudy as a volunteer and Barbara with her well-managed Volunteer Coordination program, retired from their volunteer efforts to live in Newport, Oregon. It was said of Barbara, "Turning her down was most difficult, should she call for help. She worked harder than anyone and took such good care of her volunteers we hardly knew we were working."

Director Piacentini declared in January, 1990 that the RSF had just completed its most successful year to date. At the April board meeting he reported cash on hand in the amount of $33,516 and an endowment fund of $311,567. The only negative factor was the news that the Foundation would not be managing the Bonsai Collection after all, thus quashing the possibility of income from that source. But offsetting this disappointment was news that the plant sale had generated profits of over $17,000. Officers for the previous year were carried over for an additional year with the exception of Fran Rutherford, who had resigned as Treasurer. He was replaced by Ian Walker, who had had previous experience with the job. President Mendlin cast an ominous mood over the meeting when he delivered this prophetic message:

> ... financial pressure has always been an overriding concern of the Board for the RSF. The last few years we have seen a financial turn around. We are to the point that finances have improved enough that we should now concern ourselves with having a world class garden. Still I sense some trouble. I sense that there are some personality clashes. Some of us have allowed personal feelings to dominate our thoughts and if they do, they will influence our decisions about the Foundation. Personal feelings should never interfere with business sense. We have stood shoulder to shoulder in the past and I am asking you to keep that feeling. My message today is let's all pull together and attain the heights that we know can be reached.

Dr. Herb Spady announced that Jock Brydon had just passed away at the age of 85 years. For an interesting and informative account of his life furnished by his wife, Edith, please read the first few pages of Chapter VI, "The Brydons".

The seed program had gotten off to a slow start, partially due to the fact that volunteers needed for self pollenizing plants in the collection had just not been forthcoming. Finally the program began to blossom with a seed list being distributed offering sixteen varieties from the RSF collection and an additional thirty selections of wild collected seed from China. The seed from China was a direct result of the exchange program arranged during an RSF sponsored visit to that country several years earlier.

Two important announcements were made in April. The Hardy Fern Foundation was being formed to establish a comprehensive collection of the world's hardy ferns for display, testing, evaluation, public education and introduction to the gardening and horticultural community. It was to be situated within the Foundation's gardens. And a series of new classes was being offered by the Education Committee: Introduction to Species Rhododendrons; Landscaping with Rhododendrons; Rhododendron

Identification; Spring and Fall Care and Maintenance of Rhododendrons; and Planting for Fall Color, the Deciduous Azaleas.

In April and May Director Piacentini led a group of thirteen members and friends of RSF on a visit to some of the best gardens of Scotland and England. They visited 23 gardens over a period of 24 days. The weather was ideal and the group had time to meet with and visit the directors, curators and gardeners involved with the gardens, learning something of their methods and problems. During this tour sixty-three species were identified for inclusion in the RSF collection and arrangements were made for acquiring the same. At the invitation of Mr. Keshab Pradhan, Chief Secretary for the State of Sikkim, a similar visit to Sikkim was planned for May, 1991, again to be led by Richard Piacentini.

In May, 1990 the RSF again was honored with the prestigious Institute of Museum Services award, this time in the amount of $22,017. Richard Piacentini journeyed to Washington, D. C. to accept the award from first lady Barbara Bush on the South Lawn of the White House. RSF was one of only 20 botanical gardens in the nation to be so honored. Mrs. Bush, in the presentation ceremony, stated, "You hold the cultural legacy of America, and you make unique contributions to the cultural lit-

Piacentini, far right,in Washington D.C. with Barbara Bush

eracy of our people. As museum directors, you have two major charges - to keep your collections for future generations - and to share the ideas and values they represent. And this sharing is how museums help so much to meet our country's educational challenges."

On Sunday, June 24, an open house was held to officially recognize the library in its new home. Lawrence Pierce and his family members were there to greet Foundation members and to celebrate Lawrence's 90th birthday. Lawrence and his family had collaborated in writing a book about his life, *Reminiscences and Reflections, 1900 - 1990*. Two autographed copies were placed in the library and the book was being offered in the gift shop.

David DeGroot, Curator of the Pacific Rim Bonsai Collection, had been employed by the Foundation, with his wages reimbursed by Weyerhaeuser. Now, however, the Bonsai Collection was taken over by Weyerhaeuser, who would pay DeGroot directly. This resulted in a number of staff changes for the Foundation. The Volunteer Coordinator and Education Specialist positions were consolidated into a new Program Manager position, with Suzanne Hattery in charge. Clarice Clark left the Foundation to enter business with her husband.

At a ribbon cutting ceremony on August 19, 1990 the Jane S. Rogers Visitor Center was dedicated, with remarks from Director Piacentini, President Burt Mendlin and N. Stewart Rogers. A commemorative plaque was placed on the building and guests enjoyed a pleasant time in the courtyard with refreshments and music.

At the November, 1990 meeting of the board of directors, Clarence Barrett was named Foundation Historian and directed to prepare the history of the Rhododendron Species Foundation. Membership had reached 1,036 and operating revenues had increased dramatically. Along with the increased membership and activities of the Foundation came increased need for volunteer help. The January Newsletter contained an appeal for volunteer assistance from twelve areas: plant distribution, tending exhibits at the Tacoma Garden Show, spring plant sale, tour guides, garden helpers, label making, gift sales, instructors for the education program, photographers, herbarium, office, pollen program. In addition two part time paid positions were announced, weekend assistant and office assistant.

Dr. J. Harold Clarke, former editor of the ARS Bulletin and so active in the very early activities of the RSF and a charter member of the board of directors, died November 7 at the age of 91 years. He had retired to his home in Arizona with his wife, Gretchen, in 1978.

For several years the spring plant sale had been an important fund raising event. By now it was becoming a Foundation permanent fixture, under the capable direction of Don King, who headed up a very large, active and dedicated committee. This particular spring the committee grossed over $50,000 in just five hours - an amazing feat. Over 11,000 people visited the garden this spring, with 2,451 people utilizing the guided tours in April and May.

Many classes were offered during 1991:
   Rhododendrons of the Washington Park Arboretum, Clint Smith, instructor.
   Rhododendron Identification - Bob Badger, instructor.
   Rhododendron Propagation - Dennis Bottemiller, instructor.
   Spring Flowering Trees & Shrubs - Bob Benning, instructor.
   Pruning - Bob Baines, instructors.
   Companion Plants of the RSF - Rick Peterson, instructor.
   Introduction to Bonsai - David DeGroot, instructor.
   Composting - Instructor to be announced.
   Fern Identification - Jeanette Kunnen & Mareen Kruckeberg, instructors.

Don King, left, with Esther Berry and crew

   Gardens of Bainbridge Island - Instructor to be announced.
   Field Trip to Copper Creek - George Ryan & Orris Thompson, guides.
   Two classes were offered for children: "Bugs" and "Water Detectives".

At the April, 1991 meeting of the board of directors, a new position was authorized, Second Vice President. The new slate of officers was elected, namely Don King, President; Ian Walker, 1st Vice President; Bill Lindeman, 2nd Vice President; June Sinclair, Secretary; and Jeanette Kunnen, Treasurer. They would serve for two years. In addition to these officers, the Executive Committee included Britt Smith, Marshall Majors, Clint Smith and past President Burt Mendlin, non-voting member. President King announced that the 1st Vice President would serve as liaison between the various committees and the board of directors and the membership, and as chairman of the nominating committee. The 2nd Vice President would chair the Long-range Planning Committee and work closely with the Garden Planning Committee. The remaining committees and their chairs were announced: Plant Sales, Barbara Lindberg; Photography, Dr. Keith White; Library, Fran Harrison; RSF Historian, Clarence "Slim" Barrett.

Once again, in May, 1991, the Foundation received an Institute of Museum Services award, this time in the amount of $28,268. This grant would help further improve the Foundation's operations with particular emphasis on expanding and improving the education and visitor programs.

At the fall, 1991 meeting of the board of directors, President King announced the resignation of Director Richard Piacentini, effective September 21, 1991. Appropriate action was being taken to find a qualified person to fill the position. Sadly, it was also announced that the Foundation had lost a number of loyal and active members since the last meeting, namely Helen Walker, widow of Milton V. Walker and mother of 1st Vice President Ian Walker; Mrs. Corydon Wagner, mother of board member and benefactress of the Foundation, Wendy Weyerhaeuser; Edward Dunn, RSF founding member and past President; and Jim Sinclair, husband of June Sinclair. On December 1, 1991 former Foundation Curator Kendall W. Gambrill died after a long illness.

Hoop house in summer. . .

. . .and winter

Pamela Elms, Secretary

Bill Smallwood, gatekeeper

CHAPTER XII

SECURITY

Former director Piacentini stated in his farewell message:

I would like to thank all the members, staff and volunteers of the RSF for their support during my seven years as Executive Director. It has been a pleasure working with all of you. I am very proud of the accomplishments we have made together. The RSF received national and international recognition as we expanded and improved our gardens and programs. We balanced our budget, nearly tripling our operating revenues, and have run the garden at an operating surplus in each of the past five years. We have come a long way, and none of this could have been done without your hard work, dedication and support. I wish I had time to thank each and every one of you personally. Your support really made a difference.

I resigned from the RSF on September 21, and have accepted a position as Director of the Leila Arboretum in Michigan. It has been a pleasure and honor to serve as your Director. Thank you once again. Wishing you and the Foundation the best of success. Sincerely, Richard V. Piacentini.

Following the resignation of Director Richard Piacentini President Don King undertook the additional task of acting director, while the search for a new director proceeded by means of advertisements in certain horticultural publications. A screening committee was appointed by the president, to consider qualifications of applicants and narrow the choices to two or three finalists. It was anticipated that the selection of a qualified person would take a number of months.

Meanwhile program manager Suzanne Hattery announced the initiation of an exciting new program for young people. Nature workshops were offered to scouting organizations during the week, where children could study and collect fallen leaves of azaleas, maples, dogwoods, bamboos and other species and learn to analyze and recognize them. It was anticipated that in the spring the focus would be on rhododendron identification. All local scouting groups were invited to participate in the program.

Going into the year 1992 membership stood at 1,160. Horticulturist Dennis Bottemiller reported 15,000 cuttings in the greenhouse benches for future plant sales. The hoop houses were full and the mild winter was greatly facilitating the garden operations. Clint Smith, in charge of the seed program, had reported the severe cold of December, 1990 had resulted in a low seed production for the previous year but that the present mild winter should allow the production of an abundance of seed for distribution. Almost one hundred new accessions had been made during the preceeding year, most of them via the generosity of Warren Berg, and of great importance was the fact that over 2,800 hours had been donated to the Foundation by volunteers.

Clint Smith pollinates a floret

Ernie Dzurich in hoop house

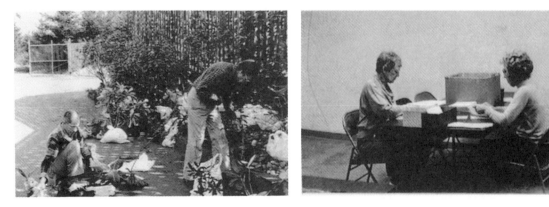

Don King and Cliff Johnson
prepare for plant sale

Kay Fasekas and Bernice Worth
in the office

Volunteerism has been and will always be a key element
in the operation of the garden

Following the death of Helen Walker, widow of founder Milton V. Walker, her son, First Vice-president Ian Walker, announced the existance of a testamentary trust to conditionally benefit the Foundation. The existance of such a trust had long been suspected but its terms and the amount of money involved had been only speculative. Ian provided some details in a memo to the board of directors dated April 24, 1992:

{President} Don King has asked me to write a brief memo regarding the trust established in my parents' will which conditionally may benefit the Foundation. I think the easiest way to do this is to use a question and answer format.

Why was the trust established?

As the Foundation was formed from a preservation and education point of view, my parents felt it appropriate that the bulk of their remaining resources be directed to this end as a return of the gifts they had enjoyed through life. Their desire also was for anonymity.

Who are the trustees and what are their functions?

The First Interstate Bank of Washington is the corporate trustee responsible for financial management. Ian Walker is co-trustee responsible for qualification determination.

How large is the trust and how is it distributed?

The trust will likely be in excess of one half million dollars. If the Foundation qualifies only the annual income will be distributed until either the earlier of the year 2051 or 21 years after the passing of Glenn, Margaret and Ian Walker. At that time the entire trust will be distributed to the Foundation.

How does the Foundation qualify to receive funds?

The Foundation qualifies if the conditions established by the will are met. These conditions include the following:

By not alienating, encumbering or hypothecating its interest in the principal or income of the Trust in any manner.

By not deviating from the specific objectives and purposes for which the Foundation was organized.

By not merging with any other organization or by becoming dominated by any other organization so that it loses its separate and distinct identity or shall become dominated by a majority of its directors who are also directors of another organization.

Ian Walker, co-trustee, or his successor co-trustee be a member of the RSF Board of Directors during the life of this Trust.

Who determines if the Foundation qualifies to receive funds?

Ian Walker or his successor co-trustee shall determine in his/her sole and absolute discretion whether or not the Foundation is carrying out its original objectives and purposes and whether or not it is maintaining its separate and distinct identity. If so, the Foundation qualifies.

What happens if the Foundation does not qualify?

The entire trust goes to the University of Western Ontario, Ontario, Canada.

If the Foundation qualifies, how are the funds to be used?

The will states, "It is my express wish that any and all funds distributed to the Foundation, whether income or principal, be specifically utilized for the promotion of educational and scientific research of species rhododendron, and for the funding of activities directly related to the location, collection, propagation and distribution of true forms of species rhododendron, as set forth in Article 1 of the original by-laws adopted by the Foundation at the time of its incorporation."

How will it be ascertained if the funds are used properly?

It is my suggestion that an advisory group be constituted which would do the following:

Working with the Board and the Director, identify projects with detailed, realistic and measurable goals in each area identified in the answer to the preceding question, which would be recommended for consideration. These would be projects which could be accomplished within a realistic and specific period of time, and when the costs are combined be within the anticipated yearly earnings of the trust.

Review the progress toward the attainment of the goals for which funding was supplied and expedite the timely completion of the projects when needed.

Develop recommendations for the following year.

Specific projects would be selected and funded. If the goals were met on a timely basis, funding would be available for future goal projects, subject to future goal attainment.

In addition to the above trust, a uni-trust was created in the Walker will which left the Foundation some $145,000 available at once for any purpose. This, of course, dramatically improved the financial condition of the Foundation. Ian Walker recommended that $40,000 of these funds be set aside for a professional fund raising effort.

It seemed apparent to Ian Walker that his position as First Vice-president of the Foundation was in potential conflict with his position as co-trustee. Accordingly he tendered his resignation as an officer of the Foundation, although he would of course remain a member of the board of directors.

On June 18, 1992 President King announced the hiring of a new executive director, John T. Fitzpatrick of Charlottesville, Virginia. John graduated with a Bachelor of Science in Horticulture from the University of Maryland. He was garden curator for Bressingham Gardens, Norfolk, England from 1980 to 1981. While there he worked under the direction of Alan Bloom and contributed to the documentation of the collection by recording and labelling more than 2,500 different perennials. In 1982 he became assistant director of horticulture for White Flower Farm in Litchfield, Connecticut. In 1986 he was appointed director of the Thomas Jefferson Center for Historic Plants, Monticello, Charlottesville, Virginia.

John had been active in professional organizations including Historic Landscapes Committee of the United States International Council on Monuments and Sites, American Association of Botanical Gardens and Arboreta, Perennial Plant Association, Southern Garden History Society and Rock Garden Society. He had been an experienced lecturer, writer and editor and had had experience in business and public administration. In applying for the position he stated, "My horticultural interests are much broader than the preservation of historic plants, the area in which I have been active since 1986. I care deeply about the preservation of 'wild' plants, those bequeathed to us by the earth. I also have a long-term commitment to reaching a wider public, sharing with them our rich garden heritage, and a vision of what horticulture can be in the future."

Delighted at the prospect of having a full time executive director, President King praised the performance of the staff members and volunteers during the absence of a director, "… speaking of a great organization, it has been quite evident over the past 12 months that the RSF is truly a great organization. The office and garden staff have performed in a very professional manner and have not hesitated to take on additional responsibilities. Through the teamwork of staff members and volunteers, all of the functions of the RSF have continued on schedule and the quality of the services and products have continued at a very high level."

Program manager Suzanne Hattery announced that the Foundation was awarded a 1992 General Operating Support Grant from the Institute of Museum Services in the amount of $34,567. This was a singular honor inasmuch as there had been 1,428 applications and the Foundation is one of only seventeen botanical gardens in the United States, and the only botanical garden in the State of Washington, to receive this award. In accordance with the terms of the grant the funds would be used to expand the visitor program, further develop the education program and expand the operating base in order to provide more income for program and exhibit maintenance.

Volunteers Bernice Worth and Adella Nestegaard "deadheading"

At the spring meeting two new names were added to the Executive Committee as members at large, namely Steve Gangsei and Clarence "Slim" Barrett. In addition to the new executive director there were now eight staff members serving the Foundation: Dennis Bottemiller, horticulturist; Pam Elms, administrative assistant; Suzanne Hattery, program manager; Steve Hootman, gardener; Rick Peterson, groundskeeper; Nyla Redford, bookkeeper; Bill Smallwood, gatekeeper and Linda Strandberg, assistant gardener.

In May nineteen members of the Foundation travelled to Southeast Asia including fifteen days in Sikkim. While in Sikkim they saw twenty-eight species of rhododendrons and had many spectacular views of the snow capped peaks of the Himalayas. After Sikkim, most of the group spent an additional five days in India and some also enjoyed four days in Thailand.

June brought the sad news of the death of Karen Gunderson, long a supporter of the Foundation, having served as member, volunteer and employee. At the urging of Fred Robbins and Esther Avery she became active in the formation and organization of the garden when it was moved to Federal Way in 1976 and she remained until October, 1985. It was said that she never asked anyone to do anything that she would not do herself.

At the October meeting of the Executive Committee the director suggested it would be appropriate to give the Foundation's garden a name that would be in keeping with its true nature. Accordingly the name 'Rhododendron Species Botanical Garden' was adopted. In announcing this change to the membership, John Fitzpatrick said, "This name should make it clear to people who don't know about the Foundation that we maintain a public garden with a serious purpose. We expect the new name to be more effective in literature and advertisements designed to attract garden visitors and new members...."

1992

News was announced that Dennis Bottemiller, foundation horticulturist, had resigned after three years of service, in order to take a position as horticultural technician with the City of Tacoma. This loss was partially offset by the hiring of Rick Peterson as the Foundation's curator and funds from the Walker estate gift were authorized to salary the new position for the following year. Bill Boggs was hired to fill the position of nursery manager and Steve Hootman was elevated to garden manager.

1992

Over the years the Foundation, like most non-profit organizations, has managed to offer periodic communications to its members in the form of a 'Newsletter'. It has been this author's experience in a number of such organizations that it is extremely difficult to find a person with the talent, intellect, dedication and spirit to undertake the position of editor, and too often the job, even when successfully carried out, goes without true appreciation. It was, therefore, quite appropriate that in the October, 1992 issue of 'The Rhododendron Species Foundation Newsletter' a tribute to the Newsletter's editor, Renee Hill appeared, authored by her daughter Nancy Nestor. It is certainly worthy of reproduction here.

"Great Things from Little Cuttings grow..and Thanks!"

A few years ago when the garden was new and gathering cuttings to enlarge the collection, one person began to start another collection - news. From what humble beginnings in Oregon and Washington came the Rhododendron Species Foundation and its "Newsletter"!

"My dear friend Marge (Baird) volunteered me for the job", said Renee Hill, "I guess she thought I'd be good at it - or maybe that I wouldn't give up". Marge was right on both counts. Now 17 years in production. (This is volume 17, but I'd been doing "Cuttings" for a while before Margaret Young suggested we number them. It had been at least three years by then, so that issue was number three.

The garden has grown and expanded in those years to become the world class collection that it is today. The Newsletter has grown, too. Early sporadic editions, "It was hard to find something to write about in the beginning - but when there was something to write about, we did!"

At first it was just a simple typed sheet with an appropriate name - "Cuttings". Through many evolutions to typed, photocopied, and computer production to a very professionally written and produced newsletter.

Through it all Renee Hill has been editor extraordinare. Editors, in general, seldom get credit for the work they do; pulling together stories (cramming long articles into tight places, and stretching small ones to fill holes). There are late nights communing (or arguing) with the typewriter (now computer) and many heated discussions with temperamental production staff.

Renee has continued to do what Marge said she would nearly twenty years ago; 1, do a good job and 2, not give up. I know because I've been there for a lot of it, helping when I could, hindering when I could not help and figuring out just why the computer wouldn't do what we thought it ought.

It has been a wonderful experience for me, learning about and loving the plants, the people, the newsletter and my mother.

I would like to say thanks to the RSF for giving us something to write about, to Marge for the original suggestion, and thanks, Mom, for doing a good job, and not giving up.

Nancy is still active in the production of the Newsletter and Renee gives her full credit for making it "pretty".

At the end of the year Suzanne Hattery announced that over 18,500 people had visited the garden during 1992! And with the annual convention of the American Rhododendron Society taking place in nearby Tacoma this spring the Foundation planned to host an open house for all ARS members and their families.

In the inaugeration day wind storm some 25 large trees blew down, causing irreparable damage to many plants and requiring extensive repairs and removal of logs and brush. The arduous task was not completed until late fall of 1993. Tracy Spier described the ordeal: "After months of raking, hauling debris and cutting logs, we are relieved to report that this area is back in order. During the storm, several root masses were thrust into the air as trees fell. We left two of these in place, as they add interest to the landscape and provide educational opportunities. Garden visitors not only see the shallow roots of these massive trees, but also the ability of rhododendrons to survive and adapt to natural disasters...." At the same time she announced that a new access path for disabled persons had been completed from the garden entrance to the gazebo.

At the April board of directors meeting the board resolved to employ the services of Mason Blacher & Associates, professional fund raisers, in an effort to bolster the finances of the Foundation. At the same meeting the slate of new officers for the ensuing two years was elected: President, Don King; 1st Vice President (pro tempore - 1 year), Britt Smith, 2nd Vice President, Fred Whitney; Treasurer, William Lindeman; Secretary, Clarence Barrett. Honore' Hacanson was elected to complete Barrett's term as member-at-large on the Executive Committee.

Staff changes were announced that spring. Tracy Spier replaced Steve Hootman as gardener and Charmaine Adsero was employed as program manager, replacing Suzanne Hattery, who had resigned. After eight years on the job Pam Elms resigned as administrative assistant. Director Fitzpatrick stated, "She was a key player and contact with our widespread membership and a reliable source of information about Foundation activities over the years. Much more than an administrative assistant, Pam set up many of our current programs. Her cheerful, energetic presence is missed." She was replaced by Deanna Hallsell, a graduate of the University of Arkansas at Little Rock.

On July 9, 1993 John Fitzpatrick announced his resignation as Executive Director, effective July 23rd. President Don King immediately called the Executive Committee into emergency session and began the search for a new director. Ultimately four resumes were submitted for consideration and two applicants appeared for interviews before the Executive Committee on July 21, 1993, a third being interviewed by telephone. On July 24, 1993 applicant Scott Vergara was hired as the new director.

Scott Vergara had been a botanist and school teacher from a family of plantspeople and brought to the Foundation technical skills as well as practical knowledge. In addition, and perhaps more important, he brought with him the ability to relate to people at all levels. Soon he was acquainted with staff, working with them at their respective jobs until he knew well their work areas and capabilities. Within a few months he introduced himself and the Foundation to a great many horticultural organizations in the Pacific Northwest, creating a rapport with the plant oriented organizations that the Foundation had never theretofore enjoyed. He addressed a number of chapters of the American Rhododendron Society, cementing relationships with these sister organizations that had long been neglected.

Staff, having inspected part of the new propagation facility. Pictured, from left to right, are Steve Hootman, curator; Tracy Spier, gardener; Deanna Hallsell, membership & development coordinator; Nyla Redford, bookkeeper; Scott Vergara, executive director; Rick Peterson, garden manager; Charmaine Adsero, program manager; Clint Smith, nursery manager. *Photo by author*

Largely as a result of Vergara's ease with people and his ability to project his genuine interest in the Foundation and its goals there soon appeared an obvious improvement in the attitudes of staff, volunteers, and board members. Clint Smith, longtime board member and activist on the Executive Committee, and a successful commercial nurseryman, was employed as plant propagator and immediately set about improving propagation facilities and techniques. A full time curator was employed, as was a second gardener.

Scott Vergara, Executive Director

A fund raising campaign authorized by the Executive Committee, employing the services of Mason Blacher & Associates brought donations of over $1,000 each from almost every member of the Executive Committee, an unprecedented occurrence. A new employee handbook was developed, along with employee grievance procedures, elements that had been anticipated but postponed for years. A new slate of officers and Executive Committee members has recently been installed:

President: Fred Whitney
First Vice-president: Honore' Hacanson
Second Vice-president: Joshua Green III
Treasurer: Bill Lindeman
Secretary: Marlene Buffington
Members at large of Executive Committee: Rollo Adams, Steve Gangsei, Moulton Prussing. Don King, ex-officio.

As this is being written a new wave of optimism and enthusiasm seems to have swept over the entire operation, an encouraging note upon which to consider termination of this phase of the Foundation's history.

It seemed appropriate in winding up this history to ask some of the long-time members of the Foundation to give a statement regarding their observations on the present condition of the Foundation and the prognosis for its future. Warren Berg, long a member of the board of directors and Executive Committee, one of the most active volunteers, a dedicated species collector and grower and a generous contributor of plants and financial support writes the following:

As I reflect on the past and all that has been accomplished by the Rhododendron Species Foundation, I think we can be proud of the role played by the many participants. There have been the usual up and downs, but the one stable factor has been the contribution of a lot of highly dedicated and talented people. Each in his or her own way has provided the strength for the Foundation to grow. At the beginning there was of course a small group of founders, led by the Walkers. As time passed the list grew to what it is today. I won't try to thank all these folks by name, but I will mention the one who got me involved, Fred Robbins. Fred was President when the rhododendron collection was moved to its present location at Federal Way and was responsible, for the most part, for obtaining the property from the Wayerhaeuser Company. I worked with Fred the first few years on my days off and I can honestly say he worked seven days a week. We certainly are indebted to him for all his efforts.

As for me and perhaps some others, there have been many challenges encountered but also many new adventures with those who have become good friends. The satisfaction of accomplishment and the sharing of so many memories has for me returned a harvest greater than what was sowed.

Warren Berg

I probably won't see all the plants bloom that I have had the good fortune to collect on my exploratory expeditions around the world. Some just take too long to flower. However, I feel good about the home given them at the botanical garden and I know that others will enjoy them long after I am gone. There are still rhododendrons to be discovered and more fun looking for them than ever imagined. In addition, there is the gift of heightened appreciation of the world and its peoples.

At the time of this writing the future of the Rhododendron Species Foundation has never look brighter. We not only have a highly experienced staff, but a truly dedicated group of volunteers. Without this volunteer program we would have to discontinue operations. They are the back-bone of the Foundation and we certainly owe them our heart-felt gratitude.

One other name must be mentioned and that, of course, is the author of this book - Clarence Barrett. There is no way we can fathom the time and talent he put into this project; it had to represent a labor of love. This book will be appreciated by rhododendron enthusiasts for years to come. Thank you, Slim.

Warren Berg

June Sinclair, long an active volunteer and financial supporter of the Foundation, as well as a member of the board of directors and Executive Committee and Secretary of the organization for a number of years, states,

Unfortunately I never met Dr. Walker. I have been lucky, however, to know Cecil Smith. His recollections of the origin of the Rhododendron Species Foundation are a tribute to the dedication and persistence of Dr. Walker or, as the founding members called him, "the needle".

According to Cecil the original collection was composed of plants imported by Dr. Walker and species donated by John and Rudolph Henny and George Grace, which had been grown from seed of Rock's 1932 exhibition. Most of the Rock plants were lost due to their difficulty and slowness in growth. This and other disasters, as chronicled in the foregoing history, discouraged the founders but failed to quench their enthusiasm. As Cecil puts it, "Wales Wood was a real nut on species, especially dwarfs." Apparently so were the others. What comes through from his recollections is that whatever the ups

191

and downs in getting the R.S.F. off the ground, there was this consuming interest and passion about the species.

To me there is a parallel between those early days and the present. We have had our suc-cesses and disappointments as the founders did. Reading the history of the Foundation it is evident that getting the garden going and keeping it going has never been easy. With our new director, present staff and eager vol-unteers, one cannot help but feel the interest and enthusiasm that must have motivated our founders. I've never been more optimistic about the future. There is no question that the grand dreams most of us share may not be realized soon, but the promise is within reach.

June Sinclair

Specifically there has been a vigorous effort undertaken to protect, verify and increase the diversity of our collection, helped tremendously by a grant from the Walker estate. An accelerated program of propagating more and rarer plants for distribution has begun, including seeds and seedlings of wild collected species. A pollen bank is being established. More and better contacts with botanical gardens, private gardens, universities and American Rhododen-dron Society chapters have been initiated, reflecting a new emphasis on science and education. Our slide collection is being updated and expanded. New programs of lectures and trips are scheduled.

These are just a few of the changes that come to mind. They represent the efforts of people who, like our founders, love species rhododendrons and are motivated and can inspire others by their enthusiasm and vision.

June Sinclair

Siegfried Berthelsdorf, M.D., long-time active rhododendron enthusiast stated in a letter to the author,

History has a multitude of interesting fragments; but one thing it offers to a few, the opportunity to hear the voices again as of Jock Brydon, Wales Wood and others as one reads through the proceedings of the International Rhododendron Conference and other earlier journals, and as one sees the pictures of those friendlies of the past. The rhododendrons were of interest to all of us, but behind the rhodies were the people who gave them ever more meaning - John Bacher, George Grace, Rudolph Henny, Ted Hansen, Harold Clarke, George Clark, Kraxberger, C. I. Sersanous and on. Maybe there is something of their immortality contained in the rhododendron, even as suggested by the moving history of Barto and his work, his gift to our gardens. It is vague, not well identified with any individual, but nevertheless sensed in a way.

The history of so viable an entity as the Rhododendron Species Foundation is never done. Time moves on, new people become involved, change is to be expected. Inevitably in a few years this history will need to be extended. Hopefully someone new will review these efforts and find in them a place to begin once more.

Benmore Castle

Heather Garden, Royal Botanic Gardens   Entrance to Rowallane

View from Terrace, Leonardslee   Rock Garden, Wisley

All photos by Jock Brydon

Some of the British gardens that are the source of many of the plants in the Species Foundation collection.

R. *macabeanum* - 77/531

R. *falconeri* - 74/006

R. *fulvum* - 77/313

R. *fictolacteum* - 77/418

All photos by F. C. Rutherford

(Note: Numbers following names are RSF accession numbers.)

R. *rothschildii*

R. *uvarifolium* - 73/291
Photo Chip Muller

R. *hodgsonii* - 65/330
Photo Rollo Adams

R. *hodgsonii* - 65/330
Photo Rollo Adams

R. *luteiflorum* - 64/103

Photo Art Dome

R. *lacteum* - 75/242

Photo Art Dome

R. *lutescens* - 74/79

Photo by Minch

R. *litiense* - 75/015

Photo Art Dome

R. *catawbiense*
Red Gable Raustien - 77/620

R. *macrophyllum* - 76/365

R. *catawbiense* "Catalga" - 75/134

R. *catawbiense* "Catalga" - 75/134

All photos by Art Dome

R. *strigillosum* - 77/233
Photo Art Dome

R. *strigillosum*

R. *strigillosum* - 75/178
Photo Chip Muller

R. *ramsdenianum* - 65/487
Photo Art Dome

R. *zoelleri* - 83/061

R. *javanicum* - 78/089

R. *xanthostephanum* - 66/667

All photos by Art Dome

R. *muchronulatum* "Cornell Pink" - 73/193

Photo Art Dome

R. *cuneatum* - 65/497

Photo Art Dome

R. *macrosepalum* 'linearifolium' - 65/447

Photo F. C. Rutherford

R. *reticulatum* - 77/040

Photo Art Dome

R. *davidsonianum* - 64/129

Photo F. C. Rutherford

R. *neriiflorum* - 76/107

R. *neriiflorum* "Rose Vallon" - 75/149

R. *campylogynum*, "Bodnant Red" -
74/061

R. *forrestii v. tumescens* - 70/175

All photos by Art Dome

R. *fulgens* - 75/065 *Photo Rollo Adams*

R. *cerasinum* - 75/043
Photo Art Dome

R. *cerasinum* "Cherry Brandy" - 83/014
Photo Art Dome

R. *yakushimanum* - 75-260
Photo Art Dome

R. *makinoi* - 74/131
Photo Rollo Adams

R. *yakushimanum*, Exbury form - 75/260
Photo Art Dome

R. *metternichii* - 65/281
Photos Rollo Adams

R. *camtschaticum* - 77/080   *Photo F. C. Rutherford*   R. *camtschaticum* - 77/080   *Photo Art Dome*

R. *ripense* in the wild   *Photo by Jock Brydon*

R. *charitopes*

R. *spinuliferum* - 69/834

Photo Art Dome

R. *japonicum* - 77/035

R. *flammeum (speciosum)* 75/030
Photo F. C. Rutherford

R. *vaseyi* foliage - 78/14
Photo F. C. Rutherford

R. *bakeri* - 77/03
Photo Art Dome

R. *wiltonii* - 75/017 *Photo F.C.Rutherford*

R. *bureavii* - 80/030 *Photo Art Dome*

R. *virgatum* - 65/404   *Photo Art Dome*

R. *smirnowii* - 77/319   *Photo Art Dome*

R. *orbiculare* - 66/542 *Photo Robert Schwab*

R. *keleticum* - 37/156   *Photo Art Dome*

R. *irroratum* "Polka Dot" - 73/145   *Photo Art Dome*

R. *irroratum* "Spatter Paint" - 64/222   *Photo Art Dome*

R. *xanthocodon* - 73/305 *Photo F. C. Rutherford*

R. *wightii* - 73/300 *Photo F. C. Rutherford*

R. *arboreum v. arboreum* - 64/118

R. *arboreum* "cinnamomeum" - 64/188
Photo Art Dome

R. *sutchuenense* v. "Garaldii" - 77/206
Photo Diane Cornish

207

R. *rude* - 65/275 *Photo F. C. Rutherford*

R. *barbatum* - 65/304 *Photo Diane Cornish*

R. *griersonianum* - 78/054
Photo Art Dome

R. *thomsonii* - 64/58
Photo Art Dome

R. *strigillosum* - 73/271 *Photo Art Dome*

R. *tephropeplum* - 65/257 *Photo Art Dome*

APPENDIX A

SPECIES LOCATION LIST

OR

SPECIES ACQUISITION LIST

Abbreviations:
R.B.G. = Royal Botanic Garden
C.H.P. = Carl H. Phetteplace
M.V.W. = Milton V. Walker
W.W. = Wales Wood

SPECIES LOCATION LIST

Species	Gardens
aberconwayii	Windsor, R.B.G., Brodick, Henny
achroanthum	Crarae, Wisley?, RBG? (purity uncertain)
adenogynum	R.B.G., Corsock, Windsor, Glendoick
adenophorum	Windsor, R.B.G., Corsock, Crarae
adenopodum	Windsor, R.B.G.?
aganniphum	R.B.G., Windsor
agastum	Glendoick, Windsor
agglutinatum	Windsor
albertsenianum	Windsor
albiflorum	Windsor
albrechtii	Trengwainton, Trewithen, Rowallane, Windsor, Bodnant
alutaceum	R.B.G., W.W.
amagianum	Windsor, Sunningdale
ambiguum	R.B.G., Windsor, Glendoick, Borde Hill, Sunningdale
amesiae	R.B.G., Windsor
annae	Windsor
anthopogon	Glendoick, R.B.G., Windsor
anthosphaerum	Leonardslee, R.B.G., Windsor, Benmore
anwheinse	Windsor, Exbury, Glendoick, Stronachullin
aperantum	Windsor, Bodnant, R.B.G., Crarae
araiophyllum	Windsor, Benmore, Eckford
arboreum	
Blood red	Exbury, Logan, Stronachullin, Brodick, Grace
White	Lochinch, Caerhays, Leonardslee
arboreum, Pink	Leonardslee, Lochinch, Glenarn, Windsor
ss. cinnamomeum	Eckford, Rowallane, Stonefield
ss. nilagiricum	
argyrophyllum	Windsor, Sunningdale, R.B.G., Hillier, Corsock
var. cupulare	R.B.G.
var. nankingense	Windsor, R.B.G.
arizelum	Windsor, R.B.G., Trewithen, Brodick, Logan
augustinii	Windsor, Sunningdale,
Exbury #1	?
Exbury #2	?
Azureum	Cole
Barto Blue	M. V. W.

Blue Cloud	M.V.W., Bovee
Caprice	M.V.W.
chasmanthum, FCC	Sunningdale
Electra	M.V.W., Brandt
Magor	M.V.W.
Marine	M.V.W.
Peter Kerr	Lancaster
Royal Purple	M.V.W.
Royston Blue	Royston
Rubrum	R.B.G., Windsor
Towercourt	M.V.W.
Unknown variety	Windsor, Sunningdale
auriculatum	Benmore, Caerhays, Windsor, Bodnant, R.B.G.
auritum	Leonardslee, Windsor, Lochinch, Exbury
baileyi	Glendoick, Glenarn, Windsor, R.B.G.
bainbridgeanum	Windsor, R.B.G.
balfourianum	Windsor, R.B.G.
barbatum	Crarae, Windsor, R.B.G., Borde Hill
basilicum	Corsock, R.B.G., Windsor, Borde Hill, Exbury
bathyphyllum	Windsor
bauhiniiflorum	R.B.G., Windsor
beanianum	Windsor, South Lodge, Stronahullin, Hillier
var. compactum	Tigh-an-rudha
Scarlet	Hillier
beesianum	Glenarn, Stronachullin, South Lodge, R.B.G.
brachyanthum	R.B.G., Windsor, Glendoick
brachycarpum	Windsor, R.B.G.
brachysiphon	Stronachullin
bracteatum	Windsor, R.B.G.
brevistylum	Windsor
bullatum (edgeworthii)	Brodick, Bodnant, Logan
bureavii	R.B.G., Windsor, Exbury, Carehays
burmanicum	Brodick, Glenarn, Glendoick, Windsor
caesium	Windsor
callimorphum	R.B.G., Windsor, Sandling Park, Glendoick
calophytum	South Lodge, R.B.G., Caerhays, Exbury, Logan, Phetteplace
calostrotum	Windsor, R.B.G., Wisley
caloxanthum	Exbury, R.B.G., Windsor, Rowallane, Benmore, Hillier
camelliaeflorum	Brodick, Glenarn
campanulatum	Exbury, Glendoick
Cooper #5768	R.B.G.
auriginosum	C.H.P., M.V.W.
campanulatum, Knaphill	Greig, Windsor
chocolate ind.	Stonefield
campylocarpum	Royston, Eckford, Exbury, Windsor, R.B.G.
campylogynum	Glendoick, Windsor, R.B.G., Beneden
var. charopoeum	Bodnant
camtschaticum	Glendoick, R.B.G., Windsor, Wisley
canadense	Windsor
capitatum	R.B.G., Windsor
carneum	R.B.G., Kew, Windsor, Brodick

carolinianum	Windsor
catacosmum	R.B.G., Windsor, Wakehurst
catawbiense	Windsor
caucasicum	Glendoick, Windsor
cephalanthum	R.B.G., Windsor, Brodick
cerasinum	Beneden, Benmore
chaetomallum	Windsor, R.B.G., Exbury
chamae-thomsonii	R.B.G., Glendoick, Windsor, Exbury
chameunum	Windsor, Glendoick
chapmanii	Windsor
charitopes	Windsor
chloranthum	Borde Hill, Windsor
chlorops	Lochinch, Lancaster, Smith
chrysanthum	Windsor, R.B.G., Royston, Glendoick
chryseum	R.B.G., Windsor, Glendoick
chrysodoron	Windsor, Bodnant
chrysolepis	Bodnant
ciliatum	Windsor, Brodick
ciliicalyx	R.B.G., Windsor, Kew, Brodick
cinnabarinum	R.B.G., Glendoick, Leonardslee
blandfordiaeflorum	Corsock
var. roylei	Windsor, McDonald
var. purpurellum	Benenden
var. aestivale	Leonardslee
var. pallidum	Leonardslee
Magnificum	Glendoick, R.B.G., Corsock
citriniflorum	R.B.G., Windsor
clementinae	Windsor, Glendoick, Leonardslee, R.B.G.
coelicum	R.B.G., Windsor
collettianum	Windsor
compactum	Windsor, Wisley
complexum	R.B.G., Windsor, Glendoick
concatenans	R.B.G., Windsor, Beneden, Caerhays ?
concinnoides	Windsor
concinnum	Windsor, R.B.G., Glendoick
v. benthamianum	Windsor, R.B.G., Glendoick
v. pseudoyanthinum	Windsor, Wisley, Tremeer, James
cookeianum	R.B.G.
coriaceum	Crarae, Benmore, R.B.G., Windsor, Borde Hill
coryanum	R.B.G., Windsor
coryphaeum	R.B.G., Exbury
cowanianum	R.B.G., Glendoick, Hillier, Windsor
crassum	R.B.G, Lochinch, Windsor, Eckford, Logan, W.W.
crinigerum	Eckford, Windsor, Exbury, R.B.G., Brodick, Lochinch
v. euadenium	Borde Hill
cubittii	Windsor, R.B.G., Kew, Brodick
cuffeanum	Stronachullin
cuneatum	Windsor, R.B.G., Glendoick
cyanocarpum	R.B.G., Windsor, Leonardslee
dalhousiae	R.B.G., Windsor, Brodick
dasycladum	R.B.G., Windsor
dasypetalum	R.B.G., Windsor, Glendoick

dauricum	Windsor, Glendoick
davidii	Windsor (maybe)
davidsonianum	Caerhays, Exbury, Windsor, Glendoick, Henny, M.V.W.
decorum	R.B.G., Glendoick, Windsor
degronianum	R.B.G., Stronachullin, Windsor
delavayi	Eckford, Brodick, Lochinch, Brodick
dendricola	Windsor
desquamatum	Exbury, Wakehurst, Windsor, Borde Hill
detonsum	Crarae, R.B.G., Windsor
diacritum	Glendoick
diaprepes	Eckford, Exbury, Windsor, R.B.G.
dichroanthum	Exbury, Windsor, R.B.G.
ss. apodectum	Brodick, R.B.G., Exbury
ss. herpesticum	Windsor
ss. scyphocalyx	Windsor, Crarae, Borde Hill
ss. septentrionale	Windsor, R.B.G.
dictyotum	Windsor, Bodnant, Exbury
dimitrum	Windsor
diphrocalyx	R.B.G., Windsor
discolor	Windsor
doshongense	Windsor, R.B.G.
drumonium	Windsor ?
dryophyllum	Windsor, R.B.G., Exbury
dumicola	Windsor
dumosulum	Windsor
eclecteum	Benmore, Borde Hill, Windsor, Exbury, Rowallane
edgarianum	R.B.G., Windsor
edgeworthii	R.B.G., Lochinch, Windsor, Leonardslee, Logan, Brodick
elliottii	R.B.G., Rowallane, Exbury, James
eriogynum	R.B.G., Windsor, Wakehurst, Exbury, Trengwainton, Bodnant
eritimum	Windsor, Glendoick,
v. heptamerum	Sandling Park
erosum	Windsor, Stronachullin
erubescens	Benmore, Windsor, Hillier, R.B.G., Brandt
erythrocalyx	Glenarn, Windsor
euchaites	(see neriiflorum)
eudoxum	Glendoick, Crarae, Windsor
ss. brunneifolium	Windsor
eurysiphon	Windsor, R.B.G.
exasperatum	Windsor, Hillier, Logan, Stronachullin
eximium	Trewithen, Windsor, Glendoick, Stonefield
faberi	Windsor ?, Hillier ?
facetum	Penjerrick, R.B.G., Windsor
falconeri	Glenarn, Brodick, Caerhays, Benmore, Stonefield, Lochinch, Lamellen
fargesii	Glendoick, Crarae, R.B.G., Corsock, Windsor
fastigiatum	Glernarn, Windsor, R.B.G., Glendoick
fauriei	R.B.G., Windsor
ferrugineum	R.B.G., Windsor, Glendoick
fictolacteum	Windsor, Crarae, R.B.G., Lochinch, Wakehurst

fimbriatum	Windsor, R.B.G., Glendoick
flavidum	Windsor, R.B.G., Hillier
flavorufum	Windsor, R.B.G.
fletcherianum	R.B.G., Glendoick, Brodick
floccigerum	Windsor, R.B.G.
floribundum	Exbury, Windsor, Borde Hill
formosum	R.B.G., Windsor, Brodick
forrestii	R.B.G., Windsor, Tremeer, C.H.P.,
v. repens	Smith
fortunei	Windsor, McDonald
fragariflorum	Windsor
fulgens	R.B.G., Windsor, Lochinch, Sandling Park
fulvastrum	Windsor ?
fulvum	Crarae, R.B.G., Windsor, Leonardslee, Sunningdale, Stronachullin. Corsock
fumidum	Glendoick, Hillier ?
galactinum	R.B.G., Windsor
genesterianum	Windsor, R.B.G., Royston
giganteum	Brodick, Logan
glaucopeplum	Windsor ?
glaucophyllum	Windsor, Corsock
v. tubiforme	R.B.G., Rowallane, Glendoick, W.W., Corsock
v. luteiflorum	R.B.G., Brodick, Logan, Benmore
glischroides	Benmore, Eckford, Windsor, Borde Hill, Wakehurst
glischrum	Borde Hill, Windsor, Stronachullin, Benmore
glischrum, v. adenosum	R.B.G.
globigerum	Windsor, W.W.
glomerulatum	R.B.G., Glendoick, Windsor
grande	Logan, Brodick, Caerhays
griersonianum	R.B.G., Windsor, Penjerrick, Trengwainton, Windsor, Logan
gymnocarpum	Exbury, Windsor , Henny, Stronachullin
habrotrichum	R.B.G., Windsor, Leonardslee, Benmore
haematodes	Windsor, R.B.G., Tremeer, Exbury, Glenarn
hanceanum	R.B.G., Rowallane, Exbury, Windsor, Glendoick
hardingii	R.B.G., Windsor
heliolepis	R.B.G., Windsor
hemidartum	Benmore, Tigh-an-rudha, Windsor
hemitrichotum	Benmore, Windsor
hemsleyanum	R.B.G.
hippophaeoides	R.B.G., Windsor, Sunningdale
hirsutum	R.B.G., Glendoick, Windsor
hirtipes	R.B.G., Windsor,
hodgsonii	R.B.G., Windsor, Benmore, Corsock, Stonefield, Logan
hookeri	Benmore, Borde Hill, Penjerrick
hormophorum	R.B.G., Windsor
houlstonii	Caerhays, Windsor
hunnewellianum	R.B.G., Wisley, Windsor, Hillier
hylaeum	R.B.G., Windsor
hypenanthum	R.B.G., Glendoick, Corsock
hyperythrum	Windsor, Exbury, Benenden, Rowallane, R.B.G.
hypoglaucum	Windsor ?, Wakehurst

hypophaeum	Windsor
idoneum	R.B.G., Windsor, Wisley, Glendoick
impeditum	R.B.G., Windsor, Towercourt
imperator	Wakehurst, Windsor, R.B.G., Glendoick
inaequale	Windsor, Kew, Trengwainton, Brodick, Glendoick
inopinum	R.B.G., Windsor
insigne	R.B.G., Glendoick, Windsor, Brodick
intricatum	R.B.G., Windsor
iodes	R.B.G., Windsor
irroratum	South Lodge, Exbury, Windsor, Lamellen, Wakehurst, Smith ?
iteophyllum	R.B.G., Windsor, Brodick
johnstoneanum	Windsor, R.B.G., Leonardslee, Trengwainton, Brodick
jucundum	Windsor
keiskei	Windsor, R.B.G., Leonardslee, Exbury
keleticum	R.B.G., Windsor, Glendoick
keysii	Exbury, R.B.G., Caerhays, Windsor
kongboense	Glendoick, R.B.G., Windsor, Bodnant
kotschyi	Windsor, R.B.G.
kyawi	Eckford, Windsor, Exbury
lacteum	Corsocsk, Windsor
F #6778	R.B.G.
lanatum	R.B.G., Dunleith, Windsor, Hillier, Bodnant
lanigerum	Windsor, Trengwainton, R.B.G., Stonehurst, Smith, Logan, Lamellin, Stronachullin
laudandum	R.B.G.
laxiflorum	Windsor, Exbury
lepidostylum	R.B.G., Windsor, Brodick
lepidotum	R.B.G., Windsor, Glendoick
leptothrium	Caerhays, Windsor, R.B.G.
leucaspis	R.B.G., Windsor, Exbury, Crarae
lindleyi	R.B.G., Glenarn, Tremeer, Brodick
linearifolium	R.B.G., Windsor, Glendoick, Leonardslee
litangense	R.B.G., Windsor, Glendoick ?
litiense	Windsor
lochae	Windsor, Kew
lochmium	R.B.G., Windsor
longesquamatum	Lamellen, Windsor, R.B.G., Dawyck
longistylum	Windsor
lophogynum	Glenarn, Stronachullin, Windsor
lowndesii	Glendoick, Windsor, Hillier
ludlowii	Glendoick, Windsor, Hillier
lukiangense	Windsor, R.B.G.
lutescens	Tremeer, Windsor, Exbury, Leonardslee
lysolepis	Windsor, R.B.G., Glendoick
lyi	Lamellen
macabeanum	Windsor, Trewithen, Trengwainton, Exbury, Lamellen, Glenarn
KW#7724	R.B.G.
maculiferum	Windsor, Stronachullin, Brandt
maddenii	R.B.G., Windsor, Kew, Caerhays, Brodick
magnificum	Brodick, Logan

makinoi	Windsor, R.B.G.
mallotum	Logan, Windsor, Borde Hill,
Farrer #815	R.B.G.
manipurense	Leonardslee, Windsor, R.G.B., Brodick
mariesii	Windsor
martinianum	R.B.G., Windsor
meddianum	Eckford, Borde Hill, Windsor
megacalyx	R.B.G., Windsor, Stonefield, Brodick
megeratum	Windsor, R.B.G., Rowallane, Bodnant
melinanthum	Windsor, R.B.G.
metternichii	Borde Hill, Windsor, R.B.G., Hillier, Stronachullin
micranthum	Windsor, Glendoick, R.B.G.
microgynum	Windsor, Exbury
microleucum	Glendoick, Windsor, Exbury, R.B.G.,Wisley, Sunningdale
micromeres	Windsor, Bodnant, Glendoick
mimetes	Windsor, R.B.G.
minus	Windsor
mishmiense	Windsor
molle	Windsor
mollicomum	R.B.G., Glendoick, Windsor
mollyanum	Benmore, Brodick, Windsor, Stronachullin
monosematum	Dawyck, Windsor, Hillier, Brandt
morii	Benmore, Benenden, Windsor, Lamellin, Bodnant
moupinense	Caerhays, Rowallane, R.B.G., Windsor
mucronatum	Windsor
mucronulatum	Windsor
myiagrum	R.B.G., Windsor
nakaharai	Glendoick, R.B.G.
nankotaisanense	Wakehurst
neriiflorum	Windsor, Royston
ss. euchaites	Windsor, Crarae
ss. phaedropum	Windsor, Stonehurst, Stronachullin
neriiflorum, ss phoenicodum	Exbury, Glendoick, Eckford, R.B.G., Windsor
nigropunctatum	R.B.G., Windsor
nipponicum	Crarae, Windsor, R.B.G., Hillier
nitens	R.B.G., Windsor
nivale	R.B.G.
niveum	Crarae, Exbury, Wakehurst, Windsor, Stonefield
nuttallii	R.B.G., Windsor
odoriferum	Windsor, R.B.G., Brodick
oldhami	R.B.G., Windsor
oporinum	Windsor, R.B.G.
orbiculare	R.B.G., Caerhays, Glendoick, Dawyck, Robbins, Sandling Park
oreodoxa	Exbury, Windsor, Borde Hill
oreotrephes	Crarae, R.B.G., Leonardslee, Sandling Park, Windsor, Glendoick, Smith
orthocladum	R.B.G., Windsor
ovatum	R.B.G., Windsor
pachytrichum	R.B.G., Benmore, Windsor, Bodnant

paludosum	R.B.G., Glendoick, Windsor, Wisley
pankimense	Crarae, Windsor
panteumorphum	R.B.G.
paradoxum	Windsor, Hillier
parishii	Windsor
parmulatum	South Lodge, Glendoick, Tremeer, Benmore
parryae	R.B.G., Windsor, Brodick
parvifolium	R.B.G., Wisley
patulum	R.B.G., Glendoick
pemakoense	Windsor, R.B.G.
pendulum	R.B.G., Glendoick, Windsor
pentaphyllum	R.B.G., Hillier, Windsor
peramabile	Windsor, Wisley
peregrinum	Lamellen, Stronachullin, Windsor
phaeochrysum	Corsock, R.B.G., Glendoick, Lochinch, Windsor, Sandling Park
pholidotum	R.B.G.
planetum	Exbury, Windsor
pocophorum	Eckford, Windsor, R.B.G.
polifolium	Windsor, Wisley
polyandrum	R.B.G., Penjerrick, Windsor, Leonardslee, Logan, C.H.P.
polylepis	Windsor, R.B.G.
praestans	R.B.G., Windsor
praevernum	Windsor
prattii	Lamellen, R.B.G., Corsock, Windsor, Brandt, Sandling Park
preptum	Windsor, Tigh-an-rudha, Lamellen
primulaeflorum	Windsor
pronum	R.B.G., Windsor
prostratum	Glendoick, Windsor
proteoides	Windsor, Hillier, R.B.G., Royston
protistum	R.B.G., Windsor, Benmore
przewalski	R.B.G., Windsor
pseudochrysanthum	Windsor, Rowallane, R.B.G., Exbury, Leonardslee, Sunningdale
puderosum	Windsor, Brodick
pumilum	Windsor, R.B.G., Glendoick, Stronachullin
puralbum	R.B.G., Windsor
quinquefolium	R.B.G., Exbury, Windsor, Leonardslee
racemosum	R.B.G., Glendoick, Crarae,Windsor
radicans	R.B.G., Glendoick, Windsor
ramosissimum	Windsor, Wisley
ramsdenianum	Crarae, Glenarn, Lamellin
recurvoides	R.B.G., Windsor, Corsock ?
reticulatum	R.B.G., Windsor, Bodnant
rex	Windsor, Tremeer, R.B.G., Bodnant
rhabdotum	R.B.G., Windsor, Brodick
rigidum	Exbury, Windsor, Glendoick, R.B.G.
ririei	Benmore, Windsor, Leonardslee, Caerhays, Tremeer
roxianum	Windsor, Corsock, Nelson, Lochinch, Stronachullin
v. oreonastes	R.B.G., Glendoick
rubiginosum	Windsor, R.B.G., Stonefield, Crarae

rubrolineatum	Benmore, Windsor, R.B.G.
rude	Tigh-an-rudha, Glenarn, Exbury, R.B.G.
rufum	Windsor
rupicola	R.B.G., Windsor, Glendoick, Wisley
russatum	R.B.G., Stronachullin, Rowallane, Windsor, Wakehurst
russotinctum	Windsor, Glendoick, Dawyck, R.B.G.
saluenense	Exbury, Windsor, R.B.G., Royston
sanguineum	Windsor, Glendoick, Benmore, R.B.G.
ss. atrorubrum	
ss. cloiophorum	Windsor
ss. consanguineum	Windsor
ss. didymum	Windsor, R.B.G., M.V.W.
ss. haemaleum	Stronachullin, Bodnant, R.B.G., Crarae
ss. mesaeum	Windsor
ss. roseotinctum	Windsor
ss. sanguinoides	
sargentianum	R.B.G., Glendoick, Windsor
scabrifolium	Windsor, R.B.G.
schizopeplum	R.B.G., Windsor
schlippenbachii	Hillier, Leonardslee, Tremeer, Bodnant
scintillans	R.B.G., Exbury, Windsor, Glendoick, Wisley (FCC)
scopulorum	Windsor, Kew
scottianum	R.B.G., Brodick
scyphocalyx	see dichroanthum
searsiae	Windsor, Dawyck, R.B.G.
seinghkuense	R.B.G., Windsor
selense	Glenarn, Windsor, R.B.G.
semibarbatum	Windsor, Glendoick
semnoides	Windsor, R.B.G.
serotinum	R.B.G., Windsor
serpylifolium	Benenden, Leonardslee, Windsor, R.B.G.
setiferum	Windsor
setosum	Glendoick?
shepherdii	Glenarn, Windsor, R.B.G.
sherriffii	R.B.G., Windsor (L & S 2751)
shweliense	R.B.G., Windsor, Glendoick
sidereum	Brodick, Wakehurst, Pack-Beresford, Logan, Stonefield
siderophyllum	Kew
sinogrande	Exbury, Logan, Caerhays, Brodick, Lochinch, Eckford
sinonuttallii	R.B.G., Windsor, Brodick
smirnowii	R.B.G., Windsor, Glendoick, Corsock
smithii	Windsor, Glendoick, Stronachullin, R.B.G.
souliei	Windsor, Sandling Park, R.B.G.
sperabile	Crarae, Windsor, R.B.G., Smith
v. weihsiense	Eckford, R.B.G., Glenarn, Windsor
v. chimiliense	Windsor
sparabiloides	Windsor
sphaeroblastum	Windsor, Benmore, R.B.G., Corsock, Glendoick
spiciferum	Windsor, Brodick, R.B.G., Leonardslee

spilanthum	R.B.G.
spilotum	R.B.G.
spinuliferum	Exbury, Windsor, R.B.G.
stamineum	Windsor
stenaulum	Caerhays, Windsor, Kew
stewartianum	Windsor, R.B.G., Eckford, Benmore
v. aiolosalpinx	Corsock
stictophyllum	R.B.G., Windsor, Wisley
strigillosum	Benmore, Borde Hill, Glenarn, Leonardslee, R.B.G., Lamellen
sulfureum	Caerhays, Lochinch, Windsor, Exbury, Borde Hill
supranubium	Brodick, Windsor, R.B.G., Kew, Logan, Crarae
sutchuenense	South Lodge, Benmore, R.B.G., Corsock, Caerhays, Borde Hill
taggianum	Windsor, Brodick, R.B.G.
taliense	Benmore, R.B.G., Windsor
tanastylum	Stronachullin, Windsor
tapetiforme	Wisley, Windsor, R.B.G.
tatsienense	R.B.G., Glendoick
telmateium	R.B.G., Windsor, Wisley
telopeum	Exbury, Windsor
temenium	R.B.G., Windsor
v. chrysanthemum	Stronachullin
tephropeplum	Eckford, R.B.G., Windsor, Stronachullin, Exbury
v. doliense	Smith
thayerianum	Caerhays, R.B.G., Brandt
thomsonii	R.B.G., Brodick, Stronachullin, Leonardslee, Windsor, C.H.P., Corsock
v. pallidum	Glenarn, Lochinch
thymifolium	Windsor, Wisley
traillianum	Corsock, Windsor, Eckford, R.B.G.
trichanthum	R.B.G., Glendoick, Windsor, Sunningdale
trichocladum	Benmore, R.B.G., Windsor, Bodnant
trichostomum	R.B.G., Exbury, Windsor, Glendoick
triflorum	R.B.G., Lamellen, Brodick, Windsor, Benmore
triplonaevium	Windsor, R.B.G.
tritifolium	Windsor
tsangpoense	R.B.G., Glendoick, Windsor
tsariense	R.B.G., Windsor, Tremeer, Hillier, Glendoick
ungernii	Glendoick, Windsor, R.B.G.
uniflorum	Windsor
uvarifolium	R.B.G., Windsor, South Lodge, Leonardslee, Smith
vaccinoides	R.B.G., Glendoick
valentinianum	R.B.G., Windsor, Hillier, Royston, Bodnant, R.T.G.
vaseyi	R.B.G., Windsor
veitchianum	R.B.G., Kew, Windsor
vellereum	Windsor, Borde Hill, Glendoick, R.B.G., Wisley
venator	R.B.G. (KW 6285), Windsor
vernicosum	Glendoick, Windsor, R.B.G., Bodnant
verruculosum	Windsor, Wisley, Glendoick, R.B.G.
vesiculiferum	Windsor, Hillier, R.B.G.

vilmorinianum	R.B.G.
violaceum	Windsor, Wisley
virgatum	R.B.G., Pack-Beresford, Windsor, Crarae
viridescens	R.B.G., Windsor
wallichii	Caerhays, Windsor, Tremeer, R.B.G.
wardii	Windsor, Glendoick, R.B.G., Glenarn, Benenden, Benmore
wasonii	Sunningdale, R.B.G., Windsor, Exbury, Glendoick, Bodnant, Stronachullin
watsonii	Windsor, R.B.G.
websterianum	Wisley
weldianum	R.B.G., Dawyck
weyrichii	Windsor, R.B.G.
wightii	R.B.G., Dawyck, Borde Hill, Windsor, Smith
williamsianum	R.B.G., Exbury, Windsor
wilsonae	Wakehurst, Windsor
wiltonii	R.B.G., Windsor, Exbury
xanthocodon	R.B.G., Windsor, Exbury, Bodnant
xanthostephanum	Lochinch, R.B.G. ?, Windsor, Benmore
yakushimanum	Wisley, Exbury, Windsor, Smith
yedoense	Benenden
v. poukhanense	R.B.G., Glendoick, Windsor
yungningense	Windsor, Wisley, R.B.G.
yunnanense	R.B.G., Glendoick, R.T.G.
zaleucum	Crarare, R.B.G., Glendoick, Pack-Beresford, Glenarn
zeylanicum	R.B.G., Benmore, Caerhays

APPENDIX   B

KEY:

V = SPECIES LOCATED AT THE UNIVERSITY OF BRITISH COLUMBIA , VANCOUVER, IN 1966.

W = SPECIES RECEIVED BY THE WALKER GARDEN, PLEASANT HILL, OREGON, FROM THE UNIVERSITY OF BRITISH COLUMBIA IN 1968.

X = SPECIES IN THE GARDEN AT JOCK BRYDON'S, SALEM, OREGON, IN 1971.

Y = SPECIES RECEIVED BY THE GARDEN AT FEDERAL WAY, WASHINGTON, FROM JOCK BRYDON IN 1974.

Z = SPECIES REPRESENTED IN THE GARDEN AT FEDERAL WAY AS OF JANUARY 1, 1994.

ABBREVIATIONS:

AC&H = Apold, Cox & Hutchinson
C&H = Cox & Hutchinson
ex Hort = Source unknown
K-W = Kingdon - Ward
L&S = Ludlow & Sherriff
LS&E = Ludlow, Sherriff & Elliot
LS&H = Ludlow, Sherriff & Hicks
LS&T = Ludlow, Sherriff &Taylor
MVW = Milton V. Walker

PSW = Polunin, Sykes & Williams
RBG = Royal Botanic Garden
SM = Smith /Mossman collection
ss. or ssp. = sub-species
SBEC = Sino-British Expedition
UBC = University of British Columbia
USDA = United States Department of Agriculture
USNA = United States National Arboretum
v. or var. = variety
W Wash Ex = Western Washington Extension Service
W Wash Re = Western Washington Research Center

Plants	Form	RSF #	Source	V	W	X	Y	Z
aberconwayii		64.204	Walker, J Henny	x	1	x	3	x
aberconwayii	'His Lordship',	64.015	Windsor, Aberconway		1	x	7	x
aberconwayii	Exbury	73.001	F Robbins, Brydon				1	x
aberconwayii		74.054	Hoitink				1	x
aberconwayii		75.287	Castle Howard					x
aberconwayii		76.334	Grieg, Phetteplace					x
aberconwayii		77.059	Granston, C. Smith					x
aberconwayii		77.536	Ex Hort					x
aberconwayii		78.015	McGuire					x
aberconwayii		92.102	Warren Berg					x
aberconwayii		92.105	C. Smith, Warren Berg					x
acuminatum		79.024						x
adenogynum		73.336					2	
adenogynum		71.619	Ex Hort					x
adenogynum		71.679	Corsock, UBC					x
adenogynum		73.002	Ex Hort					x
adenogynum		75.248	Doleshy, Berg					x
adenogynum		76.113	Delp					x
adenogynum	Forrest 21409	76.259	Windsor					x
adenogynum		76.359	Berg, Fruit Valley					x
adenogynum		92.064	Warren Berg					x
adenogynum		92.085	Berg					x
adenogynum		93.055	7 Firs Nursery, W. Berg					x
adenopodum		73.003	F Robbins, Brydon				1	x
adenopodum		76.001	Caperci					x
adenopodum		76.142	Windsor					x
adenopodum		77.352	Goheen					x
adenopodum		77.353	Ex Hort					x
adenopodum		78.004	Nelson, B. Smith					x
adenosum		75.325						x
adenosum	Rock 18228	76.138	Royal Botanic Garden					x
adenosum		76.187	Royal Botanic Garden					x
adenosum		76.211	Royal Botanic Garden					x
adenosum		77.031	Granston					x
afghanicum	Wendelbo 9706	80.083	Royal Botanic Garden					x
aganniphum	v. flavorufum	70.407	Royal Botanic Garden				1	x
aganniphum	v. flavorufum	75.097	Ex Hort					x
aganniphum	v. aganniphum	76.270	Windsor					x
aganniphum	v. aganniphum	77.771	Windsor					x
aganniphum	v. aganniphum, KW 5863	92.014	Leonardslee					x
agastum		70.181	Lamellen				1	x
alabamense	USNA 13217	76.272	USNA, Magor					x
alabamense		77.024	Granston					x
alabamense	'Fountain'	92-003	John Thornton					x
alabamense		93.001	Woodlanders, Inc					x

222

Plants	Form	RSF #	Source	V	W	X	Y	Z
albertsenianum	Forrest 14195	70.112	UBC					x
albertsenianum	Forrest 14195	75.093	Windsor					x
albiflorum		77.254	Western Wash. Ex.					x
albrechtii		69.980	Smith			x	1	
albrechtii		77.042	Granston					x
albrechtii		77.043	Granston					x
albrechtii		77.309	Baird					x
alutaceum		64.056	Wales Wood			x		
alutaceum	v. iodes	70.068	Phetteplace					x
alutaceum	v. iodes	75.199	C. Smith					x
alutaceum	v. iodes	75.321	Benmore					x
alutaceum	v. iodes, Rock	76.388	Phetteplace					x
alutaceum	v. iodes, Forrest	79.111	Borde Hill					x
alutaceum	v. alutaceum	76.202	Royal Botanic Garden					x
alutaceum	v. alutaceum	76.261	Ex Hort					x
alutaceum	v. alutaceum, F. 25738	77.656	Windsor					x
alutaceum	v. alutaceum	77.726	Royal Botanic Garden					x
alutaceum	v. alutaceum	78.074	Royal Botanic Garden					x
alutaceum	v. alutaceum	79.183	UBC					x
amagianum		73.356	Ex Hort				2	x
amagianum		75.023	Hillier					x
amagianum		77.016	Granston					x
amagianum		77.568	W. Wood					x
amagianum		80.029	Madison					x
ambiguum		00.412	Borde Hill	x	1	x		
ambiguum		73.343	Ex Hort				1	x
ambiguum		76.378	Brodick, UBC					x
ambiguum		77.099	Granston					x
ambiguum	KR 139	82.182	Jorgensen					x
amesiae		81.015	U of Newcastle					x
annae		69.072	Exbury, Walker					x
annae		70.132	Stronachullin					x
annae		73.161	Exbury, F Robbins					x
annae		76.099	Caperci					x
annae		76.143	Windsor					x
annae		79.099	Bremen Rhod.					x
anthopogon	ss anthopogon, L & S 1091	68.588	Glendoick			x	2	x
anthopogon	ss anthopogon	77.682	Brodick					x
anthopogon	ss anthopogon	80.152	UBC, Frisbee					x
anthopogon	ss anthopogon, Hed. 375	82.169	J. Henny					x
anthopogon	ss anthopogon, Hed. 397	82.171	Hedegaard					x
anthopogon	ss hypenanthum	65.492	Corsock	x	1	x	1	x
anthopogon	ss hypenanthum	79.051	Glendoick					x
anthopogon	ss hypenanthum, Cox	83.209	Cox, Gambrill					x
anthopogon		92.104	Warren Berg					x

Plants	Form	RSF #	Source	V	W	X	Y	Z
anthopogon		92.105	Warren Berg					x
anthopogon		92.106	Warren Berg					x
anthopogon		92.110	Warren Berg					x
anthopogon		92.111	Warren Berg					x
anthosphaerum	hylothreptum	64.116	Leonardslee	x	3	x	1	x
anthosphaerum	Forrest 26436	76.132	Royal Botanic Garden					x
anthosphaerum	Rock 11354	77.736	Windsor					x
anthosphaerum	Forrest 25984	77.770	Windsor					x
anwheinse		00.245	Stronachullin	x	13	x	43	
aperantum		73.004					1	
aperantum		75.094	Windsor					x
aperantum		75.332	Portland ARS Gdn.					x
aperantum		76.317	Berry					x
araiophyllum		00.527	Royal Botanic Garden					
araiophyllum		75.060	Wakehurst					x
araiophyllum	Forrest 27698	80.041	Borde Hill					x
arborescens	Skinner 1100A	76.273	USNA					x
arborescens		77.259	Tingle, W.Wash. Ex.					x
arborescens		77.260	Ex Hort					x
arborescens		77.346	Tingle, W.Wash. Ex.					x
arborescens		77.394	Calloway Gdns.					x
arborescens		77.435	Bowman					x
arborescens	Towe, C.	80.012	Towe					x
arboreum	white	66.117	Leonardslee	x	1	x	2	x
arboreum	Best pink	66.118	Leonardslee	x	2		5	
arboreum	Blood red	00.246	Stronachullin	x	2	x	2	
arboreum	AM	00.110	Logan	x				
arboreum	White	00.349	Caerhays	x				
arboreum	cinnamomeum, v roseum	71.406	Lochinch, UBC	x				x
arboreum	delavayi	00.166	Eckford	x	2			
arboreum	delavayi	73.345	Ex. Hort.				2	x
arboreum	ss. cinnamomeum	64.118	Leonardslee			x		
arboreum	ss. cinnamomeum	64.188	Rowallane	x	1		1	x
arboreum	ss. cinnamomeum	70.046	W. Wood			x	7	x
arboreum	ss. arboreum	74.002	Exbury				2	x
arboreum			USDA#358798				43	
arboreum	ss. nilagiricum	84.015	Arduaine					x
arboreum	ss. arboreum	74.132	USDA					x
arboreum	ss. arboreum	76.002	Caperci					x
arboreum	ss. arboreum	76.071	Berg, Cummins					x
arboreum	ss. arboreum	76.145	Windsor					x
arboreum	ss. arboreum	80.109	Hergerst Croft					x
arboreum	ss. arboreum	76.553	Caperci					x
arboreum	ss. arboreum, K-W 21976	79.010	Schick					x
arboreum	ss. arboreum	80.127	Trewithen					x

Plants	Form	RSF #	Source	V	W	X	Y	Z
arboreum	ss. arboreum	86.020	U of Cal Berkley					x
arboreum	ss. cinnamomeum, v roseum	76.159	Bodnant					x
arboreum	ss. cinnamomeum, v roseum	76.372	Trengwainton, Berg					x
arboreum	ss. cinnamomeum, v. cinn.	77.360	W Avery					x
arboreum	ss. cinnamomeum, v. cinn.	80.103	Killerton					x
arboreum	ss. cinnamomeum, v. cinn.	77.125	Caperci					x
arboreum	ss. zeylanicum	76.225	Brodick					x
arboreum	ss. zeylanicum	68.863				x	6	
arboreum	ss. zeylanicum	73.312					1	
arboreum	ss. delavayi, v. delavayi	77.800	Crarae				1	x
arboreum		92.020	Warren Berg					x
arboreum		92.019	Warren Berg					x
arboreum		92.021	Warren Berg					x
arboreum		92.086	Warren Berg					x
arboreum		92.087	Warren Berg					x
arboreum		91.055	Warren Berg					x
arboreum		91.056	Warren Berg					x
arboreum	Sikkim	93.074	June Sinclair					x
argyrophyllum		64.138	Corsock	x		x	7	x
argyrophyllum		00.662	Sunningdale		4			
argyrophyllum	'Chinese Silver'	64.014	Windsor			x	9	x
argyrophyllum		73.007	Caperci				11	x
argyrophyllum		70.354	Kew				1	x
argyrophyllum	var. nankingense	74.019					6	
argyrophyllum	var. nankingense	73.008	Sunningdale					x
argyrophyllum	var. nankingense	75.016	Hillier					x
argyrophyllum	var. nankingense	75.297	Phetteplace					x
argyrophyllum	ss. argyrophyllum	70.354	Kew					x
argyrophyllum	ss. argyrophyllum	73.007	Brydon, W. Wood					x
argyrophyllum	ss. argyrophyllum	76.003	Caperci					x
argyrophyllum	ss. argyrophyllum	76.176	Royal Botanic Garden					x
argyrophyllum	ss. argyrophyllum, Wilson 4276	76.263	Windsor					x
argyrophyllum	ss. argyrophyllum, Wilson 4275	77.654	Windsor					x
argyrophyllum	ss. nankingense	73.008	Sunningdale, Phetteplace					x
argyrophyllum	ss. nankingense	75.016	Hillier, Robbins					x
argyrophyllum	ss. nankingense	75.297	Phetteplace					x
argyrophyllum	ss. hypoglaucum	73.139	W Wood, Frye				5	x
argyrophyllum	ss. hypoglaucum	76.039	Caperci					x
argyrophyllum	ss. hypoglaucum	80.119	Reuthe, Croft					x
argyrophyllum	ss.omeiense, Hu 8189	79.155	Cent. for Urban Hort					x
argyrophyllum	?	93.044	June Sinclair					x
atlanticum	Skinner 10024S	73.010	USNA				1	x
atlanticum		74.023					32	
atlanticum		74.133	P. Hill					x
atlanticum	Skinner 820	76.274	USNA					x

Plants	Form	RSF #	Source	V	W	X	Y	Z
atlanticum	Skinner 550	76.275	USNA					x
atlanticum		77.434	Bowman					x
atlanticum		81.075	Biltmore					x
atropurpureum		85.044	Stanton, Cavendish					x
augustinii	ss. augustinii	63.001	Walker					x
augustinii	ss. augustinii	63.004	Windsor		4	x	5	x
augustinii	ss. augustinii	63.005	Windsor		4	x	45	x
augustinii	azuriensis	00.244	Larson	x	25			
augustinii		63.001	Windsor			x	36	
augustinii	ss. augustinii	64.206	Brandt, Walker	x		x	2	x
augustinii	ss. augustinii	64.057	Barto, Phetteplace	x	23		5	x
augustinii	ss. augustinii	70.055	W Wood					x
augustinii	ss. augustinii	70.314	Fortescue					x
augustinii	ss. augustinii	75.131	Gable					x
augustinii	ss. augustinii	75.194	C. Smith					x
augustinii	ss. augustinii	75.278	Windsor, UBC					x
augustinii	ss. augustinii	75.309	Phetteplace					x
augustinii	ss. augustinii	76.315	Berry					x
augustinii	ss. augustinii	76.207	VanWinkle					x
augustinii	ss. augustinii	77.276	W Wash Ex					x
augustinii	ss. augustinii	77.286	Pierce					x
augustinii	ss. augustinii	77.789	Caperci, Berg					x
augustinii	ss. augustinii	80.043	Borde Hill					x
augustinii	ss. augustinii	77.272	W Wash Ex					x
augustinii	ss. rubrum	76.355	Kehr, Berg					x
augustinii	ss. chasmanthum	69.092	Sunningdale					x
augustinii	ss. hardyi	78.065	Cox, Berg					x
augustinii		70.055	W Wood			x	6	
augustinii		70.025					1	
augustinii	'Fair Skies'	70.062	Phetteplace			x	2	
augustinii	dwarf	69.1156	Walker			x	6	
augustinii	chasmanthum, FCC	64.092	Sunningdale			x	19	
augustinii	chasmanthum, Blue Cloud	00.205	Bovee, Hansen	x	16			
augustinii	Electra	00.206	Brandt		6			
augustinii	Electra	00.233	Smith, Henny	x	1			
augustinii		70.314	Fortescure				1	x
augustinii		92.073	Warren Berg					x
augustinii		92.074	Warren Berg					x
augustinii	Peter Kerr	00.207	Lancaster	x	23			
augustinii		91.075	Warren Berg					x
augustinii		92.073	Warren Berg					x
augustinii		92.074	Warren Berg					x
augustinii		92.075	Warren Berg					x
augustinii		92.076	Warren Berg					x
augustinii		92.077	Warren Berg					x

Plants	Form	RSF #	Source	V	W	X	Y	Z
augustinii		92.078	Warren Berg					x
augustinii		93.041	Warren Berg					x
augustinii		93.042	Warren Berg					x
aureum	v. aureum	76.109	Berg					x
aureum	v. aureum	76.194	Royal Botanic Garden					x
aureum	v. aureum	77.150	Berg					x
aureum	v. aureum	77.648	Ex Hort					x
aureum	v. aureum	82.136	Bremen Rhod.					x
aureum	v. aureum, Wada	82.166	Birck					x
auriculatum		00.528	Eckford	x	1	x	1	
auriculatum	A.M.	67.698	Bodnant		1	x	4	x
auriculatum		76.072	Dunn					x
aurigeranum		78.104	Mossman, Winters					x
aurigeranum	USDA 354292	85.024	USDA					x
auritum		65.269	Lochinch	x	1	x	6	x
auritum		00.629	Leonardslee		1			
auritum		73.017					6	
austrinum	Skinner 96	76.276	USNA					x
austrinum	KF-Dodd 1005-100	77.398	Calloway Gdns.					x
austrinum	'Harrison's Red'	93.002	Woodlanders, Inc					x
bachii		79.157	U of Cal Berkley					x
baileyi	L & S 2869	64.146	Glenarn	x	2	x	8	x
baileyi		73.018	F Robbins, Brydon				3	x
baileyi		75.035	King & Patton					x
baileyi		76.103	F Robbins					x
baileyi	King & Patton	92.120	Warren Berg					x
bainbridgeanum	F 21821	66.535	Royal Botanic Garden	x	1	x	6	x
bainbridgeanum		77.448	F Robbins					x
bainbridgeanum	Rock 59184	77.634	Windsor, Berg					x
bainbridgeanum		77.730	Ex Hort					x
bainbridgeanum		92.080	Warren Berg					x
bakeri		73.020					18	
bakeri	Camps Red	73.019	Skinner, USNA				4	x
bakeri		77.003	Granston					x
bakeri		77.006	Granston					x
bakeri		77.369	W Avery					x
bakeri	'Sizzler' PH 68-029-03	92.115	Polly Hill					x
bakeri	'Chalif' PH 68-029-01	92.116	Polly Hill					x
balfourianum	F 16811	00.703	Royal Botanic Garden		2			
balfourianum		70.081	Phetteplace, Ex Hort			x	1	x
balfourianum		73.021	Phetteplace				2	x
balfourianum	F16316	73.335	Royal Botanic Garden				1	x
balfourianum		76.169	Phetteplace					x
balfourianum		76.251	Benmore					x
balfourianum		76.357	Berg					x

Plants	Form	RSF #	Source	V	W	X	Y	Z
barbatum		65.304	Crarae	x	3	x	4	x
barbatum		64.027	Windsor			x	2	
barbatum		64.026	Windsor			x	2	x
barbatum		70.018	W Wood			x	2	x
barbatum		70.049	C Smith			x	2	x
barbatum		70.020	Windsor			x		
barbatum		00.393	Crarae	x				
barbatum		75.253	Berry					x
barbatum		77.583	USDA					x
barbatum		78.043	Barto. Phetteplace					x
barbatum		91.051	Warren Berg					x
barbatum		91.052	Warren Berg					x
barbatum		91.057	Warren Berg					x
barbatum		91.058	Warren Berg					x
barbatum		92.025	Warren Berg					x
barbatum		92.026	Warren Berg					x
barbatum		92.027	Warren Berg					x
barbatum		92.028	Warren Berg					x
barbatum		92.029	Warren Berg					x
barbatum		92.030	Warren Berg					x
basilicum	F 17650	00.558	Windsor	x	1	x		
basilicum		00.328	Corsock	x				
basilicum		73.025	Ex Hort				2	x
basilicum		77.215	Caperci, Berg					x
basilicum	Forrest 16002	82.038	Warrington, UBC					x
basilicum	Clone A	93.083	June Sinclair					x
basilicum	Clone B	93.084	June Sinclair					x
basilicum	F24225	93.085	June Sinclair					x
bathyphyllum	F 25739	00.506	Windsor	x	1			
bathyphyllum			Berg				1	
bathyphyllum		93.099	Greer					x
beanianum		00.196	Hillier	x	1			
beanianum		74.045	F.R.				2	
beanianum	var. compactum	00.247	Stronachullin	x	2	x		
beanianum	var. compactum	74.030					2	
beanianum		73.028					2	
beanianum		73.027	Grieg, W Wood					x
beanianum		74.115	F Robbins					x
beanianum		75.143	Bodnant, F Robbins					x
beanianum		75.265	F Robbins, W. Wood					x
beanianum		77.217	F Robbins					x
beanianum		77.451	F Robbins, W Wood, Grieg					x
beanianum		77.683	Brodick, Horlick					x
beanianum		92.121	Bodnant, Warren Berg					x
beesianum		71.717	Glenarn				1	x

Plants	Form	RSF #	Source	V	W	X	Y	Z
beesianum	Rock	76.394	Phetteplace					x
beyerinkianum		85.047	Mossman, Cavendish					x
bhutanense		91.014	Warren Berg					x
bhutanense		91.015	Warren Berg					x
bhutanense		91.016	Warren Berg					x
bhutanense		91.017	Warren Berg					x
bhutanense		92.031	Warren Berg					x
bhutanense		92.032	Warren Berg					x
bhutanense		92.033	Warren Berg					x
bhutanense		93.005	Warren Berg, Dick Booth					x
bhutanense		93.006	Warren Berg, Dick Booth					x
bhutanense		93.110	Warren Berg, Dick Booth					x
bhutanense		93.111	Warren Berg, Dick Booth					x
blackii		88.044						x
brachyanthum	hypolepidotum	68.752	Caperci, Walker			x	4	x
brachyanthum	hypolepidotum		Cox				5	
brachyanthum	hypolepidotum	74.056	Glendoick					x
brachyanthum	hypolepidotum	76.096	F Robbins					x
brachyanthum	hypolepidotum	77.449	F Robbins					x
brachyanthum	ss. brachyanthum	76.095	F Robbins					x
brachycarpum		73.029					1	
brachycarpum	ss. fauriei	66.539	Royal Botanic Garden	x	3	x	6	x
brachycarpum	ss. brachycarpum	75.132	Gable					x
brachycarpum	ss. brachycarpum	77.082	Ex Hort					x
brachycarpum	ss. brachycarpum	77.420	W Wash. Ex.					x
brachycarpum	ss. brachycarpum	77.539	Ex Hort.					x
brachycarpum	ss. brachycarpum	79.056	Berg					x
brachycarpum	ss. brachycarpum	79.058	Ex Hort					x
brachycarpum	ss. brachycarpum	82.184	Jorgensen					x
brachycarpum	ss. brachycarpum	82.189	Mustila Arboretum					x
brachysiphon		70.182					1	
breviperulatum		82.088	USDA, Bovee					x
brookeanum		78.098	Mossman					x
brookeanum		82.210	Boskoop					x
bryophilum		80.141	Boskoop					x
bullatum	AM '46	65.383	Bodnant	x		x		
bullatum	K.W.20839	00.101	Brodick	x	1	x		
bullatum	large white	00.371	Brodick	x				
bullatum	pink	00.551	Logan	x				
bullatum		70.030					4	
bullatum		65.383					12	
bureavii	Brandt 1B	00.659	Brandt		2			
bureavii		00.656	Larson		2			
bureavii	Brandt 2B	00.658	Brandt		1			
bureavii	Towercourt	64.030	Towercourt, Windsor			x	1	x

Plants	Form	RSF #	Source	V	W	X	Y	Z
bureavii		00.128	Caerhays	x				
bureavii		73.034	F Robbins, Brydon				8	x
bureavii			Exb. F.R.				1	
bureavii			Grieg-Miller				1	
bureavii		73.030	C. Smith, Brydon					x
bureavii		73.031					1	
bureavii		73.032					4	
bureavii		73.033					2	
bureavii		75.011	Hillier					x
bureavii		75.138	F Robbins, Brandt					x
bureavii		76.114	Berg					x
bureavii		76.115	Berg					x
bureavii		76.190	Royal Botanic Garden					x
bureavii	McLaren 106	76.269	Windsor					x
bureavii		77.151	Berg					x
bureavii		77.574	Ex Hort					x
bureavii		80.030	Ex Hort					x
bureavii		84.147	Larson					x
bureavii	bureavioides	91.043	Warren Berg					x
bureavii	bureavioides	91.044	Warren Berg					x
bureavii		91.080	Warren Berg					x
bureavii		91.081	Warren Berg					x
bureavii		91.082	Warren Berg					x
burmanicum		66.543	Glendoick	x	1	x	15	
burmanicum	AM	00.89	Glendoick	x				
burmanicum		70.160					5	
burmanicum		77.684	Brodick, Royal Botanic Gdn					x
burmanicum	K-W 21921	81.118	Bowman, Kolak					x
burmanicum		83.164	Windsor					x
burttii		87.039	Royal Botanic Gdn, Argent					x
caesium	Forrest 26798	76.134	Royal Botanic Gdn					x
calendulaceum		76.075	Granston					x
calendulaceum		76.291	Skinner, Gable					x
calendulaceum		77.005	Granston					x
calendulaceum		77.342	W Wash. Ex.					x
calendulaceum		77.502	Baird					x
calendulaceum		77.650	Ring					x
calendulaceum		81.076	Biltmore					x
caliginis		88.046						x
caliginis		89.003						x
callimorphum		70.111	W Wood			x	24	
callimorphum		00.546	Glendoick	x				
callimorphum		73.036					5	
callimorphum	v. myiagrum	66.541	Royal Botanic Garden					x
callimorphum	v. myiagrum	76.199	Royal Botanic Garden					x

Plants	Form	RSF #	Source	V	W	X	Y	Z
callimorphum	v. myiagrum	00.541		x	1	x		
callimorphum	v. callimorphum	75.041	Nymans					x
callimorphum	v. callimorphum	77.631	UBC, Grieg					x
calophytum	v. calophytum	64.063	Barto, Walker, Phetteplace	x	1	x	1	x
calophytum		00.346	Caerhays	x				
calophytum		00.552	Logan	x				
calophytum	v. calophytum	73.039	Kehr				1	x
calophytum	v. calophytum	77.068	Granston					x
calophytum	v. calophytum	77.130	Berry					x
calophytum	v. calophytum	77.283	Pierce					x
calophytum	v. calophytum	77.462	Berg					x
calophytum	v. calophytum, Wilson 1523	82.046	Lamellen, UBC					x
calophytum	v. calophytum	82.194	Cook					x
calophytum	v. calophytum	82.196	Cook					x
calophytum	v. openshawianum	88.013	ARS					x
calophytum	Pinker, Clone A	93.067	June Sinclair					x
calophytum	Clone B	93.068	June Sinclair					x
calophytum	Clone C	93.069	June Sinclair					x
calostrotum	v. keleticum	66.595	Glendoick		2	x	27	x
calostrotum		65.502	Glendoick	x	1			
calostrotum	v. keleticum, Forrest 19919	65.503	Glendoick	x	2	x	5	x
calostrotum	v. keleticum	73.155	F Robbins, Brydon					x
calostrotum	v. keleticum	73.156	Brydon, J. Henny					x
calostrotum	v. keleticum	73.238	W. Wood, Frye				3	x
calostrotum	v. keleticum	75.196	F Robbins					x
calostrotum	v. keleticum	70.034	F Robbins			x	2	
calostrotum	v. keleticum	73.155	F Robbins, Brydon				1	x
calostrotum	v. keleticum, Rock	73.156	Brydon, J. Henny				16	x
calostrotum		66.573	Wisley		2	x	14	x
calostrotum	calciphyllum	68.779	Glendoick			x	1	
calostrotum			Cox				1	
calostrotum	v. riparium	69.779	Glendoick, Walker					x
calostrotum	v. riparium, K-W 5482	80.084	Royal Botanic Garden					x
calostrotum	v. riparium	73.198	Grieg, W Wood				3	x
calostrotum	v. riparium	73.199	F Robbins				1	x
calostrotum	v. riparium	73.200	W Wood				27	x
calostrotum		74.009					8	
calostrotum	v. calostrotum	74.059	Gigha, Brydon					x
calostrotum	v. calostrotum, Rock	74.119	Brydon					x
calostrotum	v. calostrotum	78.113	Ex Hort					x
calostrotum			Siegmund			x	14	
camelliaeflorum		00.147	Glenarn	x	1	x		
camelliaeflorum		77.686	Brodick					x
camelliaeflorum	N Sikkim	93.096	Selcer					x
camelliaeflorum	N Sikkim	93.097	Selcer					x

Plants	Form	RSF #	Source	V	W	X	Y	Z
campanulatum	ss. companulatum AM '25	64.031	Windsor			x	1	
campanulatum	ss. campanulatum	64.202	Walker, Grieg	x	2	x	7	x
campanulatum	chocolate form	65.340	Stonefield, UBC	x		x		x
campanulatum	auriginosum	68.757	Collarino, Walker			x	6	x
campanulatum		74.053	Royal Botanic Garden				2	
campanulatum	auriginosum	74.016					6	
campanulatum	Knaphill	73.042					2	
campanulatum	ss. campanulatum, Cooper 5768	71.298	Royal Botanic Garden,UBC	x				x
campanulatum	ss. campanulatum, Cooper 5768	74.053	Royal Botanic Garden					x
campanulatum	ss. campanulatum	75.009	Hillier, F Robbins					x
campanulatum	ss. campanulatum	75.082	Exbury					x
campanulatum	ss. campanulatum	75.123	Royal Botanic Garden					x
campanulatum	ss. campanulatum	75.141	F Robbins					x
campanulatum	ss. campanulatum	75.173	W. Wood					x
campanulatum	ss. campanulatum	76.126	Caperci					x
campanulatum	ss. campanulatum, PSW 9107	76.198	Royal Botanic Garden					x
campanulatum	ss. campanulatum, L & S	77.562	Caperci					x
campanulatum	ss. campanulatum	78.007	Ex Hort					x
campanulatum	ss. campanulatum	82.151	Forst Botanic Garden					x
campanulatum	ss. aeruginosum	75.244	Berg					x
campanulatum	ss. aeruginosum	76.200	Royal Botanic Garden					x
campanulatum	ss. aeruginosum	76.235	Brodick					x
campanulatum	ss. aeruginosum	92.022	Warren Berg					x
campanulatum	ss. aeruginosum	92.023	Warren Berg					x
campanulatum	ss. aeruginosum	92.024	Warren Berg					x
campanulatum	ss. aeruginosum	93.007	Warren Berg, Dick Booth					x
campanulatum	ss. aeruginosum	93.014	Warren Berg, Dick Booth					x
campanulatum	ss. aeruginosum	93.015	Warren Berg, Dick Booth					x
campanulatum	ss. aeruginosum Clone A	93.080	June Sinclair					x
campanulatum	ss. aeruginosum Clone B	93.081	June Sinclair					x
campanulatum	ss. aeruginosum Clone C	93.082	June Sinclair					x
campylocarpum	ss. caloxanthum	65.283	Eckford, R.B.G., Benmore	x	1	x	1	x
campylocarpum		73.046					1	
campylocarpum	ss. campylocarpum	73.047	F Robbins					x
campylocarpum	ss. campylocarpum	71.609	Eckford					x
campylocarpum	ss. campylocarpum	75.156	F Robbins					x
campylocarpum	ss. campylocarpum, v. elatum	73.045	W. Wood				4	x
campylocarpum	ss. caloxanthum, K-W 6868	65.522	Windsor	x	1	x	1	x
campylocarpum	ss. caloxanthum, Forrest 27123	70.355	Kew					x
campylocarpum	ss. caloxanthum	73.041					4	
campylocarpum	ss. caloxanthum	74.049					2	
campylocarpum	ss. caloxanthum	00.195		x				
campylocarpum	ss. caloxanthum, Forrest 27125	75.042	Nymans					x
campylocarpum	ss. caloxanthum, Forrest 27123	75.063	Wakehurst					x
campylocarpum	ss. caloxanthum	75.212	Portland ARS Garden					x

Plants	Form	RSF #	Source	V	W	X	Y	Z
campylocarpum	ss. caloxanthum	76.307	Fortescue					x
campylocarpum	ss. caloxanthum	77.081	Granston					x
campylocarpum	ss. caloxanthum	77.133	Ex Hort					x
campylocarpum	ss. caloxanthum	77.551	Caperci					x
campylocarpum	ss. caloxanthum, Rock 48	77.565						x
campylocarpum	ss. caloxanthum	77.669	Crarae					x
campylocarpum	ss. caloxanthum	77.685	Brodick					x
campylocarpum	ss. caloxanthum	82.173	Jorgensen					x
campylocarpum	W Sikkim	93.098	Selcer					x
campylogynum		66.664	W Wood		5	x	67	x
campylogynum	salmon pink	62.043	Glendoick			x	3	x
campylogynum	var. charopoeum		Cox				7	
campylogynum	v. cremastum	69.108!	Walker			x	14	
campylogynum	v. myrtilloides	68.772	Caperci			x		
campylogynum	v. myrtilloides	70.063				x		
campylogynum		70.321	Fortescue				2	x
campylogynum	Bodnant Red		Hydon				3	
campylogynum	leucanthum		Cox				1	
campylogynum		70.376	Wisley, UBC					x
campylogynum		73.053	Ex Hort					x
campylogynum		74.061	Hydon					x
campylogynum		74.062	Glendoick					x
campylogynum		74.063	Glendoick					x
campylogynum		75.001	Glendoick, Berg					x
campylogynum		76.084	F Robbins					x
campylogynum		76.325	Berry					x
campylogynum		77.707	Royal Botanic Garden					x
campylogynum		77.708	Royal Botanic Garden					x
campylogynum	Forrest 18030	77.709	Royal Botanic Garden					x
campylogynum		82.159	Birck, Hydon					x
camtschaticum		73.054	UBC				1	x
camtschaticum		76.009	Berg					x
camtschaticum		77.080	Granston					x
camtschaticum		77.624	Berg					x
canadense		77.345	Larson					x
canadense		77.801	Larson, W Wash Re					x
canadense		78.034	Caperci, Clarke					x
canescens	Skinner 14 (1277?)	76.277	USNA					x
canescens	Skinner 1277A	76.278	USNA					x
canescens		77.019	Granston					x
canescens		77.020	Granston					x
canescens		77.399	Calloway Gardens					x
canescens		77.400	Calloway Gardens					x
canescens		77.504	Baird					x
canescens	Gambrill	78.111	Gambrill					x

Plants	Form	RSF #	Source	V	W	X	Y	Z
canescens	'Crain's Creek'	92.001	John Thornton					x
canescens	'Cedar Creek'	92.002	John Thornton					x
capitatum			Cox				6	
capitatum		74.064	Glendoick					x
carneum		00.351	Brodick	x	2	x		
carneum		77.687	Brodick					x
carolinianum		73.055					1	
carolinianum	album	74.050					1	
carringtoniae		85.049	Schick, Cavendish					x
carringtoniae		87.040	Royal Botanic Garden					x
catacosmum	R 59543, R11185	67.689	Windsor		2	x	10	x
catacosmum		76.195	Royal Botanic Garden					x
catacosmum		82.195	Hillier, Cook					x
catawbiense		75.134	Gable					x
catawbiense		75.135	Gable					x
catawbiense		76.012	VanVeen					x
catawbiense		77.202	Sleumer					x
catawbiense		77.620	Gable, Raustein					x
caucasicum	Apold, C & H	77.601	Glendoick					x
caucasicum		79.125	Glendoick					x
cephalanthum	ss. cephalanthum	76.371	Glendoick					x
cephalanthum	ss. cephalanthum	78.076	Knightshayes, UBC					x
cephalanthum	ss. cephalanthum	79.126	Glendoick					x
cerasinum		73.057	Brydon				1	x
cerasinum		66.610	Benmore, UBC					x
cerasinum	K-W F.6923	75.043	Nymans					x
cerasinum	K-W F11011	76.167	Royal Botanic Garden					x
cerasinum		76.246	Brodick					x
cerasinum	K-W F 5830	80.046	Borde Hill					x
cerasinum	K-W F 5830	80.110						x
cerasinum		82.147	Sofiero					x
cerasinum		83.014	Berg					x
cerasinum		83.017	Berg					x
chamaethomsonii	v. chamaethomsonii	66.545	Glendoick, Glenarn	x	2	x	19	x
chamaethomsonii	v. chamaethomsonii	66.174	Royal Botanic Gdn, Salter	x		x	5	x
chamaethomsonii	v. chamaethomsonii, Rock 92	78.063	R. Henny, EP					x
chamaethomsonii		73.058					6	
chamaethomsonii		73.359					2	
chamaethomsonii	v. chamaethauma	69.1024					1	
chamaethomsonii	v. chamaethauma	70.031	F Robbins				4	x
championae		79.048	Glendoick					x
charitopes		73.061					24	
charitopes	ss. tsangpoense	73.286	Brydon, RF					x
charitopes	ss. tsangpoense, pruniflorum	68.753	Caperci			x		
charitopes	ss. tsangpoense, pruniflorum	66.676	Wales Wood			x	3	

Plants	Form	RSF #	Source	V	W	X	Y	Z
charitopes	ss. charitopes	75.320	UBC, Nymans					x
charitopes	ss. charitopes	78.072	Brodick, UBC					x
charitopes		91.026	Warren Berg					x
chlorops		64.083	Lancaster			x	2	
christi		79.031	Pukeiti Garden, Smith, E.W.					x
christi		83.055	Schick					x
christi		88.052						x
christi		88.045						x
christianae		78.101	Stanton, Mossman					x
christianae		81.027	USDA					x
christianae		82.208	Boskoop					x
christianae		83.072	Schick					x
christianae	Withers	85.029	USDA					x
chrysanthum	nikomontanum	00.661	Seattle study		1	x	3	
chrysanthum		64.208	Grieg	x		x	1	
chrysanthum		73.062					1	
chrysodoron		76.218	Glenarn					x
ciliatum		65.352	Brodick, W Wood	x	1	x	5	x
ciliatum		66.665	W Wood			x	2	
ciliatum	Hedegaard 378	82.172	Hedegaard,					x
ciliicalyx		00.666	W Wood		2			
ciliicalyx	K-W, F. 20280	82.013	Pukeiti Garden					x
cinnabarinum		70.053	F Robbins			x		
cinnabarinum		70.027	Exbury			x	4	
cinnabarinum	blandfordiaeflorum	64.139	Corsock	x	7		21	x
cinnabarinum	blandfordiaeflorum	66.630	Leonardslee			x	2	x
cinnabarinum	blandfordiaeflorum	73.065	W Wood				1	x
cinnabarinum	blandfordiaeflorum	70.019	W Wood			x	2	x
cinnabarinum	cinnebarinum, 'Mount Everest'	92.018	Leonardslee					x
cinnabarinum	var. roylei	69.243	McDonald, Walker	x	2	x	1	x
cinnabarinum	var. roylei	70.017	W Wood			x		
cinnabarinum	var. roylei	74.026	Windsor				3	x
cinnabarinum			Hydon				3	
cinnabarinum	ss. xanthocodon	66.668	W Wood		3	x	16	x
cinnabarinum	ss. xanthocodon	66.572	Bodnant			x		
cinnabarinum	ss. xanthocodon	70.023	F Robbins			x	1	
cinnabarinum	ss. xanthocodon	70.013					4	
cinnabarinum	ss. xanthocodon	70.028	F Robbins			x	7	
cinnabarinum	ss. xanthocodon	70.323	Fortescue				1	x
cinnabarinum	ss. xanthocodon	73.067					5	
cinnabarinum	ss. xanthocodon	73.068					9	
cinnabarinum	ss. xanthocodon	73.069					3	
cinnabarinum	ss. xanthocodon	73.305	Exbury, W Wood, Brydon				8	x
cinnabarinum	ss. xanthocodon, K-W 5874	75.046	Nymans					x
cinnabarinum	ss. xanthocodon	75.098	Windsor					x

Plants	Form	RSF #	Source	V	W	X	Y	Z
cinnabarinum	ss. xanthocodon	75.171	W Wood					x
cinnabarinum	ss. xanthocodon	75.251	Berg					x
cinnabarinum	ss. xanthocodon	75.275	Hydon, UBC					x
cinnabarinum	ss. xanthocodon	76.337	Phetteplace					x
cinnabarinum	ss. xanthocodon	76.386	Leonardslee, UBC					x
cinnabarinum	ss. xanthocodon	77.415	F Robbins, W Wash. Re					x
cinnabarinum	ss. xanthocodon	77.440	Ex Hort					x
cinnabarinum	ss. xanthocodon	77.670	Crarae					x
cinnabarinum	ss. xanthocodon	82.161	Birck					x
cinnabarinum	ss. xanthocodon	91.065	Warren Berg					x
cinnabarinum	ss. xanthocodon	91.066	Warren Berg					x
cinnabarinum	ss. xanthocodon, 'Copper'	92.016	Leonardslee					x
cinnabarinum	ss. xanthocodon, 'Orange Bill'	92.017	Leonardslee					x
cinnabarinum	ss. cinnabarinum,var. aestivale	64.120	Leonardslee	x	3	x	9	x
cinnabarinum	ss. cinnabarinum, LS&H 21283	73.066	W Wood					x
cinnabarinum	ss. cinnabarinum	74.066	Hydon					x
cinnabarinum	ss. cinnabarinum	75.099	Windsor					x
cinnabarinum	ss. cinnabarinum	76.087	Berg					x
cinnabarinum	ss. cinnabarinum	76.088	Caperci					x
cinnabarinum	ss. cinnabarinum	76.089	Berg					x
cinnabarinum	ss. cinnabarinum, D 24	76.256	Benmore, Berg					x
cinnabarinum	ss. cinnabarinum, Berg, W.E.	77.112	Berg					x
cinnabarinum	ss. cinnabarinum, Berg, W.E.	77.113	Berg					x
cinnabarinum	ss. cinnabarinum, Berg, W.E.	77.115	Berg					x
cinnabarinum	ss. cinnabarinum, Berg, W.E.	77.116	Berg					x
cinnabarinum	ss. cinnabarinum, Berg, W.E.	77.160	Berg					x
cinnabarinum	ss. cinnabarinum, Berg, W.E.	77.161	Berg					x
cinnabarinum	ss. cinnabarinum, Berg, W.E.	77.163	Berg					x
cinnabarinum	ss. cinnabarinum, Berg, W.E.	77.164	Berg					x
cinnabarinum	ss. cinnabarinum, Berg, W.E.	77.166	Berg					x
cinnabarinum	ss. cinnabarinum	77.442	Ex Hort					x
cinnabarinum	ss. cinnabarinum	77.558	Caperci					x
citriniflorum	v. citriniflorum	70.143	Brodick, UBC					x
citriniflorum	v. citriniflorum	76.182	Royal Botanic Garden					x
citriniflorum	v. citriniflorum	76.234	Brodick					x
citriniflorum	v. horaeum	76.139	Royal Botanic Garden					x
citriniflorum	v. horaeum	76.208	Royal Botanic Garden					x
clementinae	R 25401	00.707	Royal Botanic Garden		1			
clementinae			U.B.C.				1	
clementinae	Rock 25401	73.337	Royal Botanic Garden				2	x
clementinae		74.067	Grieg, UBC					x
clementinae	Forrest 25705	75.045	Nymans					x
clementinae		76.215	Ex Hort					x
coelicum	Forrest 25625	75.100	Windsor					x
coelicum	Forrest 25625	76.135	Royal Botanic Garden					x

Plants	Form	RSF #	Source	V	W	X	Y	Z
collettianum	Wendelbo 8975	77.710	Royal Botanic Garden					x
collettianum	Wendelbo 8975	78.069	Royal Botanic Garden, Berg					x
commonae		79.035	Pratt					x
compactum		65.455	Wisley	x	1	x	5	
concinnum	v. Chief Paulina	64.209	James	x	28	x	16	x
concinnum	v. benthamianum	64.177	Royal Botanic Garden	x			15	x
concinnum	v. benthamianum	64.180	Royal Botanic Garden		6	x		x
concinnum			H. Smith				4	
concinnum	v. pseudoyanthinum	00.180	Wisley	x	8		7	
concinnum	v. pseudoyanthinum	73.071	Exbury, Brydon, F Robbins				1	x
concinnum	v. pseudoyanthinum	73.072	Exbury, Brydon, F Robbins				9	x
concinnum		73.070	W Wood, Brydon, Wisley				9	x
concinnum	H. Sm. 12920	74.068	Goteborg Botanical Garden					x
concinnum		75.193	C. Smith					x
concinnum		75.305	Barto, Phetteplace					x
concinnum		75.313	Phetteplace					x
concinnum		77.140	Berg					x
concinnum		77.141	Berg					x
concinnum		77.516	Caperci, Suzuki					x
concinnum		91.078	Warren Berg					x
concinnum		91.079	Warren Berg					x
cookeianum		00.087	Royal Botanic Garden	x				
coriaceum		65.305	Crarae	x	2	x	2	x
coriaceum	Rock 140	73.073	Phetteplace, Brydon				1	x
coriaceum		76.171	Royal Botanic Gardens					x
coriaceum	Forrest 25622	77.672	Towercourt, Crarae					x
coriaceum	Forrest 25872	82.062	Borde Hill, UBC					x
coriaceum	Rock 11069	83.153	Windsor					x
coryanum		00.537	Royal Botanic Garden	x	1	x		
coryanum	Forrest 20932	77.711	Royal Botanic Garden					x
coryanum		80.111	Magor					x
crassifolium		87.041	Collenette, RBG					x
crassifolium		88.055						x
crinigerum		70.067	Phetteplace			x	2	
crinigerum	v. crinigerum	70.080	Ex Hort				2	x
crinigerum	v. crinigerum, Rock 100	73.076	Phetteplace				1	x
crinigerum	v. crinigerum, Rock 2	75.290	Castle Howard					x
crinigerum	v. crinigerum, Rock 2	76.018	Phetteplace, Brydon					x
crinigerum	v. crinigerum, Rock 38	76.252	Benmore					x
crinigerum	v. crinigerum, Rock 100	76.332	Phetteplace					x
crinigerum	v. crinigerum	84.148	Larson					x
crinigerum			R.B.G. seed				1	
cruttwellii		83.054	Schick					x
culminicolum	v. angiense	83.059	Schick					x
cuneatum		65.497	Glendoick	x	1	x	4	x

Plants	Form	RSF #	Source	V	W	X	Y	Z
cuneatum		69.1062	Walker			x	1	
cuneatum		73.079					4	
cyanocarpum		65.274	Leonardslee	x	2	x	1	x
cyanocarpum		75.007	Hillier					x
cyanocarpum		75.102	Windsor					x
cyanocarpum		75.209	Portland ARS Garden					x
cyanocarpum	Forrest 15570	77.731	Windsor					x
cyanocarpum		82.005	Berry, Bender					x
dalhousiae		00.354	Brodick	x				
dalhousiae	v. dalhousie	77.605	Tatum					x
dalhousiae	v. dalhousie	77.703	Brodick					x
dalhousiae	v. dalhousie	83.077	Schick					x
dalhousiae	v. dalhousie, LS&T	84.128	Borde Hill					x
dasypetalum		74.070	Glendoick				3	x
dauricum	evergreen	66.590	Glendoick		2		7	x
dauricum	"Midwinter"	74.008	Berg				2	x
dauricum		74.010					1	
dauricum		76.019	Berg					x
dauricum		76.306	Berg, Windsor					x
dauricum		76.348	Berg, Wada					x
dauricum		76.400	Berg, Kingdon-Ward					x
dauricum		77.022	Granston					x
dauricum		77.421	W Wash. Re					x
dauricum	Creech	77.600	USNA					x
dauricum		77.799	Larson, Wada					x
dauricum		82.131	Moscow Botanical Garden					x
davidsonianum	Magor	00.210	Magor, Henny	x	55			
davidsonianum		63.007	Windsor		2		2	x
davidsonianum	Caerhays pink	64.129	Caerhays	x	3	x	17	x
davidsonianum	Caerhays Pink	66.600	USNA		1	x	5	x
davidsonianum	Ruth Lyons	64.220	Walker, Childers, Lyons	x	22	x	11	x
davidsonianum		73.349	Ex Hort				1	x
davidsonianum	Serenade	73.083	Hansen, Brydon, W Wood				1	x
davidsonianum		75.188	C Smith					x
davidsonianum		75.288	Castle Howard					x
davidsonianum		77.290	Pierce					x
davidsonianum		93.106	Clint Smith					x
decorum		64.062	Glendoick, Walker, CHP	x	2	x	5	x
decorum		64.061	Glendoick			x	1	
decorum	Rock	75.170	W Wood					x
decorum		77.032	Cox, Granston					x
decorum	Forrest 30887	83.154	Windsor					x
decorum	Cox, SBEC 1225	88.003	Cox					x
decorum	Cox, SBEC 1225	88.004	Cox					x
decorum	Cox, SBEC 0439	88.005	Cox					x

Plants	Form	RSF #	Source	V	W	X	Y	Z
decorum	Cox, SBEC 0181	88.006	Cox					x
degronianum	ss. degronianum	67.708	Royal Botanic Garden		2	x	4	x
degronianum	ss. degronianum, dalriada	65.250	Stronachullin	x	1	x	4	x
degronianum		73.087					1	
degronianum	ss. degronianum, USDA 315036	73.086	USDA				1	x
degronianum	ss. degronianum	70.064	Berry, Phetteplace				4	x
degronianum	ss. degronianum	77.297	Pierce					x
degronianum	ss. degronianum,'Gerald Loder'	92.007	Leonardslee					x
degronianum	ss. heptamereum	65.281	Borde Hill					x
degronianum	ss. heptamereum	73.180	Larson, Berg					x
degronianum	ss. heptamereum, USDA330367	73.181	USDA					x
degronianum	ss. heptamereum, USDA330368	73.182	USDA					x
degronianum	ss. heptamereum	75.139	Wada					x
degronianum	ss. heptamereum	76.111	Berg					x
degronianum	ss. heptamereum	76.358	Berg, Wada					x
degronianum	ss. heptamereum	77.026	Ludlow, Sheriff & Hi					x
degronianum	ss. heptamereum	77.184	Berg					x
degronianum	ss. heptamereum	77.185	Berg					x
degronianum	ss. heptamereum	77.187	Berg					x
degronianum	ss. heptamereum	77.188	Berg					x
degronianum	ss. heptamereum	77.189	Berg					x
degronianum	ss. heptamereum	77.190	Berg					x
degronianum	ss. heptamereum	77.191	Berg					x
degronianum	ss. heptamereum	77.373	Ex Hort					x
degronianum	ss. heptamereum	77.625	Ex Hort					x
dendricola		80.137	Trengwainton					x
dendricola		81.126	Kolak, Strybing Arboretum					x
detonsum		00.164	Crarae	x				
detonsum		74.028					1	
detonsum		92.109	Warren Berg					x
detonsum		92.112	Warren Berg					x
diaprepes		83.063	Schick					x
diaprepes		65.285	Eckford	x	3	x	7	
diaprepes	Gargantua	64.034	Windsor			x	3	x
diaprepes		73.88	Exbury				1	x ·
diaprepes		75.104	Windsor					x
diaprepes	HP	77.060	Granston					x
diaprepes		83.121	Ex Hort					x
dichroanthum	ss. apodectum	65.286	Eckford, UBC	x	2			x
dichroanthum	ss. apodectum	65.336	Brodick	x		x		
dichroanthum	ss. apodectum	75.272	Goheen					x
dichroanthum	ss. apodectum, Forrest 27359	77.732	Windsor					x
dichroanthum	ss. scyphocalyx, Forrest 27089	66.560	Windsor	x	1	x	2	x
dichroanthum	ss. scyphocalyx	65.307	Crarae		10	x	2	
dichroanthum	ss. scyphocalyx	00.304	Crarae	x				

Plants	Form	RSF #	Source	V	W	X	Y	Z
dichroanthum	ss. scyphocalyx	65.397	Crarae					x
dichroanthum	ss. scyphocalyx, Rock 6	75.291	Witcher					x
dielsianum		83.060	Schick					x
dielsianum		85.019	USDA					x
dielsianum		85.022	USDA					x
diphrocalyx		73.090	W Wood				1	x
doshongense		74.038					2	
drumonium		73.091					1	
dryophyllum	F 29327	00.509	Windsor	x				
eclecteum	v. eclecteum	65.278	Borde Hill	x	2	x	1	x
eclecteum		74.022					1	
eclecteum	v. eclecteum, Rock 23512	75.121	Royal Botanic Garden					x
eclecteum	v. eclecteum, Rock 148	76.212	Royal Botanic Garden					x
eclecteum	v. eclecteum	76.364	Berg, Nelson					x
eclecteum	v. eclecteum, K-W 5732	77.735	Windsor					x
eclecteum	v. eclecteum, Forrest 21842	77.767	Windsor					x
eclecteum	v. eclecteum, K-W 6936	77.768	Windsor					x
eclecteum		92.083	Warren Berg					x
eclecteum		92.084	Warren Berg					x
edgeworthii		65.383	Bodnant					x
edgeworthii		84.038	MacKenna, RBG					x
edgeworthii	Rock	88.034	Schick					x
edgeworthii	K-W 20836	88.035	Schick					x
elegantulum		70.068	Phetteplace			x	1	
elegantulum		70.015	W Wood			x		
elegantulum		73.336	Royal Botanic Garden					x
elegantulum		75.142	Robbins					x
elegantulum		81.129	Gambrill, Cent. Urb. Hort.					x
elegantulum		93.058	June Sinclair					x
elegantulum		93.075	June Sinclair					x
elliottii		00.211	James	x	2			
elliottii		76.228	Brodick					x
elliottii	K-W 19083	76.296	Phetteplace, VanVeen					x
ellipticum	USDA 325023	73.094	USDA				2	x
ellipticum	Patrick	76.023	Caperci					x
eritimum		00.091	Glendoick	x				
erosum		65.251	Stronachullin, UBC	x				x
erosum		77.689	Brodick, Horlick					x
erosum		76.024	VanVeen, Brown					x
erosum		92.103	Warren Berg					x
erosum		92.106	Dr. Berry					x
erythrocalyx		00.293	Glenarn	x				
eudoxum	AM '60	66.547	Glendoick	x		x		
eudoxum	v. eudoxum	76.025	Glendoick, Goheen					x
eudoxum	v. eudoxum, Rock 11011	76.174	Royal Botanic Garden					x

Plants	Form	RSF #	Source	V	W	X	Y	Z
eurysiphon		77.610	King & Patton					x
exasperatum	K-W 8250	76.137	Royal Botanic Garden					x
exasperatum	K-W 8250	81.139	Royal Botanic Garden					x
exasperatum	K-W 6855	92.008	Leonardslee					x
faberi	ss. prattii	67.683	Corsock	x				x
faberi	ss. prattii	70.190	Lamellen, UBC					x
faberi	ss. prattii	76.683	Corsock					x
faberi	ss. prattii	80.115	Croft					x
faberi	ss. prattii	00.467	Sandling Park	x				
faberi	ss. prattii	00.486	Lewellen	x				
facetum		00.094	Windsor	x				
facetum		76.238	Brodick					x
facetum		79.158	U of Cal Berkley					x
facetum	SBEC 0183	88.021	Sino-British Exped					x
facetum	SBEC 0257	88.022	Sino-British Exped					x
falconeri		00.294	Glenarn	x				
falconeri		00.342	Stonefield	x				
falconeri	ss. falconeri	74.006	Robbins, Brydon				1	x
falconeri	ss. falconeri	75.250	Berg					x
falconeri	ss. falconeri	81.079	Clarke					x
falconeri	ss. falconeri	83.116	F Robbins					x
falconeri	ss. falconeri, H 6066	88.008	XH					x
falconeri	ss. eximium	00.267	Trewithen	x	2	x		
falconeri	ss. eximium	00.285	Glendoick		1			
falconeri	ss. eximium		Stonefield	x				
falconeri	ss. eximium	74.003					2	
falconeri	ss. eximium	77.510	Caperci					x
falconeri	ss. eximium	77.738	Windsor					x
falconeri	ss. eximium	87.006	Grieg, Leber					x
falconeri	ss. eximium	91.023	Warren Berg					x
falconeri	ss. eximium	91.024	Warren Berg					x
falconeri	ss. eximium	91.061	Warren Berg					x
falconeri	ss. eximium	91.062	Warren Berg					x
falconeri	ss. eximium	91.063	Warren Berg					x
falconeri	ss. eximium	91.064	Warren Berg					x
fallacinum		88.060						x
fammeum	'Hazel Hamilton'	93.101	Greer					x
farrerae		78.037	Berg, Reuthe					x
fastigiatum		73.101	Brydon, J. Henny				2	x
fastigiatum		73.100					1	
fastigiatum	Rock	75.258	Berry					x
fastigiatum	Forrest 5847	81.140	Royal Botanic Garden					x
faucium	LS&E 12045	80.089	Royal Botanic Garden					x
faucium		91.027	Warren Berg					x
faucium		91.028	Warren Berg					x

Plants	Form	RSF #	Source	V	W	X	Y	Z
ferrugineum	Album	74.034					4	
ferrugineum	Album	74.035					1	
ferrugineum		76.381	Glendoick, UBC					x
ferrugineum		77.267	W Wash. Re					x
flammeum	Galle	75.030	Galle					x
flammeum	Skinner 535B	76.286	USNA					x
flammeum		77.039	Granston					x
flammeum	'Scarlet Ibis'	93.003	Woodlanders, Inc					x
flavidum	v. flavidum	73.106	F Robbins, Brydon				7	x
flavidum	v. flavidum	75.312	Glendoick, Phetteplace					x
flavidum	v. flavidum	76.385	Stronachullin, UBC					x
flavidum	v. flavidum	77.910	Berry					x
fletcherianum		68.858	Robbins			x	2	
fletcherianum		65.355	Brodick	x		x	1	x
fletcherianum		69.831	Walker, Brandt				7	x
fletcherianum	"Yellow Bunting"		Cox				6	
fletcherianum		74.071	Glendoick					x
fletcherianum		76.104	F Robbins					x
fletcherianum		76.105	Berg					x
flinckii		91.011	Berg					x
flinckii		91.012	Berg					x
flinckii		91.013	Berg					x
flinckii		92.034	Berg					x
flinckii		92.035	Berg					x
flinckii		92.036	Berg					x
flinckii		93.008	Berg, Booth					x
flinckii		93.012	Berg, Booth					x
flinckii		93.013	Berg, Booth					x
floccigerum		00.540	Royal Botanic Garden	x	1			
floccigerum		69.763	Walker, Grieg			x	7	x
floccigerum		70.071	Phetteplace			x	1	x
floccigerum	Rock #32	68.764	Phetteplace			x	7	
floccigerum		77.572	W Wood					x
floribundum	Wilson 4266	65.279	Borde Hill	x	2	x	8	x
floribundum	'Swinhoe' AM	00.074	Exbury	x				
floribundum		79.179	Exbury, UBC					x
formosanum	USDA 325025	73.108	USDA				2	x
formosanum	Hsu, S. 69215	88.001	Ryan					x
formosum		00.356	Brodick	x	1			
formosum		69.099	Windsor	x	6	x	6	
formosum	v. formosum	65.370	Brodick					x
formosum	v. formosum	81.122	Kolak, Royal Botanic Gdn					x
formosum	v. inaequale	70.185	Lamellen				1	x
forrestii		00.030				x		
forrestii	Scarlet Runner	64.227	C. Smith	x	12	x	3	x

Plants	Form	RSF #	Source	V	W	X	Y	Z
forrestii	v. repens	73.110					14	
forrestii	v. repens	73.112					19	
forrestii	v. repens	70.030	Robbins				18	x
forrestii	tumescens	70.175					1	
forrestii	tumescens	74.012					7	
forrestii	ss. forrestii	75.263	Robbins, Grieg					x
forrestii	ss. forrestii, K-W 6832	76.146	Windsor					x
forrestii	ss. forrestii, K-W	76.373	Berg					x
fortunei	'Barto's Favorite'	69.813	Barto, Walker, Phetteplace			x	1	x
fortunei		64.055	McDonald, Walker	x	3	x	5	x
fortunei		64.021	Windsor			x	5	
fortunei	rubra		Towercourt			x		
fortunei		68.814	Bowman			x	2	
fortunei	rubra	68.809	Phetteplace			x	4	
fortunei	rubra	73.115					3	
fortunei	ss. discolor	66.561	Windsor	x	1	x	4	x
fortunei	ss. discolor	66.562	Windsor					x
fortunei	ss. discolor	66.651	Walker, Sunningdale					x
fortunei	ss. discolor	68.827	Walker, Phetteplace					x
fortunei	ss. discolor	75.064	Wakehurst					x
fortunei	ss. discolor	75.136	Gable					x
fortunei	ss. discolor, Wilson 648A	79.043	Borde Hill					x
fortunei	ss. discolor	82.140	Bremen Rhod.					x
fortunei	ss. discolor	83.042	Windsor					x
fortunei	ss. fortunei	73.113	Ex Hort					x
fortunei	ss. fortunei	76.029	VanVeen, Gable					x
fortunei	ss. fortunei	76.340	Larson, Phetteplace					x
fortunei	ss. fortunei	79.027	Byrkit					x
fortunei	ss. fortunei	82.026	Gambrill, Seigmund					x
fortunei	ss. fortunei	84.149	Larson					x
fortunei	'Mrs. Butler'	92.009	Leonardslee					x
fragariflorum		75.271	Goheen, Reuthe					x
fragariflorum	LS&E 15828	81.141	Royal Botanic Garden					x
fulgens		64.080	Royal Botanic Garden	x		x	1	x
fulgens		00.465	Sandling Park	x				
fulgens		73.116					2	
fulgens		75.065	Wakehurst					x
fulgens		75.106	Windsor, Leonardslee					x
fulgens		76.030	Caperci					x
fulgens		76.320	Berry					x
fulgens		77.507	Caperci, Frye					x
fulgens		77.555	Caperci					x
fulvum		64.028	Windsor, Towercourt, Childers			x	1	x
fulvum		00.122	Leonardslee	x	1			
fulvum		65.490	Corsock	x	2	x	1	x

Plants	Form	RSF #	Source	V	W	X	Y	Z
fulvum		64.156	Crare	x		x	5	x
fulvum		64.048	Sunningdale, Walker			x	2	x
fulvum		71.156	Crarae				1	x
fulvum	as fulvoides	73.119					3	
fulvum	Rock #1	73.117	Brydon, C. Smith				1	x
fulvum		73.118	Ex Hort					x
fulvum		76.070	Berg					x
fulvum		76.166	Royal Botanic Garden					x
fulvum		76.336	Exbury, Phetteplace					x
fulvum		76.313	Pierce					x
fumidum		69.1101	Walker			x	8	
galactinum		73.120	Brydon, W Wood				2	x
galactinum			RBG seed				1	
galactinum		74.072	Harris					x
galactinum		75.165	W Wood, Frye					x
galactinum		76.327	Ex Hort					x
galactinum		77.201	F Robbins					x
galactinum		82.095	Goteborg Bot. Gdn., RBG					x
galactinum		82.154	Goteborg Bot. Gdn., Forst B.G.					x
genesterianum		00.200	Grieg	x	1			
genesterianum	K-W 20682	77.690	Brodick					x
giganteum	FCC	00.337	Brodick	x				
glaucophyllum		65.491	Corsock	x	2	x	21	
glaucophyllum	v. tubiforme	69.776	Frye, Walker, W. Wood			x	4	x
glaucophyllum	v. tubiforme	65.475	Rowallane	x	12	x	12	x
glaucophyllum	v. tubiforme	76.233	Brodick					x
glaucophyllum	v. luteiflorum	70.061	Phetteplace			x	14	
glaucophyllum	v. luteiflorum	64.103	Brodick	x	4	x	13	
glaucophyllum	v. luteiflorum	64.114	Logan	x		x	8	
glaucophyllum		73.121					1	
glaucophyllum	v. glaucophyllum	73.122	F Robbins, Brydon				3	x
glaucophyllum		73.123					6	
glaucophyllum	v. glaucophyllum	65.491	Corsock					x
glaucophyllum	v. glaucophyllum	75.025	Hillier					x
glaucophyllum	v. glaucophyllum	76.098	F Robbins					x
glaucophyllum	'Shell Pink'	92.118	Warren Berg					x
glaucophyllum	'Shell Pink'	92.119	Warren Berg					x
glaucophyllum	Bi-color	93.047	June Sinclair					x
glischrum		65.288	Eckford, UBC	x	1	x		x
glischrum		00.529	Royal Botanic Garden	x				
glischrum	ss. rude	64.150	Glenarn, UBC	x				x
glischrum	ss. rude, K-W 10953	66.566	Windsor	x	2	x	1	x
glischrum	ss. glischrum	65.288	Eckford, UBC					x
glischrum	ss. glischrum	76.031	Caperci					x
glischrum	ss. glischrum	77.465	F Robbins					x

Plants	Form	RSF #	Source	V	W	X	Y	Z
globigerum		64.059	W Wood			x	14	
globigerum	as roxianum						2	
glomerulatum		73.125					1	
glomerulatum			Hoitink				1	
goodenoughii		83.053	Schick					x
gracilentum		78.103	Mossman, Winters					x
grande		66.554	Logan	x	1	x	2	x
grande		71.338	Brodick	x			2	x
grande	Smith, B.	81.109	B. Smith					
griersonianum		68.762	Wisley, Phetteplace			x	1	x
griersonianum		00.420	Wakehurst	x				
griersonianum		75.085	Exbury					x
griersonianum		77.284	Pierce					x
griffithianum		00.555	Logan		1	x		
griffithianum		76.033	Clark					x
griffithianum		80.099	Benmore					x
griffithianum		80.154	UBC					x
griffithianum	Smith, B.	81.112	B. Smith					x
griffithianum	Smith, B.	81.113	B. Smith					x
griffithianum	Smith, B.	81.115	B. Smith					x
griffithianum		92.053	Warren Berg					x
griffithianum		92.054	Warren Berg					x
griffithianum	#1	93.104	Bowman					x
griffithianum	#2	93.105	Bowman					x
gymnocarpum		68.212	Henny	x	2	x	17	
habrotrichum		65.275	Leonardslee		1	x	1	x
habrotrichum		65.274	Leonardslee	x				
habrotrichum		00.530	Royal Botanic Garden	x				
habrotrichum	Forrest 15778	83.052	Bender					x
haematodes	deep red	63.010	Windsor			x	18	x
haematodes			F Robbins			x	1	
haematodes		70.041	Robbins			x	2	x
haematodes		68.767	Brandt, Exbury, Walker,CHP			x		
haematodes	Rock	68.855	Robbins			x	12	
haematodes		70.039	Robbins			x	2	
haematodes		70.040	Robbins			x	3	
haematodes		70.043	W Wood, Frye			x	1	x
haematodes		68.766	Exbury, Walker, Phetteplace			x	10	
haematodes		70.005					8	
haematodes		73.129	W Wood				1	x
haematodes	ss. haematodes	75.145	F Robbins					x
haematodes	ss. haematodes, Frye	75.176	W Wood					x
haematodes	ss. haematodes	75.191	C Smith					x
haematodes	ss. haematodes	77.657	Windsor					x
haematodes	ss. haematodes	77.692	Brodick					x

Plants	Form	RSF #	Source	V	W	X	Y	Z
haematodes	ss. haematodes, McLaren S-124	77.741	Windsor					x
haematodes	ss. haematodes	77.742	Windsor					x
haematodes	ss. haematodes	77.781	UBC					x
haematodes	ss. chaetomallum	66.667	W Wood			x	1	x
haematodes	ss. chaetomallum	74.065	Glendoick					x
haematodes	ss. chaetomallum, Rock 39	75.300	Phetteplace					x
haematodes	ss. chaetomallum, For.20333	75.306	Phetteplace					x
haematodes	ss. chaetomallum, Rock 52	75.334	Castle Howard					x
haematodes	ss. chaetomallum, Rock 34	76.013	Caperci					x
haematodes	ss. chaetomallum, K-W 21077	76.206	Royal Botanic Garden					x
haematodes	ss. chaetomallum		Cox				3	
haematodes	ss. chaetomallum	00.611			1			
haematodes	(semi-double)	93.059	Windsor, Warren Berg					x
hanceanum	nanum	65.476	Rowallane	x	3	x	15	x
hanceanum	nanum	70.008	F Robbins			x	1	x
hanceanum	nanum		F Robbins			x		
hanceanum		73.131	F Robbins				3	x
hanceanum		76.034	Berg					x
hanceanum		76.383	UBC					x
hanceanum		77.052	Granston					x
hanceanum		77.298	Pierce					x
hanceanum		77.614	King & Patton					x
hardingii		70.132					1	
headfortianum			Gigha			x		
heliolepis	var. heliolepis	65.374	Royal Botanic Garden	x	1	x	1	x
heliolepis	var. heliolepis	76.302	Cox					x
heliolepis	var. heliolepis	77.323	Goheen					x
heliolepis	var. brevistylum, Forrest 6762	70.419	Royal Botanic Garden				1	x
heliolepis	var. brevistylum	66.622	F30977			x	2	
hemitrichotum		66.614	Benmore, Eckford		4	x	3	x
hemitrichotum		73.348					1	
hemsleyanum	seedlings		Robbins			x		
hemsleyanum		73.133	F Robbins				4	x
hemsleyanum		76.036	Berg					x
hemsleyanum		77.064	Granston, Heritage, ARS					x
herzogii		89.004						x
herzogii		89.008						x
hippophaeoides	v. hippophaeoides	73.135	F Robbins				5	x
hippophaeoides	v. hippophaeoides	66.592	Glendoick		2	x	4	x
hippophaeoides	v. hippophaeoides	77.611	King & Patton					x
hippophaeoides	v. hippophaeoides	78.115	Sunningdale, Phetteplace					x
hippophaeoides	v. hippophaeoides, Rock 11363	80.067	Windsor, RBG					x
hippophaeoides	Ted's form	93.056	June Sinclair					x
hirsutum		66.594	Glendoick		1	x	5	x
hirsutum		74.120	F Robbins					x

246

Plants	Form	RSF #	Source	V	W	X	Y	Z
hirtipes		64.097	Windsor	x		x	1	x
hirtipes		73.136	W Wood				5	x
hirtipes	L & S 3624	70.161	Glenarne, UBC					x
hirtipes	K-W 6223	75.049	Nymans					x
hirtipes	K-W 5659	76.186	Royal Botanic Garden					x
hirtipes		92.097	Berg					x
hodgsonii		65.330	Corsock	x	2	x	4	x
hodgsonii		65.343	Stonefield	x		x	1	
hodgsonii	Poets lawn	74.052					1	
hodgsonii		76.191	Royal Botanic Garden					x
hodgsonii		83.117	F Robbins					x
hodgsonii		91.031	Warren Berg					x
hodgsonii		91.034	Warren Berg					x
hodgsonii		91.059	Warren Berg					x
hodgsonii		91.060	Warren Berg					x
hodgsonii		92.037	Warren Berg					x
hodgsonii		92.038	Warren Berg					x
hodgsonii		92.039	Warren Berg					x
hodgsonii	Aff.	91.018	Warren Berg					x
hodgsonii	Aff.	91.019	Warren Berg					x
hodgsonii	Aff.	91.020	Warren Berg					x
hodgsonii	Aff.	92.050	Warren Berg					x
hodgsonii	Aff.	92.051	Warren Berg					x
hodgsonii	Aff.	92.052	Warren Berg					x
hodgsonii	W Sikkim	93.093	Selcer					x
hongkongense		77.779	Robinson					x
hookeri		67.711	Benmore, Eckford		1	x	1	x
hookeri			Duncan			x		
hookeri		64.049	Lem			x	1	
hookeri		73.137					2	
hookeri	K-W 13650	73.329	Nymans				2	x
hookeri	K-W 13650	75.050	Nymans					x
hookeri		76.214	Royal Botanic Gardens					x
horlickianum		84.011	Arduaine					x
horlickianum	K-W 9403	87.053	Royal Botanic Garden					x
houlstonii		66.562	Windsor	x	1	x	5	
houlstonii		68.827	Phetteplace			x	3	
hunnewellianum	ss. hunnewellianum	66.575	Wisley		2	x	4	x
hunnewellianum	ss. hunnewellianum	73.138	F Robbins				4	x
hunnewellianum	ss. hunnewellianum	75.155	F Robbins					x
hunnewellianum	ss. hunnewellianum	76.037	Berg					x
hunnewellianum	ss. hunnewellianum	84.150	Larson					x
hyacinthosmum		83.064	Schick					x
hylaeum	K-W 9322	77.743	Windsor					x
hyperythrum		64.011	Towercourt			x		

Plants	Form	RSF #	Source	V	W	X	Y	Z
hyperythrum		69.884	Nelson			x	13	x
hyperythrum			Hoitink				3	
hyperythrum	Patrick	76.038	VanVeen					x
impeditum		73.140	F Robbins, Brydon				5	x
impeditum		73.167	F Robbins, Brydon					x
impeditum		76.102	F Robbins					x
impeditum		76.379	Windsor, UBC					x
impeditum		77.617	King & Patton					x
indicum		77.304	Berg					x
indicum		81.084	Larson					x
inopinum		00.375	Royal Botanic Garden	x				
inopinum		74.039					1	
insigne		69.789	Walker, Jacobson			x	6	x
insigne		69.663	Brandt, Walker		2	x	3	x
insigne		65.259	Bodnant	x		x		
insigne		75.068	Wakehurst					x
insigne		75.110	Windsor					x
insigne		76.162	Bodnant					x
insigne		77.535	Ex Hort					x
insigne		79.097	Hobbie					x
insigne		80.120	Croft					x
insigne		82.028	UBC, Croft					x
insigne		84.151	Larson					x
intranervatum		92.110	Fran Rutherford					x
intranervatum		92.113	Chaikin					
intricatum	dark form		Bovee			x		
intricatum		73.143					2	
intricatum		73.144	F Robbins				3	x
intricatum		77.616	King & Patton					x
irroratum		66.651	Sunningdale			x	1	
irroratum	Polka Dot	69.073	Exbury, Walker	x	2	x	9	x
irroratum	Splatter Paint	64.222	C. Smith			x	10	
irroratum		00.313	Lamellen	x				
irroratum		00.423	Wakehurst	x				
irroratum		73.146					4	
irroratum		73.147					2	
irroratum		75.	Larson - WEB				1	
irroratum	ss. irroratum, Rock	75.298	Phetteplace					x
irroratum	ss. irroratum, Rock 161	75.515	Caperci					x
irroratum	ss. irroratum, Rock 161	76.100	Caperci					x
irroratum	ss. irroratum	84.018	Arduaine					x
iteophyllum		65.370	Brodick	x	4	x	18	
iteophyllum	hardier form	66.638	Brodick		1	x	2	
japonicum	USDA 315037	73.149	USDA				1	x
japonicum		77.034	Granston					x

Plants	Form	RSF #	Source	V	W	X	Y	Z
japonicum		77.035	Granston					x
japonicum	USNA 45358	81.030	USNA					x
japonicum	USNA 45358	81.031	USNA					x
japonicum	USNA 45358	81.032	USNA					x
japonicum	Creech	88.010	Creech					x
jasminiflorum	v. jasminiflorum	78.102	Mossman, Winters					x
jasminiflorum	v. jasminiflorum	82.209	Ex Hort					x
javanicum	v. javanicum	78.087	Mossman					x
javanicum	v. javanicum	78.089	Mossman, Strybing Arb.					x
johnstoneanum		65.357	Brodick	x	2	x	4	
johnstoneanum	Double	65.358	Brodick	x		x	2	
johnstoneanum		77.693	Brodick					x
johnstoneanum		86.002	Childers, Sinclair					x
johnstoneanum		87.030	Childers, Sinclair					x
kaempferi		73.380					2	
kaempferi	v. kaempferi, USDA 275535	73.202	USDA				1	x
kaempferi	v. kaempferi	73.350	Ex Hort					x
kaempferi	v. kaempferi	77.118	Berg					x
kaempferi	v. kaempferi	77.119	Berg					x
kaempferi	v. kaempferi	77.121	Berg					x
kaempferi	v. kaempferi	77.122	Berg					x
kaempferi	v. kaempferi	77.269	Ex Hort					x
kaempferi	v. kaempferi	77.659	Windsor					x
kaempferi	v. kaempferi	77.803	Berg					x
kaempferi	v. kaempferi	79.171	Berg, Suzuki					x
kaempferi	v. kaempferi	81.093	Larson					x
kanehirsi		73.151					3	
kawakamii		79.026	Larson, Bump, Smith,E W					x
kawakamii	Patrick	80.017	Van Veen					x
keiskei		70.014	W Wood			x	2	x
keiskei		66.624	Windsor		5	x	34	x
keiskei	compact	64.124	Leonardslee	x	8	x	2	x
keiskei	narrow leaf	64.125	Leonardslee	x	2	x	1	
keiskei			W Wood			x		
keiskei		73.153	F Robbins, Kingdon-Ward				3	x
keiskei	'Yaku Fairy'	74.014	Berg				8	x
keiskei		75.233	Berg, Starling					x
keiskei	Berg	76.040	Berg					x
keiskei		76.121	Berg					x
keiskei		76.299	Gambrill, VanVeen,					x
keiskei	Berg	77.104	Berg					x
keiskei	Berg	77.192	Berg					x
keiskei		77.518	Berg					x
keiskei	Berg	77.523	Berg					x
keiskei		77.537	Ex Hort					x

Plants	Form	RSF #	Source	V	W	X	Y	Z
keiskei		77.543	Ex Hort					x
keiskei		79.164	Larson, Johnson, Rokujo					x
kendrickii		64.159	Crarae		3	x	66	x
kendrickii		66.584	Crarae		4	x	19	x
kendrickii		73.254					1	
kesangiae		91.021	Warren Berg					x
kesangiae		91.022	Warren Berg					x
kesangiae		91.067	Warren Berg					x
kesangiae		91.068	Warren Berg					x
kesangiae		91.069	Warren Berg					x
kesangiae		91.070	Warren Berg					x
kesangiae		91.071	Warren Berg					x
kesangiae		91.072	Warren Berg					x
kesangiae		92.040	Warren Berg					x
kesangiae		92.041	Warren Berg					x
kesangiae		92.042	Warren Berg					x
kesangiae		92.043	Warren Berg					x
keysii		64.130	Caerhays	x	6	x	3	x
keysii	v. unicolor	70.148	Brodick				1	x
keysii		75.286	Brodick, Castle Howard					x
kiusianum			F.R.				1	
kiusianum		74.077	F Robbins					x
kiusianum		76.041	Berg					x
kiusianum		77.199	Berg					x
kiusianum		77.519	Berg					x
kiusianum		77.632	Berg, Suzuki					x
kiusianum		77.638	Ex Hort					x
kiusianum		79.059	USNA					x
kiusianum		79.061	USNA					x
kiusianum		79.062	USNA					x
kiusianum		79.063	USNA					x
kiusianum		79.064	USNA					x
kiusianum		79.065	USNA					x
kiusianum		79.066	USNA					x
kiusianum		79.067	USNA					x
kiusianum		79.068	USNA					x
kiusianum		79.069	USNA					x
kiusianum		79.070	USNA					x
kiusianum		79.071	USNA					x
kiusianum		79.072	USNA					x
kiusianum		79.073	USNA					x
kiusianum		79.074	USNA					x
kiusianum		79.167	Berg					x
kiusianum		79.172	Berg					x
kiusianum		79.181	Lohbrunner, UBC					x

Plants	Form	RSF #	Source	V	W	X	Y	Z
kiusianum	Berg	81.011	Berg					x
kiusianum		81.099	Larson					x
kiusianum		81.100	Larson					x
kiusianum		81.101	Larson					x
kongboense			Cox				3	
kongboense		74.078	Glendoick					x
konorii		78.105	Mossman, Winters					x
konorii		79.036	Pratt					x
konorii		80.143	Boskoop					x
kotschyi		73.159					2	
kotschyi		73.360					2	
kyawi		00.289	Eckford	x				
kyawi	Forrest 24542	77.745	Windsor					x
lacteum		64.141	Corsock	x	1		2	x
lacteum		00.331	Corsock	x				
lacteum		70.346	Corsock				1	x
lacteum		75.111	Windsor					x
lacteum		75.125	Royal Botanic Garden					x
lacteum		75.221	Lem, Wagner					x
lacteum		75.242	Berg, Whitney, Lem					x
lacteum		75.274	Goheen, James, Port. ARS					x
lacteum		76.101	Van Winkle, Lem					x
lacteum		77.713	Ex Hort					x
lacteum	SBEC 0345	88.023	Sino-British Exp.					x
lacteum		76.395	Phetteplace					x
laetum		77.621	Granston					x
laetum		78.088	Mossman, Strybing Arb.					x
laetum		79.156	Ex Hort					x
laetum		80.144	Boskoop					x
lanatum		76.323	Berry					x
lanatum		83.016	Berg					x
lanatum		92.082	Berg					x
lanatum		92.122	Berg					x
lanatum	Sikkim	93.087	Selcer					x
lanatum	Sikkim	93.088	Selcer					x
lanatum	Sikkim	93.089	Selcer					x
lanigerum	K-W 8251	66.615	Royal Botanic Garden		1	x	6	x
lanigerum	Sylvia	66.556	Logan	x	1	x	6	x
lanigerum	K-W 20838	00.223	Smith	x				
lanigerum		74.015					4	
lanigerum	Rock 18407A	75.010	F Robbins, Hillier					x
lanigerum	Rock 18407A	75.113	Windsor					x
lanigerum	K-W 6258	75.114	Windsor					x
lanigerum	Rock	76.044	Caperci					x
lanigerum		76.149	Windsor, Trengwainton					x

Plants	Form	RSF #	Source	V	W	X	Y	Z
lanigerum		77.318	McGuire					x
lanigerum		77.514	Caperci					x
lanigerum	K-W 6258	79.113	Borde Hill					x
lanigerum		82.042	Trengwainton, UBC					x
lapponicum		78.066	Berg, Cox					x
lapponicum		82.091	Glendoick					x
laudandum	v. temoense	75.036	King & Patton, RBG					x
laxiflorum		64.072	Exbury			x	9	
laxiflorum		73.161					1	
lepidostylum		00.104	Brodick	x	3	x		
lepidostylum		73.163					6	
lepidostylum		73.162					10	
lepidostylum		70.044	W Wood				1	x
lepidostylum		75.246	Berg					x
lepidostylum		76.382	Brodick, UBC					x
lepidotum		73.092					8	
lepidotum		75.024	Hillier					x
lepidotum	Smyth 51	76.170	Royal Botanic Garden					x
lepidotum		77.788	Ex Hort					x
lepidotum		78.078	U of Bangor, UBC					x
lepidotum		78.079	U of Bangor, UBC					x
lepidotum		79.050	Glendoick					x
lepidotum		79.053	Berg					x
lepidotum		79.054	Berg					x
lepidotum	BB 191	81.009	Schick					x
leptanthum		85.043	Cavendish, Tatum					x
leptanthum		87.042	Royal Botanic Garden					x
leptothrium		66.601	Caerhays		1		3	x
leptothrium	Rock	77.797	Berry					x
leptothrium		00.131	Caerhays	x				
leucaspis		65.398	Crarae	x	4	x	18	x
leucaspis		73.164					1	
leucaspis		77.577	Ex Hort					x
leucogigas		78.093	Mossman, UBC					x
liliiflorum		80.156	UBC					x
liliiflorum		83.002	Strybing Arboretum					x
lindleyi	GS 6562	00.718	Glenarn		3			
lindleyi		00.148	Glenarn	x				
lindleyi	L&S 6562	78.067	Glendoick, Berg					x
lindleyi		84.060	Brodick					x
linearifolium		65.447	Leonardslee	x	4	x	25	
litiense		70.514	Windsor	x			1	
lochae		78.096	Mossman, Teese					x
lochae		79.029	Stanton					x
lochae		80.145	Boskoop					x

Plants	Form	RSF #	Source	V	W	X	Y	Z
lochae		88.056						x
lochmium		65.515	Windsor	x	19	x	28	
longesquamatum		00.314	Lamellen	x	1			
longesquamatum		75.172	W Wood					x
longesquamatum		76.045	Caperci					x
longesquamatum		77.635	Magor, Berg					x
longesquamatum		79.149	Kew, Goteborg Bot Gdn					x
longesquamatum		83.010	Gambrill, VanVeen, Reuthe					x
longesquamatum		83.095	UBC					x
longesquamatum		92.081	Warren Berg					x
longesquamatum		93.057	Warren Berg					x
lopsangianum		64.149	Glenarn	x		x	1	
loranthiflorum		78.099	Stanton. Mossman					x
loranthiflorum		83.058	Schick					x
loundesii		91.088	June Sinclair					x
ludlowii		74.033	UBC				1	x
ludlowii		75.022	Hillier					x
ludwigianum		70.363	Kew			x		
lukiangense		00.376	Royal Botanic Garden	x	1	x		
lukiangense		75.071	Wakehurst					x
lukiangense		75.072	Wakehurst					x
lukiangense		75.247	Hillier, Berg					x
lukiangense		80.049	Borde Hill					x
lukiangense		81.133	Borde Hill					x
luteiflorum		70.061	Ex Hort					x
luteiflorum		73.123	Ex Hort					x
luteiflorum		75.018	Hillier, Berg					x
luteiflorum		77.430	Berg					x
luteiflorum	K-W 21040	81.124	Glendoick, Kolak, Childers					x
luteiflorum		64.103	Brodick, Corsock					x
luteiflorum		64.114	Logan					x
lutescens		70.107	Leonardslee				1	x
lutescens	Bagshot Sands'		Cox				3	
lutescens		74.079	Glendoick					x
lutescens		75.224	Wagner					x
lutescens		76.123	W. Avery					x
lutescens		77.411	Robbins, W Wash. Ex.					x
lutescens		77.432	W. Avery					x
lutescens		77.697	Brodick					x
luteum		74.080	Hydon				3	x
luteum		76.410	A. Robbins					x
luteum		77.264	Baird					x
luteum		77.265	Baird					x
luteum		77.325	Ex Hort					x
luteum		77.584	Seattle Garden Club					x

Plants	Form	RSF #	Source	V	W	X	Y	Z
lysolepis		73.167					7	
lyi		70.364					1	
macabeanum		00.268	Trewithen	x	2	x		
macabeanum		65.295	Glenarn	x	3	x	1	x
macabeanum		73.331	Nymans				6	x
macabeanum	K-W 7724	75.052	Nymans					x
macabeanum	K-W 20304	75.180	C Smith					x
macabeanum		75.227	Wagner					x
macabeanum	K-W 20304	75.245	C Smith, Berg					x
macabeanum		75.285	Towercourt, Castle Howard					x
macabeanum		76.338	Phetteplace					x
macabeanum		77.046	Granston, Magor					x
macabeanum		79.092	Ex Hort					x
macabeanum		82.039	Trewithen, UBC					x
macabeanum	K-W 20304	83.119	C. Smith, F. Robbins					x
macabeanum		83.125	Pm					x
macabeanum	Clone A	93.076	June Sinclair					x
macabeanum	Clone B	93.077	June Sinclair					x
macabeanum	Clone C	93.078	June Sinclair					x
macabeanum		93.079	June Sinclair					x
macgregoriae	v. macgregoriae	79.032	Pratt					x
macgregoriae	v. macgregoriae	83.056	Schick, USDA					x
macgregoriae	v. macgregoriae	83.074	Schick					x
macgregoriae	v. macgregoriae	85.016	USDA					x
macgregoriae	v. macgregoriae	85.020	USDA					x
macgregoriae	v. macgregoriae	85.021	USDA					x
macgregoriae	v. macgregoriae	85.026	USDA					x
macrogemmum		77.642	Berg					x
macrophyllum		77.208	B. Smith					x
macrophyllum		79.019	B. Smith					x
macrophyllum		79.020	B. Smith					x
macrophyllum	Piacentini	85.038	E W Smith					x
macrophyllum		85.050	B Smith					x
macrophyllum·		91.007	George Ryan					x
macrophyllum		91.008	George Ryan					x
macrophyllum		91.009	George Ryan					x
macrophyllum	'Forbidden Plateau	91.089	Clint Smith					x
macrophyllum	Copper Creek	93.023	Steve Hootman					x
macrophyllum	Copper Creek	93.024	Steve Hootman					x
macrophyllum	Copper Creek	93.025	Steve Hootman					x
macrosepalum		65.447	Leonardslee					x
macrosepalum		77.540	Berg					x
macrosepalum		81.102	Larson					x
maculiferum	ss. maculiferum	65.253	Stronachullin		4	x	12	x
maculiferum		00.213	Brandt	x				

Plants	Form	RSF #	Source	V	W	X	Y	Z
maculiferum	ss. anhweiense	65.245	Stronachullin					x
maddenii	pink	65.360	Brodick	x	2	x	2	x
maddenii	white	65.361	Brodick	x	1			
maddenii	Sherriff 1141	65.359	Brodick	x				
maddenii		64.051	Phetteplace			x		
maddenii	ss. crassum	64.066	W Wood			x	4	x
maddenii	ss. crassum	65.364	Brodick					x
maddenii	ss. crassum	66.633	Leonardslee					x
maddenii	ss. crassum	69.095	Windsor	x	1	x	6	x
maddenii	ss. crassum	70.183	Lamellen				1	x
maddenii	ss. maddenii	64.115	Logan	x	2	x	1	x
maddenii	ss. maddenii	77.701	Brodick					x
maddenii	ss. maddenii	78.109	Beasley, Royal Bot. Gdn.					x
maddenii	ss. maddenii	80.130	Trengwainton					x
magnificum		00.523	Brodick	x				
magnificum		77.698	Brodick					x
magnificum		81.080	Pierce, Castle Howard					x
maius		89.006						x
mallotum		66.557	Logan	x	1	x	1	x
mallotum		76.150	Windsor					x
mallotum	Farrer #815	67.712	Royal Botanic Garden		1	x	1	x
mallotum		76.229	Brodick					x
mallotum		83.018	Berg					x
mallotum		83.019	Ex Hort					x
mallotum		83.021	Berg					x
mallotum	F 17853	92.010	Leonardslee					x
manipurense		66.633	Leonardslee			x	2	
manipurense		00.362	Brodick	x				
mariesii		76.079	Berg					x
martinianum		00.100	Windsor	x				
martinianum		70.133	Stronachullin				1	x
martinianum		75.034	King & Patton					x
martinianum		75.205	W. Avery					x
maximum		75.137	Gable					x
maximum	Gambrill	76.294	Gambrill					x
maximum		77.350	W Wash Ex					x
maximum		77.564	VanVeen, Schwind					x
maximum		77.646	Leach					x
meddianum	v.atrokermesinum,	00.168	Benmore	x	1	x		
meddianum	v.atrokermesinum, For. 26495	82.060	Nymans, UBC					x
meddianum	v. meddianum	75.177	W Wood					x
meddianum	v. meddianum	75.329						x
meddianum	v. meddianum, Forrest 24104	80.080	Castle Howard					x
megacalyx		00.645	Brodick		1			
megacalyx		00.363	Brodick	x				

Plants	Form	RSF #	Source	V	W	X	Y	Z
megacalyx		80.134	Trengwainton					x
megacalyx		80.157	UBC					x
megeratum		65.477	Rowallane	x	4	x	37	x
megeratum		65.261	Bodnant	x		x	10	x
megeratum		73.176					1	
megeratum		73.178	C Smith, Brydon, W Wood				5	x
mekongense	v. rubrolineatum	66.641	Benmore, Eckford		2	x	5	x
mekongense	v. rubrolineatum	76.205	Royal Botanic Garden					x
mekongense	v. mekongense	74.111	Glendoick					x
mekongense	v. melinanthum	77.714	Royal Botanic Garden					x
mekongense	v. melinanthum		Hillier, F.R. '75				1	
mekongense	v. melinanthum, KW5489	92.011	Leonardslee					x
metternichii		65.281	Borde Hill	x	2		6	
metternichii		73.182					3	
metternichii		73.181					1	
metternichii	v. kymarouense	74.031					6	
metternichii	v. kymarouense	74.032					2	
metternichii		73.180					3	
micranthum		76.125	VanVeen, Portland ARS					x
micranthum		76.399	Portland ARS					x
micranthum		77.414	Mulligan, W Wash Ex					x
micranthum		78.001	Ex Hort					x
microgynum	Forrest 14242	74.027	Windsor				4	x
microgynum		68.212	Walker, Brydon, Exbury,					x
microgynum		77.159	Berg					x
microgynum		77.443	Ex Hort					x
microgynum		77.450	F Robbins					x
microgynum		77.461	Ex Hort					x
microgynum		77.443	Ex Hort					x
microgynum		87.054	Royal Botanic Garden					x
micromalayanum	B & M 5396	87.043	Royal Botanic Garden					x
micromeres		77.644	Berg					x
minus	v. chapmanii	73.060					1	
minus	v. chapmanii	73.059					1	
minus	v. chapmanii	76.016	Van Veen, Cline					x
minus	v. chapmanii	76.085	Brydon					x
minus	v. chapmanii	77.009	Ex Hort					x
minus	v. chapmanii	78.040	Moynier					x
minus	v. chapmanii	78.041	Moynier					x
minus	v. chapmanii	82.187	North Carolina State					x
minus	v. chapmanii	82.188	North Carolina State					x
minus	v. chapmanii	82.191	North Carolina State					x
minus	v. chapmanii	82.192	North Carolina State					x
minus	v. minus	73.055	Kehr					x
minus	v. minus	74.050	Ex Hort					x

Plants	Form	RSF #	Source	V	W	X	Y	Z
minus	v. minus	75.133	Gable					x
minus	v. minus	76.011	Van Veen					x
minus	v. minus	76.086	Cline					x
minus	v. minus	77.001	Granston					x
minus	v. minus	77.095	Granston					x
minus	v. minus	79.162	Ex Hort					x
minus	v. minus	79.163	P Hill					x
minus	v. minus	82.116	Ring					x
minus	v. minus	82.117	Ring, Deip					x
minus	v. minus	82.190	North Carolina State					x
minus	v. minus	83.009	North Carolina State					x
minus	v. minus,'Fort Gaines'	92.004	John Thornton					x
minus	v. minus,'Kolomoki'	92.005	John Thornton					x
minus	v. minus,'Rockford'	92.006	John Thornton					x
mollicomum		76.295	Gambrill, Slonecker					x
monosematum		73.186					1	
montroseanum		00.105	Brodick	x				
montroseanum	FCC	00.169	Benmore	x				
montroseanum		73.184					2	
montroseanum		74.004	Royal Botanic Garden				1	x
montroseanum	K-W 6261	80.050	Borde Hill					x
montroseanum		82.043	Lamellen, UBC					x
montroseanum		82.198	Brodick, Bender					x
morii		64.170	Benmore	x	3	x	9	x
morii		00.485	Lamellen	X				
morii		73.188					3	
morii	Patrick	77.377	Patrick, W Wash Re					x
moulmainense		80.092	Royal Botanic Garden					x
moupinense		69.1096	Caperci			x	2	
moupinense		00.478	Rowallane	x				
moupinense		73.190	C Smith				3	x
moupinense		73.191	C Smith				2	x
moupinense		69.873	Ex Hort				1	x
moupinense			Cox				1	
moupinense		74.083	Glendoick					x
moupinense		76.163	Bodnant					x
moupinense	Wilson 879	79.131	Glendoick					x
mucronatum		73.342						
mucronulatum	Cornell Pink	73.193	Brydon, Tichnor				9	x
mucronulatum		76.127	Berg					x
mucronulatum		77.661	Windsor					x
mucronulatum		78.026	Mehlquist					x
mucronulatum		79.168	Berg					x
mucronulatum		81.020	Wada, Kehr					x
mucronulatum		82.204	Berg, Suzuki					x

Plants	Form	RSF #	Source	V	W	X	Y	Z
mucronulatum		82.205	Berg, Suzuki					x
mucronulatum		82.206	Berg, Suzuki					x
mucronulatum		82.207	Berg, Suzuki					x
mucronulatum	USNA 55252	88.011	USNA					x
mucronulatum	USNA 55222	88.018	USNA					x
mucronulatum	USNA 55065	88.019	USNA					x
nakaharae		73.195	Gigha			x	18	x
nakaharae		74.085	Hydon				3	x
nakaharae		76.267	P Hill					x
nankotaisanense		70.365					1	
neriiflorum		70.045	W Wood			x	3	x
neriiflorum	ss. euchaites	68.790	Larson			x	5	
neriiflorum	ss. euchaites	65.397	Crarae	x		x	1	
neriiflorum	ss. euchaites		F.R.				3	
neriiflorum	ss. euchaites		Huey				1	
neriiflorum	maroon underleaf	74.025	F.R.				4	
neriiflorum	ss. neriiflorum	67.092	Granston					x
neriiflorum	ss. neriiflorum	69.790	Larson, Walker					x
neriiflorum	ss. neriiflorum	70.045	W Wood					x
neriiflorum	ss. neriiflorum	74.084	F Robbins					x
neriiflorum	ss. neriiflorum	74.086	Huey					x
neriiflorum	ss. neriiflorum	75.289	Castle Howard					x
neriiflorum	ss. neriiflorum	75.292	Castle Howard, Phetteplace					x
neriiflorum	ss. neriiflorum	76.107	F Robbins					x
neriiflorum	ss. neriiflorum	00.548	Glendoick	x				
neriiflorum	ss. neriiflorum, Farrer 877	77.748	Windsor					x
neriiflorum	ss. neriiflorum, SBEC 0172	88.012	Sino-British Exp.					x
neriiflorum		91.025	Warren Berg					x
nervulosum	v. nervulosum	84.165	Mossman					x
nipponicum		73.197					1	
nivale	ss. nivale	65.457	Wisley	x	4	x	21	x
nivale	ss. nivale, Cooper 3483	77.641	Berg, Royal Bot. Gdn.					x
nivale	ss. boreale	66.576	Wisley		1	x	3	x
nivale	ss. boreale	76.300	VanVeen, Reuthe					x
nivale	ss. boreale	79.141	Royal Botanic Garden					x
niveum		65.345	Stonefield	x	1	x	1	x
niveum		65.309	Crarae	x	1	x	1	x
niveum		74.013	Black				13	x
niveum		75.115	Windsor					x
niveum		76.201	Royal Botanic Garden					x
niveum		77.525	Berg					x
niveum		77.557	Caperci					x
niveum		77.676	Crarae					x
niveum	Clone A	93.062	June Sinclair					x
niveum	Clone B	93.063	June Sinclair					x

Plants	Form	RSF #	Source	V	W	X	Y	Z
niveum	Clone C	93.064	June Sinclair					x
niveum	N Sikkim	93.094	Keith White, Selcer					x
niveum	N Sikkim	93.095	Keith White, Selcer					x
noriakianum		78.036	Larson, UBC					x
nuttallii		74.005					1	
nuttallii		80.155	UBC					x
obtusum	v. amoenum		Hoitink				1	
occidentale			Hoitink				1	
occidentale	SM401		Mossman				1	
occidentale	SM604	74.089	Mossman				1	x
occidentale	'Leonard Frisbee'		Mossman				1	
occidentale		74.088	Hoitink					x
occidentale	SM 232	76.049	B Smith					x
occidentale		77.331	W Wash Re					x
occidentale		77.333	W Wash Re					x
occidentale		77.334	W Wash Re					x
occidentale		77.335	W Wash Re					x
occidentale		77.337	W Wash Re					x
occidentale		77.338	W Wash Re					x
occidentale		77.339	W Wash Re					x
occidentale		77.340	W Wash Re					x
occidentale	SM 501	77.379	Mossman					x
occidentale	SM 229	77.384	Mossman					x
occidentale	SM 408	77.395	Mossman					x
occidentale		77.499	Ex Hort					x
occidentale		77.509	Ex Hort					x
occidentale	SM 30	77.623	Mossman					x
occidentale	SM 245	81.116	B Smith					x
odoriferum		00.364	Brodick	x	2	x		
oldhami		73.203	USDA				4	x
oldhami		73.347					2	
oldhami			Hoitink				1	
oldhami		93.051	Wada, Berg					x
orbiculare		00.093	Robbins	x		x		
orbiculare		65.262	Bodnant	x	1	x	14	x
orbiculare		66.542	Royal Botanic Garden	x	4	x	11	x
orbiculare		65.350	Caerhays	x	3	x	4	x
orbiculare		67.702	Bodnant		1	x	3	x
orbiculare		00.466	Sandling Park	x				
orbiculare		73.206	Ex Hort				2	x
orbiculare		73.207					4	
orbiculare		73.205					1	
orbiculare		74.043	W Wood, Grieg				12	x
orbiculare		76.236	Brodick					x
orbiculare	ssp. cardiobasis	93.052	June Sinclair					x

Plants	Form	RSF #	Source	V	W	X	Y	Z
orbiculare	Bi-color	93.065	June Sinclair					x
orbiculatum		80.004						x
orbiculatum		83.070	Schick					x
orbiculatum		87.051	Collenette, RBG					x
oreodoxa	1524-018-70						3	
oreodoxa	v. fargesii	00.671	Barnett		1			
oreodoxa	v. fargesii	62.046	Walker, Royal Botanic Gdn		1	x	1	x
oreodoxa	v. fargesii	65.308	Crarae	x	3	x	15	x
oreodoxa	v. fargesii	65.808	Walker, Phetteplace				3	x
oreodoxa	v. fargesii	66.648	Phetteplace		3	x	2	
oreodoxa	v. fargesii	67.681	Corsock		3	x	13	x
oreodoxa	v. fargesii	67.686	Glensoick		1	x	2	x
oreodoxa	v. fargesii	67.691	Windsor		2	x	4	x
oreodoxa	v. fargesii	67.709	Royal Botanic Garden		1	x	9	
oreodoxa	v. fargesii	69.648	Ex Hort					x
oreodoxa	v. fargesii	69.670	Walker, Phetteplace		4	4	18	x
oreodoxa	v. fargesii	73.098					5	
oreodoxa	v. fargesii	73.991					11	
oreodoxa	v. fargesii	75.316	Phetteplace					x
oreodoxa	v. fargesii	76.160	Bodnant					x
oreodoxa	v. fargesii	77.354	F Robbins					x
oreodoxa	v. fargesii	83.155	Ex Hort					x
oreodoxa	v. fargesii	88.002	Ryan					x
oreodoxa	v. oreodoxa	70.395	Borde Hill					x
oreodoxa	v. oreodoxa, Wilson 4247	77.749	Windsor					x
oreodoxa	v. oreodoxa	80.121	Croft					x
oreodoxa	v. oreodoxa	82.152	Olsen, Forst Bot Gdn					x
oreodoxa		91.076	Warren Berg					x
oreodoxa		91.077	Warren Berg					x
Oreotrephes	as exquisitum	00.221	Exbury	x				
oreotrephes		70.054	Siegmund			x	8	x
oreotrephes	F 20489	66.625	Windsor		1		5	x
oreotrephes		70.032	C Smith			x	4	
oreotrephes		70.010	Royal Botanic Garden			x	2	
oreotrephes			C Smith			x		
oreotrephes		00.401	Crarae	x				
oreotrephes		70.085					3	
oreotrephes		70.053					10	
oreotrephes		73.208	Walker				5	x
oreotrephes		73.209					3	
oreotrephes		73.210	Ex Hort				3	x
oreotrephes		73.211	Exbury, Brydon, F Robbins				6	x
oreotrephes		70.027	Ex Hort					x
oreotrephes		75.261	Exbury, F Robbins					x
oreotrephes		76.335	Phettaeplace					x

Plants	Form	RSF #	Source	V	W	X	Y	Z
oreotrephes		77.139	Berg					x
oreotrephes		78.013	Jordan, Frye					x
oreotrephes		91.002	Glendoick					x
orthocladum	v. orthocladum	75.273	Goheen, Cent for Urb Hort					x
orthocladum	v. microleucum	77.216	Caperci					x
orthocladum	Clone A	93.028	Berg, Sinclair					x
orthocladum	Clone B	93.029	Berg, Sinclair					x
orthocladum	Clone C	93.030	Berg, Sinclair					x
ovatum		76.050	VanVeen, Gable					x
ovatum		81.146	Bodnant					x
ovatum	Wilson 11391	82.012	Pukeiti gdn					x
paachypodum	Forrest 7516	87.055	Royal Botanic Garden					x
pachysanthum	Patrick	78.064						x
pachysanthum		91.039	Warren Berg					x
pachysanthum		91.040	Warren Berg					x
pachysanthum	RV 72/001	92.012	Leonardslee					x
pachysanthum	'Pachy Bee'	93.043	Warren Berg					x
pachysanthum	TB 8313	93.086	Warren Berg, Fred Winter					x
pachysanthum		93.100	Greer					x
pachytrichum		65.290	Berg, Patrick	x	1	x	1	x
pachytrichum	'Sesame'	65.389	Bodnant, UBC	x	1			x
pachytrichum	Wilson 1435	70.191	Lamellen				5	x
pachytrichum		76.164	Bodnant					x
pallescens		73.352					2	
paradoxum		00.517	Windsor	x				
parmulatum		66.549	Glendoick	x	2	x	5	x
parmulatum		74.017	F Robbins				5	x
parryae		65.356	Brodick		1	x	2	
parryae		00.532	Royal Botanic Garden	x				
pauciflorum	v. pauciflorum	82.011	Baird, Strybing Arboretum					x
pauciflorum	v. pauciflorum	83.067	Schick					x
pemakoense		70.0004	F Robbins			x	5	x
pemakoense		66.596	Glendoick			2	x	28	x
pemakoense		77.268	Ex Hort					x
pendulum	LS&T 6660	76.141	Royal Botanic Garden					x
pendulum		93.053	Warren Berg					x
pentaphyllum		64.198	Hillier	x	1	x	1	x
pentaphyllum		73.214					1	
pentaphyllum		76.076	Caperci					x
pentaphyllum		77.311	Baird					x
pentaphyllum		84.160	Larson					x
peregrinum		65.316	Lamellen	x	2	x	2	
periclymenoides		76.279	Manigault, USNA					x
periclymenoides	Gambrill	76.292	Gambrill					x
periclymenoides	Gambrill	76.293	Gambrill					x

Plants	Form	RSF #	Source	V	W	X	Y	Z
periclymenoides		77.013	Granston					x
periclymenoides		77.347	W Wash Re					x
periclymenoides		93.004	Woodlanders, Inc					x
phaeochitum		87.044	Cruttwell, RBG					x
phaeochrysum	v. phaeochrysum	71.509	Windsor, UBC					x
phaeochrysum	v. phaeochrysum	75.203	Hillier, Jacobson					x
phaeochrysum	v. phaeochrysum, Forrest 19574	76.156	Windsor					x
phaeochrysum	v. agglutinatum, Rock 11335	77.653	Windsor					x
phaeopeplum		83.065	Schick					x
piercei		74.030	F Robbins					x
piercei		75.266	F Robbins					x
piercei		76.210	Royal Botanic Gardens					x
pingianum	Patrick	76.328						x
planetum		65.325	Windsor	x	1	x	1	
pocophorum		00.225	Smith	x́				
pocophorum		00.439	Royal Botanic Garden	x				
pocophorum	v. pocophorum	75.054	Nymans					x
pocophorum	v. pocophorum	75.055	Nymans					x
pocophorum	v. pocophorum	75.240	Berg					x
pocophorum	v. pocophorum	76.230	Brodick					x
pocophorum	v. hemidartum	75.107	Windsor					x
pocophorum	v. hemidartum	93.061	Warren Berg					x
polycladum		65.455	Wisley					x
polycladum		65.459	Wisley	x	5	x	41	x
polycladum		73.252					2	
polycladum		73.253					2	
ponticum		73.344	Hoitink				3	x
ponticum		76.411	A Robbins					x
ponticum		78.056	Phetteplace					x
ponticum		78.070	UBC, Royal Botanic Garden					x
ponticum		79.001	Vincent, Skirving					x
ponticum	AC&H	79.130	Glendoick					x
praestans			Hillier, F.R. '75				1	
praestans		75.074	Wakehurst					x
praestans		75.117	Windsor					x
praetervisum		87.045	Collenette, RBG					x
praetervisum		88.049						x
praevernum		66.563	Windsor	x	1	x	5	x
praevernum		80.147	Boskoop					x
preptum		00.317	Lamellen	x				
preptum		82.079	Windsor, Royal Bot. Gdn.					x
primuliflorum		77.603	Glendoick, Berg					x
primuliflorum		77.618	King & Patton					x
primuliflorum		77.715	Royal Botanic Garden					x
principis		185		x	2	x		

Plants	Form	RSF #	Source	V	W	X	Y	Z
principis		65.282	Borde Hill	x	4	x	3	x
principis		73.354	Royal Botanic Garden				2	x
principis		76.213	Royal Botanic Garden					x
prinophyllum		76.077	Granston					x
prinophyllum		77.348	W Wash Re					x
prinophyllum		77.503	M Baird					x
pronum		70.041	Windsor				1	x
pronum		74.068					1	
pronum		74.047	Berg					x
pronum		75.235	Berg					x
proteoides		65.472	Hillier	x	1	x	1	
proteoides		73.221					4	
proteoides			Hillier, F 2 '75				1	
proteoides	Rock	74.118	Brydon, F Robbins					x
proteoides	Rock	75.236	Berg, Nelson					x
proteoides		76.354	Berg					x
proteoides	(HP seed)	93.031	Sinclair					x
proteoides	(HP seed)	93.032	Sinclair					x
proteoides	(HP seed)	93.032	Sinclair					x
proteoides	(HP seed)	93.033	Sinclair					x
proteoides	(HP seed)	93.034	Sinclair					x
proteoides	(HP seed)	93.035	Sinclair					x
pruniflorum		66.676	W Wood					x
pruniflorum		74.024	USNA					x
pruniflorum		75.229	Berry					x
pruniflorum	Skinner 1111K	76.281	USNA					x
pruniflorum		77.010	Granston					x
pruniflorum		77.018	Granston, Cox					x
pruniflorum		77.402	Calloway Gardens					x
pruniflorum	KW 7038	92.013	Leonardslee					x
prunifolium		73.222					1	
prunifolium	'Hohman'	74.024					3	
przewalski		00.519	Windsor	x				
przewalski		91.041	Warren Berg					x
przewalski		91.042	Warren Berg					x
przewalski		91.083	Warren Berg					x
przewalski		91.084	Warren Berg					x
przewalski		91.085	Warren Berg					x
przewalski		91.086	Warren Berg					x
przewalski		91.087	Warren Berg					x
przewalski		92.088	Warren Berg					x
przewalski		92.089	Warren Berg					x
przewalski	?	92.090	Warren Berg					x
pseudochrysanthum		64.193	Rowallane	x	1	x	3	
pseudochrysanthum		63.036	Sunningdale, Walker		1	x	11	x

Plants	Form	RSF #	Source	V	W	X	Y	Z
pseudochrysanthum	Dwarf	65.326	Windsor	x	1	x	2	
pseudochrysanthum		73.223					1	
pseudochrysanthum		73.224	Windsor, Brydoh				5	x
pseudochrysanthum		73.226	Exbury, Phetteplace				1	x
pseudochrysanthum	USDA 325053	73.227	USDA				6	x
pseudochrysanthum		73.228	USDA				5	
pseudochrysanthum	USDA 324052	73.229	USDA				13	x
pseudochrysanthum	USDA 325055	73.231	USDA				24	x
pseudochrysanthum	USDA 325054	73.232	USDA				16	x
pseudochrysanthum							1	
pseudochrysanthum	USDA 325055	73.400	USDA					x
pseudochrysanthum	USDA 325052	73.402	USDA					x
pseudochrysanthum	USDA 325050	73.405	USDA					x
pseudochrysanthum	USDA 325050	73.407	USDA					x
pseudochrysanthum	USDA 325054	73.410	USDA					x
pseudochrysanthum	USDA 325055	73.411	USDA					x
pseudochrysanthum	USDA 325052	73.412	USDA					x
pseudochrysanthum	Wilson 10928	75.076	Wakehurst					x
pseudochrysanthum		75.189	C Smith					x
pseudochrysanthum		76.051	Berg					x
pseudochrysanthum	6718	77.637	Berg					x
pseudochrysanthum		79.002	Clement					x
pseudochrysanthum	'Komo Kulshan'	93.102	Greer					x
pubescens	'Fine Bristles'	70.114					1	
pudorosum	L & S 2752	77.716	Royal Botanic Garden					x
pulchrum	'Violet Cloud'	74.045					1	
pumilum		00.254	Stronachullin	x				
pumilum		73.233	F Robbins				5	x
pumilum		77.717	Royal Botanic Garden					x
pumilum		77.728	Ex Hort					x
quinquefolium	'Five Arrows'	73.234	Exbury				1	x
quinquefolium		77.044	Granston					x
quinquefolium		77.045	Granston					x
quinquefolium		77.433	Caperci					x
quinquefolium		80.028	Madison					x
racemosum		73.235	F Robbins, Brydon				1	x
racemosum	Rock 11403	73.236	Kehr				1	x
racemosum			Hoitink				1	
racemosum			Cox				1	
racemosum		74.097	Glendoick					x
racemosum		75.255	Berry					x
racemosum		75.293	Glendoick, Phetteplace					x
racemosum		76.367	Berg					x
racemosum		77.098	Granston					x
racemosum		77.422	W Wash Ex					x

Plants	Form	RSF #	Source	V	W	X	Y	Z
racemosum		77.446	Ex Hort					x
racemosum	Farrer	77.677	Crarae					x
racemosum	Rock 11403	79.009	Schick					x
racemosum		79.180	Nymans, UBC					x
ramsdenianum		65.487	Lamellen	x	1	x	6	x
ramsdenianum		00.310	Crarae	x				
ramsdenianum		00.067	Glenarn	x				
ramsdenianum		70.164					1	
rarum		85.001	Smith, E W					x
rarum		88.037	Schick					x
ravum		69.1068	Barto			x	13	
recurvoides		74.037					1	
recurvoides							1	
recurvoides			Hillier, F.R. '75				1	
recurvoides	K-W 7184	74.098	Grieg, UBC					x
recurvoides	K-W 7184	75.056	Nymans					x
reticulatum		76.366	Berg, Suzuki					x
reticulatum		77.021	M Baird					x
reticulatum		77.073	Granston					x
reticulatum		77.123	W Wash Re					x
reticulatum	Shikoku	77.302	Berg					x
reticulatum		79.052	Glendoick					x
reticulatum		88.007	Rhod Assn					x
reticulatum		88.014	Rhod Assn					x
retivenium		89.005						x
retusum	v. retusum	79.027	Smith, E W					x
rex	K-W 4509	00.253	Bodnant	x				
rex		73.239					2	
rex	ss. fictolacteum	73.105	F Robbins, Brydon				2	x
rex	ss. fictolacteum, Rock	75.158	F. Robbins					x
rex	ss. fictolacteum	76.091	W Wash Ex					x
rex	ss. fictolacteum	77.418	W Avery					x
rex	ss. fictolacteum	77.419	W Avery					x
rex	ss. fictolacteum	77.548	WEA, Brenden					x
rex	ss. fictolacteum, Forrest 25719	83.156	Windsor					x
rex	ss. fictolacteum, SBEC 0957	88.009	Cox					x
rex	ss. fictolacteum,	00.272		x				
rex	ss. fictolacteum,	91.001	Caperci, D. Larson					x
rex	ss. fictolacteum,	91.049	Warren Berg					x
rex	ss. fictolacteum,	91.050	Warren Berg					x
rex	ss. fictolacteum,	92.058	Warren Berg					x
rex	ss. fictolacteum,	92.059	Warren Berg					x
rex	ss. fictolacteum,	92.060	Warren Berg					x
rex	ss. arizelum	65.335	Brodick	x		x	1	x
rex	ss. arizelum	76.203	Royal Botanic Garden					x

Plants	Form	RSF #	Source	V	W	X	Y	Z
rex	ss. arizelum, Rock	76.322	Berry					x
rex	ss. arizelum	78.008	B Smith, R Henny					x
rex	ss. arizelum, Forrest 21861	82.031	Warrington, UBC					x
rex	ss. arizelumForrest 18028	82.032	Warrington, UBC					x
rex	ss. arizelum	82.035	Warrington, UBC					x
rex	ss. arizelum	65.266	Trewithen	x	2	x	3	
rex	ss. arizelum	00.550	Logan	x				
rex	ss. arizelum, clone A	93.070	June Sinclair					x
rex	ss. arizelum, clone B	93.071	June Sinclair					x
rex	ss. arizelum, clone C	93.072	June Sinclair					x
rex	ss. arizelum, clone D	93.073	June Sinclair					x
rex	ss. rex, Rock 18234	75.118	Windsor					x
rex	ss. rex	76.181	Royal Botanic Garden					x
rex	ss. rex	80.036	Brodick					x
rex	ss. rex	93.066	James Caperci					x
rhabdotum		00.366	Brodick	x				
rigidum		68.742	W Wood, James			x	4	x
rigidum		73.353	Ex Hort				2	x
rigidum		77.426	W Wash Re					x
rigidum		93.049	Mrs. Inkster, Warren Berg					x
ririei		64.133	Caerhays	x	2	x	6	
ririei		65.454	Leonardslee	x	1	x	2	x
ririei		75.013	Hillier					x
robinsonii		83.066	Schick					x
roseatum		87.058	Royal Botanic Garden					x
rothschildii	Rock 157	75.182	W Wood					x
rothschildii	HI 074	93.009	Dick Booth					x
rothschildii	HI 074	93.016	Dick Booth					x
rothschildii	HI 074	93.017	Dick Booth					x
roxieanum		00.411	Lochinch	x				
roxieanum	v. oreonastes	74.025					1	
roxieanum	v. oreonastes	74.038	Berg, Nelson				4	x
roxieanum	v. oreonastes		Hillier, PHB '75				3	
roxieanum	v. roxieanum	65.472	Hillier					x
roxieanum	v. roxieanum	64.059	Royal Botanic Garden					x
roxieanum	v. roxieanum	71.411	Lochinch, UBC					x
roxieanum	v. roxieanum	73.221	F Robbins, Hillier					x
roxieanum	v. roxieanum	74.116	Grieg, UBC					x
roxieanum	v. roxieanum	74.117	Hillier, Brydon					x
roxieanum	v. roxieanum, Rock 11292	74.128	Windsor					x
roxieanum	v. roxieanum	75.218	Nelson, Exbury,Wagner					x
roxieanum	v. roxieanum, Rock 138?	75.317	Phetteplace					x
roxieanum	v. roxieanum	76.154	Windsor					x
roxieanum	v. roxieanum,	77.126	Caperci					x
roxieanum	v. roxieanum, Rock 138	78.122	C Smith					x

Plants	Form	RSF #	Source	V	W	X	Y	Z
roxieanum	v. roxieanum, Hu	79.039	Durre					x
roxieanum	v. roxieanum	93.048	Warren Berg					x
roxieanum		92.098	Warren Berg					x
roxieanum		92.099	Warren Berg					x
roxieanum		92.101	Warren Berg					x
roxieanum		93.040	Hillier, Berg					x
roxieanum	?	93.060	June Sinclair					x
rubiginosum		00.418		x	1			
rubiginosum	Yu 14990	66.627	Windsor		1	x	3	x
rubiginosum		73.130	F Robbins, Brydon				4	x
rubiginosum	'Rosy Ball'						2	
rubiginosum		70.366	Kew				1	x
rubiginosum		71.413	Borde Hill,	x			2	x
rubiginosum		77.129	Caperci					x
rubiginosum		77.376	Ex Hort					x
rubiginosum		77.413	W Wash Re					x
rubiginosum		79.185	Berry					x
rubiginosum		80.151	Heritage Plantation					x
rubiginosum	Hu 84	82.162	Birck					x
rubiginosum		91.045	Warren Berg					x
rubiginosum		91.046	Warren Berg					x
rubiginosum		91.047	Warren Berg					x
rubiginosum		91.048	Warren Berg					x
rubiginosum		92.061	Warren Berg					x
rubiginosum		92.062	Warren Berg					x
rubiginosum		92.063	Warren Berg					x
rubropilosum	USDA 325046	73.241	USDA				2	x
rubropilosum	USDA 325049	73.242	USDA				1	x
rufum	Rock 13649	74.040	Windsor				1	x
rufum	Hummel 569	79.151	Goteburg Bot Gdn					x
rufum		80.037	Brodick					x
rugosum	v. rugosum	85.040	Cavendish,					x
rugosum	v. rugosum	85.041	Mossman, Cavendish					x
rugosum	v. rugosum	87.046	Argent, Royal Bot. Gdn.					x
rupicola	v. rupicola	65.458	Wisley	x	1	x	5	x
rupicola	v. chryseum	75.028	F Robbins					x
rupicola	v. chryseum	77.777	Berry					x
rupicola	v. chryseum, Rock	78.120	Caperci					x
rupicola	v. muliense	93.026	Berg, Sinclair					x
rupicola	v. muliense	93.027	Berg, Sinclair					x
russatum		65.479	Rowallane	x	7	x	6	x
russatum		66.602	Caerhays		1	x	8	x
russatum		73.244	F Robbins				4	x
russatum		73.245	F Robbins, Brydon				4	x
russatum	1496-049-70	70.367	Kew				2	

Plants	Form	RSF #	Source	V	W	X	Y	Z
russatum		77.412	W Wash Re					x
russatum		77.538	Ex Hort					x
russatum		78.084	C Smith, Nelson					x
russatum	Forrest 25500	79.116	Borde Hill					x
russatum		80.052	Borde Hill					x
russatum		82.202	Berg					x
saluenense		68.874	Grieg			x	18	
saluenense	ss. saluenense, Rock 110	69.876	Walker, W Wood			x	16	x
saluenense	ss. chameunum	66.597	Glendoick				9	x
saluenense		73.220					54	
saluenense	ss. chameunum	73.246	W Wood, Brydon, Exbury				10	x
saluenense	ss. saluenense	75.257	Berry					x
saluenense	ss. saluenense	76.412	Berry					x
saluenense	ss. saluenense	79.044	Borde Hill					x
saluenense	ss. chameunum	80.076	Castle Howard					x
saluenense	ss. saluenense	82.163	Birck					x
sanctum		73.250	Gigha			x	1	x
sanctum			Hoitink				1	
sanctum		76.080	M Baird					x
sanctum		77.014	Granston					x
sanctum		77.015	Granston					x
sanguineum		70.047	W Wood			x	1	
sanguineum		70.036	Phetteplace			x		
sanguineum	ss. didymum, Rock 44	68.215	Phetteplace, Walker	x		x	2	x
sanguineum	ss. didymum	69.792	Walker, W Wood, Exbury			x	10	x
sanguineum	ss. didymum	70.072	Phetteplace			x	6	
sanguineum	ss. sanguineum, v. haemaleum	70.022	Ex Hort				2	x
sanguineum	ss. sanguineum, v. haemaleum	65.403	Crarae	x		x	1	x
sanguineum	ss. haemaleum		Rock #FR				1	
sanguineum	ss. sanguineum, v. haemaleum	68.853	F Robbins			x	3	x
sanguineum	ss. sanguineum, v. didymoides	70.135	Stronachullin				1	x
sanguineum	Rock #6						3	
sanguineum	ss. didymum	70.232	Ex Hort					x
sanguineum	ss. sanguineum, v. sanguineum	77.214	Berg					x
sanguineum	ss. sanguineum, v. cloiophorum	75.231	Berry, Caperci					x
sanguineum	ss. sanguineum, v. cloiophorum	75.753	Forrest 25521, Windsor					x
sanguineum	ss. sanguineum, v. haemaleum	78.058	Rock, Phetteplace					x
sanguineum	ss. sanguineum, v. haemaleum	78.086	Rock 65, Phetteplace					x
sanguineum	ss. sanguineum, v. haemaleum	84.153	Larson					x
sargentianum	'Whitebait'		Cox				5	
sargentianum		74.104	Glendoick					x
sargentianum		75.280	Pierce					x
sargentianum		76.324	Berry					x
sargentianum	Wilson 1208	77.721	Royal Botanic Garden					x
saxifragoides		88.050						x

Plants	Form	RSF #	Source	V	W	X	Y	Z
scabridibracteum		86.022	U of Cal Berkley					x
scabridibracteum	Scarle 17	87.047	Royal Botanic Garden					x
scabrifolium	v. scabrifolium	70.155	Brodick				7	x
scabrifolium	v. scabrifolium	79.117	Borde Hill					x
scabrifolium	v. spiciferum	64.106	Brodick	x	10	x	28	x
scabrifolium	v. spiciferum, K-W 3953	70.114	Windsor					x
schizopeplum		74.042					1	
schlippenbachii		64.199	Hillier	x	1	x	2	x
schlippenbachii		77.038	M Baird					x
schlippenbachii		77.065	Granston					x
schlippenbachii		77.067	Granston					x
schlippenbachii		77.096	Granston					x
schlippenbachii		77.364	W Wash Re					x
schlippenbachii		77.569	W Wood					x
schlippenbachii		77.586	W Wood					x
schlippenbachii	Clement	79.006	Clement					x
schlippenbachii		84.154	Larson					x
schlippenbachii	'Prince Charming'	91.006	Cox, Eversole, Briggs					x
schoddei		84.167	Mossman, Tatum					x
scopulorum		80.135	Trengwainton					x
searleanum		80.148	Boskoop					x
searsiae		70.125	Glendoick				1	x
selense	ss. selense	65.296	Glenarn	x	2	x	6	x
selense	ss. selense	76.312	Windsor					x
selense	ss. selense, Forrest 14458	77.773	Berry					x
selense	ss. setiferum, K-W 7190	65.521	Windsor	x	1	x	13	x
selense	ss. dasycladum	77.766	Ex Hort					x
selense	ss. dasycladum	77.778	W Wood					x
selense	ss. dasycladum	92.055	Warren Berg					x
selense	ss. dasycladum	92.056	Warren Berg					x
selense	ss. dasycladum, Rock 11269	79.107	Borde Hill					x
selense	ss. jucundum	82.138	Bremen Rhod					x
selense	ss. jucundum, SBEC 0365	88.015	Sino-British Exp.					x
semibarbatum		75.077	Wakehurst					x
semibarbatum		81.067	USNA					x
semnoides			RBG seed				1	
semnoides		76.204	Royal Botanic Garden					x
serotinum		65.301	Royal Botanic Garden	x	1	x	1	
serotinum		00.564	Windsor	x	2			
serpylifolium		73.357					2	
serpylifolium		76.078	Berg					x
serpylifolium		76.356	Berg, Suzuki					x
serpylifolium		79.173	Berg					x
serpylifolium		79.175	Berg					x
serrulatum	Skinner 1227B	76.282	USNA					x

Plants	Form	RSF #	Source	V	W	X	Y	Z
serrulatum	Skinner 1280	76.283	USNA					x
serrulatum	Skinner 1265	76.284	USNA					x
serrulatum	Skinner 1265C	76.285	USNA					x
serrulatum		77.036	Granston					x
serrulatum		77.344	Tingle, W Wash Ex					x
setosum			Cox				1	
setosum		91.010	Warren Berg					x
setosum	Sikkim	93.092	Selcer					x
sheilae		87.048	Argent, Royal Bot. Garden					x
sherriffii		75.012	Hillier					x
sherriffii		75.238	Berg, Hydon					x
sherriffii	L&S 2751	76.155	Windsor					x
sherriffii		76.193	Royal Botanic Garden					x
sherriffii		76.237	Brodick					x
sherriffii		92.079	Warren Berg					x
shweliense		74.007					10	
sidereum		65.426	Wakehurst	x		x		
sidereum	K-W 20838	73.255	Brydon, W Wood				2	x
sidereum	K-W 20835	82.027	Phetteplace					x
sidereum	Forrest 24563	82.063	Borde Hill, UBC					x
siderophyllum		80.102	Benmore					x
sikangense	cookeanum F25622	92.015	Leonardslee					x
sikayotaizanense		79.089	Kehr					x
sikkimense	Sikkim	93.090	Selcer					x
sikkimense	Sikkim	93.091	Selcer					x
simiarum		93.050	Warren Berg					x
simsii		73.355	Ex Hort					x
simsii		80.014	USNA					x
simsii		80.018	USNA					x
simulans	Forrest 20428	76.168	Royal Botanic Garden					x
sinogrande		00.526	Brodick	x				
sinogrande	K-W 21602	73.258	F Robbins				3	x
sinogrande	K-W 6782	75.058	Nymans					x
sinogrande	Forrest 25679	79.118	Borde Hill					x
sinogrande		82.040	Trewithen, UBC					x
sinogrande		88.016	Ex Hort					x
sinogrande		91.004	Glendoick					x
sinonuttallii		65.367	Brodick	x		x		
smirnowii		65.493	Corsock, UBC	x	1	x		x
smirnowii		76.376	Berg					x
smirnowii		77.307	Miller					x
smirnowii		77.319	McGuire					x
smithii		65.255	Stronachullin	x	3	x	2	x
smithii		70.035	Robbins			x		
smithii		75.061	Wakehurst					x

Plants	Form	RSF #	Source	V	W	X	Y	Z
smithii		76.401	Benmore					x
smithii		77.004	Granston					x
smithii		88.020	Ex Hort					x
solitarium		85.042	Mossman, Cavendish					x
solitarium		88.051						x
solitarium		88.057						x
souliei	White form	00.075	Royal Botanic Garden	x				
souliei		73.261	Exbury				1	x
souliei		74.048					3	
souliei		75.005	Hillier					x
souliei		76.245	Brodick					x
souliei		76.304	Glendoick					x
souliei		77.663	Windsor					x
souliei	Hu	79.041	Durre					x
souliei		92.069	Warren Berg					x
souliei		92.070	Warren Berg					x
souliei		92.071	Warren Berg					x
souliei		92.072	Warren Berg					x
sperabile	v. sperabile	70.012	W Wood			x		x
sperabile	K-W 20260	00.228	Smith	x				
sperabile		00.160	Crarae	x				
sperabile		70.012	W Wood				3	
sperabile	v. sperabile	78.075	Brodick, UBC					x
sperabile	v. sperabile, K-W 7124	79.119	Borde Hill					x
sperabile	v. weihsiense, Forrest 26478	70.310	Nymans, UBC					x
sparabiloides	Forrest 21824	77.664	Windsor					x
sphaeroblastum		67.688	Glendoick		1	x	2	x
sphaeroblastum		64.145	Corsock	x		x	1	x
sphaeroblastum		74.021					2	
sphaeroblastum		75.187	C Smith, Nelson					x
sphaeroblastum	Forrest 17110	76.185	Royal Botanic Garden					x
sphaeroblastum		83.011	Larson					x
sphaeroblastum		84.156	Ex Hort					x
sphaeroblastum		84.157	Ex Hort					x
sphaeroblastum		84.158	Ex Hort					x
spilotum		65.302	Royal Botanic Garden	x	4	x	4	
spinuliferum		69.834	Walker, Duncan			x	4	x
spinuliferum		73.266					7	
spinuliferum	SBEC	87.012	Sino-British Exp					x
spinuliferum	SBEC	87.013	Sino-British Exp					x
spinuliferum	SBEC	87.014	Sino-British Exp					x
stamineum		70.369	Kew, UBC					x
stamineum		76.380	Kew					x
stenaulum	F 19869	00.603	Caerhays		1			
stenaulum	K-W 20679	75.040	Kew					x

Plants	Form	RSF #	Source	V	W	X	Y	Z
stenophyllum		85.046	Mossman, Cavendish					x
stenophyllum		91.015						x
stenophyllum		91.005	ex hort (Rutherford?)					x
stewartianum		65.291	Benmore		1	x	2	x
stewartianum	v. aiolosalpinx	67.684	Corsock		2	x	2	x
stewartianum		00.231	Royal Botanic Garden	x				
stewartianum	Forrest 26932	77.774	Windsor					x
stewartianum	Rock 18376	77.775	Windsor					x
stewartianum		77.802	Berry					x
strigillosum		69.836	Lyons, Walker			x	1	x
strigillosum		00.277	Leonardslee	x				
strigillosum		73.271	W Wood, Grieg				8	x
strigillosum		73.269	C Smith, Grieg				1	x
strigillosum		73.270	F Robbins				2	x
strigillosum		65.277	Leonardslee, U BC					x
strigillosum		75.169	F Robbins, Grieg					x
strigillosum		75.178	W Wood, Grieg					x
strigillosum		76.081	Berg, Phetteplace					x
strigillosum		76.222	Brodick					x
strigillosum		77.204	Van Winkle					x
strigillosum		77.627	Miller, Grieg					x
strigillosum		77.791	Crarae					x
strigillosum		82.125	Bender, Royal Botanic Gdn					x
strigillosum		83.012	Larson, Grieg					x
subansiriense	C & H 418	77.636	Berg, Glendoick					x
subansiriense		80.170	Bender, Royal Bot. Gdn.					x
succothii	K-W 13666	73.316	Nymans				3	x
succothii	LS&H 21295	75.079	Wakehurst					x
succothii		77.619	King & Patton					x
succothii		92.044	Warren Berg					x
succothii		92.045	Warren Berg					x
succothii		92.046	Warren Berg					x
sulfureum	F. 15782	00.604	Caerhays		1			
sulfureum		00.134	Caerhays	x				
sulfureum	K-W Triangle		Cox				4	
sulfureum	round leaved		Cox				2	
sulfureum		74.108	Glendoick					x
sumatranum		83.068	Schick					x
superbum		78.094	Mossman					x
superbum		83.069	Schick					x
supranubium		00.0108	Brodick	x	1	x		
supranubium		70.370	Kew			x		
sutchuenense		68.816	Phetteplace			x	3	x
sutchuenense		65.348	Caerhays	x		x		
sutchuenense		73.272	Phetteplace, Brydon				1	x

Plants	Form	RSF #	Source	V	W	X	Y	Z
sutchuenense	v. geraldii	73.273					2	
sutchuenense		76.092	Caperci					x
sutchuenense		76.330	Phetteplace					x
sutchuenense		77.205	VanWinkle					x
sutchuenense		77.224	F Robbins					x
sutchuenense		77.246	W Wash Re					x
sutchuenense		77.439	Larson, W Wash Re					x
sutchuenense		77.763	Glenarn, UBC					x
sutchuenense	Wilson 1232	79.120	Borde Hill					x
sutchuenense		82.197	Cook					x
taliense		65.292	Benmore, UBC	x	5	x		x
taliense		74.051					1	
tanastylum	v. pennivenium	75.073	Wakehurst					x
tapetiforme		66.577	Wisley		2	x	10	x
tapetiforme			W Wood				2	
tatsienense		70.422	Royal Botanic Garden				3	x
tatsienense		77.424	W Wash Re					x
tatsienense	Forrest 20482	78.048	Caerhays, Phetteplace					x
telmateium		00.578	Wisley		1			
telmateium		65.456	Wisley	x	1	x	22	x
telmateium	Forrest 21250	77.724	Royal Botanic Garden					x
telmateium	Forrest 21250	77.757	Windsor					x
telmateium	Forrest 21377	77.758	Windsor					x
telmateium	K-W 4102	77.759	Windsor					x
telmateium	Forrest 15210	80.006	Castle Howard					x
temenium	v. chrysanthemum	00.249	Stronachullin	x				
temenium	v. dealbatum	76.196	Royal Botanic Garden					x
temenium	v. gilvum	79.165	Glendoick					x
tephropeplum		70.029	Robbins			x	1	
tephropeplum	K-W 20844 pale	65.256	Stronachullin	x	1	x	5	x
tephropeplum	K-W 20844 dark	65.257	Stronachullin	x	3	x	12	x
tephropeplum	v. deliense, K-W 21000	64.230	Smith	x		x		
tephropeplum		73.275	F Robbins				13	x
tephropeplum	(as deliense)	73.276					10	
tephropeplum	(as deliense)	73.277					2	
tephropeplum							12	
tephropeplum		75.162	J Henny, W Wood					x
tephropeplum		75.183	Ex Hort					x
tephropeplum		77.578	Ex Hort					x
thayerianum		69.216	Brandt	x	4	x	9	
thayerianum		66.617	Royal Botanic Garden		1	x	6	x
thayerianum		66.605	Caerhays		1	x	6	x
thayerianum		00.135	Caerhays	x				
thayerianum		77.089	Granston					x
thayerianum		77.357	W Avery					x

Plants	Form	RSF #	Source	V	W	X	Y	Z
thomsonii	L & S 2847	67.716	Royal Botanic Garden		1	x	5	x
thomsonii		64.058	Phetteplace			x	1	x
thomsonii		73.351					1	
thomsonii		71.649					1	
thomsonii		64.239	Crystal Springs	x		x		
thomsonii	v. pallidum	00.297	Glenarn	x	12			
thomsonii	ss. lopsangianum	64.149	Glenarn					x
thomsonii	ss. lopsangianum	77.696	Brodick					x
thomsonii	ss. thomsonii	71.617	Brodick					x
thomsonii	ss. thomsonii	75.120	Windsor					x
thomsonii	ss. thomsonii	75.237	Berg, Trewithen					x
thomsonii	ss. thomsonii	76.384	Brodick, UBC					x
thomsonii	ss. thomsonii	77.522	Berg					x
thomsonii	ss. thomsonii	77.556	Caperci					x
thomsonii		91.053	Warren Berg					x
thomsonii		91.054	Warren Berg					x
tosaense		78.031	Berg, Suzuki					x
tosaense		79.016	USNA					x
tosaense		79.017	USNA				x	
tosaense		79.087	Pierce, Hillier					x
traillianum		73.281					2	
traillianum	v. dictyotum, Rock 18437	65.508	Windsor	x	1	x	13	x
traillianum	v. dictyotum	75.084	Exbury					x
traillianum	v. dictyotum	00.385		x				
traillianum	v. traillianum	76.058	Nelson, Berg					x
traillianum		92.065	Warren Berg					x
traillianum		92.066	Warren Berg					x
traillianum		92.067	Warren Berg					x
traillianum		92.068	Warren Berg					x
traillianum		92.099	Warren Berg					x
traillianum		92.100	Warren Berg					x
traillianum		92.102	Warren Berg					x
traillianum		92.104	Warren Berg					x
trichanthum		68.723	Brandt, Walker			x	5	x
trichanthum		70.016	Brandt, Walker			x	2	x
trichanthum		73.280	Brydon, W Wood				14	x
trichanthum		76.059	Caperci					x
trichanthum		76.346	Gunderson					x
trichanthum		77.287	Pierce					x
trichocladum		73.293	F Robbins, Brydon					x
trichocladum		78.091	Barto, Phetteplace					x
trichostomum	radinum	66.675	W Wood		5	x	4	x
trichostomum	v. ledoides	73.283	F Robbins				4	x
trichostomum	v. ledoides	73.284	Huey				1	x
trichostomum		75.161	W Wood					x

Plants	Form	RSF #	Source	V	W	X	Y	Z
trichostomum		76.404	Bovee					x
trichostomum		77.127	Caperci					x
trichostomum		77.909	F Robbins					x
trichostomum		80.164	Bovee					x
trichostomum		82.164	Birck					x
triflorum	v. triflorum 'mahogani'	70.026	F Robbins,			x	3	x
triflorum	v. triflorum	77.134	Berg					x
triflorum	v. triflorum	77.156	Berg					x
triflorum	v. triflorum	77.423	Larson, W Wash Re					x
triflorum	v. bauhiniiflorum	73.026	Robbins, Brydon				2	x
triflorum	v. bauhiniiflorum	77.056	Granston					x
triflorum	v. bauhiniiflorum	77.427	F Robbins					x
triflorum	v. bauhiniiflorum	77.438	W Wash Ex					x
tsariense		66.653	Grieg, Walker			x	3	x
tsariense		73.288	Nelson				4	x
tsariense		75.150	Nelson, F Robbins					x
tsariense		75.234	Nelson, F Robbins, Berg					x
tsariense	L & S 2858	77.665	Windsor					x
tsariense		82.180	Jorgensen					x
tsariense	trimoense	91.003	Glendoick					x
tschonoskii		70.035	Robbins			x	3	
tschonoskii		77.211	Caperci					x
tsusiophyllum		76.353	Berg					x
tuba		93.022	E White Smith					x
ungernii		73.290	F Robbins, Brydon				2	
ungernii		76.061	Caperci					x
ungernii	AC & H 1	76.305	Glendoick					x
ungernii		76.368	Berg, Nelson					x
ungernii		77.358	W. Avery					x
ungernii		77.368	Ex Hort					x
ungernii		77.563	Caperci					x
uniflorum	v. uniflorum	66.586	Crarae		2	x	18	x
uniflorum	v. imperator	65.422	Wakehurst	x		x	18	x
uniflorum	v. imperator	73.142					19	
uniflorum	v. imperator	77.576	Ex Hort					x
uvarifolium		64.126	Leonardslee, Ex Hort	x	1	x		x
uvarifolium		71.231	C Smith	x			1	x
uvarifolium	Rock 73	73.291	Phetteplace, Brydon				3	x
uvarifolium	Rock 73	75.308	Phetteplace					x
uvarifolium		76.062	Caperci					x
uvarifolium		76.250	Benmore					x
uvarifolium		76.319	Berry					x
uvarifolium	Rock	78.006	B Smith					x
uvarifolium	Forrest 10639	79.143	Berg					x
uvarifolium		91.029	Warren Berg					x

Plants	Form	RSF #	Source	V	W	X	Y	Z
uvarifolium		91.030	Warren Berg					x
uvarifolium		91.032	Warren Berg					x
uvarifolium		91.033	Warren Berg					x
uvarifolium	'Reginard Childs' AM 1976	92.114	Leonardslee					x
valentinianum		69.831	Brandt			x		
valentinianum		00.240	Crystal Springs	x	3			
valentinianum	AM '36	65.391	Bodnant	x		x	5	x
valentinianum		70.193	Lamellen				1	x
valentinianum		84.076	King & Patton					x
vaseyi	'White Find'	74.046					1	
vaseyi			Hydon				1	
vaseyi		75.032	Labar					x
vaseyi		76.074	Granston					x
vaseyi		77.349	W Wash Re					x
vaseyi		77.506	M Baird					x
vaseyi		78.003	Wickwire					x
vaseyi		78.014	Frisbee, WEA					x
veitchianum		70.373	Kew			x		
veitchianum		00.353	Brodick	x	2			
veitchianum	Ashcombe	74.001	Windsor				13	x
veitchianum		81.127	Kolak, Strybing Arboretum					x
venator		65.381	Royal Botanic Garden	x	4	x	19	x
venator		69.833	Grieg, Walker			x	2	x
vernicosum		00.565	Windsor	x	1			
vernicosum		00.077	Glendoick	x				
vernicosum		69.812					1	
vernicosum		73.292					2	
vernicosum		70.353	Corsock				1	x
vernicosum		75.086	Exbury					x
vernicosum		75.127	Royal Botanic Garden					x
vernicosum		75.328	Berg, Reuthe					x
vernicosum		76.177	Royal Botanic Garden					x
vernicosum	Rock 205	77.058	Granston					x
vernicosum	Rock 11328	77.760	Windsor					x
vernicosum	H. Sm. 13976	79.152	Goteborg Bot Gdn					x
vernicosum	Rock 11404	82.054	Minterne, UBC					x
vernicosum		92.091	Warren Berg					x
vernicosum	Cox 2620	93.018	Warren Berg					x
vernicosum	Cox 2620	93.019	Warren Berg					x
vernicosum	Cox 2620	93.020	Warren Berg					x
vernicosum	Cox 2620	93.021	Warren Berg					x
vernicosum		93.054	June Sinclair					x
verruculosum		65.461	Wisley	x	6	x	3	
vialii		81.078	Borde Hill, Goteborg Bot Gdn					x
virgatum	ss. virgatum	65.404	Crarae	x		x	3	x

Plants	Form	RSF #	Source	V	W	X	Y	Z
virgatum	ss. virgatum	66.672	W Wood		4	x	8	x
virgatum	ss. virgatum	80.038	Brodick					x
virgatum	ss. virgatum	84.072	Brodick					x
viridescens		73.293					10	
viridescens	'Doshong La'						3	
viscidifolium		65.297	Glenarn			x	24	x
viscosum		74.112	Hydon				3	x
viscosum		76.063	Granston					x
viscosum	Skinner 1104E	76.287	USNA					x
viscosum	Skinner 1315B	76.289	USNA					x
viscosum		77.008	Granston					x
viscosum		77.236	W Wash Re					x
viscosum		77.343	W Wash Re					x
viscosum	Gambrill	78.110						x
vitis-idaea	Wing 54	87.052	Royal Botanic Garden					x
wallichii	LS&H 17527	75.080	Wakehurst					x
wallichii	L&S 6658	75.128	Royal Botanic Garden					x
wallichii		77.070	Granston					x
wallichii		77.071	Granston					x
wallichii		82.148	Sofiero					x
wallichii		92.047	Warren Berg					x
wallichii		92.048	Warren Berg					x
wallichii		92.049	Warren Berg					x
walongense		93.103	Logan Botanical Garden					x
wardii	K-W 4170		Exbury			x		
wardii		67.721	Glenarn		4	x	8	x
wardii	L & S 15764	69.096	Windsor	x	2	x	22	x
wardii	L & S 15764 Meadow Pond	65.327	Windsor	x	1	x	3	
wardii		00.444	Royal Botanic Garden	x				
wardii	K-W 4170	73.296	Exbury, Phetteplace				6	x
wardii	K-W 4170	70.059	Exbury, Phetteplace			x	3	x
wardii		73.295	F Robbins, Hacanson					x
wardii		73.294					3	
wardii	L & S 5679	74.044	Royal Botanic Garden				1	x
wardii	v. puralbum	68.732	Grieg, Walker, RBG			x	1	x
wardii	v. puralbum	74.020					1	
wardii	v. puralbum, Forrest 10616	76.183	Royal Botanic Gardren					x
wardii	v. wardii	70.415	Royal Botanic Gardren					x
wardii	v. wardii	75.015	Hillier					x
wardii	v. wardii, Sherriff 6569	75.129	Royal Botanic Garden					x
wardii	v. wardii	76.065	Berg					x
wardii	v. wardii	76.216	Royal Botanic Garden					x
wardii	v. wardii, LS&T 5679	76.217	Berg, Royal Botanic Garden					x
wardii	v. wardii	77.088	Granston, Ub, Heritage					x
wardii	v. wardii	77.281	Ex Hort					x

Plants	Form	RSF #	Source	V	W	X	Y	Z
wardii	v. wardii	77.447	F Robbins					x
wardii	v. wardii, Rock 11147	77.678	Crarae					x
wardii	v. wardii, Gf 3	77.746	Windsor					x
wardii		91.035	Warren Berg					x
wardii		91.036	Warren Berg					x
wardii		91.037	Warren Berg					x
wardii		91.038	Warren Berg					x
wardii		91.073	Warren Berg					x
wardii		91.074	Warren Berg					x
wardii		92.092	Warren Berg					x
wardii		92.093	Warren Berg					x
wardii		92.094	Warren Berg					x
wardii		92.095	Warren Berg					x
wardii		92.096	Warren Berg					x
wasonii		65.258	Stronachullin	x	5	x	14	x
wasonii		00.267	Bodnant	x				
wasonii	v. rhododactylum, Wilson 1876	74.036	Windsor				2	x
wasonii	Wilson 1876	76.266	Windsor					x
wasonii		76.309	Fortescue					x
wasonii		76.365	Berg					x
watsonii		65.303	Royal Botanic Garden	x		x	1	x
websterianum		65.462	Wisley	x		x	1	x
weldianum		74.018					3	
westlandii		80.098	Royal Botanic Garden					x
weyrichii		73.298	USNA				1	x
wightii		00.232	Lem/Smith	x				
wightii		00.416	Borde Hill	x				
wightii		73.300	C Smith				1	x
wightii		75.006	Hillier				1	x
wightii		75.210	Portland ARS					x
wightii		78.005	B Smith					x
wightii		80.032	Larson, Miller					x
wightii	Pradhan	88.017	Pradhan					x
williamsianum		66.606	Caerhays		3	x	25	x
williamsianum		73.301	Grieg, W Wood				4	x
williamsianum		70.332					2	
williamsianum		73.302					1	x
williamsianum	F/R/ '75						2	
williamsianum		74.113	F Robbins					x
williamsianum	Hu Yu	75.277	Grieg, UBC					x
williamsianum		75.307	Barto, Phetteplace					x
williamsianum		76.165	Bodnant					x
williamsianum		77.128	Caperci					x
williamsianum		83.097	DeMezey					x
wilsonae		65.428	Wakehurst	x	5	x	18	x

Plants	Form	RSF #	Source	V	W	X	Y	Z
wiltonii		74.029					1	
wiltonii		73.303	W Wood				1	x
wiltonii		73.304	Kew, Phetteplace					x
wiltonii		75.017	Hillier					x
wiltonii		75.088	Exbury					x
wiltonii		75.148	F Robbins					x
wiltonii		75.326	Grieg, Phetteplace					x
wiltonii		76.066	Ex Hort					x
wiltonii		76.387	Phetteplace					x
wiltonii		78.060	Phetteplace, Grieg					x
wiltonii	James form	93.045	Warren Berg					x
wiltonii	Phetteplace form	93.046	Warren Berg					x
womersleyi	Mossman	84.162	Mossman					x
xanthostephanum		66.677	W Wood			x	3	
xanthostephanum	Forrest 21707	77.666	Windsor					x
yakushimanum	ss. yakushimanum FCC '47	64.012	Windsor	x		x	5	x
yakushimanum	ss. yakushimanum	64.203	Smith	x		x		
yakushimanum	ss. yakushimanum	73.308	Huey				1	x
yakushimanum	ss. yakushimanum	73.309	Walker				2	x
yakushimanum	ss. yakushimanum	73.310	Brydon, Exbury				12	x
yakushimanum	ss. yakushimanum	75.184	C Smith					x
yakushimanum	ss. yakushimanum	75.241	Berg, Exbury					x
yakushimanum	ss. yakushimanum	75.260	F Robbins, Exbury					x
yakushimanum	ss. yakushimanum	77.047	Ex Hort					x
yakushimanum	ss. yakushimanum	77.048	Granston					x
yakushimanum	ss. yakushimanum	77.169	Ex Hort					x
yakushimanum	ss. yakushimanum	77.273	F Robbins					x
yakushimanum	ss. yakushimanum	77.296	Pierce					x
yakushimanum	ss. yakushimanum	77.371	Ex Hort					x
yakushimanum	ss. yakushimanum	77.372	Ex Hort					z
yakushimanum	ss. yakushimanum	77.534	Berg					x
yakushimanum		93.037	Doleshy, Sinclair					x
yakushimanum	Taku #1	93.038	Doleshy, Sinclair					x
yakushimanum	Taku #1	93.039	Doleshy, Sinclair					x
yakushimanum	ss. makinoi	77.173	Caperci, Brydon					x
yakushimanum	ss. makinoi	73.173					2	
yakushimanum	ss. makinoi	73.174					1	
yakushimanum	ss. makinoi, seed		Wada				11	
yakushimanum	ss. makinoi, Wada	74.081	Huey					x
yakushimanum	ss. makinoi, Wada	74.131						x
yakushimanum	ss. makinoi	76.110	Cummins					x
yakushimanum	ss. makinoi	77.057	Granston					x
yakushimanum	ss. makinoi	77.370	Ex Hort					x
yakushimanum	ss. makinoi, Suzuki	82.098	Goteborg Bot Gdn					x
yakushimanum	ss. makinoi	84.152	Larson					x

Plants	Form	RSF #	Source	V	W	X	Y	Z
yakushimanum			Hoitink				1	
yedoense	v. poukhanense	77.279	W Wash Re					x
yedoense	v. poukhanense	73.355					3	
yedoense	v. poukhanense		Hoitink				1	
yedoense	v. poukhanense	78.021	Berg, Suzuki					x
yedoense	v. poukhanense	78.022	Berg, Suzuki					x
yedoense	v. poukhanense	78.023	Berg, Suzuki					x
yedoense	v. poukhanense	78.024	Berg, Suzuki					x
yedoense	v. poukhanense	81.001	Nestegaard					x
yungningense		74.073	Hoitink					x
yungningense	Forrest 29260	77.727	Royal Botanic Garden					x
yunnanense		00.241	Crystal Springs	x	4			
yunnanense	'Tower Court'	00.628	Windsor		4			
yunnanense		70.043					1	
yunnanense		70.333	Fortescue				3	x
yunnanense	Forrest 16790	76.131	Royal Botanic Garden					x
yunnanense		77.425	W Wash Re					x
yunnanense		80.033	Miller					x
yunnanense		82.107	Bremen Rhod, Goteborg					x
zaleucum		65.405	Crarae	x	2	x	4	x
zaleucum		81.014	Cook, UBC					x
zoelleri		80.150	Boskoop					x
zoelleri		81.026	USDA					x
zoelleri		83.061	Ex Hort					x
zoelleri		83.071	Schick					x
zoelleri		86.023	USNA					x

APPENDIX C

AGREEMENT

AGREEMENT, made this 13 day of June, 1974 between the RHODODENDRON SPECIES FOUNDATION (the "Foundation"), a not-for-profit Oregon corporation, and WEYERHAEUSER COMPANY (the "Company"), a Washington corporation.

WITNESSETH:

WHEREAS, the Foundation presently maintains an extensive collection of rhododendrons (such collection as it now exists or as it may be modified or enlarged in the future is referred to herein as the "collection") in a garden near Salem, Oregon, and

WHEREAS, the Foundation has determined that its present garden provides insufficient facilities and space with respect to the maintenance and future growth of the collection, and

WHEREAS, the Company is willing to make available to the Foundation land and facilities on its Corporate Headquarters' site in Federal Way, Washington to plant and maintain, on a long term basis, the Foundation's present and envisioned future collection,

NOW, THEREFORE, in consideration of the mutual covenants expressed herein, the parties hereby agree:

1. The Company shall make available to the Foundation for uses consistent with its tax-exempt activities a parcel of land located on the Company's Corporate Headquarters' site in Federal Way, Washington and marked as site 8 on the attached map, consisting of approximately 24 acres of land, to be used as a garden and display area.

In addition, the Company shall provide access to and use of a greenhouse, lath house, equipment shed and nursery area, the exact location or locations of which shall be determined by the Company as soon as feasible and which may be part of site 8. All or part of said facilities may be located elsewhere on or near the Corporate Headquarters site.

2. As soon as practicable after the date of this agreement, the Company shall, at its own expense but with the advice of the Foundation, commence site preparation work on site 8 including appropriate clearing of land, installation of necessary electrical and water connections and distribution systems, fertilization of land and fencing. In addition, the Company shall, at its own expense, but with the advice of the Foundation, construct and equip a lath house and nursery area on or near site 8 and a greenhouse and equipment shed on site 8 or elsewhere on the Corporate Headquarters site.

3. It is understood that the Company retains full right and authority to determine the manner and timing of the improvements described in paragraph 2. Nevertheless, such improvements shall be completed in a manner and at a time consistent with the projected usage of the facilities by the Foundation.

4. The Foundation shall, at its own expense and under the supervision of its own personnel cause its present collection to be removed from its present site and replanted on site 8. All plants, including future additions to the collection, and cuttings shall remain the property of the Foundation.

5. Authorized representatives of the Foundation shall have full rights of access to site 8 and the related facilities for purposes of maintaining the collection, plant propagation and sale and viewing of the collection by members of the Foundation and other interested persons and groups under the direct supervision of the Supervisor and other duly authorized representatives of the Foundation. The collection shall not be open to the public except on a limited number of predetermined dates approved in advance by the Company. The Company retains the right to have its authorized representatives go upon or cross over site 8 as may be necessary without risking damage to the collection. The greenhouse, lath house, equipment shed and nursery are intended to be used mutually by the Company and the Foundation, each for their own purposes, provided that the Company retains the right to determine, in its sole discretion, an equitable resolution of any conflicts which may arise.

6. By this agreement, the Company is granting to the Foundation the right to go upon, cross over, plant and maintain the collection and perform the other activities described in paragraphs 4 and 5 on the Company's property but is not granting to the Foundation, expressly or by implication, any other right, title or interest in the Company's property or the improvements thereof or thereon.

7. After the collection has been replanted on site 8, the Foundation shall employ at its own expense a supervisor-propagator ("Supervisor") who shall be responsible, under the direction of the Foundation, for the maintenance and growth of the collection. The Foundation shall make every reasonable effort to increase the scope of the collection in a manner consistent with its tax-exempt status. All costs and expenses associated with obtaining new cuttings, the sale of cuttings to others and, in general, the conduct of its affairs with its members and the general public shall be the responsibility of the Foundation. The Company shall, at its own expense, provide water, power and area security services and may designate certain of its employees, as may be necessary, to perform services in connection with the collection under the supervision of the Foundation and may provide the use of its heavy equipment, as may be necessary, to the Foundation; The Foundation shall be solely responsible, through its own efforts and through its direction of the Supervisor, for the maintenance (including the cost of tools, fertilizer and all other costs not borne by the Company), care and growth of the collection. The Company shall not be responsible in any way for insurance on the collection or the employees, representatives and guests of the Foundation while on Company property, it being understood that the Foundation hereby assumes the full risk of any damage or liability, except damage caused by the gross negilgence or willful misconduct of the Company or its employees, arising to the collection or said employees, representatives and guests of the Foundation. The Company shall be responsible for all property taxes on site 8 and the related facilities.

8. The Company expressly denies any warranty or representation as to the quality

or suitability of site 8 or the related facilites for the purposes intended or for any other purposes and as to the ability and performance by its employees designated to perform services under the supervision of the Foundation.

9. This Agreement may be amended only by written instrument executed by the parties. This Agreement may be terminated by either party upon giving 24 months' advance written notice. In the event the Foundation gives notice of termination under the preceding sentence, the Company shall have the right, exercisable within 6 months after the date of notice of termination, to purchase the collection from the Foundation. The purchase price shall be the fair market value of the collection, as determined by a qualified independent appraiser approved by both of the parties. Such appraisal shall take into account: (1) the ability of the Foundation, through propagation techniques, to reproduce the collection, and (2) the cost savings to the Foundation of not having to remove the then-existing collection and replanting the same at a new location.

10. The parties hereto warrant and represent to each other that all requisite corporate action required to execute and deliver this Agreement has been taken and that the Agreement is enforceable in accordance with its terms.

11. This Agreement shall be governed by the laws of the State of Washington.

IN WITNESS WHEREOF, the parties hereto have caused this agreement to be executed by their duly authorized representatives as of the date first above written.

THE RHODODENDRON SPECIES FOUNDATION

By: /s/ Fred Robbins

WEYERHAEUSER COMPANY

By: /s/ George H. Weyerhaeuser

APPENDIX D

MASTER PLAN

FOR THE DEVELOPMENT OF

THE RHODODENDRON SPECIES GARDEN

AND

EDUCATIONAL CENTER

DRAFT OF PROPOSAL

Objective: To create one of the outstanding centers in the world for the acquisition of rhododendron species and the study, cultivation, display and distribution thereof, and to disseminate knowledge relating thereto.

A. Purposes:

1. To bring together in one place, and to preserve and protect superior forms of all rhododendron species, with companion trees, shrubs and plants that originate in the same geographical region.

2. To maintain the collection under the best possible conditions so that plants may develop into mature specimens.

3. To provide space and facilities for scientific research in the field of horticulture, primarily species rhododendron and for study of the habitat, selection and propagation of superior forms.

4. To make available the knowledge of plant forms to educational institutions, libraries, horticultural organizations, garden clubs, scholars and others interested in species rhododendron.

5. To develop gardens that will be open to the public at specified times to display the plants, the environment in which they grow and methods for their propagation and culture.

6. To create an educational program that will offer information and instruction to teachers, students, and other interested persons.

7. To develop a program of public relations that will make the plans and projects of the Foundation available to those interested.

8. To stimulate a broad interest in species rhododendron, and to encourage the study, collection and propagation of these plants.

B. The Plan:

1. Present status - The Rhododendron Species Foundation grew out of dedicated interest and much hard work by a small group of members of the American Rhododendron Society. Through the years it has made significant progress in setting up the plan for the gardens and educational center.
Achievements to date:

a. Site: Twenty-three acres of beautiful wooded land have been provided by the Weyerhaeuser Company in Federal Way, Washington, on the campus of the company's international headquarters. A chainlink fence protects the area which has been carefully improved to suit the specific purposes of the gardens. Paths, roads and a sprinkler system are in place.

b. The collection: More than a decade of careful search and selection has produced a collection of more than 393 species, 13 subspecies and 46 botanical varieties for a total of some 18,000 plants. To demonstrate their geographic distribution, the species are arranged together with companion plants from the same area. A study garden has been created to illustrate, by Series, the interrelationships of the various species.

c. Present facilities: The generosity and vision of Weyerhaeuser Company has made it possible to secure some of the basic structures required by the garden.

1. A greenhouse of 2,280 sq. ft. includes the latest technology for control of climate, humidity and other factors. It provides superlative conditions for the propagation of over 10,000 plants each year.

2. A 51,400 sq. ft. lath house has been built for growing young plants.

3. A beautiful gazebo of rustic cedar provides visitors an overview of the garden.

4. The service building presently houses the Foundation office and provides storage space for tools and equipment.

d. Present staff: The staff includes a secretary who has charge of the office, maintains clerical operations and keeps the records; an experienced garden manager, a qualified propagator and two part-time laborers. Security for the entire area is provided by the Weyerhaeuser Company. In the near future a professionally qualified director will be engaged to supervise expansion of the collection and the services of the garden.

e. Volunteers: The Foundation's accomplishments, since its inception in 1964, are attributable in large part to the time and effort donated by volunteers. They will continue to make a vital contribution to the Foundation's future success.

f. Financing: Voluntary gifts, memberships and foundation grants have provided most of the funds needed to carry out the various activities proposed by the Board of Directors. The Rhododendron Species Foundation is the official tax-exempt organization for the garden. At the present time the Foundation is operating within its means. About one-third of the present income comes from Foundation grants and the remainder from memberships of various kinds. Normal escalation because of increased cost of living, expanded activities and services and the addition to the staff of a director, and most probably someone to handle memberships and fund raising will materially affect the operating budget. New sources of support must be found, and procedures developed to tap those sources. These increases in the operating budget underscore the need for a program to secure gifts from many sources that will supply operating funds and build the endowment funds (restricted and unrestricted), and thus provide strong financial support for the operating and capital budgets.

g. Education and research: The lack of facilities and staff have precluded the possibilities of establishing programs of education and research. Since they have a high priority on the schedule of future activities, they will be implemented as soon as practicable.

h. Professional affiliations: The Rhododendron Species Foundation has insisted on the highest standards for selection, verification, display and cultivation of the plants in its collection. Many superior plants have been secured from gardens throughout the world, such as, The Royal Botanic Garden in Edinburgh, Scotland;

The Queen's Garden at Windsor Great Park and Kew Gardens in England. Contact is maintained with horticulturists, scholars and other specialists throughout the United States as well as other countries. There is a need for more formalized relationships with academic institutions and horticultural groups of all types. This will be especially important when a library and educational and research programs are established.

Summary

To propose one of the finest rhododendron species gardens in the world is a bold and laudable aspiration. The garden exists. It enjoys a magnificent setting which has been properly prepared to adapt to standards set forth by the directors. An excellent representative collection of many species is being cared for and expanded under strict supervision. Four essential buildings designed for specialized needs of the garden are in use. In short, it may be said the garden is operating on schedule following the plan established by the directors. The capability to do this is important as the directors project the continuing growth and development of their program of service to the public.

2. Projection for the future - In order to achieve the objective of creating a superior rhododendron garden and educational center, the Board of Directors of the Rhododendron Species Foundation has launched a full scale development program. The long range program envisages a $6,150,000 investment in the center to provide for needed facilities and funds required to sustain and extend the program of the garden in the years ahead.

Specifics of the program are:
    a. To secure a qualified director by 1979 to ensure that the program of service grows and that the highest standards are maintained.
    b. To secure facilities presently needed:
Administration service building extension - Additional space is required for future growth as well as to meet present overcrowded conditions.
Lath house II - There is an increasing need for additional lath house space for the protection of young plants.
    c. To secure facilities for future growth as soon as funds are available:
Educational center - An educational center merits highest priority among the Foundation's major projects. Construction should be considered as soon as funds are available. This multi-purpose building will include a conference room, library, administrative office, lecture room and herbarium.
    d. To list long term needs:
Conservatory - To achieve the ultimate objectives and purposes of the Foundation, a facility should be provided which would permit the cultivation and growth of species not sufficiently hardy to survive in the climate of the Northwest.
    e. To expand the plant acquisition program:
        1. Rhododendron species - A concerted effort is needed to add to the collection first quality specimens of other rhododendron species. The present

accession plan will be expanded and gifts of plants will be encouraged.

      2. Companion Plants - To broaden the scope and to extend the season of interest for visitors, a careful selection will be required of companion trees, shrubs and herbaceous plants.

      f. To create an education and research program: In the interest of discovering and extending knowledge of rhododendron species, the Foundation needs to:

      1. Establish a program for scholarly study and research.

      2. Establish working relationships with academic institutions and horticultural organizations.

      3. Create a docents' organization which, under the supervision of the director, can help prepare educational exhibits, make presentations and demonstrations to clubs, societies and interested individuals.

      g. To extend the distribution of plant material: As the means for increasing interest in rhododendron culture and to upgrade the quality of collections, the garden will offer surplus plant material for sale and distribution.

      h. To augment the library collection: The quality of the academic program of study and research will depend very much upon the extent of the resources available in the library. Books, magazines, scientific reports and specialized records must be acquired. Special provisions must be made for the care, preservation and control of rare books and publications.

      i. To increase the endowment funds: To provide the stable financial base that the garden will need, it will be necessary to seek $5,000,000 in endowment funds over the next decade. These funds will be held in trust and only used for the purposes designated by the donors. The various funds are:

Name of Fund	Corpus	Annual earning 5%
1. General endowment	$1,500,000	$75,000

For support of general items in the annual budget.

2. Educational activities endowment	$1,500,000	$75,000

For salaries, display and demonstration costs, publications and library.

3. Capital facilities & Maintenance	$1,400,000	$70,000

For additions to the physical plant & for maintaining these structures.

4. Research endowment	$ 500,000	$25,000

5. Acquisitions endowment	$ 100,000	$ 5,000

For additional rhododendron species and companion plants.

      j. To secure additional land as required for further expansion of facilities and planting areas.

Summary:

The program of the Rhododendron Species Foundation has been dynamic and progressive. Each year there has been growth and an expansion of activities. There is every indication that the programs of the garden will continue to grow and expand. This emphasizes the need for an executive to direct and supervise the programs. As new facilities are added, the rate and type of expansion will increase. These and other factors will sharply increase the need for operating funds to continue present projects without diminishing the quality of the activities in spite of rising costs, and to respond to the increasing demand for particular services.

Budget projections have been made for the next five years. These forecasts are developed out of the experience of the past few years of operations and include safety factors to cover the costs of inflation, unforseen contingencies and expanded services including the salary of the executive director. An allowance of eight percent per year is a hedge against inflation. An allowance of twelve percent is included to cover the costs of salary increases, expanded programs and unexpected costs. The salary of the executive director is programmed for 1979.

In the five-year period, the budget will rise from $90,694 to $181,000. Securing funds to balance the budget will be an annual challenge of some dimension. To secure the needed support we propose that:

a. The membership plan for the Foundation be revised to offer these categories of annual memberships:
Individual memberships (voting)

1. Individual	$ 25.00	annually
2. Supporting	$100 to $500	"
3. Patron	$500 and up	"

Associate memberships (Non-voting) - Garden clubs and affiliates, organization chapters and study clubs, arboreta and units, and any other state, national or international horticulture group.

$ 50	(Under 50 members)
$100	(50 to 100 members)
$200	(100 to 500 members)

Corporate memberships (Non-voting) - For firms giving $100 or more annually.
Honorary life membership - For all who have given $5,000 in gifts.

IMPLEMENTING THE MASTER PLAN

To achieve a rhododendron garden and education center without peer, the directors have projected a plan of action for the next five and ten years. It is a bold program that has grown out of the hard work and dedication of many people. It is a blueprint for constructive forward movement, created out of study, research and creative planning using techniques developed by business and industry. It is a controlled forecast of the years just ahead incorporating an annual review to test the validity of the projections. The process requires an updating of any parts of the future plan that requires modification or abandonment. This provides management with an effective corrective mechanism that safeguards against gross operational errors.

The rhododendron species garden and education center will be an outstanding resource, particularly for the Pacific Northwest. Its educational program will help inform and train students and teachers in the care and culture of these unique plants. The research program will bring forth new knowledge about the plants, their care and propagation. Because it is going to have the finest and most extensive collection of rhododendron species, it will become the focal point for individuals, groups and organizations of all kinds. Scholars from all over the world will gather to observe, study, learn, discuss and debate the plants featured in the center. It will also become a great economic resource through its appeal to tourists. It will be an esthetic treasure of the highest magnitude as it attracts, delights and uplifts all who are fortunate enough to see the collection.

The values of the gardens and education center are cited as sound and logical reasons why firms, foundations, organizations and individuals will respond to an appeal for financial support. The garden and facilities present a good case to pursuade prospective donors that the Foundation is ably managed and that the Master Plan is founded on sound thinking, tested techniques for future planning, and a program with a worthy purpose.

The major negative factor in the present situation is the low profile of the Foundation. Actually in some ways, this is a benefit because there has been no advance conditioning to lead people to anticipate activities and programs before they can be properly implemented. Obviously a public relations program will be necessary, but that's normal in most campaigns.

A. Campaign goal: The following activities have been identified:

Service building extension	$ 40,000
Lath house II	5,000
Information kiosk	2,000
Education center	300,000
Conservatory	750,000

It is recommended that a campaign be developed to reach out to a selected group of people interested in species rhododendron, civic-minded firms, foundations and organizations for three-year gifts. Scheduling the campaign for early in 1978 (with the latter part of 1977 as the preparatory period) should provide enough cash and pledges so construction can begin on the education center soon thereafter.

B. Endowment funds: The endowment funds were previously listed as totaling $5,000,000:

General endowment	$1,500,000
Educational activities endowment	1,500,000
Capital building & maintenance endowment	1,400,000
Research activities endowment	500,000
Accessions	100,000

To facilitate fund raising, several different opportunities are suggested so that donors may designate their gifts to underwrite specific aspects of the program. It is likely that as the program proceeds, it will be wise to particularize gift opportunities with designations such as these:

Research associate	$500,000
Visiting scholar	500,000
Library accessions	100,000
Plant acquisition fund	50,000

Major sources for increasing endowment are:
  Outright gifts of cash or appreciated assets.
  Trusts and unitrusts.
  Wills and bequests
  Grants from foundations and firms.

To reach the $5,000,000 goal for endowment funds, a ten-year plan is proposed. This takes into account the fact that the Foundation now has a low public profile and has been without a broad fund-raising program. Therefore, modest goals are projected for the first few years with the pace quickening as people become aware of the garden and the opportunities for gifts.

In addition to concentration on raising funds to balance the operating budget and to build the new facilities, a deferred gift program will be needed. Wills, bequests and trusts of various types have the greatest potential for securing large gifts for the endowment funds. Gifts of this type generally take some time to develop. Usually a considerable period for informing and counseling prospects about the opportunities and advantages of such gifts is needed.

It is standard procedure to place funds secured through wills and bequests (unless they are specifically designated for other purposes) into the endowment funds. In addition to the obvious advantage of increasing the corpus of the funds, such gifts can be used as seed money to help influence other people to do likewise. Example is a powerful factor in stimulating people to make gifts. Since there will be separate efforts to acquire endowment gifts and to influence people to make deferred gifts (trusts, wills and bequests), annual goals for each type of fund raising have been established. Deferred gifts are only counted when received, not when they are committed by the donor. The schedule is included with this report as Appendix B.[Not included]

Predicting human response is at best a risky business. No one is wise enough to know precisely how individuals will react to a particular appeal. The schedule in Appendix B is only a suggestion. Any large gift to the endowment funds early in the process does not invalidate the program. It merely accelerates the timetable. It is also the finest kind of testimonial to the work and value of the program.

The Master Plan is an attempt to capitalize on a fortunate collection of positive factors that have come together at this moment in time. The excellent beginning that has been made in securing a first rate collection, a site and some of the essential facilities, a knowledgeable group of people interested in the gardens and education center, a record of fiscal soundness and responsibility, and an idea of great merit. These are the stuff of which successful campaigns are made. The prognosis for securing funds required to complete the program is excellent.

APPENDIX E

BY-LAWS OF

THE RHODODENDRON SPECIES FOUNDATION

AS REVISED BY THE BOARD OF DIRECTORS

APRIL 26, 1980

FOLLOWED BY BY-LAWS REVISED AS OF

NOVEMBER 10, 1990

APPENDIX E

ARTICLE I

Objectives and Purposes

The objectives of this corporation shall be: To create one of the outstanding centers in the world for the growing of rhododendron species. In pursuit of these objectives, it shall acquire, study, cultivate, display and distribute such species and disseminate knowledge relating thereto. The purposes of this corporation shall be:

1. To bring together in one place, and to preserve and protect selected forms of species rhododendron.

2. To maintain and develop the collection under the best possible conditions.

3. To provide space and facilities for research in the field of species rhododendron.

4. To make information available on species rhododendron to all interested persons and organizations through education programs and other means.

5. To develop gardens for the display of species rhododendron and suitable companion plants.

6. To stimulate a broad interest in species rhododendron, and to encourage the study, collection and propagation of these plants.

ARTICLE II

Membership

Classes: Membership in the Rhododendron Species Foundation shall be as follows:
Individual memberships (Voting)

1. Individual $ 25 up to $100
2. Supporting $100 to $500
3. Patron $500 to $5,000
4. Life $5,000 and up in one year

Associate memberships (Non-voting)

Garden clubs and affiliates, organization chapters and study clubs, and arboretum units, and any other state, national or international horticulture groups.

$ 25   (up to 30 members)
$ 50   (up to 50 members)
$100   (50 to 100 members)
$200   (over 100 members)

Arboreta and other non-membership organizations - $100 and up.

Membership contributions other than in the Life Membership category, shall be payable January 1 of each year. Membership categories and amounts may be changed by the Board of Directors. Memberships may not be transferred.

ARTICLE III

Meetings of Members

III. 1 Annual Meeting. The annual meeting of members for the election of directors to succeed those whose terms expire, and for the transaction of such other business as may properly come before the meeting, shall be held each year at such time and place as may be designated by the Board of Directors.

III. 2 Special Meetings. Special meetings of the membership for any purpose or purposes may be called at any time by the president or by not less than ten (10) members of the Board of Directors, at such time and place as the president or the Board of Directors may prescribe. Special meetings of the members may also be called by members having at least one-fifth (1/5) of the votes entitled to be cast at such a meeting; and in the event that such be the case, it shall be the duty of the Secretary, upon request of such members, to call such a special meeting of the membership to be held at such time and place as the Secretary may fix, not less than ten (10) nor more than fifty (50) days after the receipt of said request; and if the secretary shall neglect or refuse to issue such call within five (5) days of such receipt, the members making the request may issue the call, specifying therein the time and place of the meeting.

III. 3 Notice of Meeting. Written or printed notices stating the date, place and hour of the meeting and, in case of a special meeting, the purpose or purposes for which the meeting is called, shall be delivered not less than ten (10) nor more than fifty (50) days before the date of the meeting by mail to each voting member. Such notice shall be deemed to be delivered when deposited in the United States mail, addressed to the member at his address as it appears in the records of the Foundation, with postage thereon prepaid.

III. 4 Quorum. Seventy-five (75) voting members of the Foundation shall constitute a quorum. The vote of a majority of members at a meeting at which a quorum is present, shall be necessary for the adoption of any matter.

III. 5 Voting Procedure. A voice vote shall be sufficient unless an individual count is requested or deemed necessary.

ARTICLE IV

Board of Directors

IV. 1 Number and Powers. The business and affairs of the Rhododendron Species Foundation shall be managed by a Board of Directors, consisting of not less than twenty (20) nor more than sixty (60) directors, in a number which shall be determined by resolution of the Board of Directors. Directors shall be members in good standing.

IV. 2 Election of Directors.

(a) The nominating Committee shall meet and select nominees for board positions which will become vacant at the time of the annual meeting. A list of the nominees shall be included in the notice of the annual meeting of the members.

(b) Election of directors shall be by vote at the Annual Membership Meeting.

(c) At each annual meeting, one-third (1/3) of the directors shall be elected for terms of three (3) years.

(d) In case the number of directors shall be increased, a sufficient number of directors shall be elected to balance the board as previously described.

IV. 3 Honorary Director. Any person whose substantial services to the Foundation merits such recognition, may be elected by the Board of Directors as an honorary director. Honorary directors shall not have voting rights.

IV. 4 Vacancies. The Board of Directors shall have power to fill any vacancy occurring on the board. The director appointed or elected, as the case may be, to fill a vacancy, shall be elected or appointed for the unexpired term of his predecessor in office.

IV. 5 Removal. Any director elected or appointed may be removed by the Board of Directors whenever in its judgment the best interests of the Foundation will be served thereby.

ARTICLE V

Committees

V. 1 Executive Committee. The Board of Directors shall approve an Executive Committee consisting of the president, who shall be its chairperson, and six (6) members of the Board of Directors, who will serve for one year. The Executive Committee shall have all the powers of the Board of Directors between the meetings thereof on any matters requiring immediate action. All actions taken by the Executive Committee shall be by an affirmative vote of at least four members. The Executive Committee shall fill any vacancy on the Executive Committee for the duration of the unexpired term. The Executive Committee shall not have the authority of the Board of Directors in reference to amending, altering or repealing the by-laws; electing or removing any member of the Committee; electing, appointing or removing any director or electing or removing an officer of the Foundation; amending the Articles of Incorporation; adopting a plan of merger or adopting a plan of consolidation with another corporation; authorizing the sale, lease, exchange or mortgage of all or substantially all the property and assets of the Foundation; authorizing the voluntary dissolution of the Foundation or revoking proceedings therefor; adopting a plan for the distribution of the assets of the Foundation; or amending, altering or repealing any resolution of the Board of Directors which by its terms provides that it shall not be amended, altered or repealed by such committee. The designation and appointment of any such committee and the delegation thereto of authority shall not operate to relieve the Board of Directors or any individual director of any responsibility imposed upon it or him/her by law.

V. 2 Nominating Committee. The Nominating Committee appointed by the president with approval of the Executive Committee shall submit nominations for directors to the members as provided in Article IV.2. The Nominations Committee shall submit nominations for officers of the Foundation and members of the Executive Committee to the Board of Directors. The committee shall consist of a minimum of five (5) members of the Board of Directors.

V. 3 Standing Committees. The standing committees shall carry out the intent of the bylaws and are governed thereby. Standing committees are enumerated as follows:
(a) Finance committee
(b) Education committee
(c) Reference library committee
(d) Membership committee
(e) Garden committee
(f) Research committee
(g) Herbarium committee
Other standing committees may be duly appointed as may be deemed necessary. Chairpersons of the standing committees shall be appointed by the president and approved by the Executive Committee. The term of office for a chairperson shall be one (1) year.

V. 4 Other committees. The Board of Directors or the president may appoint such other committees, either standing or special, as may be deemed advisable.

ARTICLE VI

Meetings of Board of Directors

VI. 1 Annual Meetings. The annual meeting of the Board of Directors shall be held in conjunction with the Annual Membership Meeting when possible.

VI. 2 Regular Meetings. The directors shall hold regular meetings at such intervals and upon such dates and at such places as they may determine.

VI. 3 Special Meetings. Special Meetings of the Board of Directors may be held at any place, at any time, whenever called by the president or vice president, or any seven (7) or more directors.

VI. 4 Notice of Meetings. Notice of the time and place of any meetings of the Board of Directors shall be given by the secretary, or by the person or persons calling the meeting, by mail or telegram, at least ten (10) days prior to the date on which the meeting is to be held. Attendance of a director at any meeting shall constitute a waiver of notice of such meeting, except where the director attends a meeting for the express purpose of objecting to the transaction of any business because the meeting is not lawfully called or convened. Neither the business to be transacted nor the purpose of any meeting of the Board of Directors need be specified in the notice or any waiver of notice of such meeting.

VI. 5 Quorum. Fifteen (15) members of the Board of Directors shall constitute a quorum for the transaction of business. The act of the majority of directors present at a meeting at which a quorum is present shall be the act of the Board of Directors. At any meeting of the Board of Directors at which a quorum is present, any business may be transacted, and the board may exercise all of its powers.

ARTICLE VII

Officers

VII. 1 Officers Enumerated. The officers of the Foundation shall be a president, one or more vice presidents, a secretary, a treasurer, and such other officers and assistant officers as may be deemed necessary by the Board of Directors, each of whom shall be annually elected by the Board of Directors, from among its members, and shall serve until his/her successor is duly elected and qualified. Any two (2) or more offices may be held by the same person, except the offices of president and secretary. In addition to the powers and duties specified below, the officers shall have such powers and perform such duties as the Board of Directors may prescribe. The officers shall perform all the duties and functions attaching to such officers as enumerated by the Rhododendron Species Foundation Policy and Procedure Manual.

(a) Succession. In the absence, disability, resignation or removal of the president, the vice president shall succeed. In the absence, disability, resignation or removal of the president and vice president, the Executive Committee shall appoint an interim officer who shall preside until the next meeting of the Board of Directors.

VII. 2 President. The president of the Foundation shall be its presiding and chief operating officer. He/she shall preside at all meetings of the Foundation and Board of Directors, appoint all committee chairpersons and/or committees as provided herein or unless otherwise provided for, and shall perform all the other duties and functions attaching to such office. The president shall have the general authority to carry out the programs and policies approved and budgeted by the Board or the Executive Committee. The president shall not have the authority to take actions which may effect policy having long-range effects upon the operation of the Foundation without the prior approval of the Board or the Executive Committee.

VII. 3 Vice President. In the absence, disability, resignation or removal of the president, the vice president, or if more than one, as designated by the board, shall perform the duties of the president.

VII. 4 Secretary. It shall be the duty of the secretary to give notice of meetings as required hereunder, to keep records of the proceedings of the Board of Directors and of the membership, to administer the membership register, to sign and execute with the president all deeds, bonds, contracts, and other obligations, or instruments, in the name of the Foundation.

VII. 5 Treasurer. The treasurer shall receive and disburse, under the direction of the Board of Directors, funds of the Foundation, and shall prepare an annual financial report covering the fiscal year and submit it to the Foundation at the annual meeting, and shall submit such other reports as the Board of Directors may require.

VII. 6 Vacancies. Vacancies in any office arising from any cause may be filled temporarily by the Executive Committee until the next meeting of the Board of Directors.

VII. 7 Removal. Any officer elected or appointed may be removed by the Board of Directors whenever in its judgment the best interests of the Foundation will be served thereby.

ARTICLE VIII

Administrative and Financial Provision

VIII. 1 Waiver of Notice. Whenever any notice is required to be given to any member or director of the Foundation by the Articles of Incorporation or bylaws, or by the laws of the State of Oregon, a waiver thereof in writing signed by the person or persons entitled to such notice, whether before or after the time stated therein, shall be equivalent to the giving of such notice.

VIII. 2 Books and Records. The Foundation shall keep current and complete books and records of account and shall keep minutes of the proceedings of its members, Board of Directors and committees having any of the authority of the Board of Directors, and shall keep at its registered office a register of the names and addresses of its members entitled to vote. All books and records of the Foundation may be inspected by any active member, or his/her agent or attorney, for any proper purpose at any reasonable time.

VIII. 3 Amendment of Bylaws. The bylaws may be amended by a majority vote of the members of the Board of Directors present at any duly constituted meeting of the Board of Directors.

VIII. 4 Accounting Period. The yearly accounting period of the Foundation shall end on the 31st day of December of each year.

VIII. 5 Policy and Procedures. A policy and Procedure Manual shall be developed to more fully enumerate the responsibilities of the officers and committees and shall stipulate the working procedures and policies of the Foundation. The Executive Committee will have the responsibility to develop, maintain and administer the Policy and Procedure manual.

BY-LAWS AS REVISED NOVEMBER 10, 1990

ARTICLE I

Object and Purpose

The objectives of this corporation shall be to create one of the outstanding centers in the world for the growing of rhododendron species. In pursuit of these objectives, it shall acquire, study, cultivate, display and distribute such species and disseminate knowledge relating thereto. The purposes of this corporation shall be:

1. To bring together in one place, and to preserve and protect, species Rhododendron.
2. To develop gardens for landscape display and appreciation of species Rhododendron and other plants.
3. To manage the collections in the best possible manner.
4. To provide educational programs that encourage the study, collection and propagation of the collection groups.
5. To conserve species Rhododendron through the documented distribution of plant material.
6. To provide space and facilities for collections and research.

ARTICLE II

Membership

There are two classes of membership:

(a) Voting memberships: will consist of dues paying members on an individual basis. The Board will establish the categories of membership and the membership fees.
(b) Non-voting memberships: will consist of garden clubs and affiliates, organization chapters and study clubs, and arboretum units, and any other state, national or

international horticulture groups.

Membership contributions shall be payable on January 1 of each year. Membership categories and dollar amounts may be changed by the Board of Directors. Membership may not be transferred.

ARTICLE III

Meetings of Members

3.1 Annual Meeting. The Annual Meeting of the members for the election of Directors to succeed those whose terms expire, and for the transaction of such other business as may properly come before the meeting, shall be held each year at such time and place as may be designated by the Board of Directors.

3.2 Special Meetings. Special meetings of the membership for any purpose or purposes may be called at any time by the President or by not less than ten (10) members of the Board of Directors, at such time and place as the President or Board of Directors may prescribe. Special meetings of the members may also be called by members having at least one-fifth (1/5) of the votes entitled to be cast at such a meeting; and in the event that such be the case, it shall be the duty of the Secretary, upon request of such members, to call such a special meeting of the membership to be held at such time and place as the Secretary may fixl, not less than ten (10) or more than fifty (50) days after the receipt of said request; and if the Secretary shall neglect or refuse to issue such call within five (5) days of such receipt, the members making the request may issue the call, specifying therein the time and place of the meeting.

3.3 Notice of Meeting. Written or printed notices stating the date, place and hour of the meeting and, in case of a special meeting, the purpose or purposes for which the meeting is called, shall be delivered not less than ten (10) nor more than fifty (50) days before the date of the meeting by mail to each voting member on the books of the Society 60 days prior to the meeting. Such notice shall be deemed to be delivered when deposited in the United States mail, addressed to the member at his address as it appears in the records of the Foundation, with postage thereon prepaid.

3.4 Quorum. Seventy-five voting members of the Foundation or 10% of the voting membership on the membership rolls of the Foundation on the 60th day prior to the date of the meeting, whichever is less, shall constitute a quorum. The vote of the majority of the voting members at a meeting at which a quorum is present shall be necesssary for the adoption of any matter.

3.5 Voting Procedure. A voice vote shall be sufficient unless an individual count is requested or deemed necessary.

APPENDIX E

ARTICLE IV.

Board of Directors

4.1 Number and Powers. The business and affairs of the Rhododendron Species Foundation shall be managed by a Board of Directors, consisting of not less than twenty (20) nor more than sixty (60) Directors. The number of members of the Board of Directors shall be determined by resolution of the Board of Directors. Directors shall be members in good standing.

4.2 Election of Directors.

(a) The Nominating Committee shall meet and select nominees for Board positions which will become vacant at the time of the annual meeting. A list of the nominees shall be included in the notice of the annual meeting of the members.
(b) Election of Directors shall be by vote at the Annual Membership Meeting.
(c) At each annual meeting, one-third (1/3) of the Directors shall be elected for terms of three (3) years.
(d) In case the number of Directors shall be increased, a sufficient number of Directors shall be elected to balance the Board as previously described.
(e) If the membership, at its annual meeting, fails to elect the slate of Directors nominated, the prior Directors shall continue to serve until their successors are elected and qualify.

4.3 Honorary Director. Any person whose substantial services to the Foundation merits such recognition, may be elected by the Board of Directors as an Honorary Director. Honorary Directors shall not have voting rights.

4.4 Vacancies. The Board of Directors shall have power to fill any vacancy on the Board. A Director appointed or elected to fill a vacancy, or an unexpired term, shall be elected or appointed for the balance of the unexpired term.

4.5 Removal. Any Directors elected or appointed may be removed by the Board of Directors whenever in its judgment the best interests of the Foundation will be served thereby.

ARTICLE V.

Committees

5.1 Executive Committee. The Board of Directors shall elect an Executive Committee of eight (8) persons. It shall include the President, who shall be its chairperson, the other officers enumerated in Article VII of these bylaws, who shall be elected in the odd years, plus three (3) non-officers, who shall be elected in the even years, at alternate annual meetings of the Board of Directors, who shall serve for two years. The Past-President shall be an Ex-Officer member of the Executive Committee.

The term of office on the Executive Committee shall be two (2) years for the officers and two years for the non-officers. The Executive Committee shall have all the powers of the Board of Directors between the meetings thereof on any matters requiring immediate action except as limited below. All actions taken by the Executive Committee shall be by affirmative vote of at least four members. The Executive Committee shall fill any vacancy on the Executive Committee for the duration of the unexpired term.

The designation and appointment of any such committee and the delegation thereto of authority shall not operate to relieve the Board of Directors or any individual Director of any responsibility imposed upon it or him/her by law. The Committee shall not have the authority of the Board of Directors in reference to amending, altering, or repealing the bylaws; electing or removing any member of the Committee; electing, appointing or removing any Director or electing or removing an officer of the Foundation; amending the Articles of Incorporation; adopting a plan of merger or adopting a plan of consolidation with another corporation; authorizing the sale, lease, exchange or mortgage of all or substantially all of the property and assets of the Foundation; authorizing the voluntary dissolution of the Foundation or revoking proceedings thereof; adopting a plan for the distribution of the assets of the Foundation; or amending, altering or repealing any resolution of the Board of Directors which by its terms provides that it shall not be amended, altered or repealed by such committee.

5.2 Nominating Committee. The Committee shall consist of a minimum of five (5) members of the Board of Directors, the First Vice-President as chairperson and one or more past presidents when possible. The Nominating Committee shall maintain confidential records regarding each Board member and his or her activities in the Foundation. The Committee shall maintain a list of possible Board nominees and make recommendations for nomination based upon the current needs for balanced Board function and representation. The Nominating Committee shall file its list of nominees for Directors with the Board of Directors and submit it to the members as provided in Article 4.2. The Nominating Committee shall submit its list of nominations of officers of the Foundation and members of the Executive Committee to the Board of Directors.

5.3 Standing Committees. The Standing Committees shall carry out the intent of the bylaws and are governed thereby. Standing Committees are enumerated as follows:
(a) A Finance Committee will advise and assist the Treasurer and Executive Committee in the investment of the funds of the Foundation and methods of raising funds.
(b) An Education Committee will develop and make available educational materials relating to the Foundation's stated purposes.
(c) A Reference Library Committee will develop and maintain a library related to the Foundation's stated purposes.
(d) A Membership Commitee will be responsible for promoting membership in the

Foundation.

(e) A Garden Committee will be responsible for advising staff on development and maintenance of the garden(s).

(f) A Research Committee will be responsible for evaluating proposals for research carried out under the auspices of the Foundation or for proposing such research.

(g) A Board Review Committee will be responsible for monitoring the ongoing performance of the Board and making recommendations regarding such evaluations.

Other Standing Committees may be duly appointed as may be deemed necessary. The term of office for a chairperson shall be two (2) years coinciding with the term of the President or until replaced.

5.4 Other Committees. The Board of Directors or the President may appoint such other committees, either standing or special, as may be deemed advisable.

ARTICLE VI.

Meeting of Board of Directors

6.1 Annual Meetings. The Annual Meeting of the Board of Directors shall be held in conjunction with the Annual Membership Meeting when possible.

6.2 Regular Meetings. The Directors shall hold regular meetings at such intervals and upon such dates and at such places as they may determine.

6.3 Special Meetings. Special Meetings of the Board of Directors may be held at any place, at any time, whenever called by the President, or First Vice-President in the President's absence, or by any seven (7) or more Directors.

6.4 Notice of Meetings. Notice of the time and place of any meetings of the Board of Directors shall be given by the Secretary, or by the person or persons calling the meeting, by mail or telegram, at least ten (10) days prior to the date on which the meeting is to be held. Attendance of a Director at any meeting shall constitute a waiver of notice of such meeting, except where a Director attends a meeting for the express purpose of objecting to the transaction of any business because the meeting is not lawfully called or convened. Neither the business to be transacted nor the purpose of any meeting of the Board of Directors need be specified in the notice or any waiver of notice of such meeting.

6.5 Quorum. Fifteen (15) members of the Board of Directors shall constitute a quorum for the transaction of business. The act of the majority of Directors present at a meeting at which a quorum is present shall be the act of the Board of Directors. At any meeting of the Board of Directors at which a quorum is present, any business may be transacted and the Board may exercise all of its powers.

APPENDIX E

ARTICLE VII.

Officers

7.1 Officers Enumerated. The officers of the Foundation shall be a President, a First Vice President, a Second Vice President (each of whom shall be willing to succeed to the Presidency), a Secretary, a Treasurer, and such other officers and assistant officers as may be deemed necessary by the Board of Directors, each of whom shall be bi-annually elected by the Board of Directors, from among its members, and shall serve until a successor is duly elected and qualified. Any two (2) or more offices may be held by the same person, except the offices of President and Secretary. In addition to the powers and duties specified below, the officers shall have such powers and perform such duties as the Board of Directors may prescribe. The officers shall perform all the duties and functions attaching to such officers as enumerated by the Rhododendron Species Foundation Policy and Procedure Manual.

(a) Succession. In the absence, disability or resignation or removal of the President: the First Vice President shall succeed. In the absence, disability, resignation or removal of the President and the First Vice President, the Executive Committee shall appoint an interim officer who shall preside until the next meeting of the Board of Directors.

7.2 President. The President of the Foundation shall be its presiding and chief operating officer. He/she shall preside at all meetings of the Foundation and Board of Directors, appoint all committee chairpersons and/or committees as provided herein or unless otherwise provided for, and shall perform all the other duties and functions attaching to such office. The President shall have the general authority to carry out the programs and policies approved and budgeted by the Board or Executive Committee.

7.3 First Vice President. In the absence, disability, resignation or removal of the President, the First Vice President shall perform the duties of the President. If the First Vice President shall be unwilling or unable to act, the Executive Committee shall designate who shall perform the duties of the President until the next regular meeting of the Board convenes, at which time the Board shall make the designation until the next election is held.

7.4 Secretary. It shall be the duty of the Secretary to give notice of meetings as required hereunder, to keep records of the proceedings of the Board of Directors and of the membership, and to administer the membership register. These responsibilities may be delegated to professional staff. In addition, the Secretary or a Secretary pro tem, in the Secretary's absence, shall sign and execute, with the President, all deeds, bonds, contracts and other obligations, or instruments, in the name of the Foundation. These obligations shall not be delegable.

7.5 Treasurer. The Treasurer shall receive and disburse, under the direction of the Board of Directors, funds of the Foundation, and shall prepare an annual financial report covering the fiscal year andfsubmit it to the Foundation at the annual meeting, and shall submit such other reports as the board of directors may require. These powers may be delegated to bonded professional staff personnel.

7.6 Vacancies. Vacancies in any office arising from any cause may be filled temporarily by the Executive Committee until the next meeting of the Board of Directors.

7.7 Removal. Any officer elected or appointed may be removed by the Board of Directors whenever in its judgment the best interests of the Foundation will be served thereby.

ARTICLE VIII

Administrative and Financial Provision

VIII. 1 Waiver of Notice. Whenever any notice is required to be given to any member or director of the Foundation by the Articles of Incorporation or bylaws, or by the laws of the State of Oregon, a waiver thereof in writing signed by the person or persons entitled to such notice, whether before or after the time stated therein, shall be equivalent to the giving of such notice.

VIII. 2 Books and Records. The Foundation shall keep current and complete books and records of account and shall keep minutes of the proceedings of its members, Board of Directors and committees having any of the authority of the Board of Directors, and shall keep at its registered office a register of the names and addresses of its members entitled to vote. All books and records of the Foundation may be inspected by any active member, or his/her agent or attorney, for any proper purpose at any reasonable time.

VIII. 3 Amendment of Bylaws. The bylaws may be amended by a majority vote of the members of the Board of Directors present at any duly constituted meeting of the Board of Directors.

VIII. 4 Accounting Period. The yearly accounting period of the Foundation shall end on the 31st day of December of each year.

VIII. 5 Policy and Procedures. A policy and Procedure Manual shall be developed to more fully enumerate the responsibilities of the officers and committees and shall stipulate the working procedures and policies of the Foundation. The Executive committee will have the responsibility to develop, maintain and administer the Policy and Procedure Manual.

APPENDIX F
GARDEN MASTER PLAN
NOVEMBER 1, 1980

JOHN ULLMAN, LANDSCAPE CONSULTANTS
320 NATIONAL BANK BLDG.
SEATTLE, WA.

INTRODUCTION

The accompanying Master Plan Drawing is based on the directive given by the Rhododendron Species Foundation Board members to develop the Garden based on Approach Il with options A and C as presented in the June 28, 1980 Garden Master Plan Progress Report. This allowed for the following:

Re-organizing the collection botanically emphasizing microclimate potentials. Provide a path through the collection with provisions for points of emphasis and enrichment. Provide an improved area for plant sales and visitor seating inside the entry gate.

DEVELOPMENT PHILOSOPHY

The master plan has been designed to reflect the primary function of the Foundation which is the development of a comprehensive collection of species rhododendron. This has been done in a manner that meets the needs of scientists, rhododendron experts and fanciers, while accomodating the public and giving prominence to the following:

Cultural conditions of the plants
Efficient management of the collection
Conformance to taxonomic and botanical standards
Ease of comparative study

While aesthetics have not been the primary concern in this phase of the garden's development, they have been given consideration throughout the master planning process. We are confident that as the garden develops and matures it will reflect a level of aesthetics that will appeal to novice and expert alike.

FEATURES OF THE MASTER PLAN

Proper phasing is one of the most important factors in implementing the new Master Plan at the Rhododendron Species Garden. While the Master Plan has given consideration to and accomodates the following list of features, we do not suggest that they are all to be undertaken in the immediate future. Recommendations for phasing the Garden's development are in Section VII of this report. The following comprises the Master Plan Drawing and Report:

Annotated Master Site Plan
Rhododendron planting group allocations
Primary circulation routes (pedestrian and maintenance).
Locations and descriptions of site features i.e. rock outcrops, pond expansion, etc.
Description of *sub-development areas
        Companion planting descriptions for each sub-development area
Planning cost estimates
Suggested phasing for implementation

The Master Plan as presented provides a way to guide Garden development through time toward a pleasing, efficient, and cohesive completion,while anticipating and allowing for a change in attitudes and leadership.

*SUB-AREAS are naturally occuring 'places' on the site defined by their forms, location, or microclimate. The 11 sub-areas are also organizational units for phasing, location, and structure of the garden design. See Figure 1 and 2.

ARRANGEMENT OF THE COLLECTION

The sub-development area of the site presented distinct habitat potentials with a range of soil temperature, wind and sun exposures. These have been identified and utilized to re-arrange the collection botanically. The new Master Plan as shown utilizes and incorporates the work previously undertaken by the Tacoma Study Club and the contributions of the Master Plan Garden Task Force Committee and Staff.

PLANT GROUPS AND LOCATION

The plant groups on this plan are the "series" sub-division of the genus based upon the British Balfourian System used in the Species of Rhododendron. The groups have been positioned to accommodate a future shift to the Edinburgh revision. Our intent is to maximize the amount of the area for the cultivation of species rhododendrons while affording space for expansion, companion plantings and spatial variety throughout the collection. Drawn on the plan are core locations for each plant group "series". Expansion of these groups may occur generally toward the site perimeter. The space allocation for the groups is exclusive of companion plantings.

The actual area size, in square feet, allocated for plant groups is more than enough to accommodate the rhododendrons now in the collections with adequate allowance for future acquisition. The Garden Task Force established the area for each plant group. This was influenced by the relative size of the site, ultimate growth of individual plants and potential acquisitions.

Location of the plant groups on the site is based on prior work by the R.S.F. Staff, the Tacoma Study Club and the designer's overall garden concept. The committee adjusted and re-evaluated several location plans concluding with the locations illustrated in the Master Plan. One 'core' location is allocated for each plant group. The intent is to allow the second appearance of a group in the collection only if a significant rationale can be presented. Secondary locations should be kept to a minimum to maintain clarity of organization. See figure 3 .

LANDSCAPE ELEMENTS

It is the intent of the design to enhance and accentuate landscape character existing at the site. The use of open space, views, and companion trees are the core of the design as are the rhododendrons the core of the collection.

COURTYARDS

Architecture in this area should be simple and Northwest in its character and materials; appropriate scale and detail are critical. Crisp, clearly inserted forms and materials should be selected to contrast the forest outside and the collection within.

Included in this area are:

(1) Restrooms	375 SF
(2) Seating	100 SF
(3) Information Booth	100 SF
(4) Plant Sales Shelter	600 SF
(5) Courtyard Area	4800 SF
(6) Screen Trellis/Fence	120 SF

THE PRIMARY PATH is designed for people on foot and the occasional use of light service vehicles. It should not exceed 6 feet in width, owing to the nature of its proposed use. A hard surface, such as stone or brick should be applied to give definition to the path and allow it to be used comfortably in all weather conditions. A hard surface would also have the potential of providing accessibility to the handicapped.

The primary path provides a circuit through the collection which allows access to the plant groups. Secondary paths designed within the individual plant groups would interconnect to the primary path and to adjacent plant groups. This would connect all groups within the collection. See Figure 4.

SITE FEATURES - Two rock outcrops are planned. Size and stone type should be established when the features are designed. It is recommended that the rock not be stacked and that a horizontal configuration be achieved allowing ample swales between ledges for the species. See Figure 5

The existing pond should be enlarged toward the Southeast. A water feature should be created to increase the sound of running water.

GAZEBO - This structure should have display panels installed to allow for information and seasonal displays.

ROADWAYS - After much analysis, the Landscape consultants and the Garden Task Force Committee recommends deleting the 3 central portions of existing gravel road, leaving a service loop road at the Garden perimeter and thereby gaining an additional 30,000 SF optimum planting area. After the Garden's reconstruction, the need for access into the center of the Garden by heavy equipment will be minimal. Therefore the committee agreed that the Garden plan is best served by diminishing the intrusion of service roads. The RSF staff concurred that routine maintenance and emergency access can be conducted with the remaining loop road and occasional use of the proposed primary pathway. Fig. 5

MEMBERSHIP PARKING - It is recommended that an area be provided north of the Foundation office outside the fence for approximately 24 cars. This area should be further screened from the Garden and freeway.

SIGNAGE AND SEATING - Three types of signs are recommended. (1) Locational: These would be placed in each sub-area to reference the location to the entire Garden Plan. (2) Identification: These would occur within each group and should be highly visible and durable. (3) Directional: These signs should carry the RSF logo and would be primarily located in the Courtyards, Administrative Office Area, and several key points along the Primary Pathways. It is recommended that benches be provided approximately every 200 feet along the Primary Path in addition to Courtyard seating. Benches should be sited to allow examination of the collection while they are being used.

SUB-DEVELOPMENT AREAS

Within the Garden there exist inherent, identifiable natural qualities which should be retained. We have termed these sub-development areas. The Master Plan identifies and reinforces these areas through design and by recommending ways to enhance the specific landscape character of all such areas. They are as follows:

1 NORTH GATEWAY - Functions as a transition between the awesomeness of the forest and the balanced intricacy of the Garden. The North Gateway serves as an area where the anticipation of the visitor is allowed to mount while their mind clears, in preparation for the experience to follow. The intent is to present a crisp, tailored, disciplined landscape.

RECOMMENDED ACTION Grade and fill the area outside the gate to level it with the road. Continue the paving surface from the entry courtyard outside the Garden to the area between the road and the fence. Install gravel on both sides of the paved surface in this area. Plant materials in the North Gateway should be confined to deciduous canopy trees which display year-round interest. (See Companion Planting Section VI)

2   COURTYARDS - Are juxtiposed at the northern terminus of the ridge which bisects the site. This is also the highest point in the garden. The intent is to create a cathedral-like deciduous canopy of large scale trees to define the large outdoor room.

RECOMMENDED ACTION Grade and fill this area to increase its perception as the high point. This could be accomplished by contrasting the level courtyards and entry area with a mounded landform (to 5' above existing grade). Because of its prominent location, the mound would be planted primarily with plants of outstanding characteristics. Evergreen azaleas on the south and west and other species rhododendron on the north and east.

3   STUDY GARDEN - Protect and maintain intact as a major sub-area connecting it to the primary path on the North and South.

4   MEADOW - This Southeast gently sloping area requires the selective removal of Douglas Firs to increase the visibility of this prime area. The Design Intent is to create the most defined open space on the site and to emphasize the East slope.

RECOMMENDED ACTION Planting groups in this area have been located to the edges of this relatively large open space. The Master Plan is designed so that the first impression of the collection offers a spacious, open, inviting environment at the Meadow. This is a large clearing and the most open area in the Garden. The Taliense, Fortunei, Auricultatum, Falconeri and Grande are among the groups located in the Meadow Collection.

5   ALPINE OUTCROP - The primary purpose of the outcrop is to provide an optimum growing environment for the Rhododendron. The area has been planned to be open with the central focus of a rock outcropping. The design intent is to provide Alpine landscape character.

Ferrugineum, saluenense, and Anthopogon are among the groups located in this subdevelopment area.

RECOMMENDED ACTION The Alpine area will require selective removal of the Douglas Fir canopy south and west of the existing clearing to achieve the required sun exposure. (See existing vegetation Section VI) The rockwork itself should be very horizontal. Its primary purpose is to provide an optimum environment of the Alpine Collection.

6 POND - This area requires enlargement and reforming of the pond edge to enhance the unique character of this water feature. The design intent is to enhance the sense of the low point, enclosure, and confinement. The Barbatums are located in this collection.

RECOMMENDED ACTION The sound of moving water should be featured. This is the quietest part of the site in the Garden and the addition of running water would help to mask the freeway sounds.

7 FOREST GLEN - This has the development capability of becoming the most visually complex planting that visitors pass through as they proceed along the Garden path. The design intent is to create a sense of involvement within and under the dense forest canopy. Arboreum and Thomsonii are two of the principal groups in this collection.

RECOMMENDED ACTION This area has a good sense of enclosure from vegetation on the South and West but requires screening along the road.

Owing to its proximity to the heavy forest edge of primarily Douglas Fir, this area should be supplemented with only a few trees. Many of the rhododendrons to be planted in this area will ultimately reach tree height.

8 WEST HILL SLOPE - To provide interest and texture between two high canopy areas. Among this collection are the Maddenii, Moupinense and Cinnabarinum groups.

9 OLYMPIC VIEW RIDGE - Has distant Olympic Mountain views which magnify the sense of the ridge and accentuate views in all directions into the collection. The Triflorum, Ponticum, Micranthum and Heliolepis are among the groups in the Olympic View Ridge Collection.

RECOMMENDED ACTION The service areas should be screened with dense evergreen plantings. Selected view corridors down slope to the northwest should be defined and enhanced with companion tree and shrub plantings. (See Section VI)

10 OFFICE AND NURSERY - This area will not require enlargement. The companion plant materials in this area will function principally as visual screens. (See Section VI)

11 WEST OUTCROP - This final feature should be an exquisitely detailed display which culminates the visitors journey through the collection. The design intent is to provide screening and canopy which serves to provide a foreground for distinct mountain views.

RECOMMENDED ACTION The rock outcrop should be positioned on the west slope to capitalize on the distant mountain views, companion plantings should be incorporated to screen views of the maintenance area and proposed membership parking. (See Section VI)

This feature owing to its location would be visible not only from within the collection, but from adjacent proposed member parking and office area.

COMPANION PLANTINGS

DESIGN CONCEPT

The selection and use of companion plantings in the Garden is based on the following set of design criteria:

Trees should be predominantly deciduous, of small to medium height and spread. Shrubs should provide seasonal interest and where required, be rapid growing to provide screening. (Tree sizes: small - under 30', medium - 30 - 60', tall - 60'+).

Named areas in the collection (i.e. Olympic View Ridge, etc.) should be reinforced with a very limited selection of companion plants. These should serve the functional (screening, filtered sun, etc.), as well as aesthetic requirements.
Since display of species rhododendron is the primary intent, complexity of companion plantings is to be avoided.
Companion plants are always to be subordinate to the Species Rhododendron plantings.
Plants selections should be purposely limited initially to provide simplicity, not to distract from the species plantings.

DESIGN INTENT

The design intent of the companion plantings for each sub-development area is described in this section. Also included are examples of companion plantings suitable for establishing the overall character of each sub-development area. Detailed planting plans for each plant group must be developed before final selections, quantities and locations can be determined. As part of the effort to feature the collection, it is recommended that companion trees be limited to one major tree species per sub-development area. In some areas it may be desirable to include more that one companion tree species. This will be determined when the detailed planting plans are produced.

When appropriate for a specific sub-development area, examples of shrubs suitable for companion planting have also been listed. These serve as examples only, final selection of the companion plants will be made when the detailed planting plans are designed for individual sub-development areas.

While the use of bulbs and selected ground covers is recommended for certain subdevelopment areas, examples of suitable materials have not been included as part of the Master Plan Proposal.

EXISTING VEGETATION

Currently approximately 10 1/2 acres of the of the 23 acre site is influenced by Fir tree cover. The inclusion of companion plantings in the Garden necessitates an eventual removal of up to 50% of the existing Firs and Salal. The removal of these and other naturally occurring vegetation would be selective and accomplished on an area by area basis prior to planting each sub-development area.

Should the Firs not be reduced in number they will severely diminish the amount and quality of growing area available for rhododendron plantings.

In order to provide the best growing conditions for the species plantings competition for nutrients, moisture, root growth etc. must be minimal. It was therefore agreed that the gradual reduction of Firs from the Garden is essential.

SELECTION CRITERIA

While the companion plantings must first be selected for their horticultural compatability with rhododendron plantings they should also have the ability to contribute to the landscape enrichment of the sub-development areas and the overall effect of the Garden. A list of plants meeting these requirements has been included in the appendices. Other factors given consideration in the selection of companion plantings are as follows:

Hardiness
Exposure
Soil, moisture and nutrient re~uirements
Compatability with Rhododendrons
Growth rate
Growth habit
Disease and insect resistance
Maintenance requirements

APPENDIX F

DESIGN FUNCTIONS OF COMPANION PLANTINGS

The design character for each sub-development area has been described elsewhere in this report. Companion planting recommendations are based on their ability to reinforce and enhance the established design character of each sub-development area by performing one or more of the following design functions:

Background or barriers:
> Visual screens
> Wind screens
> Sun screens
> Diverters

Canopies:
> Overhead frost protection
> Shade-dense, medium, light
> Enclosure
> View articulators

Design Accents:
> Perception modification
> Visual
> Audial
> Scale
> Seasonal display

Ground covers:
> Aesthetic development and cultural practices

COMPANION PLANT CHARACTER

The following section describes the design character and intent of the companion trees and shrubs for each sub-development area. The use of companion shrubs is not being recommended for every sub-development area, in which case no examples have been listed. In all cases the materials listed are examples only, and do not represent final choices. These will be determined when the detailed plans area produced for each sub-development area.

1. NORTH GATEWAY

Design Intent: To provide a minimum of competing features and plant variety at the gate, in an effort to modify the visitors' perception before they enter the Garden.

Companion Plant Character: TREES: Small deciduous, light canopy when leafed, good form preferably with decorative bark, material must have year round interest.(i.e. Acer davidii).

2. COURTYARDS

Design Intent: To reinforce the prominence of the area as the northernmost and highest portion of the Garden. To accentuate and lend scale to the area. Since this area is at the northern perimeter, the dense shading will not effect the collection. Companion tree planting in this area may have the most dense canopy of any on the site. A dense canopy in this area will also reinforce the special nature of this area.

Companion shrubs would not be utilized in the entry courtyard. Shrub plantings in this area will be comprised principally of species rhododendron of outstanding characteristics.

Ground related floral display as can be achieved through the use of bulbs and/or selected ground covers to give added interest during periods of high visitation.

Suggested Plant Character:

TREES: Deciduous, medium height, medium to dense shade when leafed. Distinct form preferable pyramidal to oval. Good fall color essential. (i.e. Quercus coccinea).

3. STUDY GARDEN

Design Intent: To protect and maintain the area intact. Companion trees should be included to give scale and provide seasonal display.

Suggested Plant Character: TREES: Small to medium height, medium canopy, open crown, medium textured foliage, round to oval form preferred. (i.e. Magnolia Soulangiana var.).

4. MEADOW

Design Intent: To define the area yet maintain the feeling associated with open meadows.

Suggested Plant Character: TREES: A deciduous companion tree of medium foliage texture, open spreading crown, pyramidal to oval form with delicate silhouette has been recommended for this area to provide a light canopy for the collection and define the edges of the Meadow. (i.e. Cornus Kousa)

SHRUBS: Careful placement of rhododendrons within each planting group should eliminate the need to include companion shrubs as functional elements. At this point of the Garden, the visitor should be completely submerged in species rhododendron with a minimum of companion shrubs.

5. ALPINE OUTCROP

Design Intent: To create an environmental setting characteristic of Alpine plants. Companion trees should be sparingly employed to reinforce an Alpine character. True Firs and Hemlock should be featured in this area and/or deciduous trees which will work in a sparse, almost specimen planting approach, featuring high contrast and plant profile. This area is first viewed looking upslope from the path.

Companion Plant Character: TREES: Medium high, medium texture distinct form. (i.e. Tsuga mertensiana)

6. POND

Design Intent: To reinforce the aquatic nature of the area and feature the pond for its aesthetic qualities. Deciduous tree planting should be employed to shelter the species plantings near the Pond Collections and to enclose the area focusing attention on the pond and species plantings. Plant choices should reflect and respond to the aquatic aspects of this setting.

Companion shrub planting should increase in complexity in comparison to the first three sub-development areas that the path traverses.

Suggested Plant Character: TREES: Medium height deciduous, medium to fine foliage, good Fall color and Winter display, graceful, pendulous form preferred. (i.e. Betula pendula).

SHRUBS: Low to medium height, showy flowers and/or good Fall color for design accent good seasonal display. Foliage of medium texture, open form, shade tolerant, (i.e. Amelanchier lamarckii, Leucothoe keiskei and various ferns).

7. THE FOREST GLEN

Design Intent: To provide a background for the species collection and create a sense of enclosure for the visitors as they pass through this section of the Garden. The number of trees used in this area should be few due to the ultimate height of the rhododendrons. The Arboreums are included in this collection.

Companion Plant Character: TREES: Medium height, medium textured foliage upright growth, habit, distinct form. (i.e. Cornus nuttallii).

SHRUBS: Low to medium height, deciduous and evergreen, dense, medium to medium fine texture, seasonal interest. (i.e. Hamamelis mollis, Vaccinium ovatum, Pieris japonica 'Valentine').

8. WEST HILL SLOPE

Design Intent: To create the proper cultural conditions for the rhododendron in this sub-development area by providing a light canopy for sun protection and screening.

Companion Plant Character: TREES: Medium to tall, deciduous, erect habit, strong form, medium-fine foliage texture, good Fall color highly desirable.

9. OLYMPIC VIEW RIDGE

Design Intent: To reinforce the perception of being on the ridge. To provide visual screening, design accentuation and seasonal display. The ridge itself should be planted with canopy trees chosen to enhance the sounds of prevailing winds.

Shrub planting should be primarily on the West slope to modify prevailing winds. High visibility from the East down into the collection should be optimized.

Suggested Plant Character: TREES: Medium to tall height, medium-fine texture, deciduous, erect habit, strong form, good seasonal display. (i.e. Cercidiphyllum japonicum.).

SHRUBS: Evergreen and deciduous, medium to tall, dense, medium textured foliage; good screening ability and good seasonal interest. (i.e. Kalmia latifolia; Viburnum tinus 'Robustum'; Enkianthus cernuus).

10: OFFICE AND NURSERY

Design Intent: To screen the service areas from the Garden by providing an evergreen background of trees and shrubs.

Companion Plant Character: TREES: Medium to tall, evergreen, spreading habit, dense, medium fine to fine foliage; texture; ability to withstand sun and wind. (i.e. Pinus contorta or Pinus sylvestris).

SHRUBS: Medium to tall height; evergreen for year-round screening, deciduous for fall against the evergreen background. Medium to coarse textured foliage. (i.e. Myrica californica, Viburnum opulus, Garrya elliptica, Hamamelis mollis).

11. WEST OUTCROP

Design Intent: To provide year round screening of the Garden from the parking areas and to frame views to the distant Olympic Mountains. Primary trees should be Pines which are adaptable to environmental conditions of the West slope and would help modify wind and sun exposure in this difficult situation.

Companion Plant Character: TREES: Medium to tall, evergreen, upright irregular form, dense, medium fine texture, tolerance of full sun and some drought. (i.e. Pinus thunbergii).

SHRUBS: Low to medium height, evergreen for low screening, deciduous for design accent, fine, medium and medium coarse foliage texture; sun tolerant, spreading or open habit, good seasonal display essential. (i.e. Fothergilla monticola, Menziesia purpurea, Tsuga canadensis 'Cole's prostrate').

MASTER PLAN IMPLEMENTATION GUIDELINES

One of the most important factors in implementing the new master plan is proper phasing. Phasing is affected by several complex factors including: construction techniques and the associated site disruption; plant materials availability; transplanting and/or removal of existing vegetation; seasons of the year; and funding.

As a general recommendation it is agreed that the development of the Garden should proceed in a lineal progression from North to South. This represents a logical and manageable way to relocate the collection. In all cases however, detail planning must preceed planting. While the suggested phasing below gives consideration to all the factors which affect phasing it remains subject to them. Thus the following phasing is a recommendation only.

SUGGESTED PHASING

With the exception of field staking the new primary path, detailed plans must be produced for each sub-development area before it can be constructed or planted

1. Field Stake New Primary Path: Rough grading those portions of it that run through oradjacent to planting groups slated for early installation. At this time rough grading would occur only where necessary to accomodate visitors. Final paving of primary path would occur as funding becomes available.

2. Prepare Detailed Plans for North Gateway and Courtyard: Due to the functional benefits that this area would bring to the site and the degree of disruption that will be required to construct it, it is suggested that the development of the entire area be undertaken at the same time. This would involve: removal of the existing vegetation, grading, building the new fence, restrooms and sales area: installing the paving, seating, signage and all associated plantings. The actual construction and planting of this area would occur as funding becomes available.

3. Prepare Detailed Plans for and Plant the Meadow Collection: At this time only those plant groups on the East side of the meadow would be planted. This would include the following groups with associated companion plantings: Taliense, Fortunei, Auriculatum, Grande and Falconeri. This area is recommended for early installation

in that it contains some of the most significant species in the collection, and because of its proximity to the entry and the Study Garden. The Study Garden which is adjacent to this area is slated to remain intact. It will receive the addition of companion plants, seating and signage but this would be accomplished as funding becomes available.

4. Prepare Detailed Plans for and Plant the Olympic View Ridge Collection: This is the collection that will house two large groups, the Ponticums and the Triflorums. Currently the Ponticums are growing in several areas of the Garden. Planting the Olympic View Ridge at this point in the phasing would allow this major group to be permanently transplanted. Much of the area is now open and ready for planting thus it is a logical and desired progression to develop this area next.

5. Prepare Detailed Plans for and Plant the Companion Plantings on West Hill Slope: The area now lacks adequate tree cover for the rhododendrons that are slated to be planted there. It is therefore suggested that detailed plans be produced for this area in conjunction with those for Olympic View Ridge. This would allow for proper installation of the companion plantings giving them time to provide adequate cover for the species groups before they are planted.

6. Prepare Detailed Plans for and Plant the Companion Plantings for Office/Nursery and West Outcrop Collection: It is recommended that as soon as feasible companion plants be selected and installed in these areas to establish a dense screen between the garden, the freeway and the nursery area. The rock work and species plantings which are to be located in this area would be installed later in the phasing sequence as funding becomes available.

7. Prepare Detailed Plans For and Plant the Forest Glen and Pond Collections: At this time only those plantings North of the Service road would be installed. This includes: Neriiflorum, Griersonianum, Thomsonii and the associated companion plantings. The area south of the road would be installed later in the phasing sequence as funding becomes available. Ideally the pond would be enlarged and planted in conjunction with the area south of the road. This also is dependent on adequate funding.

8. Prepare detailed plans for the alpine collection. Plant it along with the West Outcrop and the West Side of the Meadow Collections: Installing these areas simultaneously would mean that major disruption in the central portion of the site would only need occur once. It would also allow the rocks for both outcrops to be purchased, delivered and installed at th same time.

Note: Areas or Landscape elements not specific would be designed, planted and/or installed as funding becomes available.

EDITOR'S NOTE: Figures 1 through 5 referred to above may be viewed in the Foundation's offices at Federal Way, Washington.

APPENDIX G

The following is a list of present and past members of the Rhododendron Species Foundation, as nearly as can be ascertained from present Foundation records. Any omissions were inadvertant.

Mrs. Jane Abbott
Mr. & Mrs. Don G. Abel
Richard & Corrine Abel
Mrs. Sally E. Abella
Mr. & Mrs. Thomas Abrego
Carolyn Acosta
Robert Adams
Rollo & Winnie Adams
Mrs. Marilyn L. Adams
Mr. & Mrs. Bruce Adams
Jane M. & Peter D. Adams
Mrs. Judy Addington
Jacob Adler
Charmaine Adsero
Mr. & Mrs. John J. Agoa
Oscar Aguilar
Mr. & Mrs. Peter Albrecht
Ms. Kerry M. Albrecht
Melvin W. Alexander
Mr. & Mrs. Henry A. Alexander
Mr. Estus Alexander
Mr. & Mrs. Donald Allan
Mrs. Rosemary Bond Allan
Mr. Lawrence Allbaugh
Mrs. Sallie D. Allen
Mrs. William M. Allen
Mrs. Harold Allen, Jr.
Dr. Brian Altenkirk
Mr. Donald F. Anderson
Mr. Howard Anderson
Mr. John Anderson
Mrs. Leonard Anderson
Mrs. Mayde C. Anderson
Ms. Harriet J. Anderson
Mr. & Mrs. Thomas Anderson
Ms. Dotty Anderson
Mr. & Mrs. Chris Anderson
Mr. & Mrs. Allan Anderson
Kathryn F. Anderson
Dr. Paul Anderson
Dr. Howard Anderson
Dr. Gregory Anderson
Darrell Anderson
Dr. & Mrs. Clarence L. Anderson
Mr. & Mrs. Henning Anderson
Mr. Johnny Andreasen
Mr. & Mrs. G. E. Andrew
Mr. & Mrs. E. W. Andrews, III
Mr. & Mrs. Edward Andrews, Jr.
Mr. & Mrs. George N. Appell
Mr. & Mrs. Louis Appell, Jr.
Mr. & Mrs. Walter Appoldt
Mr. Mike Arai
Mr. & Mrs. Robert Archer
Mrs. Dorothy M. Archibald

Mr. David K. Archibald
Mr. & Mrs. Ivan Arneson
Mr. Richard Arnold
Ms. Gayle Arnzen
Mr. & Mrs. Francis Asbury
Mr. Jason Ashford
Mrs. Mary Anne Aspinwall
Georgiana G. Aston
Mr. Robert Atherton
Bjarke Aunsbjorn
Mrs. Cleo M. Austin
Dr. & Mrs. William E. Avery
Mr. Thomas Bacon
Mr. & Mrs. Bob Badger
Mr. Lou Bagoly
Mrs. Cordell Bahn
Dr. Reid Bahnson
Mr. John B. Bailey
Mr. Robert P. Bailey
Mrs. Hugh Baird
Mrs. Charles Bakeman
Mr. Kirk Baker
Mrs. Barbara Baker
Mrs. Alton Baker
Mr. George B. Baker
Mr. & Mrs. Elbert Baker
Mr. James A. Baker
Mrs. Nancy S. Ballard
Mr. Sid Baller
Dr. James J. Ballington
Mr. & Mrs. Walter Bammann
Mr. & Mrs. E. P. Bancroft
Mrs. Lori Bancroft
Mr. R. A. Banks
Mr. Bruce Barbeau
Mr. Dean Barber
Mr. Clarence Barbre
Dr. Michael D. Barclay
Mrs. Marsha A. Barger
Mr. Chris J. Barker
Mr. Robert Barnard
Dr. & Mrs. James Barnebee
Mr. & Mrs. Clarence Barrett
Mr. David W. Barrett
Mr. Robert J. Barry
Ms. Jacqueline Bartells
Mr. & Mrs. Charles G. Bartenfeld
Mr. John P. Bartlett
Mr. & Mrs. Robert A. Bartlett, Jr.
Ms. Jeanette J. Bassetti
Dr. Kenneth J. Batker
Mr. William C. Baugh
Mrs. Charlotte Baxter
Mr. & Mrs. Dalen Bayes
Mr. Randy A. Bayes
Mr. Alec Bayless
Mrs. George Beasley, Sr.

Mr. Norman Beaudry
Mrs. Amy Beaupre
Dr. & Mrs. W. Gary Becker
Mr. & Mrs. Richard J. Becker
Ms. Judith S. Becker
Mrs. Keri Beckman
Ms. Deborah Beckman
Mr & Mrs. Scott Beckstrom
Mr. & Mrs. Sam E. Bednarski
Mr. William F. Bedwell
Mr. Walter Behrendt
A. H. Bell
Francis & Gwen Bell
Mr. Jerald K. Bell
Mrs. Dianne Bell
Dr. & Mrs. H. V. Bell, Jr.
Dr. & Mrs. J. H. Belyeu
Dr. & Mrs. John Bender
Mr. & Mrs. Larry Bender
Mr. Ed Benedict
Mr. & Mrs. Len C. Bengough
Mr. Max Benjamin
Mrs. Bonnie Marcus Bennett
Mr. & Mrs. Bob Benning
Mr. Harold J. Berg
Mr. Rudolph Berg
Mr. Walter L. Berg
Mr. Warren E. Berg
Ms. Connie Bergeron
Mr. Dave Bergstrom
Mr. & Mrs. Karel F. Bernady
Mrs. Robert T. Berry
Dr. & Mrs. Sigfried Berthelsdorf
Mr. Erik Betten
Mr. & Mrs. James P. Beury, Jr.
Dr. Eugenie Beutler
Mrs. Spencer Biddle
Ms. Carolyn J. Biedenharn
Dr. Barbara L. Billings
Mrs. Janet Binford
Mr. & Mrs. Charles W. Bingham
Nancy H. Bingham
Mr. David Binney
Mr. Jens C. Birck
Mr. R. H. Birkett
Dr. Alf Birkrem
Mr. James M. Birney
Mr. & Mrs. Alfred Bissell
Dr. R. Bissonnette
Col. & Mrs. Berne Biteman
D. G. Black
Dr. & Mrs. Stephen Black
Ms. Suzanne F. Black
Mr. James Blackford
Mr. & Mrs. W. R. Blackledge
Mr. Joel Blair, Jr.
Mr. Noble W. Blake

Mrs. Felice S. Blake
Mr. Leo Blanchette
Mr. David L. Bledsoe
Mr. & Mrs. Gerald Bleyer
Ms. Ann L. Blodgett
Mr. & Mrs. Prentice Bloedel
Mrs. Jane B. Blogg
Mr. Christian Blom
Mr. Robert L. Blough
Mr. Wilbur L. Bluhm
Mrs. R. M. Blumenthal
Mr. Bruce W. Blyth
Ms. Sarah S. Boasberg
Mr. & Mrs. R. B. Boatwright
Mr. Stephen R. Bobbink
Mr. Robert Boddy
Mrs. Pat Boehm
Dr. & Mrs. Dallas Boge
Mr. Mitchell A. Bogen
Mr. Bill Boggs
Mr. David Boggs
Ms. Dalene Boggs
Ms. Ann Bohart
Emil Bohnel
Mr. John D. Bond
Ms. Jan Bondar
Mr. Robert J. Bondira
Mr. Richard A. Booth
Mr. Donald E. Borchers
Mr. Peter Borg
Dr. Drucy Borowitz
Mr. & Mrs. Henk J. Borsje
Dr. & Mrs. Martin Borsky
Mr. John C. Bosch, Jr.
Mr. & Mrs. R. A. Boscole
Evelyn Boswell
Mr. Dennis Bottemiller
Mr. Daniel Bouchard
Mr. & Mrs. James H. Bourasa
Mr. Bill Bowlus
Jan Bowman
Dr. & Mrs. Paul J. Bowman
Mrs. Martha Box
Mr. & Mrs. Gary L. Boyd
Mr. & Mrs. Malcolm A. Boyd
Mr. Ben M. Boyd
Mr. & Mrs. Gary Boydstun
Dr. H. J. Braafladt
Mr. Werner Brack
W. H. Brackman
Ms. Kathy Bradford
Ms. Raylene Braga
Mrs. Karl Brauer
Mr. Ralph M. Bremer
Mrs. Gertrude Brenden
Mrs. Lou Brennan
Mrs. James J. Brennen

Mr. Jim Brewer
Dr. Ben Briggs
Mr. & Mrs. Bruce Briggs
Mr. Ronald G. Brightman
Mr. Richard Brinckmann
Mr. Peter W. Bristol
Ms. Anna Britt
Mr. & Mrs. Kevin Britz
Mr. & Mrs. Regnar Brochner
Dr. & Mrs. Edwin Brockenbrough
Mr. & Mrs. Harold Broman
Mr. Lawrence Brookes
Mrs. Mary Brookhyser
Dr. & Mrs. Alan Brooks
J. J. Brooks
Mr. & Mrs. Walt Brooks
Mr. Judson Brooks
Mr. Richard Brooks
Mr. William A. C. Brooks
Ms. Deanna Brooks
Mr. Jim Brotherton
Mr. Frank W. Brouse
Mrs. Mary E. Shaw Brown
Mrs. Myfanwy Scott Brown
Mr. Richard A. Brown
Mr. Garfield A. Brown
Dr. Bee Brown
Mrs. F. H. Brownell
Mr. George Brubaker
Mr. Steven G. Bruch
Mr. & Mrs. Robert B. Brunner
Mr. Malcolm Bryant
Mr. & Mrs. P. H. Brydon
Mr. Walt Bubelis
Mrs. Sammie Buben
Dr. Stephen Bubert
Ms. Christine Bublin
Mr. & Mrs. David Buchanan
Mrs. Carol Buchanan
Mr. & Mrs. Tom Buchanan
Dr. Charles A. Bucjiy
Mrs. Elwood Budil
Mrs. Marlene Buffington
Mr. & Mrs. Walter Bull
Mr. & Mrs. William Bulley
Dr. Forrest Bump
Mr. Laurence Bunner
Mr. & Mrs. Karl Burgess
Mr. Ralph E. Burgess
Mr. & Mrs. David Burns
Mrs. Frances Burns
Mr. & Mrs. Deane Burnside
Ms. Josephine E. Burr
Mr. L. P. Burris
Mr. Douglas P. Burton
Mr. Edward A. Bush
Mr. & Mrs. John Bushong

Mr. & Mrs. Paul D. Bushue
Mr. & Mrs. Joseph Butler
Mr. Don W. Butler
Mr. James Butler
Mrs. William C. Bybee
Mr. John J. Byk
Dr. Max Byrkit
Mr. & Mrs. Bernard Cabana
Mr. Francis H. Cabot
Mr. James A. Calder
Mr. & Mrs. Harrison Caldwell
Mr. Hugh A. Caldwell
Mr. Paul Caldwell
Mr. & Mrs. Clarence A. Cameron
Dr. Lee Campbell
Mr. & Mrs. Don Campbell
Mr. & Mrs. Gerald Campbell
Ms. Barbara Campbell
Mr. & Mrs. Grant W. Canfield
Mr. James K. Canfield
Mr. Allen Cantrell
Mr. & Mrs. James F. Caperci
Mr. Leamon D. Capps
Ms. Elizabeth M. Carlhian
Dr. Dorothy Carlson
Mr. & Mrs. Gary E. Carlson
Bengt Carlsson
Mrs. Joseph Carman, III
Mr. & Mrs. John W. Carnegie
Mr. & Mrs. Bob Carney
Mrs. Bessie M. Carpenter
Mr. William Carr
Ms. Marcia Carroll
Mrs. Leona P. Carty
Mrs. Dwight Cash
Mr. Tom Cashman
Mr. & Mrs. E. Scott Casselman
Ms. Ann Cassels
Dr. & Mrs. Hugh M. Castell
Mr. L. B. Caswell
Mrs. Jean Cattier
Ms. Ann Caughey
Mr. Dick Cavender
Mr. James K. Cavers
Mr. & Mrs. V. Frank Chaffin
Dr. Richard W. Chaikin
Mr. David F. Chamberlain
Mr. Patrick Chambers
Mrs. Arthur S. W. Chantry
Mrs. Carol F. Chapen
Mr. & Mrs. Howard Chapman
Mr. & Mrs. W. H. Chapman
Mr. Ralph Charbonneau
Mr. Geoffrey Charlesworth
Mr. Leonard W. Charvet
Mr. & Mrs. Clarence Chase
Mr. & Mrs. Edward Chase

Mrs. Donald Chase
Dr. Tsai Y. Cheng
Mr. & Mrs. Gerald Child
Mr. Edward C. Childs
Mr. A. Woodward Ching
Dr. Paul A. Christensen
Mr. & Mrs. R. D. Christensen
Mr. Donald Christensen
Mr. Perry Christensen
Mrs. R. E. Christensen
Ms. Cherie Christensen
Ms. Janice Christensen
Mr. Neil B. Christianson
Dr. Eric Christianson
Mr. John Christie
Mr. A. E. Church
Ms. Rebecca Church-Straka
Dr. Marie Churney
Mr. T. Bruce Clark
Ms. Barbara Clark
Ms. Ginny Clark
Ms. A. Clarice Clark
Mrs. Susan B. Clark
Mr. & Mrs. Maurie Clark
Mr. & Mrs. Mark W. Clark
Mr. & Mrs. Donald E. Clark
Dr. & Mrs. C. Spencer Clark
Paula E. Clark
Dr. & Mrs. Marion A.Clark
Mr. Andrew John P. S. Clarke
Dr. & Mrs. J. Harold Clarke
Mr. & Mrs. Craig Clarke
Mrs. Fred G. Clarke, Jr.
Mr. Leslie Clay, Jr.
Mr. Leslie Clay, Sr.
Mr. Mark J. Clements
Mr. Elbert L. Close
Mrs. Donald W. Close
Ms. Donna Cloud
Mr. & Mrs. Richard Clow
Mrs. W. J. Cloyes
Mr. Bruce Clyburn
Emilie M. Cobb
Mr. Kenneth D. Cochran
Mrs. Linda Cochran
Mr. & Mrs. Richard Coffelt
Mr. & Mrs. Wilbert J. Coffey
Mr. & Mrs. Bruce Cole
Mr. & Mrs. Charles W. Cole
Mr. Edward P. Cole
Mrs. B. S. Cole
Teden Cole
Dr. Daniel H. Coleman
Dr. Joe H. Coleman
Mr. Mark C. Collarino
Mr. & Mrs. Franklin G. Collins
Mr. William J. Collins

Mr. & Mrs. Stephen D. Collins
Mr. & Mrs. James Collins
M. et Mme. Marc Colombel
Mr. & Mrs. Robert Comerford
Mr. & Mrs. George Compton
Mrs. Mary Alice Comstock
Mrs. Helen Congleton
Mr. Robert Conklin
Mr. John R. Connelly
Mr. & Mrs. Kevin Conner
Ms. Maureen E. Connors
Mr. Thomas Conover
Mr. Norman Conrad
Mrs. Etta Cook
Mr. & Mrs. Roger S. Cook
Dr. Gary Cooley
Mr. William W. Cooley
Mr. & Mrs. Keith Cooper
Mr. & Mrs. Stanley Cooper
Baron Evence Coppee
Dr. William L. Corbin
Ms. Annabelle Corey
Mr. Jorgen Corfitzen
Mr. Landry Corkery
Mr. Royce O. Cornelius
Mrs. Erastus Corning, II
Mr. Frank H. Cornwall
Mrs. Marilyn Corum
Mr. & Mrs. Reid Cottrell
Mr. & Mrs. Art Coulter
Mr. William O. Courson
Mr. Richard Courville
Mr. Peter Cox
Ms. Jean L. Cox
Mr. James Craddock
Mr. P. L. Crafts, Jr.
Ms. Julia A. Craig
Mrs. Henry Craig
Mr. & Mrs. Clayton Crane
Mr. W. James Crawford
Mr. & Mrs. John Crawford
Dr. John L. Creech
Mr. Thomas J. Creighton
Nancy E. Crippen
Richard L. Critz
Mr. Thomas J. Cromie
Mr. & Mrs. Robert A. Crosby
Mr. & Mrs. Harold L. Crutcher
Mr. Michael D. Cullinane
Mr. & Mrs. Fred Cummings
Mr. & Mrs. Patrick Cummins
Ms. Elizabeth Cummins
Mrs. Judith V. Cundiff
Mr. & Mrs. Leo Cunningham
Mrs. Margaret Cunningham
Mr. & Mrs. William Curland
Mr. Jerry Curtis

Mr. & Mrs. Clay Curtiss
Mr. & Mrs. John A. Cyra
Mrs. Harrill Dabney
Mr. David Dahl
Helen S. Dahlberg
Mrs. Carole Dahlgard
Mr. Peter Damman
Mrs. Edward N. Dane
Mr. Dick Daniels
Ms. M. R. Daniels
Dr. Paul Dantzig
Mr. & Mrs. Edwin Darts
Mr. H. H. Davidian
Mr. Barry C. Davidson
Mr. Eugene H. Davidson
Mr. & Mrs. Lindsay J. Davies
Mr. & Mrs. George Davis
Mr. & Mrs. Marion Davis
Mrs. J. Harold Davis
Mrs. Betty V. Day
Mrs. Hollis Day
Mrs. Lucas D. De Clercq
Ms. Beth De Groen
Mr. Paul de Jager
Ms. Laurie de Paul
Mr. Philde Spoelberch
Col. & Mrs. James E. Deal
Mr. & Mrs. Glen Dealy
Mrs. Jeanne O. Dean
Mr. Michel Decalut
Mr. Jos Deen
Mr. & Mrs. David J. DeGroot
Mary F. Deihl
Mr. Polo DeLorenzo
Mr. Weldon E. Delp
Ms. Ellen Denker
Mr. & Mrs. Douglas Denkers
Mr. & Mrs. Robert E. Dennis
Ms. Kathleen Iller Depert
Mr. Gregory DerSarkisian
Ms. Gladful DerSarkisian
Mr. Clifford E. Desch, Jr.
Mr. David L. Dethero
Mr. & Mrs.Carl Deul
Mr. Mark DeVries
Mc. Charles A. Dewey, Jr.
Mr. Fred W. DeWold
Mrs. Cheryl Diamond
Mr. James Dick
Mrs. H. Lenox H. Dick
Mr. Q. Todd Dickinson
Mr. and Mrs. Lawrence Dickman
Mrs. Mary Dicks
Mr. & Mrs. John Dickson
Mr. & Mrs. Randall A. Diefendorf
Ms. Eva Diener
Mr. August A. Dietz

Mr. & Mrs. Philip Diggs
Ms. Blanche Dillon
Mrs. Don Dixon
Mr. & Mrs. J. Fred Doan
Mrs. Jeannie Dodd
Mr. Stanley Dodds
Dr. Wayne T. Dodge
Mr. & Mrs. John C. Dodge
Mr. Earl D. Dodson
Mr. John Doherty
Mr. Yasuyuki Doi`
Mrs. Ward M. Doland
Mr. Frank Doleshy
Mrs. Ida Dolphin
Mr. Arthur Dome
Ms. Tracy L. Domingues
Dr. Lawrence E. Dona
Ms. Brenda Donner
Mr. Ian Donovan
Mr. Walph W. Doty
Mrs. Percy L. Douglas
Ms. Katherine J. Douglas
Myrna Rae M. Dowsett
Ms. Chloe D. Doyle
Mr. & Mrs. Tom E. Drake
Mrs. Frederick H. Drake
M. Gilles E. Drapanaski
Ms. Patricia Drouin
Ms. Jane Drown
Ms. Gretchen Evenson Drury
Mr. Henry F. du Pont
Dr. John W. Duffield
Mr. & Mrs. Bruce Duffy
Mr. & Mrs. Alton DuFlon
Mr. & Mrs. Ronald Dulac
Mr. K. E. Duncan
Mr. Roger C. Dunlap
Mr. Edward B. Dunn
Ms. Jennifer B. Dunn
Ms. Muriel Dunn
Mr. & Mrs. Bob Dunning
Mr. & Mrs. George E. Dunning
Mrs. Lyle Dunstan
Mr. & Mrs. Joseph F. Duplinsky
Mr. Don Keck Dupree
Mr. & Mrs. Mike Durkin
Mrs. Phil Duryee
Mr. Ernest Dzurick
Mrs. James F. Early
Ms. Linda Easton
Mrs. Ella Eaton
Ms. Judy Echols
Ms. Suzanne Edison
Mr. & Mrs. F. T. Edman
Mr. Newton W. Edwards
Mr. William L. Edwards
Mr. & Mrs. Ralph W. Eells

Mr. Edward C. Egan
Mr. & Mrs. John C. Egbert
Dr. William Ehret
Ms. Hermina Ehrlich
Mrs. Shirley J. Eichelser
Geraldine L. Eilers
Mr. John Eiselein
Ms. Polly Elaidi
Mr. & Mrs. Karl H. Ellerbeck
Ms. Geraldine Ellers
Mr. Richard Ellingson
Mr. William Elliott
Mr. & Mrs. Walt Elliott
Mr. & Mrs. Keith Elliott
Dr. & Mrs. JimEllis
Mr. & Mrs. John C. Ellis
Mr. & Mrs. Steve Ellliott
Mr. & Mrs. Donald L. Elmore
Ms. Pamela Elms
Margaret Walker Emerson
Mr. & Mrs. Frank H. Emerson
Mr. Robert R. Emmerich
Mr. Charles W. Endicott
Mr. Fujio Endo
Mr. & Mrs. Henry E. Engman
Jan Erickson
Mr. Victor F. Erickson
Bent Ernebjerg
Ms. Beverly Ernst
Mr. & Mrs. Robert P. Ertel
Mr. Howard W. Escher
Mrs. Enid Parks Eshom
Mrs. Leonard Foley Eshom
Dr. Don Evans
Dr. John Evans
Mr. Matthew M. Evans
Mrs. John Evans
Dr. & Mrs. Stanton Eversole
Mr. & Mrs. Walter M. Ewing
Mr. & Mrs. Edward S. Eylander
Mr. & Mrs. B. J. Falanga
Fan Xiao Han
Ms. Catherine Fanucchi
Mr. John J. Farbarik
Mr. & Mrs. John Farmer
Mrs. Claude Farrow, Jr.
Mrs. Everett Farwell
Mr. & Mrs. William H. Fee
Mr. Domiciano Feliciano
Mr. Henning Fellenius
Mr. & Mrs. Henry R. Fenbert
Mr. Fred Fenrich
Ms. Carla Ferreira
Mr. & Mrs. Floyd Fesler, Jr.
Mr. & Mrs. William Fetterhoff
Mr. & Mrs. Jerry L. Fickes
Mr. Ken Fiedler

Mr. T. H. Findlay
Dr. Carolyn Finlay
Mr. Richard Finstuen
Mr. George Firis
Mr. Warren Fishbaugh
Mr. & Mrs. Alexander M. Fisken
Mr. Paul Fittz
Mr. & Mrs. A. R. Fitzbunol
Dr. A. L. Fitzburgh
Dr. R. Fitzburghh
Mrs. Elizabeth Fitzgerald
Mr. John T. Fitzpatrick
Mr. & Mrs. Edward R. Fitzsimmons
Mrs. Russell O. Fix
Mr. Terence J. Flanagan
Mr. Andrew Flatau
Mr. Richard A. Flavell
Ms. Lucille Fleischmann
Mr. Paul M. Fletcher
Mr. Jerry J. Flintoff
Mrs. E. F. Flohr
Marnie Flook
Mrs. Carol B. Flowers
Mr. Wing G. Fong
Mr. & Mrs. Peter Fooks
Mr. & Mrs. Edward W. Foote
Mr. & Mrs. Reavis Ford
Dr. Donald Forster
Ms. Barbara Foster
Ms. Jo Ann Foster
Mrs. J. M. Fourier
Mrs. R. L. Frackelton
Mr. & Mrs. Howard A. Frame
Mr. E. W. Frankham
Mr. Robert W. Franz
Mr. & Mrs. Tomm Frederickson
Mr. Sherwood K. Freeman
Ms. Bland Freeman
Dr. Carl Freeman, Jr.
Mrs. Archie French
Mrs. Linda French
Jo Frey
Mr. Allan K. Fry
Mr. & Mrs. Brad Frye
Mr. William Fueger
Mr. Paul D. Fullager
Mr. Henry R. Fuller
Mr. Richard E. Fuller
Mr. & Mrs. Richard Fullerton
Mr. Robert Fulton
Ms. Allison Fuqua
Mr. Frank Furman
Ms. Joelle Fustec
Dr. Henri Galibert
Ms. Eva Gallagher
Mr. Fred Galle
Mr. & Mrs. Fred W. Gallimore

Mr. Kendall Gambrill
Mr. & Mrs. Raymond Gambrill, Jr.
Mr. Robert Gamlin
Mr. & Mrs. Stephen M. Gangsei
Ms. Lynda Gardner
Mr. Robert Garriott
Ms. Jeanette Garton
Mr. James E. Garver
Mr. Milton Gaschk
Linda Gasparovic
Mrs. Charles Gates
Elaine Gauthier
Mr. James D. Gears
Dr. Arthur Gee
Mr. Herman Gehnrich
Lane Gerber
Mr. & Mrs. J. W. Gerdemann
Mr. Eugene R. German
Mr. George O. Gey
Mr. & Mrs. Thomas E. Gibson
Mr. William Gilbert
Mr. & Mrs. Russell Gilkey
Mr. Thomas D. Gillies
Mr. & Mrs. W. T. Gilmore
Mr. Art Gilmore
J. Lyell Ginter
Mr. Thomas Glade
Laurie D. Glaspey
Mr. Alvin Glaze
Mr. & Mrs. John R. Gleadle
Dr. Robert Glein
Dr. Leon Glicenstein
Dr. & Mrs. Robert Glock
Elizabeth B. Glore
Dr. & Mrs. David W. Goheen
Mr. & Mrs. Ralph Gohr
Mr. Lawrence Gooch
Mr. Wayne Stokes Goodall
Mr. & Mrs. George Goodwin
Mr. & Mrs. Glen Gordon
Mrs. Judy Gordon
Kathryn M. Gordon
Mr. & Mrs. Tom Gorey
Mr. Matthew D. Gorniak
Ms. Barbara Gorzinski
Mr. & Mrs. Richard C. Gosline
Mr. Guy H. Gottschalk
Mr. & Mrs. James K.Gottshall
Mr. Christopher Gough
Dr. William C. Govier
Mrs. Donald Graham
Dr. Donald R. Graham
Mrs. Dan A. Graham
Mrs. Dan Grahm
C. A. Granger
Mr. V. Henry Gransee, Jr.
Mae K. Granston

Mr. & Mrs. Robert W. Grant
Mrs. Gene Grant
Mr. Robert Grasing, Jr.
Mrs. Mary Gray
Mrs. Will Gray
Carol Gray
Ms. Diana Gray
Mr. & Mrs. Joshua Green, III
Mr. & Mrs. Malcolm Greenlees
Dr. Thomas Greer
Mr. Dirk Greer
Mr. Dale Greer
Mr. & Mrs. Harold Greer
Mr. & Mrs. W. S. Greer
Mr. & Mrs. Ron Gregory
Mr. & Mrs. James W. Greig
Mrs. Mary Greig
Mr. Robert Grenkowitz
Mr. & Mrs. Bud Gressman
Mr. & Mrs. Ralph Griffin
Mrs. Everet Griggs, II
Mrs. Margaret Anne Grimes
A. Grinevicius
Ms. Kristina C. Grinnell
Mr. & Mrs. William O. Griswold
Mr. & Mrs. Charlie Grods
Ms. Jane A. Groppenberger
Mr. A. N. Gross
Mr. Kenneth W. Gross
Ms. Anne Gross
Mrs. Louis Grothaus
Marjory D. Grove
Mr. & Mrs. David Gruger
Mr. & Mrs. Hugh Gruver
Jean-Pierre Gueguen
Mr. & Mrs. Daniel L. Guild
Mrs. Karen S. Gunderson
Mr. Stephen Gunderson
Mrs. Charlotte Gunderson
Mr. & Mrs. James A.Gunstone
Mr. & Mrs. Robert Gust
Ms. Cheryl A. Gween
Mr. John Gwynne
Mr. Charles R. Haag
Mr. & Mrs. Roy Hacanson
Mr. Hans Hachmann
Mr. & Mrs. Jan Hacking
Ms. Jill Haddaway
O. F. Haeffner
Mrs. William P. Hagen
Mr. & Mrs. William Hager
Mrs. Emil F. Hager
Mr. Rudolph S.Hahn
Mr. Arthur Haines
Mr. Clyde F. Haines
Mr. Edward Halas
Mr. Harold A. Hall

Prof. Benjamin D. Hall
Mr. Denis Clarke Hall
Mr. Arthur Hall
Mr. & Mrs. Stanley Hall
Mr. & Mrs. Everett G. Hall
Mr. & Mrs. Alton C. Hall
Mr. Pat Halligan
Ms. Deanna Hallsell
Mr. Donald R. Halsey
Mr. Fred Hamiltons
Mr. & Mrs. Philip D. Hamlin
K. E. Hammermeister
Mr. Brian Hammons
Mr. & Mrs. Erle Hannum
Mr. Kurt Hansen
Ms. Doris M. Hansen
Ms. Karen Hansen
Mr. & Mrs. R. J. Hansen
Mr. & Mrs. Larry J. Hansen
Mrs. Debra Hansen
Mr. Mike Hansen
Dr. William E. Hanson
E. H. Hanson
Mr. Richard E. Hanson
Mr. Henry Hanssen
Mr. Henry R. Hanssen, Jr.
Mr. & Mrs. Darrell Harber
Mr. & Mrs. Willis Harden, Jr.
Ms. Kathleen Hargrave
Ms. Gail Hargrove
Ms. Jill Harmon
Ms. Pamela J. Harper
Mr. & Mrs. Dave Harris
Mr. & Mrs. James Harris
Ms. Helen Harris
Mr. & Mrs. G. M. Harrison
Mr. & Mrs. George Harrison
Mrs. William Harrold
Mr. & Mrs. Wilson M. Harry
Mr. Clem Hartz
Dr. & Mrs. M. J. Harvey
Mr. Hans Hasche-Kluender
Mr. & Mrs. Frank Hastie
Mr. Robert W. Hastings
Mr. Miles B. Hatch
Dr. & Mrs. William Hatheway
Mrs. Suzanne Hattery
Mr. & Mrs. John H. Hauberg
Dr. Richard D. Haugen
Mrs. Harold Hawkins
Mr. & Mrs. Edmund Hayes
Mr. Robert H. Hayes
Mrs. Frederick W. Hayes
Mrs. Philip S. Hayes
Mrs. Winifred B. Hayes
Ms. Catherine W. Hayes
Mrs. Jane E. Hayter

Mr. M. Furman Haywood
Mrs. Dutton Haywood
Mrs. Ruth Head
Mr. H. W. Heath
Mr. & Mrs. Paul Heather
Dora Heckenblecher
Mr. Charles V. Heckler
Mr. Donald H. Hedges
Ms. Holly Hedges
Mrs. Virginia Heeszel
Dr. L. Heft
Mr. Donald Heil
Mrs. Helen Heiliesen
Dr. Carl G. Heller
Mr. William R. Heller
Mr. Ralph H. Heller
Mrs. David T. Hellyer
Mr. & Mrs. Henry R. Helm
Mr. & Mrs. Hugh Henderson
Mrs. Dan F. Henderson
Mr. Otto E. Henrickson
Ms. Mary D. Henry
Mr. & Mrs. David Hensel
Ms. Kathleen S. Herdiein
Mr. & Mrs. Roland C. Herman
Dr. Franklin W. Herrick
Mrs. Stephen Herron
Mr. & Mrs. David Herwick
Mrs. Daniel J. Hewitt
Mrs. David W. Hewitt
Mrs. Henry Hewitt, Jr.
Mr. & Mrs. Gordon Heyduck
Mr. George C. Hibben
Nancy Hibbing
Mr. Ohazama Hideaki
Ms. Elizabeth J. Higgins
Mr. & Mrs. Stuart Highet
Ms. Luella C. Hilby
Mr. Steven Hill
Mrs. Polly Hill
Mrs. Julian Hill
Dr. Wayne Hill
Miriam Hill
Mr. & Mrs. John Hill
Mr. & Mrs. Lloyd Hill
Mr. & Mrs. Stewart Hilscher
Mrs. Jeanne Hilterbrant
Matti Hiltunen
Mr. Daniel J. Hinkley
Mrs. Howard Hinsdale
Mr. & Mrs. Robert Hintz
Mr. & Mrs. E. D. Hirsch
Mr. Jack Hirsch
Mr. & Mrs. Douglas R. Hitchcock
Mrs. Marilyn Hite
Mr. John D. Hixson
Mr. Charles Hoag

Mr. & Mrs. W. W. Hoagland
Jane T. Hoar
Ms. Gael A. Hodgkins
Mrs. Lilliam Hodgson
Chris Hoffman
Mr. & Mrs. Carl R. Hogan
Ms. Riel Holbrook
Mr. Paul Holden
Mr. & Mrs. Mark M. Holeman
Ms. Prudence Holliger
E. A. Hollowell
Ms. Mary A. Homans
Ms. Jan J. Hook
Mr. Steve Hootman
Mr. & Mrs. Robert Hope
Mr. Michael H. Hopewell
Dr. Dale E. Hopp
Dr. Rudolph A. Hoppe
Mrs. Jocelyn Horder
Mr. & Mrs. Jack Horn
Mr. Howard S. Horner
Mrs. James Horrigan
Mr. Donald A. Horsley
Miss Mary Horstkotte
Mrs. Frederick Horstkotte, Jr.
Mr. & Mrs. Ted Hossfeld
Ms. Susan Hossfeld
Mr. Albert W. Hostek
Mrs. Hugh Hotson
Mr. Don Houghton
Mr. & Mrs. Robert Houlne
Mr. & Mrs. Harry Houston
Dr. & Mrs. C. R. Howarth
Mr. Donald A. Howe
Mr. Winfield Howe
Mr. Keith Howe
Chen-Hao Hsu
Mr. Harry Hubbard
Mr. & Mrs. Michael Hubner
Dr. Gerald Hudgens
Mr. & Mrs. Raymond C. Huey
Mr. & Mrs. Leslie D. Huff
Mr. & Mrs. William H. Huffman
Mrs. Shirley Huffman
Mogens Huge
Mr. Thomas E. Hughes
Ms. Ketty Hughes
Mr. & Mrs. Doyle Hughes
Mrs. Floyd O. Hughs
Mr. James P. Huie
Dr. Stephen Hull
Mr. & Mrs. James L. Humphrey
Mr. Brian Humphrey
Mr. Stanley W. Hungerford
Mr. Willard Hunnewell
Donna Hunt
Dr. & Mrs. David Hunt

Mr. Edward W. Hunter
Mrs. Etta Hunter
Mr. Charles S. Hunter
Dr. & Mrs. Gary Hunter
Dr. & Mrs. Wiley Hutchins
Mrs. William B. Hutchinson
Mrs. Charles Hyde
Mrs. Christy Blair Ingle
Mr. J. G. Inskip
Mr. Steve Isaacson
Mrs. Martha Isaacson
Mr. Henry C. Isaacson, Sr.
Mrs. Henry Issacson
Ms. Barbara Iverson
Dr. Peter Jackson
Mr. Ole Rolf Jacobsen
Mrs. Jane C. Jacobsen
Mr. & Mrs. Carl A. Jacobson
Mr. & Mrs. Neal M. Jacques
Mr. Frank James
Mr. & Mrs. Bernard Jarvis
Mr. Gene Jeffers
Mr. Fred R. Jelovsek
Mr. Don M. Jenkinss
Arne S. Jensen
Mr. & Mrs. Robert C. Jensen
Mr. Bernard Jensen
Mr. & Mrs. Elliott E. Jessen
Mr. & Mrs. David Jewell
Ms. Myrna Jewett
Doris R. Jewett
Mr. Clyde W. Joerg
Ms. Ilse Johansdotter
Mr. & Mrs. Ralph Johansen
Mr. Ole Johansen
Mrs. Perry Johanson
Melanie B. Johns
Mr. Donald B. Johnson
Mr. Duane R. Johnson
Mr. Harry W. Johnson
Mr. Kristan Johnson
Mr. Nick Johnson
Mr. Cletis Johnson
Mrs. Ofell H. Johnson
Mr. William J. Johnson
Ms. Diane Johnson
Ms. Phyllis Johnson
Mr. William L. Johnson
Betsy Johnson
Mr. & Mrs. Joseph A. Johnson
Mr. & Mrs. J. Clifton Johnson
Mr. & Mrs. Harold A. Johnson
Mr. & Mrs. Douglas W. Johnson
Mr. & Mrs. Cyrul Johnson
Mr. & Mrs. Charlie Johnson
Mr. & Mrs. Antone Johnson
Mary Bess Johnson

Margaret L. Johnson
E. R. Johnson
Mrs. Melba E. Johnson
Mr. & Mrs. Stan Johnson
Mr. W. J. Johnston
Mr. John D. Johnston
Mr. & Mrs. Raymond E. Johnston
Dr. Douglas K. Jolley
Mr. Gordon Jones
Ms. Jane R. Jones
Ms. Frances F. Jones
Mr. Paul Jones
Mr. Michael G. Jones
Ms. Janelle Jones
Mr. Dietrick C. Jones
Mr. Charles A. Jones
Mr. & Mrs. Joe Jones
Judith I. Jones
Admiral & Mrs. Stephen E. Jones
Faye Jones
Mr. & Mrs. Lloyd F. Jordan
Mr. Woodie Jordan
Mrs. Charles T. Jordan
Mr. Knud Jorgensen
Tue Jorgensen
Mrs. Hans Jorgensen
Ms. Lisa Jorgenson
Dr. Janice Joseph
Mr. Tiit Juhani
Bridget Jurich
Mr. Clive Justice
Mr. George Kackley
Mr. & Mrs. Clyde Kalahan
Mr. Keith T. Kalkanoff
Mrs. Ruth Kallman
Elinor Kammer
Dr. Tim Karpetsky
Mr. & Mrs. Barry S. Kast
Ms. Sally M. Katkaveck
Dr. Marvin M. Keagy
Mr. James R. Keenan
Dr. August Kehr
Mr. & Mrs. Brian T. Keim
Dr. Donald Kellam, Jr.
D. C. Kellems
Dr. Jack Keller
Mr. Augustus M. Kelley
Mr. James Kelley
Mr. Jan D. Kelley
Mr. Theodore M. Kellogg
Mr. & Mrs. Duane Kelly
Mr. Thom Kelly
Ms. Mary J. Kenady
Mr. Peter J. Kendall
Ms. Jane R. Kendall
Dr. D. Elizabeth Kennedy
Mr. Austin C. Kennell

M. Eloise Kent
Mr. & Mrs. David K. Kentala
Ms. Freda Kerman
Diane D. Kern
Mr. & Mrs. Walter Kern
Mr. Thomas Kerr
Mrs. Barbara Kerr
Ms. Kerry L. Kerston
Mr. Ron Kessel
Mr. Tim Kezele
Mr. Robert Kieckhefer
Mr. Clayton J. Kilbourne
Dr. John H. Killian
Mr. Ronald A. Killian
Mr. Kurt Kilty
Dr. A. R. Kilvert
Ms. Carol Kimbrough
Mr. & Mrs. Arthur King
Mr. Donald King
Miss Esther M. H. King
Dr. Ken King
Dr. F. Wayne King
Mr. Bob King
Mr. & Mrs. Bob Kintigh
Mr. & Mrs. Vincent Kirkwood
Mr. Richard K. Kiyomoto
Mr. Robert H. Kizer
Mr. & Mrs. Alvin M. Klass
Ruth Klawuhn
Mr. Roy Klehm
Dr. Gerald W. Klein
Mr. Eugene M. Kleiner
Ms. Karen Klemetsrud
Mr. Wayne Klemp
Mr. Marvin E. Klinect
Mr. & Mrs. Richard Klockman
Dr. & Mrs. Arthur Kluge
Mr. Fred Knapp
Mr. Dana Stephen Knickerbocker
Barbara L. Knight
Mr. & Mrs. Bob Knight
Ms. Maureen Knight
Mr. Anthony D. M. Knights
Mr. Peter Knoepfel
Mr. & Mrs. Leith Knowles
Mr. Lyle F. R. Knudson
Mr. & Mrs. William Knull
Mr. Dennis Knust
Mr. Doug Knutsen
Mr. John D. Koelsch
Mr. Thomas W. Koenig
Ms. Emily Koeniger
Mrs. Virginia Koken
Mr. & Mrs. Ernest Kolak
Mrs. Richard Kolesar
Mr. & Mrs. John D. Komen
Mr. Walter L. Koopman

Dr. Harold Koopowitz
Mr. & Mrs. Lawrence Korn
Dr. R. C. Kothenbeutel
Mr. Ryan Kothenbeutel
Mr. Robert Kothenbeutel, Jr.
Mr. & Mrs. Rex Krabbe
Mr. & Mrs. Raymond Krag
Mr. John J. Kramer
Mr. George S. Krasle
Mrs. Lisa Kraus
Mr. Stephen Krebs
Mr. & Mrs. Robert Kreiss
Mr. & Mrs. David M. Krepky
Ms. Eva Kresge
Mr. & Mrs. Frank Krieger
Ms. Margit Kristiansen
Mr. & Mrs. Jim Krob
Mr. & Mrs. Bruce Krohn
Dr. Kathleen A. Kron
Mrs. Arthur R. Kruckeberg
Mrs. Norma Krueger
Mr. & Mrs. Harold Krug
Mr. Gerhard J. Kuenecke
Mr. & Mrs. Howard Kuhn
Mr. Gerry Kuhn
Mr. William L. Kullman
Lois A. Kunkel
Mrs. S. J. Kunnen
Yuji Kurashige
Mr. & Mrs. Milo Kurie
Mrs. Marguerite Kuypers
Mr. Harley D. Kysor
Ms. Sandra F. Ladendorf
Ms. Jane Lagergren
Mr. Carlos M. Lago
Mr. John A. Laing
Mr. Lyle Lancaster
Mr. Dan Landon
Mr. & Mrs. Robert Landregan
Mr. Mitchell Langbartt
Mr. George R. Langdon
Mr. & Mrs. R. Scott Lankford
Mr. & Mrs. George Lankow
Molly D. LaPatra
Mr. & Mrs. A. LaPorte
Mr. F. Larsen
Mrs. C. F. Larsen
Ms. Jane Larsen
Dr. & Mrs. Charles H. Larson
Mr. R. H. Larson
Ms. Neva Larson
Mr. Charles T. Larus
Mr. Norval H. Latimer
Mr. Walter H. Latosh
Mr. & Mrs. S. Philip Laucks
Mr. Kenneth T. Lauhon
C. F. Laurie

Holly Hedges Laush
Dr. Edmond F. Lawrence
Mr. J. V. Lawrence
Ms. Cheryl Lawrence
Mr. & Mrs. Michael Lawson
Dr. R. Anitra Laycock
Dr. Richard W. Lazaro
Dr. David G. Leach
Mr. & Mrs. Charles Leach
Ms. M. Elaine Leahy
Mr. & Mrs. Stanley Leash
Mrs. Mary Leber
Mr. & Mrs. Bruce Leber
Mr. & Mrs. Gerald Lebert
Mrs. Ed Lebert
Ms. Gail Ledbetter
Mr. David B. Ledlie
Ms. Nancy L. Ledyard
Heeja Lee
Mr. & Mrs. G. W. LeFever
Dr. Gerald H. Leggett
Mr. Carl A. Lehman
Mr. Michael R. Lehmann
Mrs. Roy S. Leighton
Dr. Jerome LeJeune
Mr. Paul D. Leland
Ms. Maureen Lenahan
M. Jean Lennon
Mr. & Mrs. Russ Lenoir
Mr. & Mrs. Devere Leo
Mr. T. Richard Leonard
Ms. M. Sharon Leopold
Mr. & Mrs.Peter F. Leslie
Mrs. James Level
Mr. Phil Levi
Dr. & Mrs. Richard Levin
Mr. Charles S. Lewis
Mr. Mark L. Lewis
Mr. H. W. Lewis
Margaret Lewis-Gillespie
Mrs. Carolyn Lichtenwanger
Mr. & Mrs. R. Michael Ligrano
Mrs. Charles E. Lile
Mr. Mike Lilly
Mr. & Mrs. Norman Limric
Mr. & Mrs. H. C. Lindberg
Mrs. Newell Lindberg
Mr. William Lindeman
H. D. Lindquist
Mr. John R. Lindstrom
Mr. Aaron Linxwiler
Ms. Marian Little
Mr. James Livingston
R. S. Lockhart
Mr. Walter A. Loescher
Dr. Leonard Ed. Loflin
Dr. Wm. E. Lofthouse

Mr & Mrs. Henry Lohse
Mr. Charles Lonergan
Mrs. Dorothy S. Long
Mrs. Brooks Loop
Ms. Loretta Lopez
Ms. Nina A. Lopez
Mr. Irving Lord
Mr. Kenneth Lorentzon
Mr. Steven Lorton
Ms. Karla Lortz
Elizabeth Losk
Mr. Bruce Lott
Lts. Frank A. Lough
T. M. Lounsbury
Mr. Ralph Love
Ruth C. Thomas Lowe
Mr. Peter C. Lowell
Mr. & Mrs. Scott A. Lucas
Mrs. Rosina F. Lukach
J. A. Lukins
Mr. & Mrs. George Lund
Mr. & Mrs. Phil Lund
Gunnar Lundquist
Mr. & Mrs. Douglas Lundsgaard
Mr. John Lungo
Mr. & Mrs. Jay Lunn
Mrs. Frances Lust
Dr. James L. Luteyn
Ms. Pamela J. Luttrell
Mrs. M. J. Lynch
Shaun M. Lynch
Mrs. Agnes Lynn
Mr. & Mrs. Stanley W. Lyon
Ruth S. Lyons
Dr. Wolfgang Maass
Mr. Chuck Mabry
Mrs. Donald MacDonald
Mr. & Mrs. Ian MacKenzie
Mrs. R. L. MacLean
Mrs. J. Macnab
Mr. & Mrs. Daniel Macomber
Mrs. James H. Madison
Mr. Christian Madvig
Mr. Dennis Mahoney
Colonel A. Mair
Mrs. Ruby Maitland
Mr. & Mrs. Scott Maitland
Mr. & Mrs. Marshall Majors
Mrs. Mary B. Malarkey
Mr. & Mrs. John Malek
Mrs. Linda Malland
Mr. Borje Malmgren
Mr. H. R. Malone
Mrs. P. J. Maloney
Ms. Diane Mangano
Mr. William A. Mangels
Mr. Roy W. Mansfield

Mr. & Mrs. Henry Manzanares
Dr. L. Frank Maranville
Dr. James Marchand
Mr. & Mrs. Francis L. Marckx
Mr. Lynn R. Marcy
Mr. Ralph E. Markby
Mr. Doug Markle
Ms. Danelle Marks
William R.V. Marriott, M.D
Mr. & Mrs. Ted Marston
Dr. Alfred Martin
Mr. & Mrs. Robert Martin
Mr. Alfred S. Martin
Ms. Helen Martin
Ms. Joan A. Martin
Mr. Douglas Martino
Mr. Ken Marts
Mrs. Lucien Masse'
Mr. Robert F. Mast
Mr. Keith Mastenbrook
Ms. Julie Masters
Mr. & Mrs. Rudolph Mate
Mr. Robert Mathey
Ms. Shannon Matson
Mr. Edward K. Matsuwaka
Mrs. Pauline B. Matthews
Mr. & Mrs. George Mattson
Mrs. Cordelia Scaife May
Mr. Frank W. Mayer
Ruth Mayer
Mr. Dan E. Mayers
Mr. Walter Maynard
Ms. Marcia W. Maynard
Mr. Bob Mazaney
Mrs. Irene Mazer
Dr. John Mc Kinnon
Mrs. Donald M. McAusland
Mrs. D. P. McBrayer
Mr. David McCart
Dr. Jackson H. McCarter
Mr. & Mrs. Michael McCarthy
Mrs. Philip McCombs
Mrs. John McCone
Mr. & Mrs. Doug McConkey
Mr. & Mrs. Stephen McConnel
Mrs. Evan McCord
Dr. & Mrs. Mack McCormick
Mabelle C. McCornack
Edna V. McCray
W. S. McCrea
Mr. Michael A. McCullough
Mr. James McDonald
Sir James & Lady McDonald
Mr. Donald B. McDonald
Mr. & Mrs. Charles McDonald
Dr. Sandra McDonald
Mrs. Barbara McDonald

Mr. & Mrs. Kenneth McDonald, Jr.
Mr. Larry McDougald
Mr. Dean McDowell
Ms. Marta McDowell
Ms. Patricia McDowell
Mr. & Mrs. John McGrath
Mr. Patrick McGuinness
Mr. Thomas J. McGuire
Dr. W. J. McHolick
Mr. Robert McIntire
Mr. Henry McKenney
Mr. Brent McKenzie
Mr. & Mrs. David McKibben
Mr. Ernest C. McKibben
Mrs. Janet R. McKim
Mr. E. L. McKinley
Mrs. John A. McKinnon
Mr. George K. McLellan
Janet McLennon
Mrs. Cheryl McLeod
Mr. & Mrs. Larry McManus
Mr. Lawrence J. McMurtrey
Mr. Pete McNees
A. D. McNees
Mr. John H. McNeil
Mr. James J. McNeil
Mr. & Mrs. Kevin McNeil
Mr. & Mrs. Bob McNulty
Mrs. Lynn A. McNulty
Mr. Wayne A. McPherson
Mr. & Mrs. Everett McQuillen
Mr. J. F. McQuire
Ms. Sandra McShane
Mr. Joe McTyre
Mrs. Dorothy D. McVay
Mr. Shane McWilliams
Ms. Judi Meade
Mr. Anthony Meadow
Mr. & Mrs. W. H. Meadowcroft
Mrs. Albert H. Meadowcroft
Dr. James P. Meesis
Mr. Mark Megale
Dr. Gustav A. L. Mehlquist
Mr. & Mrs. Peter Melrose
Mr. & Mrs. Burt Mendlin
Ms. Joan Meneley
Mrs. Alma Menenica
Mr. Louis Mensing
Mrs. James Menzies
Dr. Donald Merkeley
Mrs. Dorothy M. Metheny
Mr. & Mrs. Carl R. Meurk
Mr. Bill Meyer
Mr. Fed Meyer
Martha Meyers
Mr. & Mrs. Max Meyers
Mr. & Mrs. R. Wayne Mezitt

Dr. & Mrs. J. C. Michel
Mr. James A. Middleton
Mrs. Barbara Miener
Mr. Bruce Mitchell
Mr. & Mrs. Nick Milfeld
Mr. Ted Millais
Mr. David Millais
Mrs. Howard W. Millan
Harold Miller
K. M. Miller
Marion S. Miller
Mr. & Mrs. George Miller
Mr. & Mrs. John Miller
Mr. & Mrs. Paul Miller
Mr. & Mrs. Pendleton Miller
Mr. William S. Miller
Dr. & Mrs. Leonard Miller
Mr. Don Milliken
Mr. & Mrs. George Milner
Ms. Mary Milton
Mr. & Mrs. Richard Milton
Ms. Virginia Minnig
Mrs. Pauline T. Mischler
Mr. & Mrs. Philip Mitchell
Mr. William Mitchell
Mrs. Harold Mitchell
Ms. Barbara H. Mitchell
Ms. Marcia Mitchell
Mr. R. A. Mitchell, Jr.
Mr. & Mrs. Chuck Mobray
Mr. & Mrs. John E. Mobray
Mr. James Moceri
Ms. Fay Mohammed
Mr. Lowell E. Moholt
Mr. & Mrs. Egon Molbak
Myrna Molberg
Mr. Paul Molinari
Cleo E. Monsees
Mr. & Mrs. G. C. Montgomery, Jr.
Mrs. Helen Marie Moodie
Mr. Mark Moore
Mr. Martin Moore
Mr. & Mrs. Ronald Moorehead
Mr. David Morel
Mrs. R. E. Morell
Mrs. Charles L. Morey
Ms. Minnie C. Morgan
Mr.. & Mrs. Harry E. Morgan, Jr.
Ms. Betsy Morgenthaler
Dr. & Mrs. Doug Morningstar
Dr. Grace E. Morris
Mr. Daniel Morris
Ms. Vicki Morris
Mrs. Sally Morrison
Mrs. Dorothy Carr Moseley
Mr. & Mrs. Allen Moses

Mrs. Gordon W. Moss
Mr. Richard A. Mossakowski
Dr. Frank D. Mossman
Dr. Irene M. Moszer
Mr. Kevin Moxon
Jane E. Moyer
Mr. Terry L. Moyer
Mr. William Moyles
Mary Ellen Mulder
Mr. Ed Mulder
Mrs. George Muller
Dr. & Mrs. Charles Muller
Dr. Patricia D. Muller
Mr. & Mrs. Brian Mulligan
Mr. & Mrs. Stephen E. Mullis
Mr. Bradley J. Mulvihill
Mr. Stanley T. Murayama
Mr. & Mrs. James A. Murchy
Mr. Richard Murcott
Mr. Brent David Murdoch
Dr. & Mrs. Gary Murphy
Mr. Irving Murphy
Jay Whitney Murray
Mr. John Murray
R. A. Murray
Mrs. L. T. Murray, Sr.
Mr. John M. Musser
Mr. Mike Muth
Mrs. Roy Myers
Mr. Ken Nahas
Mr. Glenn R. Neal
Mr. John W. Neal
Dr. John J. Neal, Jr.
Mrs. Gordon F. Nelson
Raymonde S. Nelson
Ms. Pearl W. Nelson
Ms. Sonja Nelson
Mr. Robert H. Nelson
Patricia A. Nelson
Mr. Nels Nelson
Mr. Ben Nelson
Mr. & Mrs. Robert V. Nelson
Mr. W. J. Nelson
M. & Mrs. George Nelson-Benway
Dr. & Mrs. James F. Nelwon
Mr. Albert Nerken
Mr. Alfred Nerkin
Mr. & Mrs. Sidney Nestegard
Ms. Nancy Nestor
Mr. H. E. Neumann
Ms. Peggy C. Newcomb
Mr. & Mrs. Lloyd Newcomb
Mr. & Mrs. David Nicholson
Mr. & Mrs. Kenneth Nicholson
Dr. Nickolas Nickou
Mrs. George Nickum
Mr. Phil Nicolet

Mr. Jens Nielsen
Mr. David Niemann
Ms. Jean Niemeier
A. Weston Niemela
Mr. Fredrik Nilsson
Dr. & Mrs. Mark A. E. Nixon
Mr. Mel Noble
Mr. Joseph E. Nolan
Mr. Steve Nord
Dr. William T. Norris, Jr.
Mr. & Mrs. Jack G. North
Mr. & Mrs. Flores S. Nowick
Mr. & Mrs. Neal Nunamaker
Ms. Ann Nunziata
Mr. & Mrs. James J. Nussbaum, Jr.
Ms. Shirley Nyberg
Ms. Marie Nyman
Mr. & Mrs. Philip T. O'Brien
Ms. Debbie O'Connor
Mr. Michael O'Hara
Mr. & Mrs. Eric O'Neal
Dr. & Mrs. W. F. O'Neill
Mr. & Mrs. Michael P. O'Neill
Mr. Albert D. O'Rear, Sr.
Mr. & Mrs. Carroll K. O'Rourke
Mr. William O'Rourke
Mrs. Reno Odlin
Mrs. Kathleen Ogle
Alexandra I. Olafson
Ms. Mary Oleri
Mr. H. W. Oliver
Mr. & Mrs. David M. Olsen
Mr. Ken Olsen
Mrs. Sue Olsen
Mr. & Mrs. Marshall Olson
Mr. Bjorn Olson
Mr. Oscar Oltmann
Ms. Nancy J. Ondra
Mr. Norman Orford
Mr. & Mrs. John W. Ormsby
Mr. Erik G. Ortengren
Mr. Hadley Osborn
Mrs. Helen J. Osborne
Mr. & Mrs. Larry Osterman
Mr. Melvin Osterman
Mr. Walter Ostrom
Mrs. Jonathan Ostrow
Patricia Rineheart Oswald
Ms. Ann Ottini
Mr. Robert Overstreet
Mrs. Lilliam G. Owen
Ingrid L. Owen
Mr. David Owens
Mr. Joe Ozimek
Mrs. Birdie Padavich
Mr. & Mrs. William S. Padden
N. Margaret Padelford

Mr. & Mrs. Donald W. Paden
Mr. Frank Pagliettini
Dr. & Mrs. UnoPaim
Mr. & Mrs. Thomas Paine
Mr. & Mrs. Ray Palmer
Mr. John Palmer
Mr. Michael Palmer
Ms. Lisa A. Panella
Mr. & Mrs. Max L. Panzer
Mr. & Mrs. John W. Parker
Mr. & Mrs. Rodney Parker
Mr. Edwin Parker
Mr. Tom Parker
Mrs. Phyllis Parker
C. M. Parkinson
Mr. Gordon Parkinson
Mr. Stanley Parr
Mr. Terrance M. Parr
Mr. & Mrs. James R. Parsons, Jr.
Jeanne S. Pascal
Ms. Patricia Pascoe
Mr. & Mrs. Scott Pascoe
Mrs. Ann W. Pascoe
Dr. Mavis R. Paton
Mr. & Mrs. Donald L. Patrick
Mr. & Mrs. T. Keith Patrick
Dr. Charles H. Patterson
Mr. Glen Patterson
Mr. Donald G. Paul
Mr. Georg Paulmann
Mrs. James R. Paulson
Mr. John Charles Pavlich
Dr. James C. Pearson
Ms. Karen Pease
Mr. & Mrs. William R. Peden
Mr. & Mrs. Raymond E. Pelletier
Mr. & Mrs. James Pellicer
Mrs. Francis J. Pelly
Mr. Franklin B. Pelurie
Mrs. Dina Pendleton
Mr. & Mrs. J. K. Penfield
Mr. & Mrs. Craig Penner
Ms. Shelley Penzel
Mr. Carl L. Penzer
Mr. & Mrs. Robert E. Perdue
Mr. Max C. Perena
Mr. & Mrs. John Perkins
Mr. & Mrs. Terry Perkins
Dr. P. Perlman
Mr. & Mrs. John C. Perry
Mr. Roland H. Perry
Mr. William D. Perry
Mr. Bob Person
Mr. Ted Peterschmidt
Ms. Rita Grassi Petersen
Mr. Clayton B. Peterson
Mr. Rick Peterson

Ms. Lucille Peterson
Mr. & Mrs. R. C. Peterson
Cindy Peterson
Mr. Michael Peterson
Mr. Glenn Peterson
Mr. & Mrs. Vladis Petersons
Ms. Halia Petrenko
Mrs. Hervey M. Petrich
Dr. Howard Pfeifer
Dr. & Mrs. A. Eugene Pflug
Mr. Steven C. Phare
Dr. & Mrs. Carl Phetteplace
W. W. Philip
Mr. Bruce Philip
Mr. Alan M. Phillips
Mr. Thomas Phillips
Ms. Shirley M. Phinney
Mr. & Mrs. Dante G. Piacentini
Mr. & Mrs. Vero R. Piacentini
Mr. Richard Piacentini
Dr. John H. Pierce
Mr. & Mrs. Lawrence Pierce
Mr. James C. Pierce
Mrs. Karen Pierce
Mr. Richard Pierson
Mr. & Mrs. Darrell E. Pierson
Mrs. David Pinkerton
Mrs. Mary Pinkham
Mr. George J. Pinyuh
Dr. Arnold Piper
Mr. William S. Pitt
Mr. & Mrs. John W. S. Platt
Mr. Lonnie Player
Mrs. Glen W. Player
Dr. William A. Plummer
Ms. Frances Plunkett
Mr. Graham A. Podd
Mr. Dwayne Podd
Ms. Doreen V. Pohlman
R. P. Pohlmann
Mr. Frank Polefka
Dr. Steven Hayden Pollock
W. L. Pomeroy
D. M. Poole
Mr. Richard E. Poole
Mrs. Linda Popp
Mr. Ward Porter
Mr. Robert W. Porter, Jr.
Mr. L. Norris Post
Mr. Basil C. Potter
Mr. & Mrs. Jeffrey Powel
Mr. & Mrs. Monte Powell
Susan K. Powers
Mrs. Archie Pozzi, Jr.
Mr. & Mrs. J. Dean Prater
Mr. J. Scott B. Pratt, III
Mr. & Mrs. Richard Presley

Mr. Orlando S. Pride

Ms. Aloha Pridmore

Martha Prince

Dipl.-Ing. Helmut Prinz

Mr. William M. Proebsting

Ms. Margaret Proud

Mr. & Mrs. E. Moulton Prussing

Mr. & Mrs. Otto Prycl

Mr. & Mrs. Harry Pugatch

Mrs. Nayadean Pundsack

Mr. David Purdy

Mr. Dallas J. Purnell

Mr. & Mrs. Dallas M. Purnell

Mr. & Mrs. Calvin C. Putman

Mr. & Mrs. John Putnam

Mr. Ronald R. Rabideau

Mr. & Mrs. Garnett Radebaugh, Jr.

Mr. & Mrs. David Raden

Mrs. Jean F. Radford

Ms. Susan Rakley

Mr. & Mrs. V. V. Ramayya

Mr. John Randall

Mr. Charles Ransone

Dr. & Mrs. Philip J. Rasic

Mr. James A. Rassmann

Mr. James E. Ratcliff

Mr. Derek Ratcliffe

J. C. Raulston

Mr. Alfred A. Raustein

Mr. & Mrs. John Ravenscroft

Dr. Lee Rawlings

Mrs. Nan E. Ray

Mrs. Hazel Raymond

Nancy Katherine Read

Dr. & Mrs. Robert Read

Mrs. Joseph P. Reath

Mr. Richard Redfield

Mrs. Nyla Redford

Mr. Richard R. Reding

Mr. M. Chandler Redman

Mr. Emerson A. Reed

Mrs. D. L. Reed

Mr. & Mrs. Hal Rees

Mr. Fred Rees

Mr. Ken. Reese

Dr. Melvin M. Reeves

Mr. & Mrs. Frank Reichl

Elsa Berry Reid

Mrs. Kurt Reil

Mr. & Mrs. H. Edward Reiley

Mr. Paul Reimann

Mrs. Mary A. Reisse

Mr. & Mrs. Robert A. Remole

Mrs. Eldean B. Rempel

Mr. Fred Renich

Mrs. Isetta M. Renton

Mr. Jerry Retzloff

Mrs. John W. Reynolds

Dr. Robert Rhoades

Ms. Peg Rhoades

Mr. & Mrs. Raymond Rhoads

Ms. Emilie B. Rhoads

Dr. Olaf K. Ribeiro

Mr. & Mrs. Leverett Richards

Mr. Joe A. Richardson

Mr. R. Garratt Richardson

Mr. William Richmond

Mrs. Howard E. Richmond

Mr. & Mrs. Terry A. Richmond

Ms. Linda Richmond

Mr. & Mrs. Robert Riddell

Dr. Robert Jon Riechers

Mrs. E. Madison Riehl

Dr. & Mrs. William O. Rieke

Mr. Michael Riley

Dr. Thomas Ring

Mr. & Mrs. George Ring, III

Mr. Herb Rinn

Mr. Finn Ritslev

Mr. James M. Roach, Jr.

Mr. & Mrs. Gary R. Robbins

Mr. Fred M. Robbins

Ms. Martha Robbins

Miss Grace Roberson

Mrs. L. N. Roberson

Dr. Irving Roberts

Mr. & Mrs. Jack Roberts

Mr. Roger R. Robinson

Newton Y. Robinson

Mr. Herbert Robinson

Heather Robinson

Nollie Robinson, Jr.

Mr. Merrill Robison

Mr. & Mrs. Gerald E. Rock

Dr. Keith A. Rodaway

Mr. Bjoern Roepstorff

Mrs. Jane S. Rogers

Frances M. Rogers

Mr. & Mrs. Henry C. Rogers

Mr. N. Stewart Rogers

Mr. & Mrs. George Rojas

Dr. Joseph Ronsley

Ms. Susan I. Roop

Mr. & Mrs. John W. Root

Ms. Mary Root

Mr. & Mrs. R. H. Rosenberg

Mr. Theodore M. Rosenblume

Mr. Charles S. Rosenfeld

Mr. & Mrs. Jack Rosenow

Mr. Jacob Rosenthal

Mr. Harlan Rosford

Mr. Greg Ross

Mrs. Florence M. Ross

Mr. Peter F. Ross

Mrs. Charlotte Ross

Mr. & Mrs. Bill Rossiter

Mr. & Mrs. R. Jerry Rosso

Mrs. William P. Roth

Ms. Connie Roth

Mr. F. Marion Rothrock

Mr. Gene Round

Dr. John L. Rouse

Mrs. Richard Rouzie

Mrs. H. K. Rowe

Ms. Linda L. Royer

Mr. David C. Royster

Mr. Joseph M. Ruddy

Mr. Andrew Rudko

Mr. Richard Ruess

Mr. Larry Rueter

Mrs. James Ruggles

Mr. George E. Rush

Helen S. Russell

Mr. & Mrs. George Russell

Mrs. James S. Russell

Mr. Glenn W. Russell, Jr.

Mr. & Mrs. Fran C. Rutherford

Mr. Colman Rutkin

Dr. & Mrs. George F. Ryan

Dr. & Mrs. Richard R. Ryan

Mrs. John E. Ryan, Jr.

Mrs. Gordon Sahnow

Mary C. Sainsbury

Mr. Charles G. Sale

Dr. & Mrs. Homer E. Salley

Mr. David Salmon

Ms. Cindy Salmon

Marjorie Salo

Dr. John R. Salzman

Virginia Salzman

Mrs. Ruth E. Samotis

Ms. April Sanborn

Mr. Merle Sanders

Susan F. Sanders

Mr. & Mrs. Spencer C. Sanders

Mr. Graham Sanderson

Ms. Evelyn Sandifur

Mr. Louis W. Sandine

Mr. Wayne M. Sandstrom

Mr. Ikuo Sasaki

Ms. Anne Sather

Dr. Roger E. Sauer

Mr. Richard Saulsman

Dr. Norma Saunders

Mr. George E. Saunders

Dr. Brian Saunders

Dr. Hans J. Sauter

Sir Eric Savill

Mr. & Mrs. Jeffrey Savin

Mr. & Mrs. Richard L. Savold

Ms. Dianne Sawyer-Doescher

Mr. Richard L. Scales
Mr. Stanley D. Schaad
Mrs. June Schaertl
Ms. Carole Schaffner
Mr. Henry A. Schannen
Dr. Alexander Schauff
Ms. Maryonda Scher
Mr. & Mrs. Peter A. Schick
Mrs. Joan Schiff
Mr. Rudolph E. Schild
Mrs. Hugo Schlaikjer
Mr. Ernest L. Schmidt
Mr. Fred Schmidt
Mrs. Ferdinand Schmitz, III
Mr. Franz M. Schneider
Gen. & Mrs. William M. Schoning
Dr. H. Roland Schroeder, Jr.
Mr. & Mrs. James Schubert
Mr. Joseph Schugmann
Mrs. John S. Schultz
Mr. & Mrs. Richard Schusler
Mr. David O. Schussolin
Mr. John E. Schutz
Mr. Robert William Schwab
Mrs. Siegfried Schwendtke
Mr. & Mrs. Irv Schynert
Mr. & Mrs. Mike Scott
Mrs. James E. Scott
Mrs. Sidney Scott, Jr.
Mr. Robert Scotton
Mr. & Mrs. Elmer E. Sears
Ms. Elaine Sedlack
Mr. Louis F. Seeds
Dr. & Mrs. Edward Seigmund
Ms. Virginia Seitz
Dr. Donald Selcer
Mr. Rick Sellers
Mr. & Mrs. James F. Senko
Mr. Harold Senn
Mr. & Mrs. Larry Senters
Dr. A. Frederick Serbin
Mr. & Mrs. Peter J. Serko
Mr. & Mrs. B. Vernon Severance
Mr. Anthony M. Shammarello
Mrs. Frederick Shanaman
Mrs. William M. W. Sharp
Ms. Betty Carlson Shaub
Mr. Robert G. Shaver
Mr. Kevin Shea
Ms. Sheri Shea
Mr. Charles Sheaffer
Ms. Elizabeth Sheedy
Ms. Maxine Shelly
Mr. Philip Sheridan
Mr. & Mrs. Scott Sherman
Mr. & Mrs. Thomas Sherrard
Mr. & Mrs. Richael Shestopal, Jr.

Dr. Charles J. Sheviak
Dr. T. M. Shimshak
Mr. Gary F. Shirley
Mr. & Mrs. Martin Sholomskas
Ms. Nancy Davidson Short
Mr. Lewis R. Shortt
Mr. Headley Shouse
Mr. Jack Shrauger
Mrs. J. J. Shultz
Mr. & Mrs. Ralph H. Shumm
Mr. Richard W. Shuttleworth
Ms. Deborah L. W. Siefert
Mr. & Mrs. Edward Siegmund
Mr. & Mrs. Sidney Silber
Mr. & Mrs. Don Silberman
Mr. Thomas E. Sill
Mr. Russell F. Silva
Charlotte H. Simpers
Mr. & Mrs. James E. Sinclair
Mr. & Mrs. Mickey Sinclair
Mr. & Mrs. Jeff Sires
Mrs. W. W. Sisson
Dr. Mark Sivak
Mr. & Mrs. James Skaggs
Mrs. Willard Skeel
Thurston Skei
Mr. & Mrs. Frank J. Skerbeck
Dr. Henry T. Skinner
Mr. Don Skirving
Mr. & Mrs. Wayne Sladek
Leslie G. Slater
Mr. B. P. Sleeper
Mr. Barry Sligh
Mr. & Mrs. John Slikas
Mr. & Mrs. William C. Sloan
Ms. Sharon Sloan
Mr. H. J. Slonecker
Mr. & Mrs. Robert E. Small
Mr. & Mrs. Bill Smallwood
Mr. & Mrs. Richard F. Smart
Mr. Theo C. Smid
Mr. C. N. Smit
Mr. E. Parker Smith
Ms. Mary Lou Smith
Mary L. Smith
Ms. Claire A. Smith
Ms. Pamela A. Smith
Mrs. Jeanine P. Smith
Mr. Wilburn S. Smith
Mr. R. Nelson Smith
Mr. Joe R. Smith
Mr. Graham F. Smith
Mr. & Mrs. Britt M. Smith
Mr. Bryant Smith
Mr. & Mrs. William E. Smith
Mr. & Mrs. Richard Smith
Mr. & Mrs. Ray C. Smith

Mr. & Mrs. David Smith
Mr. & Mrs. Cecil Smith
Mr. & Mrs. Alan I. Smith
Dr. John Allen Smith
Mr. Clint Smith
Mr. E. White Smith, Jr.
Mr. Raymond C. Smith, Jr.
Mrs. Robyn Smith-Bronstein
Mrs. William E. Snell
Faith Snider
Ms. Marilyn Snodgrass
Mr. & Mrs. Eugene L. Snow
Mr. Moeljo Soetrisno
Mr. Charles E. Sohl
Ms. Ann Solomon
Mr. & Mrs. Mani Soma
Mr. E. J. Somers
Ms. Danielle Somers
Mr. David Sommerville
Mr. Earl A. Sommerville
Vagn Sondergaard
Ms. Lynn Sonneman
Mr. Kurt Sorensen
Ms. Lucie Sorensen
Mr. Allan Sowinski
Dr. & Mrs. Herbert A. Spady
Mr. Dave Spangler
Mrs. Doreen Spellmann
Ms. Sandra Spencer
Ms. Tracy Spier
Mr. Herbert J. Spier, Jr.
Mr. Ulrich Spies
Ms. Caroline C. Spiller
Ms. Phyllis Spinning
Philippe de Spoelberch
Mr. John J. Spring
Mrs. John A. Sprouse
Mr. & Mrs. Ben W. Staab
Mr. Leon Stamatis
Mr. Paul Stamets
Mr. & Mrs. Malcolm T. Stamper
Ms. Mary Standaert
Mr. Alfred B. Stansbury
Mr. & Mrs. David Starr
Mr. Robert L. Staton
Mr. Claus J. Staune
Mr. & Mrs. Gerhard Stavney
Mr. & Mrs. Conrad L. Stayton
Mr. & Mrs. James Stearns
Mr. Ted Stecki
Ms. Nancy Steel
Mr. Richard Steffen
Mr. Bill Steil
Mr. L. William Steil, Jr.
Helen W. Stein
Mrs. Carolyn J. Steiner
Mrs. Zee Stella

Eleanor Stelling
Mr. & Mrs. Robert Stelloh
Mary Ann Stephens
Ms. Linda Bronwen Stephens
Deanna Stevens
Mr. John J. Stevens
Mr. Larry Steward
Mr. Francis E.Stewart
Mr. & Mrs. Roger Stewart
Mr. & Mrs. Clinton F. Stewart
Mr. & Mrs. Coulter Stewart
Mr. Mike Stillwell
Mr. W. A. Stipe
Dr. Joseph R. Stone
Lora Stonefeld
Professor Allan Stoops
Priscilla P. Storer
Ms. Irene Storkan
Mr. William Storms
Mr. M. Dean Stout
Mrs. Janice Strand
Evelyn A. Strawbridge
Ms. Alice Strong
Ms. Susan Stubbs
Mrs. Donald Sturdivant
Mrs. Julian Sturtevant
Mr. Barry Sugnet
Mrs. H. Suhr
Mr. Dale Sullivan
Mrs. Barbara R. Sullivan
Mrs. Charles D. Sully
Mr. & Mrs. Maurice H. Sumner
Ms. B. J. Suse
Mr. Hideo Suzuki
P.J.J. Swanepoel
Mrs. Maureen Swanson
Mr. & Mrs. Don Swanson
Mr. & Mrs. Raymond L. Swanson
Mr. Bill Swanson
Mr. & Mrs. Thomas Sweeney
Mr. Harold E. Sweetman
Mr. Bernard M. Swenson
Mr. & Mrs. Dale Swier
Ms. Sue Sykes
Mr. & Mrs. Ed Szlosek
Mr. Gerald Taaffe
Mr. & Mrs. Milton B. Tanggard
Mr. Tom Tanton
Mr. Larry Tardaewether
Mr. & Mrs. Wes Tarpley
Mr. J. Patrick Tatum
Mr. & Mrs. Al Taylor
Mr. & Mrs. Arthur R. Taylor
Mr. & Mrs. Paul F. Taylor
Mr. Allan R. Taylor
Mr. John L. Taylor
Mr. Richard H. Taylor

Mrs. Margaret B. Taylor
Dr. Roy L. Taylor
Miss Cora Ten Eych
Mrs. Vanda P. Terilli
Ms. Marie Terryll
Mrs. Louise Teubner-Rhodes
Mr. William S.Thackray
Mrs. H. L. Thiederman
Carmen Thomas
L. A. Thomas
Mr. & Mrs. Dwight Thomas
Mr. & Mrs. Leo A. Thomas
Mr. Kevin S. Thomas
Ruth C. Thomas
Mr. & Mrs. Donald C. Thompson
Ms. Adrienne W. Thompson
Mr. Jeffrey T.Thompson
Mr. Dave Thompson
Mr. & Mrs. Stephen E. Thompson
Mr. & Mrs. Neil W. Thompson
Mr. & Mrs. Orris E.Thompson
Mr. & Mrs. Wirt L. Thompson, Jr.
Mr. Dave Thorbeck
Dr. & Mrs. John T. Thornton
Mr. & Mrs. Allen Thorsett
Mr. G. J. Throop
Mrs. Paul E. Thurston
Mr. C. L.Thurston
Judith Freriks Thut
Mr. & Mrs. Max Tietjens
Mr. & Mrs. Warren F. Timmons, III
Mr. & Mrs. John F. Tinker
Dr. & Mrs. David L.Tison
Mrs. Paul H. Titus
Mr. & Mrs. Ross Tocher
Mrs. Anne G. Todd
Dr. Norman Todd
Mr. James R. Todd, Jr.
Mrs. Thor C. Tollefson
W. L. Tolstead
Mr. & Mrs. Martin Torklep
Ms. Mary A. Torklep
Mr. Ty L.Treddenbarger
Mr. & Mrs. Patrick A. Trembley
Mrs. Glen Kerry Trimble
Mr. Steven Trout
Mr. Tandy Trower
Mr. John N. Trudell
Mr. Murray Turoff
Mrs. Robert Tweddle
Ms. Linda L. Tynes
Mr. Ray H. Tyson
Mrs. Suzanne S. Underwood
Mr. Joseph W. Upton, II
Dr. P. G. Valder
Mr. Jon Valigorsky
Mr. James W. Valliant

Mr. Mike van Buskirk
Dr. Robert L. van Citters
Mr. Jerry van de Sande
Mr. John van den Meerendonk
Mr. Jens van Draby
Mr. & Mrs. Roger van Gelder
Mr. J. Van Meulder
Mr. & Mrs. P. Van Royen
Mr. Theodore Van Veen
Mr. Gary B. Van Winkle
Mr. & Mrs. Dirk Van Woerden
Mr. Andrew VanCleve
Mr. & Mrs. Herman Vandenboom
Mrs. Gerrit Vander Ende
Mr. & Mrs. Steven Vanderveen
M. & Mrs. Alan Vandevert
Mrs. Dorothy Van Duynhoven
Hakon Vangsnes
Mr. & Mrs. Lou Vargha
Marian L.Vaughan
Dr. James H. Venable
Scott Gregory Vergara
Katherine & RodolfoVergara
Mr. & Mrs. Vern Verhei
Mr. Kaare Einar Vetaas
Ms. Marianne Victor
Mr. Richard G.Vincens
Mr. M. S.Viraraghavan
Mr. John H. Vogel
Mr. Wade Volwiler
Mr. Paul K. von Bergen
Mrs. Margaret Von Hacht
Mr. Donald H. Voss
Dr. L. Keith Wade
Mr. & Mrs. Corydon Wagner
Mr. David E. Wagner
Mr. Robert H. Wagner
Mr. Corydon Wagner, III
Mr. & Mrs. Charles V. Waid
Mr. Geoffrey Wakefield
Dr. Phillip M.Waldman
Miss Gladys Waldron
Mr. & Mrs. Alan R. Walker
Ms. Marilyn Walker
Mr. W. A.Walker
Mr. Sharon Walker
Mr. Ian P. Walker
Mr. & Mrs. Cyrus Walker
Dr. & Mrs. Milton V. Walker
Mr. & Mrs. Larry L.Walker
Mr. Don Wallace
Mr. Harry E. Wallace
Mr. Michael W. Wallace
Fern Wallenstrom
C. G. Wallis
Mr. Guy Wallis
Mr. & Mrs. Kevin Wallis

Mr. Charles G.Wallis, Jr.
Mr. Curtis S. Walseth
Mr. Tim Walsh
Mrs. Kathleen Walsh
Mr. Douglas W.Waltenburg
Mr. David Walton
Mrs. James R. Walton
Patricia Walton
Mr. & Mrs. Jerry Wanaka
Mr. & Mrs. Robert W. Ward
Mrs. J. M. Waters
Mr. Conrad A. Watne
Mr. & Mrs. TomWatson
Mr. Edward Watson
Mrs. R. D. Watson
Mr. & Mrs. Lynden M. Watts
Mr. John K. Weagle
Mr. Jemmie Wear
Mr. Greg Weatherford
Mr. Daniel C. Weaver
Mr. & Mrs. Bruce Weber
Mr. John D. Weeden
Mrs. Catherine Weeks
Mr. & Mrs. Charles L. Wegener
Ms. Barbara D.Weinz
Mr. Vernon E. Weis
Mr. Harvey Welch
Mr. James R. Welch
Mr. Robert L. Welch
Mrs. Pauline Weller
Mr. R. W.Wellman
Mr. Richard H. Wellman
Mr. & Mrs. Robert Wells
Ms. Deborah Wendel
Dr. Franklin H. West
Duncan West
Mr. & Mrs. Horace E. West
Mr. Morris West
Ms. Margaret West
Mr. & Mrs. Norman L. Westlake
Mr. & Mrs. C. David Weyerhaeuser
Mr. & Mrs. George H. Weyerhaeuser
Mr. & Mrs. Halvor G. Wheeler
Mr. Steve Wheeler
Mr. Steve D. Whitcher
Ms. Joyce M. White
Dr. Keith White
H. W. White
Mr. & Mrs. Thomas White
Mr. Elmer J. White
Mrs. Robert York White
Mrs. Stewart W. White
Dr. John Whitelaw
Ms. Carol Whitney
Mr. & Mrs. Fred B. Whitney
Mr. & Mrs. James H. Wiborg
Mrs. Boyd Wickwire

Ms. Veronica Wieniewski
Mr. J. Wieting
Mrs. Warland Wight
Mr. Frank A. Wilber
Mr. Douglas P. Wilbur
Mrs. Leonard M. Wilcox
Mr. David Wilde
Ms. Madeline Wilde
Ms. Carol Wilder
Mrs. Gloria F. Wildharber
Mr. & Mrs. Arthur Wiley
Mr. & Mrs. Water B.Wilkes
Mrs. Barbara Wilkins
Mr. George L. Wilkinson
C. D. Will
Dr. & Mrs. Don G. Willard
Ms. Edith Willard
Ms. Ann R. Williams
Dr. & Mrs. David J. Williams
Dorothy Williams
Ms. Emeline R. Williams
Maxine D. Williams
Kathy L. Williams
Mr. Fred Williamson
Mr. Lloyd L. Willis
Mr. & Mrs. George V. Willoughby
Mrs. Maurine Willoughby
Dr. Howard Wilson
Mr. William George Wilson
Mr. Robert B. Wilson
Dr. I. B.Wilson
Mr. & Mrs. Gary Wilson
Mr. Gerry E. Wilson
Mrs. C. R. Winger
Mr. Jack E. Winn
Wanda A. Winner
Dr. John Wister
Mr. Glenn Withey
Mr. Frank E. Witt
Mr. Robert W. Witt
Mr. & Mrs. George A. Wolf
Mr. & Mrs. John W. Wolfe
Ms. Glenda Wonders
Mr. & Mrs. Edward G. Wood
Mr. & Mrs. George L. Wood
Mr. & Mrs. Wales Wood
Mr. Phillips Foss Wood
Mr. R. MacFarlene Wood
Mr. & Mrs. Warren C. Woodard
Mr. George Woodard
Mr. & Mrs. Joe Woods
Mr. & Mrs. Robert Workman
Dr. Ann J. Worth
Mr. & Mrs. W. T. Worth
Mr. William Wrede
Mr. & Mrs. Gordon L. Wright
Mr. & Mrs. William Wright

Mr. Harry Wright
Mr. Steve Wright
Mr. Edmund A. T. Wright, Esq.
Mr. & Mrs. C. Bagley Wright, Jr.
Mr. Robert I. Wright, Jr.
Mrs. Jayne Wuerth
Mrs. William A. Wurster
Mr. & Mrs. Wendell Wyatt
Mrs. Walter Wycoff
Mr. Gordon Wylie
Mr. Steve Yeatts
Dr. Ernest Yelton
Mr. Roger Yerke
Mr. Thomas York
Yamada Yoshio
Mrs. Glen B. Youell
Mr. Andrew H. Young
Mr. Howard S. Young
Mr. Stanford Young
Mrs. Judith Y. Young
Mrs. Margaret A. Young
Willena Youngblood
Mrs. Andrew J. Yuhl
Mrs. Lois Yuhl
Mr. Mathias C. Zack
Mr. & Mrs. Philip J. Zeller, Jr.
Dr. C. C. Zibbeveld
Brig. Gen D. Z. Zimmerman
Dr. Michael J. Zimmerman
Mr. Robert Zimmerman
Ms. Melinda Zoehrer
Mr. Andrew Zoltay
Mr. & Mrs. Shim Zudekoff
Dr. William M. Zurich, Jr.
American Bamboo Society, Pacific
    Northwest Chapter
American Rhododendron Society
American Rhododendron Society
    Research Foundation
Andover Terrace Garden Club
Arnold Arboretum
ARS-Birmingham Chapter
ARS-California Chapter
ARS-Cascade Chapter
ARS-Central Gulf Coast Chapter
ARS-Connecticut Chapter
ARS-Corvallis Chapter
ARS-De Anza Chapter
ARS-Denmark Chapter
ARS-Eugene Chapter
ARS-Eureka Chapter
ARS-Fraser South Rhododendron
    Society
ARS-Grays Harbor Chapter
ARS-Great Lakes Chapter
ARS-Greater Philadelphia Chapter

ARS-Indiana Chapter
ARS-Juan de Fuca Chapter
ARS-Komo Kulshan Chapter
ARS-Leigh Valley Chapter
ARS-Lewis County Chapter
ARS-Long Island Chapter
ARS-Massachusetts Chapter
ARS-Middle Atlantic Chapter
ARS-Monterey Bay Chapter
ARS-Mount Arrowsmith Rhodo-
	dendron Society
ARS-New Jersey Chapter
ARS-New York Chapter
ARS-North Island Chapter
ARS-North Kitsap Chapter
ARS-Noyo Chapter
ARS-Olympia Chapter
ARS-Olympic Peninsula Chapter
ARS-Peace Arch Rhododendron
	Society
ARS-Philadelphia Chapter
ARS-Piedmont Chapter
ARS-Pine Barrens Chapter
ARS-Portland Chapter
ARS-Potomac Valley Chapter
ARS-Princeton Chapter
ARS-S.W. Oregon Chapter
ARS-San Mateo Chapter
ARS-Seattle Rhododendron Society
ARS-Shelton Chapter
ARS-Siuslaw Chapter
ARS-So. California Chapter
ARS-Southeastern Chapter
ARS-Tacoma Chapter
ARS-Tappen Zee Chapter
ARS-Tennessee Valley Chapter
ARS-Tualatin Valley Chapter
ARS-Valley Forge Chapter
ARS-Vancouver (BC) Chapter
ARS-Victoria Chapter
ARS-Willamette Chapter
ARS-William Bartram Chapter
Assoc. des Parces Botanique de
	France
Atlanta Botanical Garden
Australian Rhododendron Society
Azalea Study Group
Bayley Landscaping
Beckstrom Rhododendron Growers
Berry Botanic Garden
Bleddso Farms
Bloedel Foundation
Bovees Nursery
Brooklyn Botanic Garden Library
Callaway Gardens
Canton Custom Landscaping

Capitol District Washington Fed-
	eration of Garden Clubs
Cascade Heather Society
Center for Urban Horticulture, Univ.
	of Washington
Charles E. Merrill Trust
City Wide Garden Club
Coe Foundation
Cougar Hills Blooming Beauties
Denver Botanic Gardens Library
Edmonds Community College
Edmonds Methodist Church
Evergreen Fund
Evergreen Trailways
Fisher's Nursery
Fred G. Meyer Foundation
Glenridge Garden Club
Goddard Garden Club
Goteborg Botanical Garden
Growth Nursery Farm
Hardy Fern Foundation
Hendricks Park Rhododendron
	Garden
Huckleberry Unit #59
Issaquah Garden Club
Killarney Garden Club
Kunming Institute of Botany,
	Academia Sinica
Lady Bugs Garden Club
Lake Washington Garden Clubs
Le-Mac Nurseries, Inc.
Lindberg Foundation
Longwood Gardens
McConkey J.M. & Company, Inc.
Mendocino Coast Botanical Garden
New York Botanical Garden
New Zealand Chapter
Norfolk Botanical Garden
Norman Archibald Charitable Trust
North American Rock Garden
	Society
Northwest Ornamental Horticultural
	Society
Pacific Rhododendron Society,
	Auburn Chapter
Pacific Rhododendron Society, Gig
	Harbor Chapter
Pacific Rhododendron Society,
	Tacoma Chapter
Pacific Tropical Botanical Garden
Park Garden Club
Phipps, Howard Phipps Family
	Charitable Foundation
Pierce County Iris Society
Planting Fields Arboretum
Port Angeles Garden Club
Portland Garden Club

Pukeiti Rhododendron Trust
R. D. Merrill Foundation
Rare Plant Group Garden Club of
	America
Rhododendron Club
Rhododendron Society of Canada
RHS Garden
River Road Garden Club
Rockefeller Center Properties
Seattle Foundation
Seattle Garden Club
Senior Center of West Seattle
Simpson Reed Fund
Smith College
So. Seattle Community College
Species Associate Group
Stanley Smith Horticultural Trust
Strybing Arboretum Society
Sunnydale Garden Club
Swedish Rhododendron Society
Tacoma Garden Club
Tacoma Rhododendron Study Club
Tacoma Species Associate Group
Tam Engineering Corporation
The Longview Rhododendron
	Society
The New Zealand Rhododendron
	Association
The Norwegian Arboretum
Thomas Jefferson Garden Club
Thomas L. Berger Associates, P.S.
Univ. of Calif. Berkeley Botanical
	Garden
Univ. of Wash., Washington Park
	Arboretum
Univ. of Wash., Washington Park
	Arboretum Unit # 06
Univ. of Wash., Washington Park
	Arboretum Unit # 09
Univ. of Wash., Washington Park
	Arboretum Unit # 19
Univ. of Wash., Washington Park
	Arboretum Unit # 39
Univ. of Wash., Washington Park
	Arboretum Unit # 83
Univ. of Wash., Washington Park
	Arboretum Unit # 98
Van Dusen Botanical Gardens
Wagner Fund
Washington Jockey Club Longacres
Washington State Nurserymen's
	Association
Webbers Booksellers
Weyerhaeuser Company Foundation
Williamsburg Nursery
Winterthur Museum & Gardens
Woodland Creek Rhododendron
	Gardens